JESUS OF NAZARETH

JESUS OF NAZARETH

MILLENARIAN PROPHET

DALE C. ALLISON

FORTRESS PRESS
MINNEAPOLIS

JESUS OF NAZARETH
MILLENARIAN PROPHET

Book and cover design by Joseph Bonyata.
Cover art: *Cristo Benedicente*. Martini, Simone (1284–1344). Pinacoteca, Vatican Museums, Vatican State. Courtesy of SEF/Art Resource, N.Y. Used by permission.

Library of Congress Cataloging-in-Publication

Allison, Dale C.
Jesus of Nazareth : millenarian prophet / Dale C. Allison.
   p. cm.
Includes bibliographical references.
ISBN 0-8006-3144-7 (alk. paper)
1. Jesus Christ—Prophetic office. 2. Millennialism—Palestine—History
3. Jesus Christ—Historicity. I. Title.
BT252.A44 1998
232.9'08—dc21   98-21602

                                                                CIP

Manufactured in the U.S.A.   AF1-3144

02   01   00   99   98   1   2   3   4   5   6   7   8   9   10

For
JOEL

שנים שיושבין ויש ביניהם דברי תורה שכינה שרויה ביניהם

CONTENTS

PREFACE

I USED TO TELL FRIENDS that I wanted to write a book on the historical Jesus, but that I would not know enough or be wise enough to do so until I was in my fifties. Well, I am still in my forties, and here is a book on Jesus. The reason is not that I have gained sufficient knowledge and wisdom but rather the opposite. The years have bestowed some humility and taught me that, partly because of an inability to make up my mind about so many things, I shall never be able to write the sort of thorough tome I once envisaged. I shall instead always be limited to seeing and writing about only fleeting glimpses of the past—and to making guesses about all too much. These three chapters, then, are fragments that have fallen from the ruins of a project that the builder has abandoned.

Chapter 1 sets out to discover how we might come to knowledge of the historical Jesus and ends up concluding that the tradition about him is best understood on the supposition that he was, among other things, what sociologists and anthropologists call a millenarian prophet. Chapter 2 considers what we can know about Jesus' millenarian vision and how his eschatological language should be interpreted. Chapter 3 argues that Jesus was, despite so much written to the contrary, a sort of millenarian ascetic whose words and behavior are illuminated through comparative materials.

As a whole, this book functions as a belated prologue to my earlier contribution, *The End of the Ages Has Come: An Early Interpretation of the Passion and Resurrection of Jesus* (Philadelphia: Fortress, 1985; Edinburgh: T. & T. Clark, 1987). In that volume I sought an explanation for the so-called realized eschatology of the New Testament. During graduate days the study of millenarian movements persuaded me that the early Christian interpretation of the death and vindication of Jesus in eschatological categories was due in the first place to a post-Easter reinterpretation of Jesus' own eschatological prophecies. Of that I remain persuaded. But the book's reception has disappointed. The problem is not that it has gone unnoticed but that, when it has been referred to, the cause has been for almost everything except the main thesis and the comparative materials on which it is based. It is my hope that the present volume will be more persuasive than its predecessor and encourage other students of Jesus and early Christianity to pay more attention to worldwide millenarian movements and comparative messianism.

All three chapters appear here for the first time. The opening chapter, however, grows out of two panel discussions, both moderated by Amy-Jill Levine. The first was held at the SECSOR meeting in Macon, Georgia, in March 1997, the second at the annual AAR/SBL meeting in San Francisco in November of the same year. On both occasions I enjoyed profitable encounters with John Dominic Crossan and Gerd Lüdemann.

Quotations from the Bible are most often from the RSV and NRSV, but I have sometimes offered my own translations.

I should like to thank John Barclay, John J. Collins, W. D. Davies, and Amy-Jill Levine for commenting on portions of the manuscript. The whole was read by Joel Marcus, and to him I dedicate this book. His encouragement first led me to think I should write it. His learned criticism much improved the final product. And his good humor and friendship made life easier during a most difficult and confusing time.

ABBREVIATIONS

AGJU	Arbeiten zur Geschichte des antiken Judentums und des Urchristentums
ALGHJ	Arbeiten zur Literatur und Geschichte des hellenistischen Judentums
ATR	*Anglican Theological Review*
BBB	Bonner biblische Beiträge
BETL	Bibliotheca ephemeridum theologicarum Lovaniensium
Bib	*Biblica*
BR	*Bible Review*
BTB	*Biblical Theology Bulletin*
BZ	*Biblische Zeitschrift*
BZNW	Beihefte zur Zeitschrift für die neutestamentliche Wissenschaft
CBNT	Coniectanea Biblica, New Testament Series
CBQ	*Catholic Biblical Quarterly*
CIJ	Corpus Inscriptionum Judaicarum
CRINT	Compendia Rerum Iudaicarum ad Novum Testamentum
DSD	*Dea Sea Discoveries*
EB	Echter Bibel
EKK	Evangelisch-katholischer Kommentar
ETL	*Ephemerides theologicae Lovanienses*
ExpT	*Expository Times*
FRLANT	Forschungen zur Religion und Literatur des Alten und Neuen Testaments
HeyJ	*Heythrop Journal*
HTKNT	Herders Theologischer Kommentar zum Neuen Testament
HTR	*Harvard Theological Review*
IBS	*Irish Biblical Studies*

ICC	International Critical Commentary
Int	*Interpretation*
JAAR	*Journal of the American Academy of Religion*
JBL	*Journal of Biblical Literature*
JJS	*Journal of Jewish Studies*
JQR	*Jewish Quarterly Review*
JR	*Journal of Religion*
JSJS	*Journal for the Study of Judaism* Supplement
JSNT	*Journal for the Study of the New Testament*
JSNTSS	*Journal for the Study of the New Testament* Supplement Series
JSP	*Journal of Social Psychology*
JTS	*Journal of Theological Studies*
NovT	*Novum Testamentum*
NovTSup	*Novum Testamentum* Supplements
NTAbh	Neutestamentliche Abhandlungen
NTOA	Novum Testamentum et Orbis Antiquus
NTS	*New Testament Studies*
NTTS	New Testament Tools and Studies
QD	Quaestiones Disputatae
RAC	*Reallexikon für Antike und Christentum*
RevBib	*Revue biblique*
RevQ	*Revue de Qumran*
RSR	*Recherches de science religieuse*
SB	Strack/Billerbeck, *Kommentar zum Neuen Testament aus Talmud und Midrasch*
SBLDS	Society of Biblical Literature Dissertation Series
SBS	Stuttgarter Bibelstudien
SJT	*Scottish Journal of Theology*
SNTSMS	Society for New Testament Studies Monograph Series
SNTU	Studien zum Neuen Testament und seiner Umwelt
TDNT	*Theological Dictionary of the New Testament*
TGI	*Textbuch zur Geschichte Israels*
TSAJ	Texte und Studien zum Antiken Judentum
TT	Theologisk Tidskrift
TU	Texte und Untersuchungen
TZ	*Theologische Zeitschrift*
VC	*Vigiliae christianae*
WUNT	Wissenschaftliche Untersuchungen zum Neuen Testament
ZNW	*Zeitschrift für die neutestamentliche Wissenschaft*
ZTK	*Zeitschrift für Theologie und Kirche*

JESUS OF NAZARETH

1

THE JESUS TRADITION AND THE JESUS OF HISTORY

HOW TO FIND A MILLENARIAN PROPHET

Introduction

Dozens of ancient sources tell us what Jesus supposedly said and did. But what did he really say and what did he really do? This question stalks all modern Jesus research, and, to understate the matter, it is not easy to answer. Hagiographical traditions and sacred biographies written by the devotees of a founder or religious savior are notoriously unreliable. Tradents gather what they can and concoct what they cannot gather, often reaping where their founder did not sow. The result is that everywhere history coalesces with myth.[1] Nothing is more common than the putting of words into the mouth of one's religious authority.[2] That this was true in Jesus' native religion, Judaism, appears from both the Pentateuchal legislation, which attributes itself in its entirety to Moses, as well as from the abundance of intertestamental pseudepigraphical writings

---

1. Instructive here are *The Biographical Process: Studies in the History and Psychology of Religion*, ed. Frank E. Reynolds and Donald Capps (The Hague: Mouton, 1976), and Geo Widengren, "Prolegomena: The Value of Source-Criticism as Illustrated by the Biographical Dates of the Great Founders," in *Historia Religionum: Handbook for the History of Religions, volume 1: Religions of the Past*, ed. C. Jouco Bleeker and Geo Widengren (Leiden: E. J. Brill, 1969), pp. 1–22.

2. Documentation seems almost needless; but for two good examples see Ilya Gershevitch, "Zoroaster's Own Contribution," *Journal of Near Eastern Studies* 23 (1964), pp. 12–33, and Annemarie Schimmel, *And Muhammad Is His Messenger: The Veneration of the Prophet in Islamic Piety* (Chapel Hill: University of North Carolina Press, 1985).

still in existence. Once we doubt, as all modern scholars do, that the Jesus tradition gives us invariably accurate information, unvarnished by exaggeration and legend, it is incumbent upon us to find some way of sorting through the diverse traditions to divine what really goes back to Jesus.

Contemporary scholarship has not backed down from this daunting assignment. Early in the twentieth century, after faith in the existence of Q and belief in the priority of Mark cast off rival hypotheses, some imagined that source criticism would solve our problem. C. H. Dodd believed that "from the data attested by Mark and 'Q' in conjunction we can derive a clear and relatively full picture of the character of the ministry of Jesus."[3] The skepticism of the form critics, however, gradually abraded this sort of confidence, which now strikes so many as naive. Scholars have accordingly been moved to devise alternative means of fishing dominical items out of the sea of traditions. The result has been the invention of so-called criteria, that is, tests with which we can assay the extant traditions and determine which inform us about the Jesus of history.[4]

These criteria appeal to common sense. For instance, that a tradition should not be thought authentic unless it coheres with other traditions already regarded as genuine—the criterion of consistency—seems self-evident. Again, that we may feel confident in assigning a unit to Jesus if it is "dissimilar to characteristic emphases both of ancient Judaism and of the early Church"[5]—the criterion variously known as dissimilarity or distinctiveness or double discontinuity or dual irreducibility—has an initial plausibility. So too does the criterion of embarrassment, according to which a fact or saying is original if there is evidence that it embarrassed early Christians.

Reflection, however, creates more than a little unease. Coherence, for example, is a rather subjective thing. Two things that fit together according to one exegete may seem irreconcilable according to another. If, for Hans Conzelmann, the "structure" of Jesus' thinking would not "tolerate

---

3. C. H. Dodd, *History and the Gospel* (New York: Charles Scribner's Sons, 1938), pp. 85–86.

4. For a survey and references to secondary literature see John P. Meier, *A Marginal Jew: Rethinking the Historical Jesus* (New York: Doubleday, 1991), pp. 167–95. Also particularly helpful are R. S. Barbour, *Traditio-Historical Criticism of the Gospels* (London: SPCK, 1972), and M. Eugene Boring, "Criteria of Authenticity: The Lucan Beatitudes as a Test Case," *Forum* 1/4 (1985), pp. 3–38. For an annotated bibliography on the subject see Craig A. Evans, *Life of Jesus Research: An Annotated Bibliography* (Leiden: E. J. Brill, 1996), pp. 127–46.

5. The words are those of Norman Perrin, *Rediscovering the Teaching of Jesus* (New York: Harper & Row, 1967), p. 39.

the synthesis of the Kingdom of God and Son of Man," [6] other scholars cannot see the point, which the authors of Q, Mark, Matthew, and Luke also apparently missed. Again, if for Stevan Davies the kingdom's presence and its futurity are two things that sit uncomfortably side by side,[7] others have had no difficulty imagining that Jesus spoke of both at the same time because his "eschatology [was] in the process of realization." [8] Perhaps the problem here is that one can always, as should be obvious in this age of deconstructionism, find tensions or contradictions between two texts. Long ago F. C. Burkitt made the point with the following illustration:

> "The Kingdom of Heaven is like leaven," said Jesus once; very well, we may say, the Kingdom of Heaven is therefore something essentially alive, working within that in which it is placed, something immanent. But Jesus also said, "The Kingdom of Heaven is like a treasure hidden in a field." According to this it is something essentially external, accidental, transcending the ordinary features and contents of its surroundings. Here is a patent contradiction, a contradiction as uncompromising as could anywhere be found.[9]

The issue is not whether we can find tensions but whether they mean much. Consistency and inconsistency are very much in the eye of the beholder.

Even though some espy contradiction where others see harmony, perhaps we can all concur that even the more reflective of us "are neither perfectly rational nor perfectly irrational but imperfectly both." [10] Human beings are not Vulcans. Why have critics asked whether Paul's views on

---

6. Hans Conzelmann, "Present and Future in the Synoptic Tradition," in *God and Christ: Existence and Province*, ed. Robert W. Funk and Gerhard Ebeling (New York: Harper & Row, 1968) = *Journal for Theology and the Church* 5 (1969), p. 30.

7. Stevan L. Davies, *The Gospel of Thomas and Christian Wisdom* (New York: Seabury, 1983), p. 48.

8. The famous phrase ("sich realisierende Eschatologie") is from Joachim Jeremias, *The Parables of Jesus*, 2d rev. ed. (New York: Charles Scribner's Sons, 1972), p. 230.

9. F. C. Burkitt, "The Parables of the Kingdom of Heaven," *The Interpreter* 7 (1910–1911), p. 132. He went on to add: "The contradiction does not come from the Parables, but from the use we have made of them."

10. David Hackett Fischer, *Historians' Fallacies: Toward a Logic of Historical Thought* (New York: Harper & Row, 1970), p. 214. This certainly includes New Testament scholars. I remember my bewilderment when, as an undergraduate, I read p. 452 of Lloyd Gaston's *No Stone on Another: Studies in the Significance of the Fall of Jerusalem in the Synoptic Gospels*, NovTSup 23 (Leiden: E. J. Brill, 1970), because while that page assigns the original saying behind Mk 9:1; 13:30; and Mt 10:23 to a Christian prophet, p. 38 credits Jesus as the author.

eschatology evolved with time and whether Romans and Galatians say different things about the law? The reason is that the apostle, who was surely a more orderly thinker than Jesus, said some things that do not obviously go together. Why should we believe that Jesus was any different? Do we have here a holdover from the old systematic theology? Surely if Jesus was, as so many have held, an eschatological prophet who lived in the imaginative world of the apocalypses, we should not expect much consistency from him, for the essential irrationality of apocalyptic is manifest from the history of messianic and millenarian movements.[11] Who could turn the words and actions of the seventeenth-century Jewish Messiah, Sabbatai Ṣevi, into a coherent system of thought? One cannot disagree when Gerd Theissen affirms that "we have to develop a historical sense for the degree of coherence and incoherence which we may expect in a given epoch and in the writings of an individual author or in his orally transmitted words." [12] But such "historical sense" is an elusive thing that varies greatly from historian to historian.

The criterion of dissimilarity, whose implicit notion that the new is good may be the offspring of the modern idea of progress, is no less troublesome than the criterion of consistency. As others have often remarked, it can at best tell us what was distinctive, not what was characteristic of Jesus. Because Jesus lived and moved and had his being within the Jewish tradition, the criterion is not a net that catches fish of every kind; it can only find things that Jesus did not take from elsewhere. All too often, however, dissimilarity has been misused as a means of separating the authentic from the inauthentic, that is, a way of eliminating items from the corpus of authentic materials.[13] The result is a Jesus who "is necessarily a free-floating iconoclast, artificially isolated from his people and their Scripture, and artificially isolated from the movement that he founded." [14]

---

11. It is useful to recollect contradictions that critics have found in some of the old Jewish and Christian apocalypses, contradictions that have been the basis for dubious compositional theories (for example, G. H. Box's analysis of *4 Ezra* and R. H. Charles's analysis of Revelation, in *The Apocrypha and Pseudepigrapha of the Old Testament*, 2 vols. [Oxford: Clarendon, 1913]). See also Jack T. Sanders, "The Criterion of Coherence and the Randomness of Charisma: Poring through some Aporias in the Jesus Tradition," *NTS* 44 (1998), pp. 1–25.

12. Gerd Theissen, "Historical Scepticism and the Criteria of Jesus Research," *SJT* 49 (1996), p. 156, n. 10.

13. See further my critique of Norman Perrin's method in "A Plea for Thoroughgoing Eschatology," *JBL* 113 (1994), pp. 664–67.

14. Richard B. Hays, "The Corrected Jesus," *First Things* (May 1994), p. 45. Long ago Oscar Cullmann, *Salvation in History* (London: SCM, 1967), p. 189, observed the obvious: "The Church probably did put some words in Jesus' mouth to make clear its idea of Jesus,

Beyond this, the objection of Morna Hooker, first raised three decades ago, has never been successfully answered.[15] We just do not know enough about first-century Judaism[16] or early Christianity[17] to make the criterion very reliable. Why pretend to prove a negative? I remember W. D. Davies once advising me never to use the word *unique* in connection with Jesus. His reason was very simple: How can we claim anything to be without parallel when so little is known about antiquity? The recent publication of old Palestinian prayer texts which address God as "my Father" (4Q372 and 4Q460) has vindicated the wisdom of his warning. Joachim Jeremias's confident and influential conclusions about Jesus' use of *abba*, conclusions built upon a claim to distinctiveness, have been discredited.[18]

The criterion of embarrassment is more promising. Certainly historians in other fields have often reasoned according to its logic, as when scholars of Islam have affirmed that the "Satanic verses" rest upon a historical episode, because Muslims did not invent a story in which Mohammed mentions the names of three goddesses.[19] And yet there is a problem. We must face the surprising fact that all of the supposedly

---

but it also used genuine sayings of Jesus for this purpose. It *selected such genuine* sayings of Jesus *as accorded with its own tendencies*, ones that specially emphasized what seemed to it to be of central importance. . . ."

15. Morna Hooker, "Christology and Methodology," *NTS* 17 (1971), pp. 480–87; idem, "On using the Wrong Tool," *Theology* 75 (1972), pp. 570–81. For an attempted rebuttal see R. H. Fuller, "The Criterion of Dissimilarity: The Wrong Tool?" in *Christological Perspectives*, ed. Robert F. Berkey and Sarah A. Edwards (New York: Pilgrim, 1982), pp. 42–48.

16. Certainly if we confine ourselves to Jewish sources known to have been composed in the first century and before the Jewish War we have very little to work with. If, on the other hand, we enlarge the comparative materials by including, as is often done, the Hebrew Bible, all the Dead Sea Scrolls, and rabbinic texts, then there is hardly anything that does not have some sort of parallel.

17. Here it is rewarding to read F. Gerald Downing, *The Church and Jesus: A Study in History, Philosophy and Theology*, SBT 2/10 (London: SCM, 1968). This book argues that "we do not know enough about Jesus to allow us to construct a clear account of the primitive Church because we do not know enough about the primitive Church to allow us to construct a clear account of Jesus" (p. 51; italics deleted). No doubt we all sometimes forget that our knowledge of early Christianity is woefully incomplete. Maybe one can, with a holographic plate, reconstruct the whole image from a part; but it is otherwise with our fragmentary knowledge of the early church.

18. For further discussion of the criterion of dissimilarity and its problems see now especially Gerd Theissen and Dagmar Winter, *Die Kriterienfrage in der Jesusforschung: Vom Differenzkriterium zum Plausibilitätskriterium*, NTOA 34 (Göttingen: Vandenhoeck & Ruprecht, 1997).

19. Compare the argument of Arthur Jeffery, "The Quest of the Historical Mohammed," *The Moslem World* 16 (1926), pp. 328–29, that Ibn Isḥāq's lost work on Mohammed must have contained valuable information because so many of the surviving quotations are unfavorable to later piety.

embarrassing statements or words are found in the Jesus tradition itself. This means that they were not sufficiently disconcerting to be expurgated. Perhaps this "reminds us that beside a creative thrust there was also a conservative force in the Gospel tradition." [20] But does it not also strongly hint at the pluralism of the early church [21] and reveal that what may have flustered some may have left others unperturbed?

P. W. Schmiedel famously claimed that Mk 13:32, where Jesus says that neither the angels in heaven nor the Son knows the day of the consummation, should be one of the "foundation pillars for a truly scientific life of Jesus," because Christians would not have attributed ignorance to their Lord. [22] The argument is worth considering. Patristic writings vainly strive to evade the plain sense of the saying. [23] Textual authorities for both Mt 24:36 and Mk 13:32 omit "nor the Son." Luke drops the saying altogether. Yet Mark and Matthew passed it on, the latter at least without making any significant modification. Moreover, Paul (in 1 Cor 15:28) and John (in 14:28) were able to subordinate "the Son" to the Father, and in like manner others may have had no difficulty with the thought that the Father knew things the Son did not. So what decision should one make? [24]

Whether or not one shares my misgivings about dissimilarity, coherence, and embarrassment, it is certain that they and other criteria have not led us into the promised land of scholarly consensus. If our tools were designed to overcome subjectivity and bring order to our discipline, then they have failed.

This state of affairs does not, however, mean that we should lay them aside. For in truth we have nothing better in the scholarly toolshed; at least I have not turned up anything better. Apparently we must reconcile

---

20. Meier, *Marginal Jew*, vol. 1, p. 170.

21. The modern discovery of pluralism in the early church is akin to the modern discovery of pluralism among the Puritans or among ancient Jews. Everywhere, monolithic entities have been fractured. The rule is: the more that historical research progresses, the more complex things seem to be.

22. See P. W. Schmiedel, "Gospels," in *Encyclopaedia Biblica*, ed. T. K. Cheyne and J. Sutherland Black (London: Adam and Charles Black, 1901), vol. II, col. 1881.

23. Ambrose, *De fid.* 5:16; Athanasius, *C. Ar.* 1–3:42–50; Basil, *Ep.* 236; Chrysostom, *Hom. on Mt.* 77:2; Cassiodorus, *Exp. Ps.* on 9:39, among others.

24. Robert J. Miller, "Can the Historical Jesus Be Made Safe for Orthodoxy? A Critique of *The Jesus Quest* by Ben Witherington III," *The Journal of Higher Criticism* 4 (1997), p. 129, finds it "quite believable that early Christians might well have invented this saying as a way of explaining why Jesus had not been more precise in his predictions, or as a way of taking out insurance on his credibility, just in case the End proved tardy."

ourselves to the unhappy fact that our methods are defective and may often mislead us. Probably, as will be explained later, our best recourse is to figure out how to improve and use our existing indices, unwieldy as they are, under the guidance of an interpretive model established independently of those indices. Perhaps this will help us stay a little closer to the truth. Such, at any rate, is the main purpose of this chapter.

But, however much we better our methods for authenticating the traditions about Jesus, we are never going to produce results that can be confirmed or disconfirmed. Jesus is long gone, and we can never set our pale reconstructions beside the flesh-and-blood original. We should not deceive ourselves into dreaming that methodological sophistication will ever eventuate either in some sort of unimaginative scientific procedure or in academic concord. Rudolf Bultmann was right to assert that often we are left with only a "subjective judgment."[25] Until we become literal time travelers, all attempts to find the historical Jesus will be steered by instinct and intuition. Appeals to shared criteria may, we can pray, assist us in being self-critical, but when all is said and done we look for the historical Jesus with our imaginations—and there too is where we find him, if we find him at all.

An Imaginary Case Study

I should like to explore further the hazards that accompany all attempts to authenticate Jesus traditions by considering a hypothetical scenario. Imagine with me that, in the year 35 C.E., there lived in Jerusalem a Jewess named Faustina. A recent and enthusiastic convert to Peter's preaching, she soon found she had the gift of prophecy, and in Christian services she began uttering oracles in the name of the risen Lord. Faustina was, moreover, a very charismatic figure, and her ecstatic speech was greatly esteemed over a wide area.

Because Faustina's listeners took her prophetic claims at face value, that is, because they believed that her words were truly those of the resurrected Jesus, some of her sentences were passed down with the preface, "Jesus said." Indeed, if truth be known, it was she who introduced the apocalyptic Son of man sayings into early Christianity. She was quite fond of the book of Daniel, and picking up on Jesus' innocent use of an Aramaic

---

25. Rudolf Bultmann, *History of the Synoptic Tradition*, rev. ed. (New York: Harper & Row, 1963), p. 102.

locution ("son of man"), she authored all the nonredactional sayings in which Jesus prophesies the future coming of the Son of man.

The fictional case of Faustina is not far-fetched. It rather gains its force from its resemblance to nonfictional narratives some scholars have produced. So it is appropriate to ask how we, two thousand years later, can play Sherlock Holmes and follow the long cold trail of subtle clues to the place where we might see what Jesus said and what someone else said in his name. Are we clever enough to solve the case of the Faustina sayings?

What about the criterion of multiple attestation, which maintains that a saying attested in two or more independent sources has a better chance of being authentic than one attested only singly? Two facts about Faustina show us that in this matter it is a poor guide. First, our prophetess flourished very soon after Jesus' ministry ended, and, second, she was a person of far-flung influence, whose prophetic logia were widely distributed. The result of these two circumstances is that her sayings entered the Jesus tradition very near its beginning, early enough in fact to have been in the main tributary before it split off into the Q tradition, the Markan tradition, the Thomas tradition, and whatever other Jesus tradition one wishes to speak of. Thus many of Faustina's sayings are attested more than once in our earliest sources. For this reason the criterion of multiple attestation will not screen out her materials.

Does it help that, according to the experts, some of her sayings show signs of having been composed in Aramaic? No, because Faustina herself spoke the language of Jesus. Further, as she had grown up in Galilee and then later moved to the environs of Jerusalem, some of her sayings, just like those of her Lord, naturally enough exhibit Palestinian touches. So the rule that a saying has higher odds of telling us about Jesus if it reflects religious or social or economic or political conditions within first-century Palestine does not aid us here. In addition, matters are all the more difficult for us because Faustina steeped herself in the primitive Jesus tradition and liked to imitate it. She loved, for instance, to use the prefatory "amen" and to arrange her thoughts in poetic parallelism. In other words, like Luke imitating the Septuagint, she made Jesus' style her own style.[26]

Will the criterion of dissimilarity find Faustina's fingerprints? Let us consider her apocalyptic Son of man sayings. They distinguish themselves

---

26. "If the early Church did, in fact, create traditions about Jesus (and it surely did), it would no doubt have attempted, at least for the most part, to create such traditions as would fit 'reasonably well' into the general picture of Jesus which it had received through the prior traditions." So William O. Walker, "The Quest for the Historical Jesus: A Discussion of Methodology," *ATR* 51 (1969), p. 50.

from non-Christian Jewish traditions in two conspicuous ways. (1) They equate the Son of man with Jesus of Nazareth. (2) They (in contrast with the closest parallels in Daniel, *1 Enoch*, and *4 Ezra*) use "the Son of man" in a titular fashion. So this group of sayings might be thought to satisfy half of the criterion of dissimilarity, even though Jesus was not the author. What about the other half? Faustina's Son of man sayings also differentiate themselves from early Christian tradition. For despite Faustina's popularity, titular usage of "the Son of man" never grew beyond the Jesus tradition. The peculiar phrase failed to establish itself as a christological title. So Faustina's apocalyptic Son of man sayings are not quite like anything else in early Christian tradition (certainly there is no trace of them in the epistles) and so they appear to meet the other half of the criterion of dissimilarity.[27]

The lesson for us is that Faustina was just as capable as Jesus of composing sayings that seem to distinguish themselves from what we know of both Jewish and Christian tradition. This must have been true of all sorts of people in the early church. Certainly the apostle Paul produced, to use Perrin's phrase, quite a few sentences that are "dissimilar to characteristic emphases both of ancient Judaism and of the early Church." So too the author or authors of the *Gospel of Thomas*. Does not the criterion of dissimilarity make the curious assumption that Jesus alone, but not any contributor to the Jesus tradition after him, said distinctive things?

Some scholars have mistakenly authenticated Faustina's apocalyptic Son of man sayings by the criterion of embarrassment. Surely, they say, early Christians did not formulate for Jesus false prophecies. The promise, now found in Mt 10:23, that the persecuted disciples will not complete their missionary task in Israel before the Son of man comes— one of Faustina's sayings—has been proclaimed indubitably dominical because, in the event, it was falsified. The difficulty with this argument, however—a difficulty so fundamental that one wonders how anyone could ever have missed it—is that Faustina's comforting prediction of imminent salvation became problematic only later, long after it had established itself in the tradition as an authentic word of Jesus. There it remained, not forgotten (it was, after all, prefaced with "Jesus said") but reinterpreted (compare Jn 21:23).

The criterion of consistency is perhaps no more helpful than any of our other tools, for, as already observed, Faustina was steeped in the Jesus

---

27. See further John G. Gager, "The Gospels and Jesus: Some Doubts about Method," *JR* 54 (1974), pp. 265–66.

tradition. Not only had she made Jesus' style her own, but she had meditated profoundly upon the content of his speech. Thus, much that she said was in continuity with what he had said. The criterion of consistency will accordingly not catch her out. To illustrate: It is easy to imagine that Jesus (1) never said anything about the coming of the Son of man and yet, at the same time, (2) never said anything that would contradict or even stand in noticeable tension with such a belief; Jesus accordingly could have had an eschatological scenario that Faustina enlarged in a creative but fairly faithful fashion, with the result that we can no longer discern who said what. One thinks of our difficulty in seeing where, in the early Platonic dialogues, Socrates ends and Plato begins.

The Method of John Dominic Crossan

John Dominic Crossan has thought about the problem of finding the original Jesus as long and as hard as anyone. Examination of his creative and intriguing proposals is an instructive exercise.

Crossan opines that "historical Jesus research is becoming something of a bad joke."[28] The diversity of reconstructions creates the "suspicion that historical Jesus research is a very safe place to do theology and call it history, to do autobiography and call it biography."[29] The remedy for this embarrassing situation, a situation which conveys "the impression of acute scholarly subjectivity," lies in reconsidering our methods.[30] Archaeologists no longer loot mounds at random but assign every item from a site to its proper chronological layer. Jesus researchers need to do something similar. They need to employ a scientific stratigraphy.

Crossan declares that his procedure is triadic. First, he seeks to put his reconstruction in context by way of cross-cultural anthropology and Greco-Roman history. Second, he offers a formal inventory of the Jesus tradition. This means (1) dating the relevant sources, (2) grouping them then into four chronological strata (30–60, 60–80, 80–120, and 120–150 C.E.), and (3) arranging the individual units into one of four categories: those attested only once, those independently attested twice, those independently attested three times, and those independently attested more than three times. Crossan's third step is to determine what precisely goes back to Jesus. For this he believes that we should begin with his first stratum, and that even on that level it is methodologically wise to bracket

---

28. John Dominic Crossan, *The Historical Jesus: The Life of a Mediterranean Jewish Peasant* (San Francisco: HarperCollins, 1991), p. xxvii.

29. Ibid., p. xxviii.

30. Ibid.

material attested in one source alone. For "something found in at least two independent sources from the primary stratum cannot have been created by either of them. Something found there but only in single attestation could have been created by that source itself." [31]

Crossan's method nonetheless "postulates that, at least for the first stratum, everything is original until it is argued otherwise." [32] This seemingly includes even the materials attested in a single source. He also, however, goes on to say that the greater the attestation, the more seriously we should reckon with an origin with Jesus. He illustrates his method with an example:

Kingdom and Children [1/4]
(1) Gos. Thom. 22:1–2
(2) Mk 10:13–16 = Mt 19:13–15 = Lk 18:15–17
(3) Mt 18:3
(4) Jn 3:1–10

We have here a "complex" constituted by six units (Gos. Thom. 22: 1–22; Mk 10:13–16; Mt 19:13–15; Lk 18:15–17; Mt 18:3; Jn 3: 1–10). These units come from four independent "sources" (Thomas, Mark, M, John). One of these sources (Thomas) belongs to Crossan's first stratum. So "Kingdom and Children" is followed by [1/4], 1 signifying that the complex is attested in the first stratum (30–60 C.E.), 4 indicating that there are four independent witnesses to it. The upshot of this way of displaying things is that the lower the number on the left and the higher the number on the right, the greater the chance we are dealing with something that originated with Jesus himself.

The results of Crossan's method are on display throughout his engaging book The Historical Jesus. Jesus turns out to be a Cynic-like Jewish peasant who early on abandoned John the Baptist's imminent apocalyptic expectation for an egalitarian social program. For our purposes the main interest is an appendix, "An Inventory of the Jesus Tradition by Chronological Stratification and Independent Attestation." This displays in comprehensive fashion the results of Crossan's method and includes his judgment on the origin of every complex catalogued. The + sign marks those that go back to Jesus, the − sign those that do not. The ± sign is placed in front of complexes "whose metaphorical or metonymical content rendered such positivistic simplicities magnificently irrelevant." [33] Although Crossan himself does not offer the statistics, an examination of his inventory shows, among other things, that approximately 54% of the

31. Ibid., pp. xxxii–xxxiii.
32. Ibid., p. xxxii.
33. Ibid., p. xxxiv.

units in Q, 52% of the units in the *Gospel of Thomas*, and 41% of the units in Mark are marked with the + sign.

There is much to admire in Crossan's book, which has garnered so much attention, even outside the guild.[34] The concern for method is commendable, as is the openness to noncanonical sources. Further, the application of cross-cultural anthropology is stimulating and, we hope, will be taken up by others. My purpose here, however, is not to praise Crossan but to criticize him. For, despite the methodological finesse, one is left with many questions.

1. *Scholarly diversity.* How troubled should we be by the different pictures of Jesus modern historians have developed? It is the rule rather than the exception that the sources for important historical figures do not allow definitive reconstructions but rather generate abiding contention. This is simply the reality of the humanities, in which the interpretations of individuals and texts are always up for grabs. What in the book of Jeremiah goes back to Jeremiah? Which fragments did Heraclitus himself author? What was really in the mind of Alexander the Great or Claudius Caesar? Again, what did Paul believe about the law of Moses, and how much of it did he practice? And what is the chief lesson of *Hamlet?* The failure of scholars to answer these questions conclusively, and to create some sort of consensus is just the inevitable consequence of limited historical sources and limited human abilities: it is "the historicity of historical work."[35] Uniform interpretation is found nowhere, provisional and conflicting interpretation everywhere.

Of what figure of note do we *not* have contending representations? Was Shelley above all a Platonist or above all a political radical or above all a skeptical empiricist? The experts tell different stories. Who was the real Gandhi? Was he the brilliant saint of Louis Fischer's popular biography or the tyrannical and superstitious political opportunist depicted in Richard Grenier's well-known *Commentary* piece?[36] When there are even very disparate biographies of modern figures who have left us their own written materials, how could it be any different with Jesus, who wrote nothing at all? Crossan himself says near the end of his book that "there

---

34. Note *Jesus and Faith: A Conversation on the Work of John Dominic Crossan*, ed. Jeffrey Carlson and Robert A. Ludwig (Maryknoll: Orbis, 1994).

35. Leander E. Keck, *A Future for the Historical Jesus: The Place of Jesus in Preaching and Theology* (Nashville: Abingdon, 1971), p. 24.

36. Louis Fischer, *Gandhi: His Life and Message for the World* (New York: Mentor, 1954). See also *Commentary*, March, 1983; reprinted as Richard Grenier, *The Gandhi Nobody Knows* (Nashville: Thomas Nelson, 1983).

will always be divergent historical Jesuses."[37] That, it seems, is the one sure fact. The quest for the historical Jesus will ever be a book without its final chapter. Perhaps, then, we should make the best of it by recalling the story of the blind men and the elephant: We can at least hope that most of the contributors have some piece of the truth to share with us.

2. *Stratification.* Crossan comes to the sources as a geologist who seeks to map the strata. This is understandable. Just as sedimentary rock forms in layers, surely the bedrock of the Jesus tradition was covered, as time went on, by layers of secondary materials. So we need to expose the various deposits to get to the original. In trying to dig down to Jesus, however, Crossan makes an exceedingly high number of controversial judgments. His stratigraphic view looks like this:

Fourth stratum, 120–150 C.E.

2d ed. of John, Acts, *Apocryphon of James,* 1 and 2 Timothy, 2 Peter, Polycarp, *Philippians,* 2 *Clement, Gospel of the Nazoreans, Gospel of the Ebionites, Didache* 1:3b—2:1, *Gospel of Peter*

Third stratum, 80–120 C.E.

Matthew, Luke, Revelation, *1 Clement,* Barnabas, *Epistle, Didache* 1:1–3a; 2:2—16:2; *Shepherd of Hermas,* James, 1st ed. of John, the letters of Ignatius, 1 Peter, Polycarp, *Philippians* 13–14, 1 John

Second stratum, 60–80 C.E.

Gospel of the Egyptians, Secret Gospel of Mark, Mark, P. Oxy. 840, 2d ed. of the *Gospel of Thomas, Dialogue of the Savior* 124.23–127.18; 131.19–132.15; 137.3—147.22, the Signs Gospel embedded in John

First stratum, 30–60 C.E.

the authentic Paulines, the 1st ed. of the *Gospel of Thomas,* the *Egerton Gospel* (= Pap. Eg. 2 + Pap. Köln 255 (Inv. 608)), the Fayum Fragment (P. Vienna G. 2325), P. Oxy. 1224, *Gospel of the Hebrews,* Q, a miracle collection that lies behind the Signs Gospel and Mark and

---

37. Crossan, *Historical Jesus,* p. 423. But in "Jesus and the Kingdom: Itinerants and Householders in Earliest Christianity," in *Jesus at 2000,* ed. Marcus J. Borg (Boulder: Westview, 1997), pp. 32–33, he writes: "Without the strictest possible methodology, scholars will disagree not only on the interpretation of any given text but also on what texts are in the original historical Jesus layer of the tradition to be interpreted." But will we not continue to disagree about texts even if we adopt a common and strict methodology? Contrast Stevan L. Davies, *Jesus the Healer: Possession, Trance, and the Origins of Christianity* (New York: Continuum, 1995), who supports his novel thesis that Jesus was not primarily a teacher by referring to the failure of scholars to agree about the content of Jesus' proclamation. By the same sort of reasoning one could argue that the pre-Socratic philosophers were not teachers because the experts disagree so much about what they had to say—an obvious absurdity.

Secret Mark, a sayings source used by *Didache* 16 and Matthew 24, the Cross Gospel (embedded in the Gospel of Peter)

The questions are manifold. What is the justification for sorting the sources into four periods? Why not three, or five, or six? And why are the lines drawn where they are? Why not a line at 50 or 70 c.e. or one at 100 c.e.? Crossan may have good reasons for his choices, but he does not, so far as I can see, let us know what they are.[38] N. T. Wright is correct to observe: "Crossan's cut-off points for dating are of course arbitrary. The first two strata consist of twenty years each, the third forty, thus enabling him to imply, say, that a document written in 81 belongs with one written in 119 rather than with one written in 79."[39]

Problems also attend the individual documents themselves. A survey of the secondary literature reveals no agreement at all among the specialists regarding the dates of, for example, the *Apocryphon of James*,[40] the *Gospel of the Egyptians*,[41] the *Secret Gospel of Mark*,[42] the *Egerton Gospel*,[43] the *Gospel of Thomas*,[44] or the *Gospel of the Hebrews*.[45] And

---

38. At an earlier time Crossan offered a different stratigraphy: (1) 40s–50s, (2) 60s–70s, (3) 80s–90s, (4) 40s–90s. See "Materials and Methods in Historical Jesus Research," *Forum* 4/4 (1988), pp. 9–10.

39. N. T. Wright, *Jesus and the Victory of God* (Minneapolis: Fortress, 1996), p. 49, n. 102.

40. According to Helmut Koester, *Ancient Christian Gospels* (Philadelphia: Trinity Press International, 1990), p. 200, "It is still too early to draw final conclusions concerning the character and date of the Apocryphon of James."

41. "The time of composition cannot be determined exactly. The Gospel of the Egyptians belongs in the second century, presumably the first half." So W. Schneemelcher, "The Gospel of the Egyptians," in *New Testament Apocrypha, Volume One: Gospels and Related Writings*, vol. 1., rev. ed., ed. Wilhelm Schneemelcher and R. McL. Wilson (Louisville: Westminster/John Knox, 1992), p. 215. According to Ron Cameron, *The Other Gospels: Non-Canonical Gospel Texts* (Philadelphia: Westminster, 1982), p. 50, "a date in the late first or early second century is most likely."

42. Great controversy has surrounded this document; some have suggested that it might be a modern forgery. See Morton Smith, "Clement and Secret Mark: The Score at the End of the First Decade," *HTR* 75 (1982), pp. 449–61 (arguing for authenticity) and H. Merklein, in *New Testament Apocrypha*, vol. 1, pp. 106–109 (urging reservations); also Robert H. Gundry, *Mark: A Commentary on his Apology for the Cross* (Grand Rapids: Eerdmans, 1993), pp. 603–23.

43. Although Crossan thinks this could be as early as the fifties, many (with some justification) have seen dependence upon both the Synoptics and John; see, e.g., Frans Neirynck, "Papyrus Egerton 2 and the Healing of the Leper," *ETL* 61 (1985), pp. 153–60, and D. F. Wright, "Apocryphal Gospels: The 'Unknown Gospel' (Pap. Egerton 2) and the *Gospel of Peter*," in *Gospel Perspectives: The Jesus Tradition outside the Gospels, Volume 5*, ed. David Wenham (Sheffield: JSOT, 1985), pp. 210–21

44. According to Crossan, *Gospel of Thomas I* was composed ("possibly in Jerusalem, under the aegis of James' authority") in the 50s, *Gospel of Thomas II* ("under the aegis of the Thomas authority") in the 60s or 70s perhaps. The two layers "are identified, but

Crossan's early dating of many sources is idiosyncratic. Furthermore, the experts express widely divergent opinions regarding the evolution and sources of the *Gospel of Thomas*. Can we really reconstruct an early version of it? Did it draw upon the Synoptics? Much doubt likewise besets the very existence of both the Signs Gospel that may lie behind John [46] and the so-called Cross Gospel.[47]

What happens to those of us who cannot come to any firm judgment on the dating of a document or the existence of a hypothetical source? If, for instance, one cannot decide even to what century *Thomas* belongs, how do we utilize Crossan's method? Should we still not be able to use those complexes within *Thomas* that appear to us to be independent and primitive even when we are unable to plug the document into a chrono-

---

tentatively and experimentally, as follows: the earlier James-layer is now discernible primarily in those units with independent attestation elsewhere . . . the Thomas-layer is now discernible primarily in that which is unique to this collection. . . ." (*Historical Jesus*, p. 428). Crossan himself admits that this stratification is "crude." One may add, without discourtesy, that it is also highly speculative. What is the justification for the precise dating? How does Crossan know that *Gospel of Thomas I* was not composed in the 60s or 70s (and so belongs to his second stratum), *Gospel of Thomas II* in the 70s or 80s? Others date *Thomas* to the second century and see dependence upon the Synoptics; note especially C. M. Tuckett, "Thomas and the Synoptics," *NovT* 30 (1988), pp. 132–57; idem, "Das Thomasevangelium und die synoptischen Evangelien," *Berlin Theologische Zeitschrift* 12 (1995), pp. 186–200. In "The Historical Jesus in Earliest Christianity," in *Jesus and Faith*, p. 5, Crossan writes: "Those Christians whom Paul is strongly opposing during the winter of 53 to 54 CE in writing 1 Corinthians make eminent sense as Thomas-type Christians." He then refers to others (Helmut Koester and Stephen Patterson) who have made this suggestion. If this is one of Crossan's reasons for putting *Thomas* in the 50s, it is not compelling. At best one might be able to show, through an examination of 1 Corinthians, that a Thomas-like Christianity existed in the 50s, but surely not that the *Gospel of Thomas* itself had already then been composed. Scholars have also observed some interesting connections between Q and Paul's opponents. Do we then infer, on this basis, that Q also must have been circulating in the 50s and that among Paul's opponents were both Q Christians and Thomas Christians? Again, why not take the fascinating links between *Thomas* and John's Gospel (see Gregory J. Riley, *Resurrection Reconsidered: Thomas and John in Controversy* [Minneapolis: Fortress, 1995]), as evidence that *Thomas* was written at the end of the first century?

45. Crossan dates this to the 50s and says it is independent of the Synoptics. But surely this is one point at which we simply have to confess ignorance. The date of the *Gospel according to the Hebrews* and all but seven short fragments of it are things lost to history. Any time between 50 and 150 C.E. is possible, and no decade more likely than any other.

46. For a survey of the history of this hypothesis followed by critical evaluation see Gilbert Van Belle, *The Signs Source in the Fourth Gospel: Historical Survey and Critical Evaluation of the Semeia Hypothesis*, BETL 116 (Leuven: Leuven University Press, 1994).

47. Crossan has an entire book on this source: *The Cross that Spoke: The Origins of the Passion Narrative* (San Francisco: Harper & Row, 1988). For criticism see A. Kirk, "Examining Priorities: Another Look at the *Gospel of Peter*'s Relationship to the New Testament Gospels," *NTS* 40 (1994), pp. 572–95.

logical sequence? And if this is the case, have we not admitted that what matters is not a document's date but our estimation of the traditions within it?

One must allow Crossan his judgments about dates, many of which he has argued for in various publications. But one wonders how he dares to be so confident about such uncertain things. Is it not ironic that he has chosen to erect his project upon assertions that are no less controverted than his subsequent pronouncements about what traditions do or do not go back to Jesus? Far too much depends upon conjectures, not established conclusions. To illustrate: if one were to put Q in the 60s instead of 40s or 50s, then by my count almost a third of the items in the first stratum would be moved to the second stratum. That is no small change. Similarly, even if we buy into the hypothesis of a primitive *Thomas*, dating it just a decade later would require serious revision, for then *Thomas* and so twenty-eight complexes would be moved out of the first stratum. Is it not strange that so much hinges upon putting Q and *Thomas I* in the 50s and not later? Obviously, those of us who disagree with significant aspects of his stratigraphical analysis, or are just uncertain about it, will not agree that he has reached bedrock. We will need to build our houses upon some other foundation.

Crossan freely confesses that his "methodology does not claim a spurious objectivity." In line with this, he challenges others to accept his "formal moves or. . .to replace them with better ones. They are, of course, only formal moves, which then demand a material investment. Different scholars might invest those formal moves with widely divergent sources and texts, but historical Jesus research would at least have some common methodology instead of a rush to conclusion. . . ."[48] I should like to take up this challenge.

If we are going to insist upon sorting the sources into strata, then we might well locate the first break at the destruction of the second temple. For whether or not the story of the flight to Pella (Eusebius, *H.E.* 3:5:3) is apocryphal, a break in the sociological continuity of Jewish Christianity clearly occurred then; and from that point on the law-free version of Christianity seems to have gained the upper hand. So 70 C.E. (unlike Crossan's first suggested break, 60 C.E.) marks a major turning point in the history of the church.

What then would go into that first stratum, into the period 30–70 C.E.? The authentic Paulines and Q would have to be included. So too also probably Mark, for those who now date it after the destruction of

---

48. *Historical Jesus*, p. xxxiv.

Jerusalem think it was composed very shortly thereafter, and so its traditions go back at least to the 60s. Crossan would further include *Thomas*, the *Egerton Gospel*, the Fayum Fragment, P. Oxy. 1224, the *Gospel of the Hebrews*, a sayings source common to *Didache* 16 and Matthew 24, the Cross Gospel, the *Gospel of the Egyptians*, and a miracle collection used by the Signs Gospel as well as by Mark and the *Secret Gospel of Mark*. This, however, is to be both perilously exhaustive and unduly speculative. It is surely better to be circumspect in this matter and err on the side of caution. If a document can be plausibly dated later rather than earlier, is it not safer, on methodological grounds, to prefer the later date? For this reason many of us would exclude all of Crossan's noncanonical proposals from the first stratum. Also, for many of us, too much doubt surrounds the reality of the Cross Gospel and a miracle collection allegedly used by the Signs Gospel, Mark, and *The Secret Gospel of Mark* for them to be placed in any stratification. They are interesting hypotheses, but one is reluctant to do anything with them.

Whereas (with the exception of Paul's epistles) the members of Crossan's first stratum are all noncanonical and/or hypothetical, my much shorter list of sources certainly composed before 70—Paul, Q, Mark—contains two canonical sources and one hypothetical source reconstructed from the Synoptics (Q). This is not the result of a personal bias in favor of the canon. For I do indeed find some independent traditions about Jesus outside the canonical Gospels, including *Thomas*. It is simply my honest conclusion that Paul, Mark, and Q are probably our earliest sources, and that nothing noncanonical can be confidently placed before 70 C.E.

Whether or not this is the correct judgment, the recent fuss over the value of extracanonical sources has perhaps been, if not much ado about nothing, then much ado about not too much. Crossan is a champion of noncanonical sources. He does not believe that the canonical Gospels should have pride of place in reconstructing the historical Jesus. He and others have even sometimes impugned the integrity of scholars who have not seen the extracanonical light.[49] But if one carefully scrutinizes where he puts his + signs in his data base, it becomes apparent that, when all is said and done, he has a mostly Synoptic Jesus.[50] On pp. xiii–xxvi of *The Historical Jesus*, Crossan offers a reconstructed inventory of the

---

49. See, e.g., "Materials and Methods," pp. 6–7, where he speaks of Jeremias's "prejudice," and "Responses and Reflections," in *Jesus and Faith*, p. 13.

50. Compare Robin Scroggs, in his review of Crossan's *Historical Jesus*, in *Int* 47/3 (1993), p. 301: "I have tried to pay especial attention to Crossan's appropriation of the apocryphal materials he considers authentic, and I am not certain whether such appropriation significantly affects . . . [the] picture."

authentic sayings of Jesus. Of the one hundred and four sayings printed, only six or seven are unattested in the canon. It is true that his tradition-histories often use noncanonical variants,[51] and also true that he frequently finds the earliest version of a saying in *Thomas*. Still, it is perhaps surprising that Crossan's scouring of extracanonical sources has not, by his own accounting, added much that is truly new.

The preceding discussion began with a conditional: *if* one is going to insist upon sorting the sources into strata. . . . But should we so insist? I am hard pressed to say for sure. It certainly makes sense to suppose that time dimmed and distorted memories and even crafted false ones. Still, there is not really much time between, say, Q and Mark or between Mark and L (all of which Crossan assigns to separate strata). We are talking here about years, not centuries. Further, as everyone recognizes, genuine sayings of Jesus appear in what are Crossan's second and third strata,[52] and in his words, "in abstract theory, a unit from the fourth stratum could be more original than one from the first stratum."[53] Many in fact have argued that in several places where Q (from Crossan's first stratum) overlaps with Mark (from Crossan's second stratum), the latter is sometimes more primitive.[54]

Moreover, is it not possible that, "in abstract theory," our earliest source could have been a tendentious production that subsequent sources improved upon? Students of Buddhism hold that probably "the first items of the sacred biography to appear within the Buddhist tradition were the Jākata stories which recount events in the previous lives of the Founder. In fact, it is quite possible that such stories were told by the Buddha himself to illustrate a point or to drive home a moral."[55] Historians of Alexander the Great maintain that Arrian's *Anabasis*, written in the second century C.E., is probably more reliable than the works of Onesicritus of Astypalaea and Cleitarchus, which were written close to the lifetime of Alexander,[56] and that, in general, Arrian's prudent evaluation of his sources enabled him often to improve upon his predecessors.

---

51. One noteworthy example: on pp. 360–67 of *The Historical Jesus*, Crossan uses the *Didache* to argue that the tradition of the last supper did not originate with Jesus.

52. According to Crossan's inventory, stratum 2 has 18 complexes with the + sign and stratum 3 has 18 with the + sign.

53. Ibid., p. xxxii.

54. See Rudolf Laufen, *Die Doppelüberlieferungen der Logienquelle und des Markusevangeliums*, BBB 54 (Bonn: Peter Hanstein, 1980), and the interesting review of Charles E. Carlston, *CBQ* 43 (1981), pp. 473–75.

55. Frank E. Reynolds, "The Many Lives of Buddha: A Study of Sacred Biography and Theravāda Tradition," in Reynolds and Capps, *The Biographical Process*, p. 42 (see n. 1).

56. Lionel Pearson, *The Lost Histories of Alexander the Great* (New York: American Philological Association, 1960), pp. 83–111, 212–42.

Crossan's stratigraphical method, on the contrary, might mislead one into supposing that there is a correlation between the date when a document appeared and the age of the traditions preserved in that document. But if someone were to establish beyond reasonable doubt that all of the parables in Q entered only at a second or third stage of Q's development, that would be nothing more than an interesting fact about the evolution of Q. We would still not know anything more about where those parables came from originally. Coming into a textual tradition is not always the same thing as coming into being. Crossan himself knows this. He holds that the apocalyptic sayings of the Baptist entered Q only at a secondary stage, but he nonetheless thinks them reliable testimony to what John was all about.[57]

Geologists refer to inverted strata and thrust faults: some things are not in the expected order. In like manner, historians of Jesus know all too well that the historical figure they seek is not, so to speak, really confined to the bottom; he is scattered throughout the different layers of the first and early second century. So how much are the uncertain dates of sources not much separated in time going to help us in our quest for Jesus? Is a stratigraphical procedure really required for "scholarly discipline and investigative integrity"?[58] Crossan finds at least 22% of the sayings singly attested in L—a third-stratum source—to go back to Jesus, whereas he finds approximately 28% of the sayings singly attested in Q—a first-stratum source—to have such an origin. That is not much of a difference—and reason for wondering whether stratigraphy really discloses important truths.

If our methods work with material in a supposed early stratum, will they not work equally well with materials in later strata? And if so, what is gained by privileging one stratum? Does it not make sense instead to apply our indices of authenticity to all complexes no matter where they come from? Crossan would respond that he has nowhere released himself from such an obligation. But then why does he so emphasize the importance of stratigraphy? One recalls that New Testament textual critics have found that the oldest witnesses are not always the best.

Imagine that Mark and Luke but not Matthew had survived. We would then sunder Luke into Mark and L material; Q would for us be gone. But would this make much difference in our reconstruction of the historical Jesus? We would not be lacking any material, just the knowledge that some of it came from a lost sayings source. Whether Crossan

57. *Historical Jesus*, pp. 228–38.
58. Ibid., p. xxxii.

would still come up with the same Jesus under such circumstances is an interesting question.[59] I think he might. If so, what does this mean for stratigraphy?

3. *Multiple attestation.* In addition to relying upon early attestation, Crossan also pays much attention to how often a complex is independently attested. Does it appear only in one source or in two or in three or in more than three? His principle is that the more widely attested a complex is in independent sources, the more likely it is to have originated with Jesus. In affirming this, Crossan seems to be making common sense. The scholar looking for the historical Buddha typically begins with the items shared by the various Buddhist schools: such items come from a time before those schools diverged. According to an old rule of journalism, each fact should be attested by at least two firsthand witnesses.

But common sense can mislead, and it may mislead us here. The more frequently a complex is attested, the more congenial, one naturally infers, it was to early Christians. But the more congenial a complex was to early Christians, surely the less likely it is that Jesus composed it. Conversely, the less congenial a tradition, the more likely its origin with Jesus and the less likely its multiple attestation. Here the criterion of multiple attestation is in a tug-of-war with the criterion of dissimilarity: they pull the same unit in opposite directions.

The problem becomes acute when we contemplate the complexes that are attributed to Jesus in one source but not so credited in another. There are many of these. Surely this is an interesting fact that demands attention (although it is not reflected in Crossan's appendix). Consider the sayings now collected in Q 6:27–38. Parallels appear in the following places: Rom 2:1; 12:14, 17, 21; 1 Cor 4:12; 1 Thess 5:15; *1 Clem.* 13:2; Polycarp, *Ep.* 2:2–3; and *Did.* 1:3–5. Q and *1 Clement* ascribe the relevant words to Jesus himself. Paul and the *Didache* do not, and Polycarp quotes only some of them as having Jesus' authority. What follows? Jürgen Sauer has argued that the early church created the imperative to love one's enemy and the sayings popularly associated with it.[60] The attribution to Jesus was secondary. Most would dispute this verdict. But Sauer's reasoning is understandable. Not only do the relevant sayings appear with

---

59. In personal conversation Crossan has indicated that he himself is unsure of the answer: he might need to rethink everything.

60. J. Sauer, "Traditionsgeschichtliche Erwägungen zu den synoptischen und paulinischen Aussagen über Feindesliebe und Wiedervergeltungsverzicht," *ZNW* 76 (1985), pp. 1–28.

sufficient frequency to enable him to say that here the criterion of dissimilarity fails to point to Jesus, but those sayings are not always passed down under Jesus' name. So in this case multiple attestation becomes part of the case *against* derivation from Jesus.

Strangely enough, Crossan's work itself makes one query the claim that the more attestation something has the more confident we can be about its origin. Consider the following chart, constructed on the basis of Crossan's inventory for his first stratum. The numbers represent the percentages of authentic complexes. That is, the 70 in the Q column on the row for multiple attestation means that, of the Q complexes that are attested more than three times, 70% are marked with the + sign.

	Q	Mk	M	L	Thomas
multiple attestation	70%	75%	40%	60%	77%
triple attestation	70%	74%	25%	0%	62%
double attestation	72%	75%	63%	75%	89%
single attestation	28%	—	—	—	—

Given Crossan's stated method, one would expect the highest numbers to be at the top. This is not the case. In four of the sources cited (Q, M, L, *Thomas*), the highest number is on the row for double attestation. The exception is Mark, for which the numbers for all three strata are nearly identical. The implication is that, when Crossan has finished with the material, although single attestation turns out to be a rather bad thing (note the 28% for single attestation in Q in the above chart), nothing seems to be gained when something is witnessed to three times instead of two, or four times instead of three, or five times instead of four.

Why should this be the case? When two independent sources attest a complex, that is valuable information. For it proves that, for both sources, that complex was tradition. But it does not disclose anything more. When Tom, Dick, and Harry tell the same joke even though they have never spoken to one another and have no common acquaintances, we may infer that none of them made it up. But we still have no information about who *did* make it up. Consider the following diagram, which returns Faustina, as well as her husband Justus, another post-Easter contributor to the Jesus tradition, to the argument:

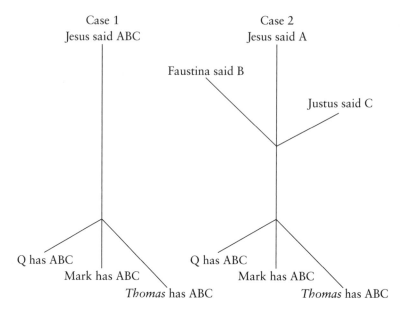

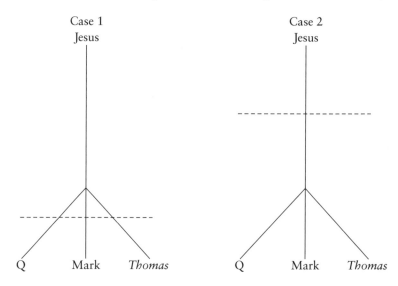

Multiple attestation cannot distinguish between these two cases. It cannot tell us who said what. It does nothing more than demonstrate that A, B, and C already belonged to the Jesus tradition before the earliest of our three sources.

The point may be further illustrated with a second diagram, one which has to do not with individual sayings or complexes but with the broader streams of tradition that flowed into Q, Mark, and *Thomas*. The horizontal line marks the death of Jesus and the subsequent birth of the church:

Multiple attestation establishes a probable origin with Jesus only if the three streams separated before Easter (case 1). But whether they in fact separated then or sometime later (case 2) is a separate issue that has to be independently determined. If the evidence is consistent with case 2, then we remain in the dark because we do not know whether what we are examining entered the tradition before or after the dotted line that represents the birth of the church.[61]

One final point regarding multiple attestation: Crossan's wont is to confine it to sayings or complexes, not ideas.[62] Thus he attributes no apocalyptic Son of man saying to Jesus, partly because none has multiple attestation.[63] But certainly the *idea* of the apocalyptic Son of man appears independently in several sources. Ben Witherington has observed that Crossan himself, when discussing the contrast between John the Baptist and Jesus in Mk 2:18–20, takes the saying into account because of its thematic parallel in Q 7:31–35.[64] In Crossan's words, "We have. . .only single attestation for the contrast on fasting between John and Jesus in 144 *Wisdom Justified* [1/1] and 106 *Fasting and Wedding* [1/2], but I cannot ignore them, because they evince double attestation not of the same text but of the same theme."[65] What are we supposed to think? Does multiple attestation include themes, or should it be confined to complexes?

The question is crucial if there are things that turn up again and again in the Jesus tradition but which may, upon critical analysis, never appear in a complex one takes to be original. Consider the proposition that Jesus had a pre-Easter follower named Peter. Let us say that, after examination of all the relevant materials, someone decides that every single story or saying in which he appears is a creation of the community and without pre-Easter foundation. What would follow? While the evidence would be consistent with denying to Peter a pre-Easter role, would one have good reason for thinking this to be the case? Could one not rather take Peter's frequent appearance in various complexes from various sources to be best explained on the supposition that Peter did follow Jesus? Here one would

---

61. In order to make my point I have assumed that apocryphal Jesus traditions emerged only after Easter; but that probably was not the case; see below, pp. 70–72.

62. Contrast the still interesting work of Dodd on this subject: *History and the Gospel,* pp. 91–103 (see n. 3).

63. On this see further below, pp. 115–20.

64. *The Jesus Quest: The Third Search for the Jew of Nazareth* (Downers Grove: Inter-Varsity, 1995), pp. 66–67.

65. *Historical Jesus,* p. 260.

have to choose between multiple attestation of complexes and multiple attestation of themes or motifs.

4. *Single and double attestation.* The preceding pages indicate that the chief service of multiple independent attestation is to exclude a redactional origin and so establish the traditional nature of a complex prior to its earliest witness. It takes us this far and no farther. When Crossan instead offers that it can up the odds that something comes from Jesus, he is not obviously correct. This judgment not only, as observed, goes against his own conclusions but makes a very strange assumption. Why should he in effect assume that the popularity of a complex bespeaks authenticity? Maybe, as already indicated, this turns everything upside down. Perhaps the popularity enjoyed by a complex should be proportional to our suspicion that it was a Christian creation or has at least been much meddled with by the church.

Let me return to Q 6:27–38 and its parallels within and without the canon. Only in Q do we find the straightforward imperative, "Love your enemies." It does not appear in Rom 2:1; 12:14, 17, 21; 1 Cor 4:12; 1 Thess 5:15; *1 Clem.* 13:2; Polycarp, *Ep.* 2:2–3; or *Did.* 1:3–5. But "Love your enemies" is precisely the most memorable and provocative phrase in the entire network of related texts. Further, one would be hard pressed to find many who doubt that Jesus authored the strange and demanding imperative. Our conclusion should probably be that the modification of "Love your enemies" was deliberate. Christians were understandably uncomfortable with the apparent implications of this radical imperative, and so the paraenetical tradition displaced it with the easier and more realistic order to "*Pray* for your enemies." [66] In such a case as this, the singly attested Q saying gets our vote even though it is missing from half a dozen other witnesses to the same tradition. Here we prefer the testimony of the one over the testimony of the many.

If we are going to be mechanical or statistical about things, those complexes attested precisely twice are those with the highest claim to authenticity. For when a complex is attested by two and only two independent sources this means that it was not created by either and further that Christians found it far less useful than many other parts of the Jesus tradition. Indeed, the chart on p. 21 above shows that even for Crossan it is sayings with double attestation that fare best.

But then what about those sayings that are only singly attested? This is

66. See Heinz-Wolfgang Kuhn, "Das Liebesgebot Jesu als Tora und als Evangelium," in Hubert Frankemölle and Karl Kertelge, eds., *Vom Urchristentum zu Jesus: Für Joachim Gnilka* (Freiburg: Herder, 1989), pp. 194–230.

where Crossan's method, at least to judge by his results, works well. The following statistics, which reckon the percentages of authenticity for five sources in four strata, are based upon his inventory:[67]

	all	Q	Mk	M	L	Thomas
1st stratum						
multiple attestation	48%	70%	75%	40%	60%	77%
triple attestation	55%	70%	74%	25%	0%	62%
double attestation	62%	72%	75%	63%	75%	89%
single attestation	21%	28%	—	—	—	—
2d stratum						
multiple attestation	(0%)	(0%)	(0%)			
triple attestation	40%	—	66%	(50%)	66%	—
double attestation	11%	—	38%	—	(0%)	0%
single attestation	9%	—	10%	—	—	16%
3d stratum						
multiple attestation	(0%)	—	—	—	—	—
triple attestation	(0%)	—	—	(0%)	—	—
double attestation	14%	—	—	20%	20%	—
single attestation	15%	—	—	9%	22%	—
4th stratum						
multiple attest			N O N E			
triple			N O N E			
double			N O N E			
single	0%	—	—	—	—	—

It is immediately apparent that, for Crossan, it is not good for a saying to be alone. The rates of authenticity fall off precipitously when one moves from double or triple or multiple to single attestation. For example, 70% or more of the Q complexes attested elsewhere are from Jesus, but when they have no companionship authenticity falls below 30%. Similarly, L and *Thomas* fare rather well when standing with others, but when alone their numbers plummet.

What is the correct interpretation of Crossan's result? Seemingly implicit in his method is the presumption that most of the traditions attested singly may have been created by the particular community that handed them on, and so they were not widely known. Perhaps this presumption is correct. Who among us would assign to Jesus sayings singly attested in

67. The number under "all" is obtained by dividing the number of + signs by the total number of complexes for each stratum. The numbers in parentheses indicate that the category contained five or fewer cases and so may be statistically insignificant.

sources as late as John or the *Dialogue of the Savior*? We assume they were created by the author of John or of the *Dialogue* or by their communities or by those communities' special tradition.

But matters may be different with a source as early as Q. If Crossan could argue that the Q community was a distinct entity whose singly attested sayings were produced by and largely confined to that entity, others could urge that contributors to Q knew some things that Jesus said and did that other tradents of the Jesus tradition just did not know. One could also argue—and this I do argue here—that many of the singly attested Q sayings do not appear elsewhere because (1) they became potential theological problems (Q 9:59–60;[68] 11:24–26;[69] 13:28–29;[70] 16:17;[71] 22: 28–30[72]), (2) they were no longer understood (Q 16:16;[73] 17:37[74]), and (3) they were not relevant apart from an ongoing dialogue with scribes and/or Pharisees (Q 11:39–41,[75] 42,[76] 43,[77] 46,[78] 47–48,[79] 52[80]). So one wonders about the disparity between the high percentage of authentic complexes Crossan finds in Q complexes attested two or more times, on the one hand, and the low percentage he finds in Q complexes attested only once, on the other. Maybe the relative reliability of Q when it is

68. Jesus' call for a man to follow him and leave the dead to bury their own dead has often been thought to contradict the commandment to honor parents.

69. Exegetes have sometimes wondered whether Q 11:24–26 might not reflect Jesus' own experience of having a demon return to a person he had exorcized. See, e.g., Joel Marcus, "The Beelzebul Controversy and the Eschatologies of Jesus," in *Authenticating the Words of Jesus*, ed. Craig A. Evans and Bruce Chilton (Leiden: E. J. Brill, 1998, forthcoming). Some early Christians might have been unhappy with the thought that an exorcism of Jesus was not permanently effective.

70. This saying was originally about the return of Israel from the diaspora; see Dale C. Allison, Jr., *The Jesus Tradition in Q* (Valley Forge: Trinity Press International, 1997), pp. 177–92. Outside of Jewish Christian circles, such a belief had to be either dropped or spiritualized.

71. Christians with a relaxed view of the authority of the Mosaic Torah would have had difficulties with an assertion about the law's inviolability.

72. The promise to sit on twelve thrones might be thought to include Judas—a troublesome thought.

73. The difficulties in interpreting "the kingdom of God has suffered violence and the violent take it by force" are notorious.

74. The meaning of "Where the corpse is, there the eagles will be gathered together" is anyone's guess.

75. This woe is addressed to the Pharisees and refers to their practice of cleansing dishes.

76. This woe is addressed to the Pharisees and is about tithing mint and dill and cummin.

77. This woe is addressed to the Pharisees and refers to seating arrangements in synagogues.

78. This concerns Pharisees who put hard burdens on others.

79. This is about building memorials to the prophets.

80. This woe is about the Pharisees not allowing others to enter the kingdom.

backed up by other witnesses should encourage us to trust it when it is not so backed up. So I am unsure whether the disparity in Crossan's results is due to the creativity of Q's tradition or to his excessive skepticism regarding singly attested complexes.

5. *Tradition-histories and the burden of proof.* One of the most remarkable statements in *The Historical Jesus* appears on p. xxxii: "My method postulates that, at least for the first stratum, everything is original until it is argued otherwise." In the past a few New Testament scholars have urged that a saying attested in the Synoptics should be presumed authentic until it is proved otherwise.[81] But there have also been those who have claimed just the opposite, that a saying should be presumed inauthentic until one brings forth good arguments to the contrary.[82] The response to both of these judgments is that the burden of proof should always be on the one making an argument.[83] The one who wants to use a complex to say something about Jesus should show that it originated with Jesus. And the one who wants to use a complex to say something about the church should establish its communal *Sitz-im-Leben*. Why should this demand vary from stratum to stratum? "What makes a datum reliable is not the document in which it is found but its intrinsic authenticity as established by careful testing."[84]

Aside from the issue of the burden of proof is the problem of how Crossan typically establishes to his satisfaction that a complex did not originate with Jesus. His primary method is tradition-history. Let us consider, as an illustration, his tradition-history of Q 12:8–9, a complex denied to Jesus, even though it is attested in several sources and belongs to Crossan's first stratum. His case can be outlined as follows:

Before the Angels [1/4], attested in Q 12:8–9 (compare Mt 10:32–34); Mk 8:38; Rev 3:5; 2 Tim 2:12

Stage I

Proposition: The church formulated the following saying: "Every one who acknowledges me before men will be acknowledged before the

---

81. So, e.g., Stewart C. Goetz and Craig L. Blomberg, "The Burden of Proof," *JSNT* 11 (1981), pp. 39–63, and R. H. Stein, *Gospels and Tradition: Studies on Redaction Criticism of the Synoptic Gospels* (Grand Rapids: Baker, 1991), pp. 153–87. Harvey K. McArthur, "The Burden of Proof in Historical Jesus Research," *ExpT* 82 (1971), pp. 116–19, endorses the principle, but only in relation to the criterion of multiple attestation.

82. So, e.g., Perrin, *Rediscovering*, p. 15.

83. So Hooker, "Wrong Tool," p. 580; Ben F. Meyer, *The Aims of Jesus* (London: SCM, 1979), pp. 81–83; E. P. Sanders, *Jesus and Judaism* (Philadelphia: Fortress, 1985), p. 13.

84. Keck, *Future*, p. 30.

angels of my Father; but he who denies me before men will be denied before the angels of my Father."

Justification: (a) The church composed what Ernst Käsemann termed "sentences of sacral law," and this is an example of one.[85] (b) The other "sentences of sacral law" in the Jesus tradition are community creations.[86]

Stage II

Proposition: The passives were replaced by references to the speaker himself (Jesus). Matthew has, "I also will acknowledge" and "I also will deny." 2 Tim 1:12 has, "If we deny him, he also will deny us." Rev 3:5 has, "I will confess your name before the Father and his angels."

Justification: One would expect the tradition to make Jesus' role more and more explicit.[87]

Stage III

Proposition: Mark added "the Son of man" to his variant: "For whoever is ashamed of me and of my words in this adulterous and sinful generation, of him will the Son of man also be ashamed." Luke followed Mark in inserting "the Son of man."

Justification: Versions of the saying without "the Son of man" exist, and "because of the formal matrix, it is God or the passive voice that one expects to find as the original protagonist."[88]

What shall we say of this reconstruction? It is one thing to observe that a process may have occurred and quite another to establish that it in fact did occur. We should respect the critical distance between possibility and probability. Crossan could be right. But he also could be wrong. It is not apparent that he has here obviously crossed the line between the possible and the probable. Others have offered equally plausible tradition-histories for the very same complex. Let me outline a tentative alternative of my own:

Stage I

Proposition: Jesus said something close to this: "Every one who acknowledges me before human beings, the Son of man will acknowledge

---

85. See Ernst Käsemann, "Sentences of Holy Law in the New Testament," in *New Testament Questions of Today* (Philadelphia: Fortress, 1969), pp. 66–81.

86. This is probably a fallacious generalization; see David E. Aune: *Prophecy in Early Christianity and the Ancient Mediterranean World* (Grand Rapids: Eerdmans, 1983), pp. 166–68, 237–40.

87. Crossan does not say this, but the point seems implicit in his argument.

88. *Historical Jesus*, p. 249.

before the angels of God; but the one who denies me before human beings, the Son of man will deny before the angels of God."

Justification: (a) Jesus composed a good number of sayings in which
the first part relates a circumstance in the present and the second part a
correlative circumstance in the eschatological future.[89] (b) Early Christians are unlikely to have created a saying which might be taken to mean
that someone other than Jesus is "the Son of man."

Stage II

Proposition: Luke or his tradition turned the second appearance of "the
Son of man" into a passive ("will be denied").

Justification: (a) The omission destroys what must have been an original symmetry. (b) Luke often avoids verbatim repetition. (c) Luke may
have wished to avoid depicting Jesus as an accuser.

Stage III

Proposition: Mark or his tradition dropped the first part of the saying
(that about acknowledging Jesus) and retained only the second.

Justification: (a) Abbreviation has taken place to serve the purpose of
Mark's immediate context, which is moral warning. (b) Mark's saying is
otherwise obviously secondary ("ashamed of me and of my words").

Stage IV

Proposition: Matthew replaced "the Son of man" with "I."

Justification: (a) κἀγώ is elsewhere redactional (Mt: 9; Mk: 0; Lk: 6).
(b) Matthew replaced "the Son of man" in Mk 8:31 = Mt 16:21 and
probably Lk 6:22 = Mk 5:11.

Stage V

Proposition: The saying is alluded to outside the Jesus tradition without
the title, "the Son of man" (Rev 3:5; 2 Tim 2:12).

Justification: Early Christian sources outside the Jesus tradition generally avoid "the Son of man."

The issue here is not whether this second tradition-history is better
than Crossan's. The point rather is how easily one can come up with
something else, how almost effortlessly one can imagine that history followed another path.

Let me try an analogy. My children play with jigsaw puzzles. Sometimes

---

89. Recall the beatitudes and see David E. Aune, *Prophecy*, p. 166.

they begin by collecting all the pieces with straight edges and then making the frame. Other times they start with all the pieces of the same color, put them together to make a portion of the whole, and then work outward. Once the picture is done I cannot tell which method they used. A completed jigsaw puzzle leaves no clues as to the order in which its pieces were assembled. The very same puzzle can be put together in countless different ways. Although we are reluctant to admit it, maybe the Jesus tradition is similar. We have the finished Gospels. But can we really draw up in any reliable detail, as Crossan has attempted to do, the multitudinous tradition histories that presumably lie behind them?

Writing a commentary on Matthew has given me the opportunity to review the sundry tradition histories that have been offered by divers scholars for all the material in the First Gospel, and I have often offered my own speculative histories. But as my experience has grown my ambition has narrowed. The overwhelming impression I have after studying the vast secondary literature is that all too often we have been trying to know the unknowable. Was the saying preserved in Mk 10:15 ("Truly I tell you, whoever does not receive the kingdom of God as a little child will never enter it") the original core from which the complex in Mk 10:13–16 par. was spun,[90] or did the story in Mk 10:13–14 + 16 draw to itself the saying in 10:15?[91] Did someone fabricate Mk 2:15 ("Jesus in Levi's house with toll collectors and sinners") out of 2:14 (the call of Levi) in order to introduce 2:16–17 (Jesus' response to the accusation that he eats with sinners),[92] or did someone fabricate 2:14 on the basis of 2:15?[93] Again, regarding the different versions of the last supper preserved in Mk 14.23–26; Lk 22.19–20; and 1 Cor 11.23–25, did Luke conflate the tradition in Paul with the more primitive tradition of Mark?[94] Or did Luke preserve an early tradition that developed in two different directions, one represented by Mark, the other by Luke?[95] Or is Paul's account

---

90. So John Dominic Crossan, "Kingdom and Children," *Semeia* 29 (1983), pp. 75–95.

91. So R. Busemann, *Die Jüngergemeinde nach Markus 10: Eine redaktionsgeschichtliche Untersuchung des 10 Kapitels im Markusevangelium*, BBB 57 (Bonn: Hanstein, 1983), pp. 119–28.

92. So John Dominic Crossan, *In Fragments: The Aphorisms of Jesus* (San Francisco: Harper & Row, 1983), pp. 213–20.

93. So Rudolf Pesch, "Levi-Matthäus (Mc 2.14/Mt 9.9; 10.3): Ein Beitrag zum Lösung eines alten Problems," *ZNW* 59 (1968), pp. 40–56.

94. So Rudolf Pesch, *Das Abendmahl und Jesu Todesverständnis*, QD 80 (Freiburg: Herder, 1978), pp. 26–69.

95. So Heinz Schürmann, *Der Einsetzungsbericht Lk 22,19–20*, NTAbh 20/4 (Münster: Aschendorff, 1955).

the most primitive and Luke's more primitive than Mark's? [96] Or are these solutions simplistic because all three accounts preserve early tradition and have original and secondary elements in more or less equal measure? [97]

With regard to these and hundreds of comparable questions, modesty becomes us. We may well have our convictions (I usually, despite everything, do), but whether our convictions constitute knowledge we can never discover. We just do not know. It should trouble us that none of our speculative tradition-histories can ever be falsified. One can put together the myriad pieces of the Synoptic puzzle in just about any order. And our sources, being inanimate, cannot protest.

Pascal wrote, concerning the proofs for the existence of God known to him, that they were complicated and made little impression upon him, and, although he might have thought them of service during the moment of their demonstration, an hour afterwards he feared he had been mistaken. This is like my experience with complex tradition-histories. I can remember occasions on which I went through someone's hypothetical stages and said to myself that it all made sense. But later, after quitting the pages in which I found the tradition-history, doubts began to assail me. And then, when I later ran across a competing and no less plausible tradition-history for the very same material, I questioned whether I had gained any knowledge in the first place.

It is not here proposed that New Testament scholars quit writing tradition-histories; nor do I myself forswear the exercise. Our curiosity is too great, as is our vanity; and there is also the likelihood that sometimes we actually get to the truth. But good sense should compel us to admit how fragile and uncertain our hypothetical histories usually are. This includes Crossan's histories as well as those of everyone else.

The lesson is this: We would like to identify what facts we can reasonably know and what generalizations we can plausibly make about Jesus before we enter the congested realm of conjectural tradition-histories. Perhaps one problem with Crossan's reconstruction of the historical Jesus is that too much hangs upon his ability to divine how a completed puzzle was put together. [98]

6. *Uncertainty.* Each complex in Crossan's inventory comes prefaced

---

96. So Eduard Schweizer, *The Good News according to Mark* (Atlanta: John Knox, 1970), pp. 300–302.

97. So I. Howard Marshall, *Last Supper and Lord's Supper* (Grand Rapids: Eerdmans, 1980), pp. 40–53.

98. In fact, much can be said about Jesus without attempting intricate tradition-histories; see E. P. Sanders, *The Historical Figure of Jesus* (London: Penguin, 1993).

with a positive sign (+) or a negative sign (−). As already indicated, the former means that a complex or its core is from the historical Jesus, the latter that it is not. There is also the ± sign, which means that the "metaphorical or metonymical content" makes irrelevant "such positivistic simplicities." While there is some uncertainty about what this means, one wants to ask, Where are all the question marks? Experience informs us that there are limits to the powers of our historical-critical methods. Some things cannot be known. Surely Jesus said some of the things attributed to him. And surely Jesus did not say some of the things attributed to him. And just as surely there must be occasions on which we cannot tell the difference.[99] Doubt must surround our historical conjectures as shadow does light. Should we all not be more skeptical about our ability to divine the past? Should question marks not be scattered throughout Crossan's appendix? One would trust Crossan more if he would more often confess to be within the cloud of unknowing.

Crossan might respond that this criticism misses the mark because it misinterprets his negative sign. He could retort that it indicates only that a complex cannot be safely attributed to Jesus, that it might come from Jesus but we just cannot know this. Crossan, however, does not say this. He says that a negative sign stands for his judgment that a unit does not come from the historical Jesus. Beyond this, *many*—not a few, but many—of the units which carry the negative sign contradict, as Crossan himself freely confesses, his own reconstruction of the historical Jesus. Many of them, for example, would turn Jesus into an apocalyptic prophet. For Crossan such units just cannot be authentic.

Crossan might also respond that the historian has no business playing it safe. In *Who Killed Jesus? Exposing the Roots of Anti-Semitism in the Gospel Story of the Death of Jesus*,[100] he argues that "historical scholarship is not called to absolutes or to certitudes but only to its own best reconstructions given accurately, honestly, and publicly. Even in our courts, with life and death in the balance, our best judgments are given 'beyond a reasonable doubt.' We seldom get to beyond *any* doubt. But, in the end, judgments must be made. . . ."[101] He goes on to say that "historians

---

99. Compare Meyer, *Aims*, p. 84: There should be three columns for historicity: yes, no, and question marks. He goes on to add, rightly, that "the quest of evidence pertinent to historicity will necessarily be open, supple, and delicate, and judgments of historicity qualified by nuances over the scale of probability."

100. John Dominic Crossan, *Who Killed Jesus?* (San Francisco: HarperCollins, 1995).

101. Ibid., p. x.

should be ready and willing to say, This, in my best professional reconstruction, is what happened; that did not."[102]

Many of us, however, may honestly believe that sometimes the evidence is truly equivocal and that there is nothing wrong with saying so. One concedes that there may well be, as Pascal urged, times when, although reason remains uncertain, one must nonetheless wager. Yet that there is some need for historians to bet on each and every origin of a complex in the Jesus tradition is hardly manifest.

After laying down Crossan's learned and sophisticated book one might feel that the Jesus tradition is an intricate mess beyond our ability to sort it. Crossan's methods, however cleverly designed, raise many questions, and they cannot invert the circumstance that our ignorance exceeds our knowledge. Maybe Crossan's *The Historical Jesus* is a monument not to his own failure but to the inevitable failure of all of us. Maybe our reach for the historical Jesus must always exceed our grasp.

We cannot separate chemical compounds with a knife. Nor can we tell at the end of a river what came from the fountainhead and what from later tributaries. Once the streams mingle they cannot, by human means, be divided into their previous component parts. Aristotle seemingly preferred to speak of Pythagoreans in general instead of Pythagoras in particular because he found it too hard to extract the historical philosopher from the apocryphal material assigned to him. Might not an analogous circumspection be called for from historians of early Christianity? The Canadian mounted police can claim, "We always get our man," but we all know that some crimes go unsolved. Why should we think that contributing apocryphal material to the Jesus tradition is something that, two thousand years after the fact, we can regularly detect?

Quandaries, Alternatives, Paradigms

In theory it is conceivable that Jesus uttered a very high percentage of the sayings the Synoptics impute to him. If such were indeed the case, then obviously we could know a good deal about him and perhaps even sort out some of the secondary additions. But it is also in theory conceivable that Jesus authored, let us say, only six of those sayings. In this second case the tradition would be so thoroughly corrupt that our knowledge about him would be minimal and surely insufficient for us to figure out

102. Ibid., p. 37.

what six sayings it was that he did utter. Sometimes we can scrape off corrosion and get to the metal; other times the corrosion is such that the metal is no longer there.

The question then is this: Where, between the first hypothetical situation (a high percentage of the tradition goes back to Jesus) and the second (only six sayings go back to him) is the point at which our sources become sufficiently unreliable so as to put the quest beyond our ability? In order to solve a criminal case one must have some decent witnesses. In like manner the sources for the Jesus tradition must give us enough truth to work with: they need to tell the truth often enough for us to figure out when they are not telling the truth. If it is otherwise we are out of luck and cannot make up the lack.

Consider the issue of eschatology.[103] Many of us have, since Johannes Weiss and Albert Schweitzer, been persuaded that Jesus was an eschatological prophet with an apocalyptic scenario.[104] Our judgment is consistent with the Synoptics' testimony. They contain numerous statements about punishment and reward, about divine judgment and supernatural vindication. They also contain sayings about the coming Son of man and sayings about the coming kingdom of God. Then there is Mark 13, a lengthy prophecy of the latter days, and Q 17:22–37, which depicts eschatological catastrophe. There are also the prophetic woes cast upon those who reject Jesus' mission as well as the promises of eschatological comfort for the poor and the hungry. Those of us in Schweitzer's camp do not claim that all of this material goes back to Jesus. But we do affirm that much of it does, and that much of the remainder is in continuity with Jesus' own outlook.

Some, however, deny that Jesus' eschatology involved an imminent, apocalyptic expectation with tribulation, resurrection, and final judgment. What do they do with the materials referred to in the previous paragraph? Although they can interpret some of it in a nonapocalyptic sense, much of it—including sayings and themes attested more than once in the

---

103. Throughout this book the word "eschatology" has to do with history's consummation and the events directly associated with it, such as the resurrection and final judgment. Different writers, however, have given the term different meanings. Crossan's Jesus, for example, is eschatological by his (Crossan's) understanding of "eschatology" (having to do with a divine utopia, not necessarily the end of the world) but not by mine.

104. Herein I shall, with reference to Jesus and early Christianity, use "apocalyptic" to designate a cluster of eschatological themes and expectations—cosmic cataclysm, resurrection of the dead, universal judgment, heavenly redeemer figures, etc.—that developed, often in association with belief in a near end, in postexilic Judaism.

earliest sources—they must deny to Jesus.[105] But is not the excision of so much a dangerous procedure? One can only amputate so much before the patient is killed. If we really decide that our earliest sources—here I have in mind Q and Mark—are so misleading on this one topic, then maybe they cannot lead us to Jesus at all. Similarly, if it turns out that, in accord with the voting of some of the more skeptical members of the Jesus Seminar, Faustina, or someone like her, or several someones like her, really authored the vast majority of sayings in Q and Mark, then one wonders whether we can ever establish what Jesus, as opposed to his early followers, said.

The conclusion would seem to be that the historical Jesus cannot be caught if we are left only to our own historical-critical devices. As in the fairy tale, if the birds have eaten too many of the crumbs, the trail cannot be found. Indeed, one might go so far as to urge that, if the sayings in the earliest Jesus tradition, taken in their entirety, are not roughly congruent with the sorts of things Jesus tended to say, then our task is hopeless.

Even if we were to come to such a conservative conclusion, it must immediately be added that we can never demonstrate that our sources do in fact contain enough authentic material—however much that might be— to make questing a promising activity. There is no way around Faustina, no way ever to establish beyond hesitation that Jesus and no one else said or did such and such. Doubt will never leave us nor forsake us.

This chapter is not, however, a plea to give up the quest in favor of agnosticism about Jesus. Our criticism need not become cynicism, and I am not urging that the ax of skepticism must be laid unto the root of the trees in the Jesus tradition. The point is rather that as historians we do something different from mathematicians, who since Thales have eschewed intuition and demanded proofs. Unlike them we cannot formulate proofs for our theorems. We are also unlike scientists, if by that is meant people who fashion experimental trials which allow predictions to be concretely falsified. Certainly we will never be able to program a computer with perfected criteria of authenticity, run the Jesus tradition through it, and learn what Jesus did and did not say. There is no foreseeable victory over uncertainty and no way around subjectivity. "Persistently personal judgements have to be made about the nature of the gospel material."[106]

As historians of the Jesus tradition we are storytellers. We can do no

105. On Crossan's treatment of the apocalyptic Son of man sayings see Chapter 2 herein.
106. D. G. A. Calvert, "An Examination of the Criteria for Distinguishing the Authentic Words of Jesus," *NTS* 18 (1972), p. 219.

more than aspire to fashion a narrative that is more persuasive than competing narratives, one that satisfies our aesthetic and historical sensibilities because of its apparent ability to clarify more data in a more satisfactory fashion than its rivals.

But how is this done? The contention of this chapter is that our first move is not to discover which sayings or even what complexes are authentic.[107] Rather, we should be looking for something akin to what Thomas Kuhn once called a "paradigm," an explanatory model or matrix by which to order our data (see note 114). The initial task is to create a context, a primary frame of reference, for the Jesus tradition, a context that may assist us in determining both the authenticity of traditions and their interpretation. Most of us have probably been doing something like this all along anyway, even when we have pretended to get our results by using criteria of authenticity. We do not come to our task with nothing more than the Jesus tradition, a knowledge of first-century history, and our criteria in hand. We also always bring with us a story, formed or half-formed, a story about Jesus, a story made up of expectations and presuppositions that tacitly guide us in our use of criteria. This is one reason we have such a variety of results from various scholars.

It would seem to follow that we should initially be concerned less with refining our criteria of authenticity than with worrying about how to establish a story that can usefully arrange our mass of data into coherent patterns. If we do not and cannot come to our data with a *tabula rasa*, we might as well examine the slate. Here Crossan is correct:

> Nobody initiates historical Jesus research without any ideas about Jesus. It is therefore a little ingenuous to start from certain texts and act as if one discovered the historical Jesus at the other end of one's analysis. There is and should be always an initial hypothesis that one tests against the data.[108]

But what should be our "initial hypothesis" that we can "test against the data"? The works of modern scholarship offer us a selection. We can

---

107. Sanders, *Jesus and Judaism*, also refuses to begin with the sayings.

108. Crossan, "Materials and Methods," p. 10. He goes on, on p. 11, to state his working hypothesis: "Jesus proclaimed the unmediated presence of God to each and every individual and thus the concomitant unmediated presence of each individual to every other individual." This is offered as a summary of the original Jesus that explains the later tradition in all its multiplicity—a proposal discussed at length in "Divine Immediacy and Human Immediacy: Towards a New First Principle in Historical Jesus Research," *Semeia* 43 (1988), pp. 121–40. But in "Responses and Reflections," in *Jesus and Faith*, pp. 146–47, he discards this approach as "too subjective."

interpret the tradition on the supposition that Jesus was an eschatological prophet.[109] Or we can make sense of it by maintaining that he was a Zealot and revolutionary. The Jesus tradition can also be analyzed according to the notion that Jesus was first of all a magician, or first of all a Pharisee, or first of all a Jewish peasant Cynic, or first of all a healer and exorcist. It is possible to construe the data—to interpret, on the one hand, and to discard, on the other—in accord with each explanatory model. Reasonable people have done so.

This should not surprise, for "at any given time infinitely many mutually incompatible hypotheses are each compatible with any finite amount of data."[110] One can draw any number of curves through a finite set of points to create a thousand different pictures. Recall the two very different stories told to explain the evidence at the O. J. Simpson murder trials. One account held that all the evidence pointed to Simpson because he was guilty. The other claimed that all the evidence pointed to him because the police set him up. It is always possible to explain one set of facts with more than one story. How do we choose which story to believe?

Philosophers of science, largely in response to Kuhn's work, have much discussed the nature of competing paradigms or explanatory models in science and how shifts of vision occur—how, for instance, the Aristotlean theory of motion gave way to Galileo's theory of motion. What changes during most scientific revolutions is not the extant data but their interpretive context. There is a switch in visual gestalt: what was once seen as a duck is now seen as a rabbit.

To what extent this is a rational enterprise, and to what extent our paradigms actually correspond to reality, are involved philosophical questions beyond the scope of this chapter. I must be content with remarking that, even if some philosophers are now conceptual relativists and in general deny "that some *one* way of seeing, some one sort of theory, has any exclusive claim to be the *right* way,"[111] most New Testament scholars still share a universe of discourse, and within that discourse it makes sense to ask whether one paradigm or interpretive norm is better than some other. Not all of our pertinent facts are "theory-laden" in a debilitating sense, nor do most New Testament scholars live in truly different conceptual

109. This is what Sanders, *Jesus and Judaism*, does. See especially p. 10: "Enough evidence points towards Jewish eschatology as the general framework of Jesus' ministry that we may examine the particulars in the light of that framework."

110. Hilary Putnam, *Mathematics, Matter and Method: Philosophical Papers, Volume I*, 2d ed. (Cambridge: Cambridge University Press, 1979), p. 352.

111. G. J. Warnock, *English Philosophy since 1900* (London: Oxford University Press, 1958), p. 144.

worlds.[112] It seems reasonable to hope that the common sense of John Wisdom holds for Jesus research: "We can all easily recollect disputes which though they cannot be settled by experiment are yet disputes in which one party may be right and the other wrong and in which both parties may offer reasons and the one better reasons than the other."[113]

For the last hundred years perhaps most New Testament scholars have approached the sayings of Jesus with the paradigm of Jesus as eschatological prophet. To borrow from Kuhn's analysis of scientific revolutions, the works of Weiss and Schweitzer brought "a relatively sudden and unstructured event like the gestalt switch."[114] Many scholars underwent a sort of conversion experience (one which is still replayed today, when someone brought up in church with a noneschatological understanding of the kingdom of God goes off to college or graduate school and becomes convinced that Jesus was an eschatological prophet). Despite both initial and continued resistance, more and more scholars came to see that the story of Jesus as eschatological prophet offered, to use Lakotas's expression, the best research program. Its simplicity, scope, explanatory power, and parallels in the history of religion commended it.

The basic eschatological paradigm has been in place now for a century. It has become an academic tradition that has enabled its social constituency to order its reading of New Testament texts; and its proponents remain many. It indeed still holds its proud place. But some now think that, although it has lived a useful life, the old paradigm now needs to be retired. Few deny that the eschatological interpretation of the Jesus tradition has brought us much illumination, for it has revealed once and for all that many sayings contain an apocalyptic eschatology. But Crossan and others believe that many of those sayings are secondary and that their addition greatly distorted things. So these scholars are offering us a new paradigm—Jesus as aphoristic sage (Borg) or as Jewish peasant Cynic (Crossan).

112. Helpful here is Karl R. Popper, *The Myth of the Framework: In Defence of Science and Rationality*, ed. M. A. Notturno (London: Routledge, 1994), especially pp. 33–64. In my experience many critical New Testament scholars began life as fundamentalists but then, at least in part through rational reflection, changed their outlook—a circumstance that suggests that Popper is right when he argues that one can transcend a framework through what he calls "criticism."

113. John Wisdom, *Philosophy and Psycho-Analysis* (Oxford: Basil Blackwell, 1964), p. 156 (italics deleted). Helpful here is Peter Lipton, *Inference to the Best Explanation* (London: Routledge & Kegan Paul, 1991).

114. Thomas S. Kuhn, *The Structure of Scientific Revolutions*, 2d ed. (Chicago: University of Chicago Press, 1970), p. 122.

Max Planck ruefully observed that "a new scientific truth does not triumph by convincing its opponents and making them see the light, but rather because its opponents eventually die, and a new generation grows up that is familiar with it."[115] Although I think it an unlikely eventuality, I can imagine the new, nonapocalyptic paradigm establishing itself as the new orthodoxy when those of us who grew up on Schweitzer have died out. It is my conviction, however, that, if the old paradigm is ever discarded, a grave error will have been made. The proposition that Jesus was an eschatological prophet with an apocalyptic scenario should remain the matrix within which the authentic traditions are embedded.

The Best Research Program

We cannot confirm the new paradigm or refute the old one by sharpening the traditional criteria of authenticity any more than by doing exegesis or creating tradition-histories. For how we perform these tasks always depends upon the assumptions we bring to them. To repeat, our paradigm should, if possible, be settled upon prior to and independently of our evaluation of the historicity of individual items in the Jesus tradition. Our goal is not to be free of prejudices but to have the right prejudices. Can this be done?

It is indeed possible to say a good deal about Jesus apart from detailed evaluation of the province of various complexes. Moreover, when we undertake this endeavor we are back with the conventional paradigm of Jesus as eschatological prophet. I have set forth the reasons in other publications.[116] Let me here offer a summary of some of them.

1. Passages from a wide variety of sources show us that many early followers of Jesus thought the eschatological climax to be approaching.[117] We also know that, in the pre-Easter period, Jesus himself was closely associated with John the Baptist, whose public speech, if the Synoptics are any guide at all, featured frequent allusion to the eschatological judgment, conceived as imminent.[118] Jesus indeed was baptized by John.

115. Max Planck, *Scientific Autobiography and Other Essays* (New York: Philosophical Library, 1949), pp. 33–34.

116. Dale C. Allison, "A Plea for Thoroughgoing Eschatology," *JBL* 113 (1994), pp. 651–68, and "The Eschatology of Jesus," in *The Encyclopaedia of Apocalypticism, Volume 1: The Origins of Apocalypticism in Judaism and Christianity*, ed. John J. Collins (New York: Continuum, 1998), pp. 267–302.

117. Examples include Acts 3:19–20; Rom 13:11; 1 Cor 16:22; 1 Thess 5:1–11; Heb 10:37; Jas 5:8; 1 Pet 4:17; 1 John 2:8; Rev 22:20; and *Didache* 16.

118. See especially Q 3:7–17. It might be argued that one should follow not the Gospels but Josephus, whose John is not an apocalyptic prophet but a social reformer (*Ant.* 18:

Obviously, then, there must have been significant ideological continuity between the two men. So, as many have repeatedly observed, to reconstruct a Jesus who did not have a strong eschatological orientation entails unexpected discontinuity not only between him and people who took themselves to be furthering his cause but also between him and the Baptist, that is, discontinuity with the movement out of which he came as well as with the movement that came out of him. Presumption is against this. The argument is valid, and it is pursued at length in chapter 2 herein.[119]

2. The canonical Gospels, traditions in Acts, and the letters of Paul are united in relating that at least several pre-Easter followers of Jesus, soon after his crucifixion, declared that "God [had] raised Jesus from the dead,"[120] vindicated him by "the resurrection of the dead ones" (Acts 4:2).[121] Their combined testimony on this matter is not doubted by anyone, so we may ask why people made this claim, why they affirmed the occurrence of an eschatological event. The best explanation is that several influential individuals came to their post-Easter experiences (whatever they were) with certain categories and expectations antecedently fixed, that they already, because of Jesus' teaching, envisaged the general resurrection to be imminent. This is why "resurrection" was the chief category by which they interpreted Jesus' vindication.[122]

3. According to Mk 15:33, when Jesus died there was strange darkness (compare Amos 8:9–10). According to Mt 27:51–53 there was also a strong earthquake (compare Zech 14:5) and a resurrection of the dead

---

116–19). Josephus, however, sought to underplay the eschatological fervor of Judaism. It is telling that his portrait of the Essenes includes nothing about the restoration of Israel, cosmic dualism, or messianic hope. Only from the Dead Sea Scrolls—presumably written by Essenes—do we learn these things.

119. Crossan has, in public debate, disputed this argument with the observation that with it one could demonstrate that Gandhi was not a pacifist, for he came out of an environment of violence and after he was gone violence ruled. The illustration does show that individuals can stand against and above their times. But the difference between Jesus and Gandhi is that whereas the evidence for the pacifism of the latter is massive and overwhelming, the evidence that Jesus forsook the scenario of John the Baptist is nil or close to it.

120. For this formula and its antiquity see W. Kramer, *Christ, Lord, Son of God*, SBT 50 (London: SCM, 1966), pp. 19–44.

121. On the related, pre-Pauline expression in Rom 1:4 see H.-W. Bartsch, "Zur vorpaulinischen Bekenntnisformel im Eingang des Römerbriefes," *TZ* 23 (1967), pp. 329–39.

122. Compare Paula Fredriksen, "What You See Is What You Get: Context and Content in Current Research on the Historical Jesus," *Theology Today* 42/1 (1995), p. 94: "The disciples' experience of Jesus' resurrection points indisputably to the Christian movement's origins in the eschatological hopes of first-century Judaism—the resurrection of the dead, the vindication of the righteous." She plausibly adds: "The disciples' choice to remain in Jerusalem rather than return to Galilee suggests further that they continued to expect *something* to happen, and soon. . . ."

(compare Ezek 37; Zech 14:4–5). According to John's Gospel, Jesus' death was "the judgment of the world" (12:31) and brought down the reign of Satan (16:11). According to Paul, Jesus is "the first fruits of those who have died" (1 Cor 15:20)—a metaphor which assumes that the eschatological harvest is underway, that the resurrection of Jesus is only the beginning of the general resurrection of the dead. Given its multiple attestation in Paul, the Synoptics, and John, the habit of associating the end of Jesus with eschatological motifs must go back to very early times.[123]

What explains the habit? The best answer is that, while Jesus was yet with them, his followers—as Luke 19:11 plainly tells us—"supposed that the kingdom of God was to appear immediately."[124] They foresaw eschatological suffering followed by eschatological vindication, tribulation followed by resurrection. So when Jesus was, in the event, crucified and seen alive again, his followers, instead of abandoning their eschatological hopes, did what one would expect them to do: they sought to correlate expectations with circumstances. This is why they believed that in Jesus' end the eschaton had begun to unfold, and why early Christian texts associate the death and resurrection of Jesus with what appear to be eschatological events.

4. The Roman world of the first century was, in the words of Helmut Koester, "dominated by prophetic eschatology," and the apocalyptic writings of Judaism, which share "the general eschatological spirit" of the Roman imperial period,[125] put us in touch with a type of eschatology that was well known in Jesus' time and place.[126] Not only did the sacred collection itself contain apocalyptic materials—for example, Isaiah 24–27, Daniel, Zechariah 9–14—but portions of 1 Enoch, some of the Jewish Sibylline Oracles, and the Testament of Moses[127] were in circulation in Jesus' day; and the decades after Jesus saw the appearance of 4 Ezra,[128] 2 Baruch, and the Apocalypse of Abraham. His time was also when the

123. See further my book, The End of the Ages Has Come: An Early Interpretation of the Passion and Resurrection of Jesus (Philadelphia: Fortress, 1985).
124. This may be Lukan redaction, but Mk 10:37 presupposes the very same expectation on the part of Jesus' disciples. Compare Acts 1:6.
125. The quoted words are from Helmut Koester, "Jesus: The Victim," JBL 111 (1992), pp. 10–11.
126. See further S. E. Robinson, "Apocalypticism in the Time of Hillel and Jesus," in Hillel and Jesus: Comparisons of Two Major Religious Leaders, ed. James H. Charlesworth and Loren L. Johns (Minneapolis: Fortress, 1997), pp. 121–36.
127. T. Mos. 7:1 says that "the times will quickly come to an end" after the events of chapter 6, which clearly have to do with Herod the Great.
128. 4 Ezra 14:44–45, incidentally, refers to seventy noncanonical books that presumably belong to the apocalyptic tradition. While the number is likely to be exaggerated, it does point in a certain direction.

Dead Sea Scrolls, so many of which are charged with eschatological expectation, were presumably being composed or copied and studied. The point, reinforced by Josephus's remarks on the general popularity of Daniel (*Ant.* 10.268),[129] is simply that the sort of eschatology Schweitzer attributed to Jesus was indeed flourishing in Jesus' day. Social and political circumstances were probably ripe for the production of a millenarian movement;[130] and the sense of an imminent transformation, perhaps partly due "to the prevalent belief induced by the popular chronology of that day that the age was on the threshold of the Millennium,"[131] ap-

129. Many no doubt understood the fourth kingdom of Daniel 2 to be the Roman empire, after which the God of heaven would rule (2:36–45; see Josephus, *Ant.* 10.276; *4 Ezra* 12:10). Moreover, Christians have often construed Daniel's "seventy weeks of years" so that they come to fulfillment in Jesus' day (e.g., Tertullian, *Adv. Jud.* 8; Jerome, *Comm. Dan.* on 9:24–27). Did some Jews before Christianity do the same? See further William Adler, "The Apocalyptic Survey of History Adapted by Christians: Daniel's Prophecy of 70 Weeks," in *The Jewish Apocalyptic Heritage in Early Christianity*, ed. James C. Vander-Kam and William Adler, CRINT III/4 (Assen: Van Gorcum/Minneapolis: Fortress, 1996), pp. 201–38.

130. Here I can appeal to the first two parts of Crossan's *Historical Jesus*.

131. Abba Hillel Silver, *A History of Messianic Speculation in Israel* (Boston: Beacon, 1959), p. 5 (italics deleted). Relevant are Tacitus, *Hist.* 5:13 ("The majority were convinced that the ancient scriptures of their priests alluded to the present as the very time when the Orient would triumph and from Judaea would go forth men destined to rule the world"), and Suetonius, *Vesp.* 4 ("An ancient superstition was current in the East, that out of Judaea would come the rulers of the world. This prediction, as it later proved, referred to two Roman Emperors, Vespasian and his son Titus; but the rebellious Jews, who read it as referring to themselves. . ."). On this neglected topic see Roger T. Beckwith, *Calendar and Chronology, Jewish and Christian: Biblical, Intertestamental and Patristic Studies*, AGJU 33 (Leiden: E. J. Brill, 1996), pp. 217–75; L. L. Grabe, "The End of the World in Early Jewish and Christian Calculations," *RevQ* 11 (1982), pp. 107–108; and Ben Zion Wacholder, *Essays on Jewish Chronology and Chronography* (New York: KTAV, 1976), pp. 240–57. The messianic movement that broke out in Crete in the fifth century C.E. (see Socrates, *H.E.* 7:38) appears to have been related to a messianic calculation (compare *b. Sanh.* 97b; *b. 'Abod. Zar.* 9b); see Salo Wittmayer Baron, "Messianic and Sectarian Movements," in *Essential Papers on Messianic Movements and Personalities in Jewish History*, ed. Marc Saperstein (New York: New York University Press, 1992), pp. 162–63. Even the sober Maimonides, who knew of many falsified calculations of the end and wrote that no one knows the date of the Messiah's coming, offered his own calculation; see his *Iggeres Teiman*. For early Christian calendars and eschatology see Richard Landes, "Lest the Millennium Be Fulfilled: Apocalyptic Expectations and the Pattern of Western Chronography 100–800 C.E.," in *The Use and Absue of Eschatology in the Middle Ages*, ed. Werner Verbeke, Daniel Verhelst, and Andries Welkenhuysen (Leuven: Leuven University Press, 1988), pp. 137–211. For the importance of calendrical calculation for the nineteenth-century Millerites—something which may give us a taste for how things were in certain circles in antiquity—see Stephen D. O'Leary, *Arguing the Apocalypse: A Theory of Millennial Rhetoric* (New York: Oxford University Press, 1994), pp. 120–25. Even though the year 1000 did not witness widespread eschatological expectation—see A. Vasiliev, "Medieval Ideas of the End of the World: West and East," *Byzantion* 16/2 (1943), pp. 462–502—there is no denying

pears to have been shared by many.[132] So to propose that Jesus thought likewise is just to say that he believed what many others in his time and place believed.

5. Several New Testament texts compare Jesus with some of his contemporaries:[133]

Q 7:33–34: Jesus compares his ministry with the ministry of John the Baptist.

Mk 6:14: Herod Antipas says that Jesus is John the Baptist risen from the dead.

Mk 8:28: "People" say that Jesus is like John the Baptist.

Acts 5:35–39: Gamaliel compares Jesus and his followers with Theudas and his movement.

Acts 5:35–39: Gamaliel compares Jesus and his followers with Judas the Galilean and his movement.

John the Baptist, Theudas, and Judas the Galilean were moved by eschatological expectation or hope for Jewish restoration. John proclaimed a near end and was thought of as a prophet. Theudas claimed to be a prophet, acted as a new Moses, and was viewed as a threat by the Romans.[134] Judas the Galilean, according to Josephus, *Ant.* 18:5, sought independence for the Jewish people with the help of God. Now the comparisons in the canonical Gospels and Acts, most of which are attributed to outsiders, would be natural if Jesus was remembered as an eschatological

---

the importance of dates for the psychology of eschatological expectation during the last millennium; see Hillel Schwartz, *Century's End: A Cultural History of the Fin de Siècle from the 990s through the 1990s* (New York: Doubleday, 1990).

132. The arguments of Richard A. Horsley to the contrary, in *Sociology and the Jesus Movement*, 2d ed. (New York: Continuum, 1994), pp. 96–99, do not persuade. Among other things, he neglects or too lightly passes over the significance of the Dead Sea Scrolls, the Baptist, and the *Testament of Moses*. Historians have often failed to see just how prevalent apocalyptic speculation was in all classes during the Middle Ages (see Bernard McGinn, *Visions of the End: Apocalyptic Tradition in the Middle Ages* [New York: Columbia University Press, 1979]) or how important a role it has played and continues to play in American culture (see Paul Boyer, *When Time Shall Be No More: Prophecy Belief in Modern American Culture* [Cambridge: Harvard University Press, 1992]). Matters may be similar with the first century C.E., especially as our major source for the period, Josephus, was not interested in highlighting apocalyptic fervor (recall his treatment of John the Baptist).

133. In addition to what follows see J. A. Trumbower, "The Historical Jesus and the Speech of Gamaliel (Acts 5:35–39)," *NTS* 39 (1993), pp. 500–517.

134. See Josephus, *Ant.* 20:97–99, and Dale C. Allison, Jr., *The New Moses: A Matthean Typology* (Minneapolis: Fortress, 1993), pp. 78–79.

prophet who proclaimed that God's kingdom would replace the Roman kingdom. They are not easily explained if he was not so remembered.

The arguments just introduced are straightforward and powerful. They involve no special pleading nor any questionable argumentation. They are, moreover, mutually reinforcing. That Jesus was baptized by an eschatological prophet and had among his followers people who proclaimed a near end, that certain followers of Jesus proclaimed his resurrection soon after the crucifixion, that his passion and vindication were associated with eschatological motifs, that many first-century Jews expected an apocalyptic scenario to unfold in their near future, and that our sources compare Jesus with others who believed in such a scenario or at least expected God soon to rule Palestine—these indisputable facts together tell us that Jesus held hopes close to those attributed to him by Weiss and Schweitzer. The evidence is, to be sure, circumstantial, but then one recalls what Thoreau famously said: "Some circumstantial evidence is very strong, as when you find a trout in the milk."

The conclusion that Jesus was an eschatological prophet establishes itself, let me emphasize, apart from detailed evaluation of the Jesus tradition. Further, this result is sufficiently forceful that, were the sayings attributed to Jesus to suggest some other conclusion, the correct inference would probably not be that Jesus was not an eschatological prophet but rather that the sayings tradition is unreliable, that Christians expunged from it the eschatological elements in order to protect Jesus from being viewed as a false prophet.

Fortunately for us, however, the sayings only confirm what we can infer on other grounds. For in our sources Jesus seemingly speaks of the consummation as temporally near[135] and admonishes people to watch for the coming of the Lord or of the Son of man.[136] He also pronounces eschatological judgment on contemporaries[137] and otherwise announces or presupposes that the final fulfillment of God's saving work is nigh.[138] How came all this matter into the Jesus tradition? Does not the agreement between the sayings tradition and what we otherwise know of Jesus constitute an initial reason for hope that the sayings tradition preserves some authentic material?

135. Q 10:9; Mk 9:1; 13:30; Mt 10:23; Gos. Thom. 111.
136. E.g., Q 12:39–40, 42–46; Mk 13:33–37; Mt 25:1–13; Lk 12:35–38.
137. See below, n. 142 and pp. 131–36.
138. E.g., Q 17:23–37; Mk 1:15; 13:28–29, 33, 37; Lk 18:1–8; 21:34–36.

Themes and Rhetorical Strategies

My task to this point has been fourfold: first, to underscore the hazards of the popular criteria for authenticity; second, to display the weaknesses of Crossan's methodological proposals; third, to contend that we should not attempt to determine the authenticity of items within the Jesus tradition until we have established an interpretive framework; and, fourth, to argue what that one particular interpretive framework should be. One more preliminary requires attention before we take up again the problem of passing individual traditions through the sieve constituted by the indices of authenticity.

When we look back on our encounters with others our most vivid and reliable memories are often not precise but general. I may, for instance, not remember exactly what you said to me last year, but I may recall approximately what you said, or retain what we call a general impression. It is like vaguely recollecting the approximate shape, size, and contents of a room one was in many years ago—a room that has, in the mind's eye, lost all color and detail. After our short-term memories have become long-term memories they suffer progressive abbreviation. I am not sure I remember a single sentence that either of my beloved grandparents on my father's side ever said to me. But I nonetheless know and cherish the sorts of the things that they said to me.

All of this matters for study of the Jesus tradition, because it goes against universal human experience to suppose that early Christians, let us say, accurately recorded many of Jesus' words but somehow came away with false general impressions of him. If the tradents of the Jesus tradition got the big picture or the larger patterns wrong then they almost certainly also got the details—that is, the sentences—wrong. It is precarious to urge that we can find the truth about Jesus on the basis of a few dozen sayings deemed to be authentic if those sayings are interpreted contrary to the general impressions conveyed by the early tradition in its entirety. If Jesus was, for example, either a violent revolutionary or a secular sage, then the tradition about him is so misleading that we cannot use it for investigation of the pre-Easter period—and so we cannot know that Jesus was either a violent revolutionary or a secular sage. Here skepticism devours itself. The conclusion refutes the premises.

The first-century Jesus tradition is, to state the obvious, not a collection of totally disparate and wholly unrelated materials. As everyone knows, certain themes and motifs and rhetorical strategies are consistently attested over a wide range of material. It is in these themes and motifs and rhetorical strategies, if it is anywhere, that we are likely to have an accurate memory. Indeed, several of these themes, motifs, and strategies are sufficiently well attested that we have a choice to make. Either they tend to preserve pre-Easter memories or they do not. In the former case we know enough to begin to authenticate individual items: the general will help us with the particular.[139] But in the latter case our questing for Jesus is not just interminable but probably pointless and we should consider surrendering to ignorance. If the tradition is so misleading in its broad features, then we can hardly make much of its details.

Any objective inventory of the major themes and motifs that appear again and again in the Jesus tradition would surely include the following:

1. The kingdom of God[140]
2. Future reward[141]
3. Future judgment[142]
4. Suffering/persecution for the saints[143]

139. A. E. Harvey, *Jesus and the Constraints of History* (Philadelphia: Westminster, 1982), pp. 4–5, thinks that the attention of modern New Testament scholars "has moved away from establishing the truth or falsity of any particular report about Jesus, and is now directed more towards the impression made by the narrative as a whole." Compare the proposal of John Riches, *Jesus and the Transformation of Judaism* (New York: Seabury, 1982), p. 53: "It is not simply a matter of finding individual sayings which are beyond doubt authentic and moving out from these to those which are closest to them. What one is looking for is a *group* of sayings sufficiently distinctive that, although one cannot be sure of the authenticity of any one of them, one can say with some confidence that, taken as a group, they represent characteristic features of Jesus' teaching."

140. For the canonical data see Jeremias, *Theology*, pp. 31–35. His figures are as follows: Mk: 13; logia common to Matthew and Luke (Q): 9; M: 27; L: 12; Jn: 2. For the *Gospel of Thomas* see 3, 20, 22, 27, 46, 49, 54, 57, 76 82, 96, 97, 98, 99, 107, 109, 113, 114. See also the catalogue of Wright, *Jesus and the Victory of God*, pp. 663–70.

141. See Q 6:20–23; 12:8–9, 42–44; 13:30; 14:11; 17:33; 19:26; 22:28–30; Mk 8:35; 9:41; 10:28–39; Mt 5:7–10, 19; 6:1–6, 17–18; 23:12; 25:14–30, 31–46; Lk 6:20–23, 37–38, 46–49; 14:14; 18:14; Jn 5:29; 6:40; 14:2–3; *Gos. Thom.* 2, 18, 19, 22, 49, 76, 114; etc.

142. See Q 6:46–49; 10:12–15; 11:31–32, 47–51; 12:8–9, 10, 45–46; 13:23–27, 28–29, 30; 14:11; 17:2, 33; 19:26; Mk 3:29; 8:35, 38; 9:42–48; Mt 5:19; 23:12; 25:14–30, 31–46; Lk 6:24–26; 18:14; 19:41–44; 23:27–31; Jn 5:29; 12:48; *Gos. Thom.* 42, 59, 70; etc.

143. See Q 6:22–23, 28–30; 10:3, 10–11; 11:49–51; 12:4–7, 11, 51–53; 13:34–35; Mk 8:31; 9:12–13, 31; 10:20, 35–40; 12:1–10; 13:9–13, 14–20; Mt 5:10; 7:15; 10:23, 25; 24:10–12; Lk 13:31–33; 22:31; Jn 15:18–25; 16:1–4, 16–24; *Gos. Thom.* 58, 68, 69, 82, 86; Justin, *Dial.* 35:3; etc.

5. Victory over evil powers [144]
6. A sense that something new is here or at hand [145]
7. The importance of John the Baptist [146]
8. Reference to "the Son of man" [147]
9. God as Father [148]
10. Loving/serving/forgiving others [149]
11. Special regard for the unfortunate [150]
12. Intention as what matters most [151]
13. Hostility to wealth [152]
14. Extraordinary requests/difficult demands [153]
15. Conflict with religious authorities [154]

144. See Q 4:1–13; 11:14, 17–20, 22; Mk 1:12–13, 21–28, 34, 39; 3:20–27; 5:1–20; 6:7, 13; 7:24–30; 9:14–29, 38; Mt 7:22; 9:32–34; Lk 13:15–17, 32; 10:17–20; 22:31–32; Jn 12:31; 14:30; 16:11, 33; *Gos. Thom.* 35; etc.

145. See Q 7:22; 10:9, 21–22, 23–24; 11:20, 31, 32; 12:54–56; 16:16; Mk 1:15, 27; 2:18–20, 21–22; 4:10–12; Mt 12:6; 13:34–35; 16:17; Lk 5:39; 10:18; 13:6–9; 17:20–21; Jn 1:51; 5:31–38; 14:8–14; *Gos. Thom.* 17, 46, 47, 51, 62, 91.

146. See Q 3:7–17; 7:19–35; 16:16; Mk 1:1–8, 14; 2:18; 6:14–29; 9:9–13; 11:27–33; Mt 3:14–15; 11:14–15; 21:28–32; Lk 3:10–14; 7:29; 11:1; Jn 1:6, 15, 19–42; 3:22–4:3; 5:31–38; 10:40–41; *Gos. Thom.* 46, 78 (?); etc.

147. See Q 6:22; 7:34; 9:58; 11:30; 12:8, 10, 40; 17:24, 26; Mk 2:10, 27–29; 8:31; 9:9, 12, 31; 10:33–34, 45; 13:26; 14:21, 41, 62; Mt 10:23; 13:37, 41; 16:13, 27, 28; 24:30, 39; 25:31; 26:2; Lk 17:22, 25, 30; 18:18; 19:10; 21:36; 22:48; 24:7; Jn 1:51; 3:13–15; 5:27; 6:27, 53, 62; 8:28; 12:23, 34; 13:31–32; *Gos. Thom.* 86; etc.

148. The canonical data are collected in Joachim Jeremias, *The Prayers of Jesus*, SBT 2/6 (London: SCM, 1967), pp. 11–65. *Thomas* uses "Father" often of God—e.g., 3, 40, 44, 50, 79, 83, 98, 99.

149. See Q 6:27–28, 31, 32–36; 11:4; 17:3–4; Mk 9:35; 10:41–45; 12:28–34; Mt 5:23–24; 6:14–15; 18:23–35; 19:19; 23:11–12; 25:31–46; Lk 10:25–28, 29–37; 13:15–17; 22:24–26; Acts 20:35; Jn 13:1–35; 14:15–17; 15:12–17; *Gos. Thom.* 25, 26, 48, 95; *Gos. Heb.* according to Jerome, *Comm. Eph.* 5:4; etc.

150. See Q 6:20–21; 7:22; 11:14; 13:30; 14:15–24; Mk 1:40–45; 2:15–17; 3:1–6; 5:1–20, 25–34; 7:31–37; 8:22–26; 9:14–29; 10:46–52; 14:3–9; Mt 25:31–46; Lk 13:10–17; 14:1–6, 12–14; Jn 4:1–38; 5:2–9; 9:1–12; 13:29; *Gos. Thom.* 54, 69; etc.

151. See Q 6:43–45; 11:34–36, 39; Mk 7:1–8, 15; 12:30; Mt 5:5:8, 21–23, 27–28; 6:1–4, 5–6, 16–18; 12:34–37; Lk 16:15; Codex D for Lk 6:4; *Gos. Thom.* 22, 45, 89; etc.

152. See Q 6:20, 30; 10:4; 11:34–36; 12:22–31, 33–34; 16:13; Mk 1:16–20; 2:14; 4:19; 6:8–9; 8:34–37; 10:17–31; 12:41–44; 14:3–9; Mt 13:44–46; Lk 6:24–26; 11:41; 12:13–21; 14:12–14; 16:1–9, 10–12, 19–31; *Gos. Thom.* 36, 42, 54, 56, 63, 64, 78, 81; P. Oxy. 655; etc.

153. See 1 Cor 7:10; 9:14; Q 6:27–30, 37–38; 9:57–60; 14:26, 27; 16:18; 17:3–4; Mk 1:16–20; 2:14; 6:8–9; 8:34, 35; 9:42–48; 10:11–12, 17–27; Mt 5:33–37; 19:10–12; 23:9; Lk 14:12–14, 23, 28–33; *Gos. Thom.* 42, 55, 95, 101; P. Oxy. 1224; etc.

154. See Q 11:39–41, 42, 43, 44, 46, 47–48, 52; Mk 2:15–17, 23–28; 3:1–6; 7:1–23; 12:13–17, 18–27; 14:53–65; Mt 15:12–13; 23:8–12, 15, 16–22; Lk 11:37–38, 53–54; 13:10–17; 14:1–6; 16:14–15; 18:9–14; Jn 4:1–3; 7:32, 45–52; 9:13–34; 11:45–53; 18:1–32; *Gos. Thom.* 39, 102; P. Oxy. 1224; etc.

16. Disciples as students and helpers[155]
17. Jesus as miracle worker[156]

The first seven items as well as the eighth (at least according to some interpretations of the evidence) readily invite an eschatological interpretation. When put together they foretell a utopia, labeled "the kingdom (of God)," that is already manifesting itself notwithstanding great opposition.[157] We have here the standard pattern of Jewish messianism, which is also found in millennial movements worldwide—a time of tribulation followed by a time of unprecedented blessedness. To this extent, then, the Jesus tradition seems to be in line with our earlier conclusion that Jesus was an eschatological prophet who expected God's rule to come shortly.

Items 9–11, if they preserve historical memory, tell us that Jesus the eschatological prophet was, like the Buddha, a teacher of compassion. God's status as father is, in several of the sayings, particularly associated with special care for human beings.[158] And the demands to love others and to attend especially to the marginal are the concrete human correlates of the divine charity (compare Q 6:33). They are, in the idiom of the Lord's Prayer, a way of making things on earth more like they are in heaven.

Entries 12–14 suggest that Jesus was a moral rigorist. The focus upon intention, the insistence that one serve God instead of mammon, and the demand that certain individuals follow him immediately and unconditionally indicate that, whatever he may have taught about compassion, he made uncommonly difficult demands upon (at least some) people.[159] It is likely that his moral radicalism was, as Albert Schweitzer famously argued, related to his belief in a near end. It is just common sense, confirmed by the experience of those who are told that they have little time to live, that the present takes on added seriousness if the end is felt to be near. Moreover, it seems a very good guess that not just Jesus' prohibition of

155. See Q 6:20; 9:57–10:15; 22:28–30; Mk 3:7–12; 4:10; 6:6–13, 35–41; 7:17–23; 8:27–38; 9:30–41; 10:10–12, 23–31; 13:1–37; Mt 10:5–6, 23, 40–42; 13:36–43, 51–52; 15:12–13; 16:17–19; Lk 9:51–56; 10:17–20; 11:1–2; 22:35–38; Jn 4:2; 6:60–71; 11:7–16; 13:1–17:26; Gos. Thom. 6, 12, 13, 18, 20, 22, 24, 37, 43; etc.

156. See Q 7:1–10, 19–22; 10:9; 11:14–20; Mk 1:21–28, 29–31, 32–34, 40–45; 2:1–12; 3:1–6, 22; 5:1–20, 21–43; 6:30–44, 47–52; 7:24–30, 31–37; 8:22–26; 9:14–29; 10:46–52; Mt 9:27–31; 14:28–33; 26:53; Lk 13:32; 14:1–6; Jn 2:1–11; 5:2–9; 9:1–12; 11:28–44; etc.

157. Jesus' focus on the intention of the heart should also, in my judgment, be associated with eschatological expectation; see Wright, Jesus and the Victory of God, pp. 282–87.

158. E.g., Q 6:35; 11:2–4, 9–13; 12:22–31; Mk 14:35–36; Lk 12:32.

159. See further Chapter 3 herein.

divorce (see chapter 3) but also his critique of wealth and his call to freedom from care were all related to a programmatic belief in the eschatological restoration of paradise (compare Mk 10:6–9).[160]

Items 15–16 tell us that Jesus was a well-known teacher, a fact otherwise confirmed by Josephus[161] as well as by the very existence of the multitudinous sayings in the Jesus tradition.[162] And the very last feature—Jesus as miracle worker—probably explains in great measure Jesus' great popularity and helps us understand why people paid attention to what he had to say.

If certain themes and motifs tend to appear regularly in the sayings tradition, the same is true of certain formal literary features, or what may be called rhetorical strategies. The following eight are among the more prominent:

1. Parables[163]
2. Antithetical parallelism[164]
3. Rhetorical questions[165]
4. Prefatory "amen"[166]

160. See further Jürgen Sauer, *Rückkehr und Vollendung des Heils: Eine Untersuchung zu den ethischen Radikalismen Jesu*, Theorie und Forschung 133/Philosophie und Theologie 9 (Regensburg: S. Roderer, 1991). Sauer also relates Jesus' understanding of the Sabbath and his teaching on fasting to eschatology.

161. *Ant.* 18:63: Jesus was "a wise man" and "a teacher of people." On this see Meier, *Marginal Jew*, vol. 1, pp. 56–88. That some of Jesus' followers were known as *mathētai* = *talmîdîm*, that is, learners, is significant.

162. Interesting here are Samuel Byrskog, *Jesus the Only Teacher: Didactic Authority and Transmission in Ancient Judaism and the Matthean Community*, CBNT 24 (Stockholm: Almqvist & Wiksell, 1994), pp. 199–236, and R. T. France, "Mark and the Teaching of Jesus," in *Gospel Perspectives, Volume I: Studies of History and Tradition in the Four Gospels*, ed. R. T. France and David Wenham (Sheffield: JSOT, 1980), pp. 101–36.

163. The catalogue of Andrew Parker, *Painfully Clear: The Parables of Jesus* (Sheffield: Academic Press, 1996), pp. 119–21, lists a total of sixty-two parables from the Synoptics and Q. Many of these also appear in *Thomas*.

164. Jeremias, *Theology*, pp. 14–20, offers these numbers: Mk: 30; logia common to Matthew and Luke (Q): 34; M: 44; L: 30. Note also Codex D for Lk 6:4 and *Gos. Thom.* 82 = Origen, *Hom. Jer.* 20:3. On the related phenomenon of compound parallelism see T. W. Manson, *The Teaching of Jesus* (Cambridge: Cambridge University Press, 1967), pp. 54–56.

165. See Q 6:32, 39, 41–42, 44, 46; 7:24, 31; 10:35; 11:11–13, 18, 19, 40; 12:23, 25, 42; 13:18, 20; 14:34; 15:4; Mk 2:8, 9, 19, 25; 3:4, 23, 33; 4:21, 30; 5:39; 8:36; 12:24, 26; Mt 12:5, 11–12, 34; 21:28; 23:17, 19; Lk 13:2, 4; 13:15; 14:5, 31; 16:11; 17:7–9; 23:31; *Gos. Thom.* 18, 78, 89; etc.

166. The canonical statistics are, according to Jeremias, *Theology*, pp. 35–36, as follows: Mk: 13; logia common to Mt and Lk (Q): 9; M: 9; L: 3; Jn: 25.

5. The divine passive [167]
6. Exaggeration/hyperbole [168]
7. Aphoristic formulation [169]
8. The unexpected or seemingly paradoxical [170]

No one can dispute that the themes and motifs and strategies just listed are widely attested in the Jesus tradition. The relevant question is what we should make of this fact. My own conviction, which others may regard as naive and precritical, is that, for reasons given above, we should probably either accept almost all of them or reject them in their entirety.[171] Sometimes, as with what engineers call a statically determinate structure, everything stands or falls together. It can be all or nothing. In the present instance, either the tradition instructs us that Jesus spoke often about the kingdom of God and about God as Father and typically used parables and asked rhetorical questions and so on, or the tradition is not a useful source for Jesus[172] and we should start questing for someone or something else. It is my working hypothesis that the former is the case.

Although my working hypothesis is not groundless, it is not the result

167. The count of Jeremias, *Theology*, p. 11, is: Mk: 21; logia common to Mt and Lk (Q): 23; M: 27; L: 25.

168. See Q 6:41–42; 12:46; 14:26, 27; 17:6; Mk 4:8, 31–32; 8:34; 9:42–48; 10:25; Mt 5:22, 29–30; 6:3; 23:8–10, 15, 24; Lk 16:31; 19:40; *Gos. Thom.* 26, 48, 55, 101; etc.

169. On this see especially David E. Aune, "Oral Tradition and the Aphorisms of Jesus," in *Jesus and the Oral Gospel Tradition*, ed. Henry Wansbrough, JSNTSS 64 (Sheffield: JSOT, 1991), pp. 211–65. He defines "aphorisms" as pithy expressions "of personal insight and vision, attributed to particular individuals . . . often reflecting specific situations." He counts 44 in Mark, 49 in Q, 32 in M, 22 in L, 8 in John, 4 in *Thomas*, and 8 in other sources and rightly comments: "While it may be difficult to argue that this or that particular saying is 'historical' or 'authentic' . . . the sheer number of such aphorisms together with their persistent attribution to Jesus makes it certain that Jesus regarded himself and was regarded by his followers and later Christian generations as a Jewish sage and teacher of wisdom."

170. Note, e.g., Q 6:20–23 (being poor, hungry, in mourning, and reviled are made out to be good things); 10:21 (revelation is not for the learned but for babes); 12:51 (Jesus has not come to bring peace but a sword); 13:19 (the kingdom is like corrupting leaven); 13:30 (the last will be first, the first last); Mk 2:17 (Jesus calls not the righteous but sinners); 7:15 (things going in do not defile); 8:35 (saving life will lose it, losing life will save it); 9:12–13 (eschatological Elijah did not succeed in his ministry of reconciliation); 10:45 (the Son of man came not to be served but to serve); Lk 10:25–37 (the Samaritan is the hero); Lk 16:1–8 (commendation of a dishonest character).

171. This is of course not a statement about the authenticity of any particular text cited in the previous footnotes. Here it is the collective weight of the evidence, the pattern created by the multitude, that is being considered; the accuracy of any particular witness is another matter. Compare Nils A. Dahl, *The Crucified Messiah and Other Essays* (Minneapolis: Augsburg, 1974), p. 67, and Riches, as in n. 139.

172. This is the view of G. A. Wells, *The Jesus Legend* (Chicago: Open Court, 1996).

of an irrefutable argument, nor can it be vindicated by a few observations. It is not a verdict reached by self-evident steps from self-evident truths and clear observations. It is rather informed guesswork, a postulate with which to work. This means that "its evidence is seen in its consequences."[173] That is, its claim to truth lies in its explanatory power as time goes on and it is applied to ever enlarging arrays of texts and observations. If we can tell good stories with this working hypothesis, then well and good. But if we could not tell such good stories, or if we could tell better stories with some other working hypothesis, then we would have to reconsider.

Running the Gauntlet

We may now turn to the problem of authenticating individual complexes and topics. The following five indices,[174] it must be emphasized, assume the discussion to this point. They are not to be employed in isolation but are rather to be guided by the paradigm of Jesus as eschatological prophet and the working hypothesis that the themes, motifs, and strategies highlighted in the previous section go back to Jesus himself. Further, it must be underlined that these indices are fallible. They cannot be stated in such a way as to avoid ambiguity or subjectivity in application. New Testament scholars can no more produce universally valid rules of evidence than philosophers can successfully formalize induction. The indices of authenticity inevitably employ what has been called an informal rationality, that is, a logic that cannot be precisely explicated.[175] As with chaotic systems, which are too complex to describe fully, so the process of making informed inferences about history is too complicated to be reduced to formulation. Put simply, our indices may help us arrange some of our clues, but they can only take us so far. They are suggestive, not demonstrative. They are tools, which do not do the labor for us but only make it a little bit easier for us to do. Our informed imaginations, working with a thousand variables in ways we ourselves probably cannot fully explicate, still have plenty to do.

Here then are my suggestions:[176]

---

173. W. V. Quine and J. S. Ullian, *The Web of Belief* (New York: Random, 1970), p. 43.
174. With Meyer, *Aims*, p. 86, I prefer "index" over "criterion." The former is an indicator, the latter a standard to be passed or failed.
175. On this see David Hodgson, *The Mind Matters: Consciousness and Choice in a Quantum World* (Oxford: Clarendon, 1991), pp. 114–56.
176. The date of the source in which the complex is found does not matter. Also irrelevant is whether something has multiple attestation.

1. The plausibility that a complex or topic originated with Jesus is increased if it illumines or is illumined by the paradigm of Jesus as eschatological prophet or known biographical information about him[177] or one of the major themes enumerated on pp. 46–48. Jesus' ruling on divorce, preserved in 1 Cor 7:10–11; Q 16:18; and Mk 10:2–12, is a case in point. It not only epitomizes Jesus as moral rigorist, but the justification given in Mk 10:2–12, that at creation male and female were one flesh, gains its force from the standard apocalyptic linkage between *Urzeit* and *Endzeit* and so falls in line with Jesus' eschatological outlook.[178] Similarly, the beatitudes in Q 6:20–23 (compare *Gos. Thom.* 54, 68–69) coincide at so many points with themes presumably characteristic of Jesus that they likely descend from him. They allude to an eschatological Scripture (Isa 61:1–3), promise future reward, comfort the unfortunate, and implicitly disparage wealth.[179]

2. The plausibility that a complex or topic originated with Jesus is, nothwithstanding the caution expressed earlier in this chapter, increased if the Christian tradition has seemingly struggled with it, and especially if there are signs that the early Jesus tradition itself sought to domesticate or reinterpret the item. This is a restatement of the so-called criterion of embarrassment. One example is Jesus' prophecy of the destruction and rebuilding of the temple, which receives more than one reinterpretation and is in Mark attributed to false witnesses.[180] A second example is Q 6:27, the imperative to love one's enemy. It has, because of its extreme demand, been modified in or dropped altogether from the paraenesis in the canonical and extracanonical parallels to Q 6:27–38.[181]

3. The plausibility that a complex or topic originated with Jesus is increased if one cannot concoct a persuasive narrative explaining its emergence in the post-Easter period. This is perhaps akin to the criterion of dissimilarity but omits altogether any contrast with Judaism.[182] To illus-

---

177. Almost everyone regards as indisputable a rather long list of particulars, including that Jesus was baptized by John, that he was a Galilean miracle-worker, that he was known as a teacher, that he was crucified in Jerusalem under Pontius Pilate in the reign of Tiberius, and that shortly after his death some of his followers claimed he had risen from the dead.

178. See further below, p. 210.

179. See further chapter 3 of my *The Jesus Tradition in Q*.

180. See the discussion on pp. 98–101 below.

181. See further p. 24.

182. Compare Meyer, *Aims*, p. 86: "The requirement of simultaneous discontinuity with Judaism and the post-paschal church errs by excess. That the community should gratuitously adopt from Judaism elements in discontinuity with its own concerns, practices, and tendencies simply does not make sense. Discontinuity with the post-paschal church is sufficient by itself to establish historicity."

trate: Arland J. Hultgren has argued that Christians constructed Mk 12:18–27, where Jesus argues against the Sadducees in favor of resurrection, in order to answer questions about remarriage and mourned loved ones.[183] But surely Mk 12:18–27 is a rather roundabout and obscure way of addressing such questions. If no better post-Easter tale can be told, are we not invited to seek some genesis in the life of Jesus? The early church, moreover, did not, as far as we know, engage the Sadducees in debate,[184] and, outside the Gospels, Christian texts argue for the resurrection and speculate on its nature by reference to Jesus' resurrection, not Scripture.[185]

Consider, as another example, the topic of Pilate as Roman governor when Jesus was crucified. Even if one were to attribute all of the post-Markan references to Pilate to Markan influence and further deny a historical core to the story in Mk 15:1–15, it would be difficult to offer a convincing explanation of why Christian legend landed upon Pilate in particular. Here is a case where a topic—Jesus crucified under Pontius Pilate—seems historical apart from the issue of whether it appears in any authentic complexes.

4. The plausibility that a complex or topic originated with Jesus is increased if it exhibits a confluence of several of the formal features listed on pp. 49–50. Mt 21:28–32, for instance, is a parable, contains antithetical parallelism, and ends with a rhetorical question. Thus it has some initial claim, on formal grounds, to come from Jesus. Consider also Q 12:51–53. This unit, with its end-time application of Mic 7:6, not only (a) harmonizes with the paradigm of Jesus as eschatological prophet who saw the present as a time of crisis and (b) is illumined by the biographical fact that members of Jesus' own family were hostile to him but also (c) contains antithetical parallelism, a rhetorical question, and a contrast with a scriptural expectation (eschatological peace).[186]

5. The plausibility that a complex or topic originated with Jesus is increased if it has inconspicuous or unexpected connections with a complex

183. Arland J. Hultgren, *Jesus and His Adversaries: The Form and Function of the Conflict Stories in the Synoptic Tradition* (Minneapolis: Augsburg, 1979), pp. 123–31.

184. There is no evidence of real Christian debate with Sadducees in any of the four Gospels, and they are missing entirely from all the New Testament epistles. They are only marginal in Acts (4:1–2; 5:17–18; 23:6–10).

185. See further below, pp. 177–78.

186. For the reconstruction of this Q text, the value of the parallel in *Gos. Thom.* 16, and an origin with Jesus, see my article, "Q 12:51–53 and Mk 9:9–11 and the Messianic Woes," in *Authenticating the Teaching of Jesus*, ed. Craig Evans and Bruce Chilton (Leiden: E. J. Brill, forthcoming, 1998).

already thought, on other grounds, to be dominical. This may be called the index of intertextual linkage. Q 12:51–53, which for reasons just given should probably be attributed to Jesus, has intriguing connections with the notoriously obscure Mk 9:11–13. They say very much the same thing—the present is not the time of eschatological peace and reconciliation but of eschatological suffering—and they both say it by setting one scriptural text or expectation against another.[187] Beyond these correlations, the two chief Scriptures beneath the texts—Q 12:51–53 draws upon Mic 7:6; Mk 9:9–11 refers to Mal 4:6—are probably intertextually related in the Hebrew Bible[188] and have in any case been read together in exegetical history. Surely, then, if Q 12:51–53 rests on dominical tradition, we are at least invited, despite all the learned opinion to the contrary, to consider that Mk 9:11–13 may too.[189]

Mk 10:45 also, just as Mk 9:9–11, shows an interesting relationship with the authentic complex Q 12:51–53. It may be depicted visually:

Q 12:51–53
a. an "I came" saying
b. a contrast with eschatological expectation ("not peace")
c. a surprising antithesis ("but a sword")
d. a reference to suffering (familial strife)
e. a warrant from Scripture (use of Mic 7:6)

Mk 10:45
a. a "Son of man came" saying
b. a contrast with eschatological expectation (Dan 7:13–14)
c. a surprising antithesis ("but to serve")
d. a reference to suffering ("give his life")
e. a warrant from Scripture (allusion to Isa 53:10–12)[190]

Once more one must at least ask whether there is not significance in this sort of concurrence, whether such inconspicuous but nonetheless real correlations are better explained by happenstance or by a common origin.

187. In Q 12:51–53, Mic 7:6 is played off against the well-attested expectation of eschatological peace. In Mk 9:9–11 the end-time suffering of the saints in Daniel 7 (there identified with or closely associated with "the one like a son of man") is played off against the promise of eschatological reconciliation in Mal 4:6.
188. Pierre Grelot, "Michée 7,6 dans les évangiles et dans la littérature rabbinique," *Bib* 67 (1986), p. 375.
189. See further my article, "Q 12:51–53 and Mk 9:9–11 and the Messianic Woes."
190. An allusion to Isaiah 53 has sometimes been denied but remains likely; see W. J. Moulder, "The Old Testament Background and Interpretation of Mark x.45," *NTS* 24 (1977), pp. 120–27.

Because scholars have insufficiently utilized the index of intertextual linkage, I should like to offer further examples of its application. Q 7:22–23, Jesus' recitation of miracles in response to a question from John the Baptist, refers to seeing and hearing, borrows from Isa 61:1, and ends with a beatitude. These three features link it with two other complexes that are widely accepted as dominical:

Q 6:20–23	Q 7:22–23	Q 10:23–24
Isa 61	Isa 61	
makarism	makarism	makarism
	see and hear formula	see and hear formula

Do these parallels to Q 7:22–23 not raise a bit the odds—I do not say establish authenticity but only raise the odds—that the text in the middle had the same origin as those to its right and left?

Q 9:58 ("Foxes have holes, and birds of the air have nests, but the Son of man has nowhere to lay his head") = Gos. Thom. 86 is commonly attributed to Jesus, whereas Mk 10:45 ("The Son of man came not to be served but to serve and to give his life as a ransom for many") is most often assigned to the community. But the former probably alludes ironically to Psalm 8, where God has put the beasts of the field and "the birds of the air" under the feet of "the son of man." [191] This is interesting, because Mk 10:45 has often been thought, and I think rightly, to refer ironically to Daniel 7, where the "one like a son of man" is served.[192] That is, in both Q 9:58 and Mk 10:45, "the Son of man" is the subject, in both texts he is humbled, and in both cases this humility apparently stands in ironic contrast with a Hebrew Bible passage about the exalted status of "the son of man" or "one like a son of man." Is this a coincidence or an intimation of common authorship?

According to Q 16:13, "No servant is able to serve two lords; for either (the servant) will hate the one and love the other or be devoted to the one and despise the other. You cannot serve God and mammon." [193] We

191. M. H. Smith, "No Place for a Son of Man," Forum 4/4 (1988), pp. 83–107.

192. Compare C. K. Barrett, "The Background of Mark 10:45," in New Testament Essays: Studies in Memory of Thomas Walter Manson, ed. A. J. B. Higgins (Manchester: Manchester University Press, 1959), pp. 8–9, and Peter Stuhlmacher, Reconciliation, Law, and Righteousness (Philadelphia: Fortress, 1986), pp. 20–22.

193. The differences between Matthew and Luke are minimal. The variant in Gos. Thom. 47 ("It is impossible for a man to mount two horses and to stretch two bows, and it is impossible for a servant to serve two masters, otherwise he will honor the one and offend the other") seems secondary: the end has been truncated and the beginning has drawn to

have here a secular proverb[194] followed by two lines of sharp antithetical parallelism—no middle case is allowed—followed by the religious or ethical application; and the whole unit has to do with wealth. The very same pattern shows up in another quatrain, Q 11:34–35: "The eye is the lamp of the body. Whenever your eye is sound also your whole body will be lit up. But whenever (your eye) is bad your body will be dark. Watch then lest the light that is in you be darkness."[195] As in Q 16:13 the unit opens with a secular proverb. Then come two lines in antithetical parallelism that set forth two extremes. And the complex ends with the religious or ethical application, which again has to do with wealth (the "sound eye" is generous whereas the "bad eye" is selfish). It seems highly unlikely that Q 16:13 is a conscious imitation of Q 11:34–35 or *vice versa*. A better explanation of the commonality is that the same person authored both units; and since Q 16:13 is widely ascribed to Jesus, the implication is obvious: he also authored Q 11:34–35.

As a final example of intertextual linkage, consider Mk 10:25 ("It is easier for a camel to go through the eye of a needle than for someone who is rich to enter the kingdom of God")[196] and Mt 23:24 ("You strain out a gnat and swallow a camel"). Well nigh everyone accepts the former as a saying of Jesus. The latter does not enjoy such favor. This is because it is, to use Crossan's categories, a third stratum complex with single attestation. But in Matthew the logion appears in a block of Q material, and if the saying—which is hard to imagine as an isolated unit—had stood in Q, would we not expect Luke to have deleted it? The third evangelist often altered or dropped things that might not have been understood by a non-Jewish audience. And here one must wonder what a Gentile would have made of a saying that presupposes knowledge of how Lev 11:41[197] was traditionally understood: one should strain wine to get out small bugs (*m. Šabb.* 20:2; *b. Hull.* 67a). Moreover, the possibility of a neat wordplay in Aramaic—"gnat" = *qalmāʾ*/"camel" = *gamlāʾ*[198]—should *perhaps* encourage us to suppose that the saying could be old.

itself two related proverbs. Further, "servant" might betray Lukan influence (it appears in Luke but not Matthew).

194. See Plato, *Rep.* 8.555C; Cicero, *Balbo* 11.28; Philo, frag. 2.649; *Poimandres* 4:6b; *T. Jud.* 18:6.

195. For the reconstruction of the Q text and justification for the following remarks see my *Jesus Tradition in Q*, pp. 134–68.

196. This also appeared in the *Gospel of the Nazaraeans* according to Origen, *Comm. on Mt.* 15:14.

197. "All creatures that swarm upon the earth are detestable; they shall not be eaten."

198. Matthew Black, *An Aramaic Approach to the Gospels and Acts*, 3d ed. (Oxford: Clarendon, 1967), pp. 175–76.

Be that as it may, proof of a redactional or late origin is lacking, and with that in mind the parallels between Mk 10:25 and Mt 23:24 may be worth considering. Each contains (a) a humorously absurd image that (b) involves a contrast between the very large and the very small[199] and that (c) mentions the proverbial enormous camel and that (d) does this in order to characterize an error of certain individuals who are outside the circle of Jesus' followers. Is this coincidence? Or was Mt 23:24 modeled upon Mk 10:25? Or did Jesus author both?

Four remarks need to be subjoined to my all-too-brief exposition of my five indices of authenticity. First, each index has its contrary. That is, the plausibility that a complex originated with Jesus is decreased if it neither illumines nor is illumined by the paradigm of Jesus as eschatological prophet or a known biographical fact or one or more of the themes listed on pp. 46–48;[200] and/or if the Christian tradition has not struggled with it;[201] and/or if one can concoct a persuasive narrative explaining its emergence in the post-Easter period;[202] and/or if it does not exhibit any of the formal features listed on pp. 49–50;[203] and/or if it does not have significant connections with a complex already thought, on other grounds, to be dominical.[204]

Second, even after we have passed portions of the Jesus tradition through our five indices we should feel no moral certainty about the outcome. We still have nothing more than pliable texts and indeterminate arguments. A confluence of indicators may raise the level of plausibility— but that is all historians will ever have, higher and lower levels of plausibility. Further, we have no antecedent reason either to hope that all authentic sayings will successfully run the gauntlet nor to expect that all secondary additions will fail. And it takes very little effort to learn that sometimes our indicators send conflicting signals.[205] Nothing, to revert to

199. A striking contrast between small and large also appears in the parable of the mustard seed (Q 13:18–19; Mk 4:30–32; *Gos. Thom.* 20) and the parable of the leaven (Q 13:20–21; *Gos. Thom.* 96).

200. Mt 18:15–17, which offers instructions on ecclesiastical excommunication, is an obvious example.

201. Q 10:22 (only the Son knows the Father), so far from being a stumbling block, probably contributed much to the theology of John's Gospel.

202. *Gos. Thom.* 22, which speaks of the two becoming one, by which is meant male and female becoming one, can be explained as a development of baptismal doctrine (compare Gal 3:27–28; Col 3:9–11).

203. Mt 3:15 ("Let it be so now; for it is proper for us in this way to fulfill all righteousness") is an example.

204. Here one may cite Mt 18:20 ("For where two or three are gathered in my name, I am there among them") and *Gos. Thom.* 38 ("There will be days when you seek me but will not find me").

205. So it is with Mk 10:45. It may have connections with dominical texts (see above),

our earlier discussion, guarantees that we will not be forever confusing Jesus with Faustina or Justus. Perhaps the tares and wheat have grown together, and maybe we cannot pull out one without uprooting the other.

Third, we do not have Jesus' original utterances but only their descendants. It is not just that we have lost the (presumably) Aramaic originals but that the tradition apparently did not treasure pristine purity or verbatim reproduction. Matthew and Luke felt free to rewrite the sayings of Jesus in Mark and Q, and Paul's versions of Jesus traditions do not show word-for-word agreement with our other sources.[206] If we needed confirmation, the *Gospel of Thomas* supplies it. So we should be hunting for the *sense* of something that Jesus said, not for his words as such.

Finally, our indices often leave a hung jury. Many tradtions allow us no conclusion at all, except that an origin with Jesus or an origin with the church are equal possibilities. Did Jesus utter the golden rule (Q 6:31; *Gos. Thom.* 6; *Did.* 1:2)? Did he say that a disciple is not above the teacher (Q 6:40; Jn 13:16)? Is the picture of the last judgment in Mt 25:31–46 partly based upon something Jesus said? Did he perhaps prophesy to his disciples, "The heavens and earth will roll back in your presence" (*Gos. Thom.* 111)? How could one ever decide? We can no more answer these questions with conviction than we can determine whether Jesus ever really witnessed a herd of swine rushing down a steep bank to drown in the sea. It may be frustrating to leave so much undecided; but where the data are not conclusive, our conclusions should be modest. And sometimes we may not be able to make up our minds. The past is often inscrutable.

Some Results

Although it is obviously far beyond the scope of this chapter or book to evaluate the Jesus tradition in its entirety, it would perhaps be anticlimactic not to give the reader some idea of where the application of the various indices takes us.

1. *The Problem of "Authenticity."* The most important result is that we can say a good deal about Jesus. It is not, however, possible to offer, as one can with Crossan's inventory, statistical generalizations. This is because one hesitates to put + or − or even ± or *?* in front of every com-

---

but it involves a concrete prediction of death and harmonizes with the post-Easter understanding of Jesus' death as an atonement.

206. For Paul see especially 1 Cor 7:10–11, 25; 9:14; 11:23–26; 1 Thess 4:15–17.

plex. On the one hand, traditions that originated with Jesus were refor-
mulated, translated, modified through additions, and given new meaning
through secondary contexts.[207] On the other hand, community produc-
tions must have partly evolved out of and in close connection with other
materials already in the tradition.[208] The categories of "authentic" and
"inauthentic" or (as Crossan prefers) "original" and "not original" can
be misleading; we do not find Jesus through the simple exercise of sub-
tracting ecclesiastical accretions to get back to the pristine performances.
Rather, in most cases we are dealing with mixed products, and the contributions of Jesus and the tradition are inextricably intertwined. Almost
everything, one could contend, merits Crossan's ± sign.

To underscore the point, let me offer three illustrations, two from
Mark and one from Q. Mk 1:9–11 recounts the story of Jesus' baptism.
Here three things are said: (a) John baptized Jesus; (b) the heavens were
torn apart and the Spirit descended as a dove; and (c) and a heavenly voice
proclaimed Jesus to be beloved Son. It is usual to regard (a) as an historical fact and (b) and (c) as Christian interpretations of that fact. Assuming this view to be correct, should the complex get (as it does in Crossan)
a plus sign (for the fact that John baptized Jesus) or rather a negative sign
(for the dove and the voice) or maybe, because of the mixture of history
and myth, the ± sign? One might also consider a question mark if one
were to entertain the possibility that Mark's story preserves traces of a visionary experience Jesus had at his baptism.

Shortly after the baptismal story Mark tells us that Jesus came into
Galilee proclaiming the good news of God and saying, "The time is
fulfilled, and the kingdom of God has come near; repent, and believe in
the good news" (1:14–15). What do we make of this unit? Many now ascribe it to Markan redaction, so it might earn the minus sign, which it
does in Crossan. But those of us who believe that Jesus (a) taught in
Galilee, (b) thought that the time of Satan's rule was coming to its end,[209]

---

207. For this and what follows I borrow from Ferdinand Hahn, "Methodologische
Überlegungen zur Rückfrage nach Jesus," in *Rückfrage nach Jesus: Zur Methodik und Be-
deutung der Frage nach dem historischen Jesus*, ed. Karl Kertelge, QD 63 (Freiburg: Herder,
1974), pp. 29–30.

208. Compare Dahl, *Crucified Messiah*, p. 67: "Whether the historicity of individual
words or episodes remains uncertain is consequently of lesser importance. The fact that the
word or occurrence found a place within the tradition about Jesus indicates that it agreed
with the total picture as it existed within the circle of the disciples."

209. For this interpretation of Mk 1:15 see Joel Marcus, "'The Time Has Been Fulfilled!' (Mark 1:15)," in *Apocalyptic and the New Testament: Essays in Honor of J. Louis
Martyn*, ed. Joel Marcus and Marion L. Soards, JSNTSS 24 (Sheffield: JSOT, 1989),
pp. 49–68.

(c) proclaimed the imminence of the kingdom of God, (d) called for repentance, and (e) associated his ministry with the prophecies of Deutero-
Isaiah[210] might well regard Mk 1:14–15 as a fair summary of Jesus'
proclamation. So should we bestow upon it, even if it is redactional, the
+ sign? Or should it have the ± sign?

Consider also Q 4:1–13, the temptation story. Most modern scholars
have rightly judged this to be unhistorical, a haggadic fiction produced
through reflection upon scripture. But whoever composed it clearly did
so in the knowledge that Jesus was (a) a miracle-worker who (b) sometimes refused to give signs, (c) thought himself victorious over demonic
forces, (d) was steeped in the scriptures, (e) had great faith in God, and
(f) was a person of the Spirit. So what we seem to have in Q 4:1–13 is an
illustration of the obvious fact that historical fiction can instruct us about
history.[211]

The point of all this is just to underline how facile is the usual assumption that a complex either originated with Jesus or with the church.
It follows that statistical generalizations regarding authenticity will also
be facile.[212]

2. *Eschatology, christology, soteriology.* Jesus turns out to have been
the proponent of an apocalyptic eschatology. This result is of course contained in the methodological premise, according to which Jesus was an eschatological prophet. But in this regard history is not different from hermeneutics: circularity we will always have with us.[213] At the same time,

210. For the dependence of "believe in the good news" upon Deutero-Isaiah see Bruce
D. Chilton, *God in Strength: Jesus' Announcement of the Kingdom*, SNTU B/1 (Freistadt:
F. Plöchl, 1979), pp. 92–95.

211. See further my article, "The Temptations of Jesus," in *Authenticating the Deeds of
Jesus*, ed. Bruce Chilton and Craig A. Evans (Leiden: E. J. Brill, forthcoming 1998).

212. There may be a parallel here with a Pauline conundrum. John Barclay, *Colossians
and Philemon*, New Testament Guides (Sheffield: Sheffield Academic Press, 1997), p. 35, has
written: "It turns out. . .that the differences are not large between Paul himself writing this
letter [Colossians], Paul writing with the aid of a secretary, Paul authorizing an associate
to write it, and the letter being composed by a knowledgeable imitator or pupil of Paul. Perhaps with our intense concern to demarcate 'Paul' from 'non-Paul' we are working with an
artificial or anachronistic notion of individual uniqueness: was Paul completely different
from his contemporaries and associates, or did he typically work with others, influencing
them and being influenced by them? Have we created a Paul of utter uniqueness in line with
the peculiarly modern cult of the individual? Whether by Paul, by a secretary, by an associate or by a pupil, Colossians is clearly a 'Pauline' letter."

213. Compare Hahn, "Methodologische Überlegungen," pp. 37–38, who observes the
problem of interpreting the individual pieces of the Jesus tradition without first having a total picture of Jesus and the problem of having a total picture of Jesus without first interpreting the individual pieces. His method is similar to my own in that he enters the circle
from generalizations about Jesus and the Jesus tradition.

some sayings with an apocalyptic worldview may be deemed authentic not just because they illuminate or are illumined by the paradigm of Jesus as eschatological prophet but also because they satisfy other indices. For instance, and as already observed above, Q 12:51–53 is not just consistent with an eschatological outlook but further harmonizes with a biographical fact about Jesus—his own familial conflict—and contains several of the formal features characteristic of Jesus. So the conclusion that certain apocalyptic sayings go back to Jesus is not just a product of the premise: the final conclusion also fortifies the opening supposition.

The attribution of apocalyptic sayings to Jesus is further vindicated because it enables us to understand why Jesus' program exhibits so many striking parallels with worldwide millenarian movements.[214] Like many Pacific cargo cults, Jewish messianic groups, Amerindian prophetic movements, and Christian sects looking for the end of the world, Jesus' program

- addressed the disaffected or less fortunate in a period of social change that threatened traditional ways and symbolic universes;[215]

214. Documentation for the following may be found in the detached note that follows this chapter.

215. Crossan has argued that John the Baptist and Jesus appeared when Jewish peasants were suffering mounting taxation, indebtedness, and land expropriation within a context of expanding commercialization. There was accordingly an increasing sense of deprivation and much disillusionment with the status quo. People were ready and willing to listen to individuals who set themselves against present circumstances—including the Roman order—and spoke of a better future. For a different view see Thomas E. Schmidt, *Hostility to Wealth in the Synoptic Gospels*, JSNTSS 15 (Sheffield: JSOT, 1987), pp. 17–37. One should be cautious here. "The mechanistic theories of apocalypse's appeal based in economic circumstances that prevail in much current scholarship fail to account for. . .[the] wide variety of class and education in apocalyptic audiences," and "the omnipresence of such emotions as anxiety, apprehension, and dissatisfaction present an inherent difficulty to those who attempt to account for the appeal of apocalypse by linking fluctuations in its historical popularity to intangible societal moods"; so O'Leary, *Arguing the Apocalypse*, pp. 9–10. It nonetheless seems safe to believe that many first-century Jews would presumably have perceived the present as unsatisfactory, simply because the Jewish tradition, for which land and God were inextricable, made any form of foreign pagan rule unacceptable; and "it is clear that wherever a long-established tradition of hope exists, one that gives a dramatic explanation of the cosmos and allows of active participation in the drama in such a way as to fulfil people's fantasies and to take them out of the daily toil or routine of their lives, there any change in social, economic or cultural conditions will favor the rise of a messianic movement" (René Ribeiro, "Brazilian Messianic Movements," in *Millennial Dreams in Action: Studies in Revolutionary Religious Movements*, ed. Sylvia L. Thrupp [New York: Schocken, 1970], p. 65). Alan F. Segal, *Rebecca's Children: Judaism and Christianity in the Roman World* (Cambridge: Harvard University Press, 1986), p. 72, observes that, in Jesus' time, all the factors requisite for a millenarian movement were in place in Jesus' time and place. Compare John G. Gager, *Kingdom and Community: The Social World of Early Christianity*

it indeed emerged in a time of aspiration for national independence[216]

• saw the present and near future as times of suffering and/or catastrophe[217]

• was holistic, that is, envisaged a comprehensive righting of wrongs[218] and promised redemption through a reversal of current circumstances[219]

• depicted that reversal as imminent[220]

• was both revivalistic[221] and evangelistic[222]

(Englewood Cliffs: Prentice-Hall, 1975), pp. 22–28. Note that the original Jesus tradition says much about the poor and oppressed, who are never content with their lot; and it further (like the Dead Sea Scrolls) contains polemic against Jewish leaders, who had power over others. Indeed, one should at least ask, since there is so much more in the early Jesus tradition about the scribes and Pharisees than about the Roman overlords, whether Jesus' millenarianism may have been as much a response to alienation from leaders of his Jewish community as to the problem of foreign oppression. However that may be, Albert Schweitzer, *The Quest of the Historical Jesus* (New York: Macmillan, 1968), pp. 369–70, was probably wrong in urging that the "apocalyptic enthusiasm" of Jesus' day was "called forth not by external events, but solely by the appearance of two great personalities [the Baptist and Jesus]. . . ."

216. Surely whatever success the pre-Easter Jesus movement enjoyed was partly due to dissatisfaction with Roman rule, a dissatisfaction that grew into violent revolt thirty years later.

217. Jesus saw difficulties all around him (Q 6:20–23; 10:3; 11:23; 14:15–24, 26; Mk 8:34); and he evidently interpreted the Baptist's death, his own present, and the near future in terms of the eschatological woes; see further Chapter 2.

218. In the Jesus tradition in Q we find teaching having to do with money (Q 6:20), food (Q 6:21a; 11:3; 12:23–25; 13:28), clothing (Q 12:26–29), emotional well-being (Q 6:21b), physical illness (Q 7:22), injustice (Q 6:22), knowledge (Q 10:21, 23–24), religious forgiveness (Q 11:4), religious salvation (Q 12:4–7, 8–9), and politics (God will rule instead of Caesar).

219. Probably most characteristic of all of Jesus' sayings are those that feature reversal: the hungry will be filled (Q 6:21); the exalted will be humbled and the humbled exalted (Q 14:11); those who try to make life secure will fail and those who lose life will find it (Q 17:33); many who are first will be last whereas the last will be first (Mk 10:31). Segal, *Rebecca's Children*, p. 82, suggests that "the presence of prostitutes and tax collectors among Jesus' supporters is probably symbol as well as actual, vividly expressing the apocalyptic ethic of overturning the established order." For a modern messianic parallel to this see Joel Marcus, "Modern and Ancient Jewish Apocalyptic," *JR* 76 (1996), pp. 23–25.

220. See Chapter 2 below.

221. By this is meant deepening the piety of the faithful and stirring up religious faith among the indifferent. See further Marcus Borg, *Jesus, A New Vision: Spirit, Culture, and the Life of Discipleship* (San Francisco: Harper & Row, 1987), pp. 125–49.

222. On Jesus as a missionary see Martin Hengel, *The Charismatic Leader and His Followers* (New York: Crossroad, 1981), pp. 73–80, and Laufen, *Doppelüberlieferungen*, pp. 260–68.

- may have promoted egalitarianism[223]
- divided the world into two camps, the saved and the unsaved[224]
- broke hallowed taboos associated with religious custom[225]
- was at the same time nativistic[226] and focused upon the salvation of the community[227]
- replaced traditional familial and social bonds with fictive kin[228]
- mediated the sacred through new channels[229]
- demanded intense commitment and unconditional loyalty[230]
- focused upon a charismatic leader,[231]
- understood its beliefs to be the product of special revelation[232]
- took a passive political stance in expectation of a divinely wrought deliverance[233]

223. On egalitarianism and Jesus, Crossan, *Historical Jesus*, pp. 295–302, offers material to think about. But for justified caution see Amy-Jill Levine, "Second Temple Judaism, Jesus, and Women: Yeast of Eden," *Biblical Interpretation* 2 (1994), pp. 8–33.

224. On this see my article, "Jesus and the Covenant: A Response to E. P. Sanders," *JSNT* 29 (1987), pp. 57–78.

225. The several stories of Jesus' conflicts on the Sabbath probably record the memory that, even if he did not set himself against Moses, he was intentionally provocative regarding Sabbath customs.

226. Jesus' use of "kingdom of God" was an implicit rejection of the kingdom of Caesar and an implicit endorsement of Jewish kingship. Further, his almost exclusive focus upon his own people (see especially E. P. Sanders and Margaret Davies, *Studying the Synoptic Gospels* [London: SCM, 1989], pp. 305–12), his lack of teaching about Gentiles (see Allison, *The Jesus Tradition in Q*, pp. 183–86), his interest in the Hebrew Bible (see below, p. 68), and the Jewish features in his eschatological promises (e.g., Q 13:28, which says that being in the kingdom means enjoying the presence of Abraham, Isaac, and Jacob) leave no doubt that Jesus was, in his own way, seeking to uphold his Jewish heritage.

227. On Jesus' hopes for Israel see pp. 141–45 below. Note the plurals in Q 6:20–22 and the collective judgments in Q 10:13–15.

228. See, e.g., Q 12:51–53; 14:26; Mk 3:31–35.

229. With Jesus the sacred appears to have been experienced primarily in his healings and meals.

230. Note Q 9:60; 10:4; 12:22; Mk 1:16–20.

231. The Romans arrested Jesus but not those around him. Note also the meager number of stories in the Jesus tradition that do not put Jesus front and center.

232. For the presence of this motif in the Jesus tradition see n. 145.

233. Jesus' pacifism is apparent from both Q 6:27–36 and the tradition that he did not resist once arrested (Mk 14:43–52; 15:1–15). Other Jews near Jesus' time were willing to die for their religious convictions without fighting; note Josephus, *Bell.* 2:169–74; *Ant.* 18:261–78. According to Michael Barkun, *Disaster and the Millennium* (New Haven: Yale University Press, 1974), p. 19, "passivity is often a sign that a movement has already had its moment of confrontation with existing institutions and has been defeated." Did the memory of the failure of Galilean uprisings in the wake of Herod the Great's death affect Jesus?

- expected a restored paradise that would return the ancestors[234]
- insisted on the possibility of experiencing that utopia as a present reality[235]
- grew out of a precursor movement[236]

Finally, it is significant that any millenarian movement that survives has to come to terms with disappointed expectations, since the mythic dream or end never comes. The evidence that this happened in early Christianity is substantial.[237] In sum, then, we may fairly conclude that Jesus was the leader of a millenarian movement.[238]

234. On the resurrection in Jesus' proclamation see Chapter 2 below.

235. On the presence of the kingdom of God (which stands beside its futurity) in Jesus' words and work, see Meier, *Marginal Jew*, vol. 2, pp. 398–506.

236. Jesus was baptized by John and may even, at his baptism, have experienced some sort of foundational religious experience. In addition, Q has Jesus speaking to people who believed in John (7:24–34), Mark has the two figures being conflated in some people's minds (6:16; 8:28), and John has Jesus drawing disciples from the Baptist movement (1:29–51).

237. See further below, pp. 98–101.

238. The attempt of Horsley, *Sociology and the Jesus Movement*, pp. 90ff., to dissociate the early Jesus movement from millenarian movements is unconvincing. The differences between Christianity and cargo cults do not eliminate the similarities, which also appear in ancient, medieval, and modern European and American millenarianism.

There are additional features of the Jesus tradition that one might relate to millenarianism. E.g., if Jesus may have had a special place for women within his movement (although this is not quite as obvious to me as it seems to be to others), one could relate this to the special attraction of females to many millennial movements; recall the importance of women in Montanism, and see further Norman Cohn, *The Pursuit of the Millennium: Revolutionary Millenarians and Mystical Anarchists of the Middle Ages*, rev. ed. (New York: Oxford, 1970), pp. 160–61, 261; Hillel Schwarz, "Millenarianism: An Overview," in *The Encyclopedia of Religion*, ed. Mircea Eliade (New York: Macmillan, 1987), vol. 9, p. 528; idem, *The French Prophets: The History of a Millenarian Group in Eighteenth-Century England* (Berkeley: University of California, 1980), especially pp. 134–46, 191–215; George Shepperson, "The Comparative Study of Millenarian Movements," in *Millennial Dreams in Action: Studies in Revolutionary Religious Movements*, ed. Sylvia L. Thrupp (New York: Schocken, 1970), pp. 47–48; and Peter Worsley, *The Trumpet Shall Sound: A Study of "Cargo" Cults in Melanesia*, 2d ed. (New York: Schocken, 1968), p. xl.

Again, because the tradition has Jesus spending most of his time in rural Galilee, it may be worth noting that some millenarian movements have been concentrated in rural areas. On this see Barkun, *Disaster and the Millennium*, pp. 66–74, and idem, *Crucible of the Millennium: The Burned-Over District of New York in the 1840s* (Syracuse: University Press, 1986), pp. 140–41 (arguing against Cohn, *Pursuit of the Millennium*). It may also be relevant, when considering early Christianity, to note the generalization of Hillel Schwartz, "Millenarianism: An Overview," in *The Encyclopedia of Religion*, ed. Mircea Eliade (New York: Macmillan, 1987), vol. 9, p. 529: millenarian movements are often "founded on the fringes of empire or at the fracture line between competing kingdoms."

Some recent reconstructions of Jesus tend to eliminate not only apocalyptic eschatology but also Christology and soteriology from the original tradition. Do we not all know that saints and religious heroes are regularly divinized, exalted with mythic titles, and interpreted within traditional mythic patterns after their deaths? And how could Jesus have interpreted his death before it happened?

It may, however, be worth observing that eschatology, Christology, and soteriology are among the things that Christian fundamentalists hold dearest. Is detaching these things from Jesus sometimes encouraged by a personal dislike of conservative religion? However that may be, the elimination of apocalyptic eschatology from the earliest tradition is utterly implausible. Further, and as we have seen, Mk 10:45, with its soteriological interest, *might* go back to Jesus; and, because one can, beyond that, make a strong case that the various versions of the last supper reflect something Jesus said,[239] it is a reasonable surmise that Jesus, at least near the end, envisaged his death and gave some meaning to it.[240] Important people in hazardous circumstances have occasionally had intimations of an untimely death and ruminated upon it: Abraham Lincoln was so anxious about the possibility of assassination that he had nightmares about it, which he shared with others.[241]

As for Christology, whether Jesus spoke of "the Son of man" with reference to a redeemer yet to come (so Bultmann and others) or instead used the expression to refer to the suffering and vindication of the saints in the latter days,[242] he must have held himself to be a

239. See H. Merklein, "Erwägungen zur Überlieferung der neutestamentlichen Abendmahlstraditionen," *BZ* 21 (1977), pp. 88–101, 235–44. Contrast Crossan, *Historical Jesus*, pp. 360–67.

240. See further Heinz Schürmann, "Wie hat Jesus seinen Tod bestanden und verstanden? Eine methodenkritische Besinnung," in *Orientierung an Jesus: Zur Theologie der Synoptiker*, ed. Paul Hoffmann et al. (Freiburg: Herder, 1973), pp. 325–63, and idem, "Jesu Todesverständnis im Verstehenshorizont seiner Umwelt," *TGI* 70 (1980), pp. 141–60.

241. Roy P. Basler, *The Lincoln Legend: A Study in Changing Conceptions* (New York: Octagon, 1969), pp. 185–91. One also recalls Swedenborg's famous letter to John Wesley, wherein the former predicts his own death.

242. These are the two most likely options. For the former see Adela Yarbro Collins, "The Apocalyptic Son of Man Sayings," in *The Future of Early Christianity*, ed. Birger A. Pearson (Minneapolis: Fortress, 1991), pp. 220–28. The collective interpretation of "the Son of man" in the Jesus tradition was once popular with British exegetes (e.g., J. R. Coates, A. T. Cadoux, T. W. Manson, C. J. Cadoux, C. H. Dodd, the later Vincent Taylor) but has fallen out of favor lately (although Morna Hooker and C. F. D. Moule have still promoted it). It deserves reexamination. (1) If Jesus did not use "the Son of man" as an exclusive self-designation, this would help explain why, outside the Jesus tradition, the term never became

prophet.[243] Not only does the tradition report that this is what people made of him,[244] but Mk 6:4[245] probably and Lk 13:32–33[246] possibly rest upon words of Jesus.[247] In addition, the use of Isa 61:1–3 in both Q

---

a christological title. (2) In general, many of Jesus' sayings have in view what Gerd Theissen calls "Gruppenmessianismus"; see his article "Gruppenmessianismus: Überlegungen zum Ursprung der Kirche im Jüngerkreis Jesu," *Jahrbuch für Biblische Theologie* 7 (1992), pp. 101–23. And Judaism knew of such "Gruppenmessianismus"; see Hartmut Stegemann, "Some Remarks to 1QSa, to 1QSb, and to Qumran Messianism," *RevQ* 65–68 (1996), pp. 479–505, and Annette Steudel, "The Eternal Reign of the People of God—Collective Expectations in Qumran Texts (4Q246 and 1QM)," *RevQ* 65–68 (1996), pp. 507–25. (3) In Daniel 7 "the one like a son of man" can be identified with the saints of the Most High, and some premodern exegetes read it this way; see Maurice Casey, *Son of Man: The Interpretation and Influence of Daniel 7* (London: SPCK, 1979), pp. 51–98. (4) If "the Son of man" for Jesus meant the saints of the latter days, then we can understand why, in a text such as Q 12:8–9, Jesus is closely associated with "the Son of man" and yet the two do not seem identical. (5) The collective interpretation explains why some interpreters have been able to find in many Synoptic "Son of man" texts a generic sense. (6) This interpretation also clarifies the mysterious Mk 9:12b; see my article, "Q 12:51–53 and Mk 9:9–11 and the Messianic Woes." (7) 1 Thess 4:15–17 is closely related to Mk 9:1; 13:24–27; and Mt 24:30–31. But whereas in the Synoptic texts it is the Son of man who comes on the clouds, in Paul it is the Lord Jesus and the saints, both resurrected and alive. That is, in 1 Thess 4:15–17 the saints do not wait for Jesus to come to earth but join him on the clouds. This makes sense if the early tradition envisaged the coming of the Son of man as the coming of the saints. (8) The "thrones" (plural) of Dan 7:9 can be understood to refer to the thrones of God and "the one like a son of man." This matters because Q 22:30, which could go back to Jesus, probably alludes to Daniel 7, and it puts a collectivity (the followers of Jesus in Luke, the twelve in Matthew) on "thrones." In other words, the text can be taken to mean that the disciples will have the role of "the one like a son of man" (compare Rev 20:4). (9) In Lk 12:32, which may also go back to Jesus, Jesus' disciples are told that they will be given the kingdom. In Dan 7:14 the son of man is given the kingdom, as are the saints in verses 18 and 27. Again one can understand the saying to mean that the remnant around Jesus fulfills the role of the figure in Daniel. (10) As T. W. Manson observed long ago, there is a striking correspondence "between the 'Son of Man' predictions and the demands made by Jesus on his disciples. Again and again it is impressed upon them that discipleship is synonymous with sacrifice and suffering and the cross itself. This at once suggests that what was in the mind of Jesus was that he and his followers *together* should share that destiny which he describes as the Passion of the Son of Man, the Remnant that saves by service and self-sacrifice. . ." (*The Teaching of Jesus*, 2d ed. [Cambridge: Cambridge University Press, 1935], p. 231).

243. Compare Wright, *Jesus and the Victory of God*, pp. 162–96.

244. Compare Mk 6:15; 8:27–28; Mt 21:11, 46; Lk 7:39; 24:19.

245. "Prophets are not without honor, except in their hometown, and among their own kin, and in their own home"; compare *Gos. Thom.* 31 = P. Oxy. 1:31; Jn 4:44.

246. "Yet today, tomorrow, and the next day I must be on my way, because it is impossible for a prophet to be killed outside of Jerusalem."

247. Mk 6:4, which harmonizes with what we otherwise know of Jesus' strained relationship with his family, is widely reckoned original; compare Crossan, *Historical Jesus*, p. 347. Lk 13:32–33 is more difficult, for it is singly attested and there are signs of Lukan redaction in v. 33. Nonetheless, the complex does rest upon pre-Lukan tradition; see

6:20–23 (the beatitudes)[248] and 7:22–23 (Jesus' answer to John's question)[249] strongly implies that he associated himself with the eschatological figure who is anointed with the Spirit in that Hebrew Bible text.[250] And this in turn helps explain why early Christians came to confess him as "the Messiah." For no persuasive purely post-Easter explanation for confession of Jesus as "the Messiah" has been forthcoming. If, however, Jesus' followers already, in his own lifetime, identified him as an eschatological figure "anointed" by God (Isa 61:1), then the step to confession of him as "the Anointed One" would not have been large.[251]

Joachim Jeremias, *Die Sprache des Lukasevangeliums*, MeyerK (Göttingen: Vandenhoeck & Ruprecht, 1980), p. 234, and Matthew Black, *An Aramaic Approach to the Gospels and Acts*, 3d ed. (Oxford: Clarendon, 1967), pp. 206–8. The unit is consistent with the paradigm of Jesus as eschatological prophet and Jesus' status as healer and exorcist; and it expounds on the theme, attested throughout the Jesus tradition, of the suffering of the saints. The church, moreover, used the three-day idiom with reference to Jesus' resurrection, whereas here it is used in connection with his death. See further John M. Perry, "The Three Days in the Synoptic Passion Predictions," *CBQ* 48 (1986), pp. 637–54, and Kim Huat Tan, *The Zion Traditions and the Aims of Jesus*, SNTSMS 91 (Cambridge: Cambridge University Press, 1997), pp. 57–77.

248. On the beatitudes see my *Jesus Tradition in Q*, pp. 97–104.

249. "The poor have good news brought to them" takes up Isa 61:1. For discussion of the origin of Q 7:22–23 see W. D. Davies and Dale C. Allison, Jr., *A Critical and Exegetical Commentary on the Gospel according to St. Matthew*, ICC, 3 vols. (Edinburgh: T. & T. Clark, 1988, 1991, 1997), vol. 2, pp. 244–45; Ulrich Luz, *Das Evangelium nach Matthäus (Mt 8–17)*, EKK 1/2 (Neukirchen-Vluyn: Neukirchener, 1990), pp. 164–66; and Walter Wink, "Jesus' Reply to John," *Forum* 5/1 (1989), pp. 121–28.

250. The Dead Sea Scrolls (11QMelchizedek and the fragmentary 4Q521) use Isa. 61:1–3 to portray the eschatological liberation of Israel's captives, and an eschatological interpretation of these verses also appears in the targum to Isaiah.

251. See further Harvey, *Jesus*, pp. 120–53. The question of what Jesus might have made of the promises to David is more difficult to answer. Mk 12:35–37 (on David's son and Lord) does not help, for even if it preserves an argument from Jesus, the point has been lost. Whether Mk 8:27–30 (the confession at Caesarea Philippi) and 14:53–65 (the Jewish trial in which Jesus acknowledges his messiahship) contain historical memory is difficult to establish. Still, the issue needs to be pursued. (1) The Romans executed Jesus as a "king" (Mk 15:26); and "some people besides the Romans must have understood Jesus as a messianic candidate, for neither the Romans nor their administrative advisers among the aristocrats in Judea would have fabricated a messianic role for Jesus, were he not already perceived to be a messianic threat" (Segal, *Rebecca's Children*, p. 85). (2) If either Q 22:28–30 or Mk 10:35–40 contains authentic material, it would seem to follow that Jesus thought of himself as a king (compare the royal aspirations of Judas son of Ezekias in Josephus, *Ant.* 17.271–73; of Simon in Josephus, *Bell.* 2.57; of Athrongaeus the shepherd in Josephus, *Bell.* 2.60–65; of Menahem son of Judas in Josephus, *Bell.* 2.434; note also the general statement in *Ant.* 17.285 and the discussion of popular kingship in Richard A. Horsley and John S. Hanson, *Bandits, Prophets, and Messiahs: Popular Movements in the Time of Jesus* [Minneapolis: Seabury, 1985], pp. 88–134). For the possibility that Q 22:28–30 goes back to Jesus see V. Hampel, *Menschensohn und historischer Jesus: Ein Rätselwort als Schlüssel*

3. *Jesus the Jew.* The late Ben Meyer, in a rather uncharitable review of Crossan's *The Historical Jesus*, claimed that the leading themes of the traditional quest for Jesus have been "eschatology, fulfillment of scriptural promise, prophecy, type, messianic consciousness, and so on." In Crossan's book, however, "Judaic tradition is not in evidence: neither covenant, nor election, nor Torah, nor prophecy has any bearing on Jesus' mission." [252] Whether this is a fair estimate of Crossan may be left to others to decide. [253] The only point here is that the methodology promoted in this chapter produces a thoroughly religious [254] and thoroughly Jewish [255] Jesus who belongs with Meyer's traditional quest. Jesus was much concerned with the prophetic tradition and with the interpretation of Torah. [256] His thought focused on the culmination of Israel's story and

---

zum messianischen Selbstverständnis Jesu (Neukirchen-Vluyn: Neukirchener, 1990), pp. 140–51. On Mk 10:35–40 see Davies and Allison, *Matthew*, vol. 3, pp. 85–86. That Jesus, if he thought himself a king, did not speak openly about it, is understandable in view of the potential dangers (compare Jn 6:15). (3) If Jesus spoke of rebuilding the temple (see pp. 97–101), the implications are large. 2 Sam 7:4–17 foresees a descendant of David who will build God's house. This was an eschatological prophecy in first-century Judaism; see Donald Juel, *Messiah and Temple*, SBLDS 31 (Missoula: Scholars Press, 1977), pp. 169–97. The targum on Zech 6:12 bestows upon the temple builder of 2 Samuel 7 the title "Messiah." For further discussion see Craig A. Evans, *Jesus and His Contemporaries*, AGJU 25 (Leiden: E. J. Brill, 1995), pp. 437–56, and Gerd Theissen and Annette Merz, *Der historische Jesus* (Göttingen: Vandenhoeck & Ruprecht, 1996), pp. 462–70 (ET: *The Historical Jesus* [Minneapolis: Fortress, 1998]).

252. Ben Meyer, *CBQ* 55 (1993), pp. 575–76. Compare Witherington, *Quest*, p. 74: "To judge from Crossan, Jesus had little or nothing to say about the future of Israel, the law, the covenants, eternal life, resurrection, last judgment or salvation as more than just a social adjustment." The same complaint appears in Leander E. Keck, "The Second Coming of the Liberal Jesus?" *Christian Century* Aug. 24–31, 1994: 786: "There is virtually nothing particularly Jewish left in Crossan's portrait of this Mediterranean peasant."

253. One does, however, sympathize with Alan F. Segal, "Jesus and First-Century Judaism," in *Jesus at 2000*, p. 66. He cautions that the tag "Cynic" tends to dissolve Jesus' Jewish identity.

254. There is a current tendency among some—altogether expected in a secular age—to interpret portions of the Jesus tradition in secular as opposed to religious categories; compare Birger A. Pearson, "The Gospel according to the Jesus Seminar," *Religion* 25 (1995), p. 334. Robert W. Funk, *Honest to Jesus: Jesus for a New Millennium* (San Francisco: HarperCollins, 1996), more than once refers to Jesus as "secular sage."

255. Compare James H. Charlesworth, *Jesus' Jewishness: Exploring the Place of Jesus in Early Judaism* (New York: Crossroad, 1996).

256. In just the few texts briefly reviewed on pp. 52–57 herein there are citations of or allusions to Genesis (Mk 10:2–12), Exodus (Mk 12:18–27), Psalms (Q 9:58), Isaiah (Q 6:20–23; 7:22–30; Mk 10:45), Daniel (Mk 10:45), Micah (Q 12:51–53), and Malachi (Mk 9:9–11). For a thorough overview see Bruce Chilton and Craig A. Evans, "Jesus and Israel's Scriptures," in *Studying the Historical Jesus: Evaluations of the State of Current Research*, NTTS 19, ed. Bruce Chilton and Craig A. Evans (Leiden: E. J. Brill, 1994), pp. 281–335.

so his speech was dominated by the hope of salvation and the threat of judgment. His summons to repentance[257] was an urgent plea for the spiritual reformation that was widely expected to herald the advent of the Day of the Lord.[258] Jesus, in sum, was a Jewish prophet who demanded repentance in the face of the eschatological crisis and interpreted his own person and ministry in terms of scriptural fulfillment. And his chief goal, as an actor in the cosmic drama, was "the eschatological restoration of Israel."[259]

Speculations on the Evolution of the Tradition

The suggestions offered so far for reconstructing the historical Jesus might be represented by three concentric circles. The outermost circle is the primary frame of reference, the paradigm of Jesus as eschatological prophet. The second circle contains the facts all but universally agreed upon as well as an inventory of the major themes and motifs and rhetorical strategies that appear repeatedly in the traditions. The innermost circle then encompasses the assorted complexes which do not flunk the various indices of authenticity. But because a reconstruction of Jesus and the pre-Easter Jesus movement will seem feeble unless it can find significant parallels elsewhere, the last move is to step out of the circles to seek confirmation of the whole through history-of-religion parallels. Many of these parallels, as observed in the previous section, turn out to be found above all in millenarian movements.

But one final issue needs to be raised, if only briefly. If the Jesus tradition does indeed contain reliable information about Jesus and not just later invention, how were the memories preserved? If we no longer believe that the authors of our sources or their immediate predecessors were eye-witnesses, and if Birger Gerhardsson's interesting attempt to relate the transmission of the Jesus tradition to rabbinic memorization[260] fails to persuade,[261] then how do we explain the frequent retention of authentic materials?

---

257. On this theme see pp. 103–104 herein.

258. See Deut 4:30–31; Hos 3:4–5; Acts 3:19–21; *As. Mos.* 1:18; *T. Dan.* 6:4; *T. Sim.* 6:2–7; *T. Zeb.* 9:7–9; *T. Jud.* 23:5; *Apoc. Abr.* 29; *Sipre Deut.* 41 (79b); *b. Sanh.* 97b; and *b. Yoma* 86b.

259. So Meyer, *Aims*, p. 239.

260. Birger Gerhardsson, *Memory and Manuscript: Oral Tradition and Written Transmission in Rabbinic Judaism and Early Christianity*, 2d ed. (Uppsala and Lund: C. W. K. Gleerup, 1964); *Tradition and Transmission in Early Christianity* (Lund: C. W. K. Gleerup, 1964); *The Origins of the Gospel Tradition* (Philadelphia: Fortress, 1979); *The Gospel Tradition* (Lund: C. W. K. Gleerup, 1986).

261. See Werner Kelber, *The Oral and the Written Gospel* (Philadelphia: Fortress, 1983).

The place to begin is at the beginning, which was not Easter. Jesus, like Francis of Assisi, was a popular holy man and no doubt well on his way into legend in his own time. A miracle-worker with an apocalyptic message that generates enthusiasm is immediately going to be the center of stories both true and apocryphal. Anyone who has read Gershom Scholem's work on Sabbatai Sevi probably has a feel for the kinds of tales and rumors that must have trailed Jesus wherever he went.

Many of those tales were undoubtedly miracle stories: there is no reason to believe that such stories were told only after Easter or only by disciples. Etienne Trocmé once argued that the miracle stories "originated and were handed down for a time" not in a Christian setting but in "the village society of north-eastern Galilee or the area immediately surrounding Lake Tiberias. Storytellers at markets and during the winter evenings found a ready audience for narratives with no literary pretensions, but too sensational to leave a popular audience unmoved."[262] Although Trocmé's theory that Mark first inserted the miracle stories into Christian tradition is without real evidence, it remains true that most of those stories have little or nothing to say about the kingdom of God or repentance or anything eschatological; and in only one do we find the demand to follow Jesus (Mk 10:52). These striking facts demand explanation.

More recently, Gerd Theissen has also concluded that most of the miracle stories were originally told by people who were interested above all in Jesus' healings and exorcisms, not his religious proclamation.[263] This hypothesis explains their popular character and the relative paucity of specifically Christian themes (compare the popular tale about John the Baptist in Mk 6:17–29). It is also congruent with the Christian stories in which outsiders know and/or tell about Jesus' miracles.[264] Theissen's hypothesis should probably be accepted.

Once the popular and non-Christian origin of the bulk of the miracle stories is considered plausible, a pre-Easter pedigree would seem to follow. It does not make sense to suppose that storytellers outside the church began to entertain people with Jesus' miracles only after he had died or only after some people began to proclaim his resurrection from the dead. Most of the stories may have come into being and were then retold in

262. Etienne Trocmé, *Jesus as Seen by His Contemporaries* (Philadelphia: Westminster, 1973), p. 104. See further Trocmé's *The Formation of the Gospel according to Mark* (Philadelphia: Westminster, 1975), pp. 45–54.

263. *The Gospels in Context: Social and Political History in the Synoptic Tradition* (Philadelphia: Fortress, 1991), pp. 97–112.

264. Note Q 7:3; Mk 1:28, 45; 3:8; 5:14, 19–20, 27; 6:2, 14; 7:25, 36. While some of these notices may well be redactional, how could the historical reality have been otherwise? A wonder-worker generates stories.

anticipation of Jesus' arrival in a particular village, or soon after his departure.

The pre-Easter Jesus tradition did not, however, consist only of a popular, uncontrolled folklore. A special group of itinerant missionaries surrounded Jesus,[265] and much of the original tradition must have once functioned as advice and encouragement for them in particular.[266] The missionary discourse in Q 10:2–16 (compare Mk 6:6–13), the counsel on care in Q 12:22–31,[267] the Lord's Prayer in Q 11:2–4,[268] the call stories in Mk 1:16–20; 2:13–14; and Q 9:57–60 (+ 61–62?), and the exhortation to faithfulness in Q 12:2–12[269] are all likely examples of complexes that preserve Jesus' demands of and guidance for those he called to "fish for people" (Mk 1:17; compare Jer 16:16).

These pre-Easter itinerants, according to Q 10:9, were instructed to proclaim the kingdom of God and its imminence (10:9). We are not told beyond that what specifically they were to say. But one cannot imagine that their message differed much from that of Jesus. Certainly their other activities were in imitation of his, for their purpose was to enlarge his influence (Q 10:3–8). This is why he could say: "Whoever receives you receives me; whoever receives me receives the one who sent me."[270] So *their* proclamation of the kingdom must have been *his* proclamation. It would seem to follow that if Jesus, in addressing crowds, used parables to communicate his message[271] and made moral demands in the face of the

265. Hengel, *Charismatic Leader*, pp. 71–80; Meyer, *Aims*, pp. 153–54.

266. One cannot, despite all the distortions of the tradition, avoid seeing in the words of Jesus two sorts of imperatives, one for itinerant missionaries—"the heroic absolute for the *corps d'elite* on whom fell the terrible responsibility of sharing directly in the Messianic crisis" (C. H. Dodd)—and one for everyone else—a more general call to repentance. The hermeneutical implications of this recognition are considerable. For instance, Q 12:22–31 means one thing if interpreted as encouragement for a select group in a difficult situation and quite another if construed as general religious instruction applicable to all of Jesus' hearers.

267. See my discussion and references to secondary literature in *Jesus Tradition in Q*, pp. 21–24.

268. Lk 11:1 plausibly introduces the prayer as being for Jesus' disciples: "Teach us to pray, as John taught his disciples."

269. The themes of proclamation (12:3), fear of persecution (12:4–7), and confession before authorities (12:11–12) would be relevant to missionaries but not all believers or people in general. On the likely dangers of a pre-Easter mission see Jonathan A. Draper, "Wandering Radicalism or Purposeful Activity? Jesus and the Sending of Messengers in Mark 6:6–56," *Neotestamentica* 29 (1995), pp. 183–202.

270. Q 10:16; compare Mk 9:36–37; Jn 5:23; 12:44–50; 13:20; *Did.* 11:4–5. See Crossan, *Historical Jesus*, pp. 347–48.

271. We can infer that the parables of the kingdom, or at least most of them, originally served missionary proclamation. (1) The tradition tells us that Jesus addressed the public and opponents with parables (Q 11:21–22, 24–26; Mk 4:1–2, 33–34; Mt 12:33–37; Lk 15:3–7; etc.). (2) Joachim Jeremias, *The Parables of Jesus*, 2d rev. ed. (New York: Charles

end, then his disciples used those same parables and moral demands.[272] That is, the materials in the Jesus tradition that originally had a missionary setting were not spoken by Jesus alone but also by the group associated with him. Again, then, we may speak of the pre-Easter Jesus tradition.[273]

If the Jesus tradition once consisted of a popular folk-tradition full of miracle stories on the one hand and of materials directed to and used by itinerant missionaries on the other, things changed with Jesus' death and the proclamation of his resurrection from the dead. Although missionaries continued to remember and live by Jesus' words to them, the content of their good news changed. The proclaimer became the proclaimed, and the announcement of the kingdom was eclipsed by the announcement of Jesus' vindication and exaltation.[274] In this altered situation new materials were needed, and old ones required emendation. Thus the parables, to take one example, seemingly ceased to function as missionary proclamation and became instead instruction and paraenesis for those within the community.[275]

Scribner's Sons, 1972), pp. 33–42, demonstrated the tradition's strong tendency to turn parables addressed to crowds or opponents into parables addressed to disciples; this makes point (1) all the more forceful. (3) Most of the parables of the kingdom can be directly related to themes that must have dominated Jesus' public proclamation—the nearness of the end (e.g., Q 12:39 = Gos. Thom. 21, 103; Mk 13:28; Lk 12:16–21 = Gos. Thom. 63; Lk 13:6–9), the surpassing value of the kingdom (e.g., Mt 13:44 = Gos. Thom. 109; Mt 13:45–46 = Gos. Thom. 76), the need for preparation (e.g., Q 6:47–49; 11:24–26; 19:14–26; Lk 16:19–31; Mt 25:1–13; Gos. Thom. 97), and the mercy and compassion of God (e.g., Q 15:4–7; Mt 20:1–15; Lk 15:8–10, 11–32). (4) The parables compare this to that in order to illuminate and clarify, so one imagines that they functioned as illustrations and expansions of Jesus' fundamental statements about the kingdom and its requirements.

272. Compare Gerhardsson, Origins, p. 73: "Jesus presented meshālim for his hearers, and the disciples were the first to memorize them, to ponder them, and to discuss together what they meant." I would add that they also preached them.

273. Compare Burton Scott Easton, "The First Evangelic Tradition," JBL 50 (1931), pp. 148–49, and see further Heinz Schürmann, "Die vorösterlichen Anfänge der Logientradition: Versuch eines formgeschichtlichen Zugangs zum Leben Jesu," in Der historische Jesus und der kerygmatische Christus, ed. H. Ristow and K. Matthiae (Berlin: Evangelische Verlagsanstalt, 1962), pp. 342–70. It should be stressed that to find pre-Easter tradition is not necessarily to find Jesus. Not only must the miracle stories have been subject to exaggeration and distortion from the first, but we have no reason to believe that the disciples did not make their own contributions and alterations. Gerhardsson's idea of a "holy word" being memorized is implausible. Recall that already in the lifetime of St. Francis his rule was being changed and even moved in directions he did not like, and that some of the Sioux disciples of Wovoka wrongly added a militant note to his message.

274. Recall the speeches in Acts and the traditional confessional formulas in Paul's epistles.

275. Pertinent observations in Jeremias, Parables, pp. 42–48.

Jesus' death also led to the creation of new traditions. Just as Buddhists, not long after Gautama's death, compiled an account of his final journey and departure,[276] so the followers of Jesus, using the Hebrew Bible[277] and Jewish traditions about the suffering of the righteous,[278] did the same thing. The result was recitation of the institution of the Lord's Supper and the pre-Markan passion narrative,[279] which were presumably used in primitive Christian liturgies.[280] This could only have been expected, for, in Gerhardsson's words, Jesus' execution "cried out for another explanation than the official one that the authorities had silenced a deceiver. . . . Here the adherents of Jesus needed an interpretation 'from within' to set up against the official declarations of outsiders."[281]

The post-Easter situation was also different in that the one community around Jesus soon became a number of different communities with various leaders, including scribes and teachers.[282] Such scribes and teachers—who perhaps put together the passion narrative—apparently first formulated the apothegms or pronouncement stories, which supply brief settings for pregnant and memorable sayings.[283] These apothegms most resemble the (expanded) chreias of Greek tradition, which were the product of rhetoricians and their students.[284] A few parallels appear also in the

276. Reynolds, "The Many Lives of Buddha," pp. 48–51.

277. D. J. Moo, *The Old Testament in the Gospel Passion Narratives* (Sheffield: Almond, 1983).

278. George W. E. Nickelsburg, "The Genre and Function of the Markan Passion Narrative," *HTR* 73 (1980), pp. 153–84; Lothar Ruppert, *Jesus als der leidende Gerechte? Der Weg Jesu im Lichte eines alt- und zwischentestamentlichen Motivs*, SBS 59 (Stuttgart: Katholisches Bibelwerk, 1972).

279. Although the extent of the pre-Markan passion narrative and its evolution are legitimate topics for debate, the occasional doubt as to its very existence is excessive; see Theissen, *Context*, pp. 166–99. He plausibly places the origin of the passion narrative in the Jerusalem of the 40s.

280. We know next to nothing about the format of early Christian services. But one wonders whether the sort of "informal controlled oral tradition" Kenneth E. Bailey finds in modern Middle Eastern villages should be related to Christian retelling of Jesus' passion; see his article, "Informal Controlled Oral Tradition and the Synoptic Gospels," *Asian Journal of Theology* 5 (1991), pp. 35–54.

281. *Gospel Tradition*, p. 42.

282. Compare Mt 13:52; 23:34. On the existence of "schools" in the early church see C. K. Barrett, "School, Coventicle, and Church in the New Testament," in *Wissenschaft und Kirche: Festschrift für Eduard Lohse*, ed. K. Aland and S. Meurer (Bielefeld: Luther, 1989), pp. 96–110.

283. For further discussion see Theissen, *Context*, pp. 112–22 (although I hesitate to follow him in associating the *chreia* not only with scribes and teachers but also with missionaries and wandering charismatics).

284. See George Wesley Buchanan, *Jesus: The King and His Kingdom* (Macon: Mercer, 1984), pp. 43–74; R. F. Hock and E. N. O'Neil, eds., *The Chreia in Ancient Rhet-*

rabbinic corpus, where again they are the product of the learned;[285] and it is telling that, in the pronouncement stories, the most frequent players are, besides Jesus, the scribes and Pharisees, that is, learned opponents.[286] Christian scribes or teachers, in competition with other leaders, apparently formulated many or most of the apothegms, and their goal in so doing was to arm themselves with polemic and apologetic.[287]

The post-Easter community, in addition to preserving old traditions and creating new ones, also brought together things that were once separate when it joined the popular traditions of Jesus' miracles with the missionary traditions of the itinerants.[288] This is the only supposition that explains why those two traditions are found together in both Q and Mark. When Abraham Lincoln died, not only did his life draw to itself mythological motifs so that he became in effect the first American deity,[289] but his martyrdom was the catalyst for bringing together the Eastern biographical tradition, which depicted an innate loftiness dedicated to the common good, with the Western biographical tradition, which made Lincoln a folk hero and product of the frontier.[290] In like fashion, the early Jesus people, whose hero was even more larger than life after his martyrdom and exaltation, adopted the popular miracle stories as their own, turned them into evangelistic propaganda,[291] and combined them with the rest of the growing ecclesiastical tradition.

---

oric. Volume I. *The Progymnasmata* (Atlanta: Scholars Press, 1986); Burton L. Mack, *A Myth of Innocence* (Philadelphia: Fortress, 1988), pp. 172–207; and Burton L. Mack and Vernon K. Robbins, *Patterns of Persuasion in the Gospels* (Sonoma: Polebridge, 1989).

285. Henry A. Fischel, "Story and History: Observations on Greco-Roman Rhetoric and Pharisaism," in *American Oriental Society, Middle West Branch, Semi-Centennial Volume*, ed. Denis Sinor (Bloomington: Indiana University, 1969), pp. 59–88, and Gary G. Porten, "The Pronouncement Story in Tannaitic Literature: A Review of Bultmann's Theory," *Semeia* 20 (1981), pp. 81–99. For chreias in Philo and Josephus see Leonard Greenspoon, "The Pronouncement Story in Philo and Josephus," *Semeia* 20 (1981), pp. 73–80.

286. By contrast, the popular early Christian apocryphal literature features very few pronouncement stories; see William D. Stroker, "Examples of Pronouncement Stories in Early Christian Apocryphal Literature," *Semeia* 20 (1981), pp. 133–41.

287. This is in line with Theissen, *Context*, p. 116: "In the Synoptic apothegms one group affirms its own convictions and behavior by differentiating itself from other surrounding groups."

288. Relevant here is Bernd Kollmann, *Jesus und die Christen als Wundertäter*, FRLANT 170 (Göttingen: Vandenhoeck & Ruprecht, 1996), pp. 355–62.

289. Lloyd Lewis, *Myths after Lincoln* (New York: Harcourt, Brace and Company, 1929), pp. 347–56.

290. Donald Capps, "Lincoln's Martyrdom: A Study of Exemplary Mythic Patterns," in Reynolds and Capps, *The Biographical Process*, pp. 393–412.

291. See further Gerd Theissen, *The Miracle Stories of the Early Christian Tradition* (Philadelphia: Fortress, 1983), pp. 259–64.

Unscientific Postscript

When Descartes sat down and tried to do epistemology from scratch, he deceived himself. The philosopher thought in a human language, argued by the hazy principles of induction, and moved forward toward an implicit set of goals. He did not begin from nowhere. Maybe in like fashion those of us who quest for Jesus sometimes fool ourselves into thinking, or at least carelessly leaving the impression, that we are starting with nothing and arriving at our results in such a way that anyone with sufficient intelligence should be able to follow our arguments and come to agree with us.

But each of us, to state the obvious, carries out our investigations within an infinitely complex web of personal beliefs that influences all our thinking. Further, we all, in our daily lives, are constantly evaluating people, trying to figure out what they are thinking or what they are feeling. No doubt our constant experience in doing this must, on some level, affect how we handle the Jesus tradition. Whether we know it or not, the sorts of tacit skills that we employ to size up, for example, the character of a new neighbor are probably operating when we go on the quest for Jesus—when we, in Bultmann's phrase, look for "a characteristically individual spirit."[292]

The often-maligned Jesus Seminar published the results of its voting over the years in *The Five Gospels*.[293] In this the sayings of Jesus are printed in red, pink, gray, and black. The introduction offers this possible interpretation:

Red: That's Jesus!
Pink: Sure sounds like Jesus.
Gray: Well, maybe.
Black: There's been some mistake.

Without here debating the merits of voting and printing things in color, I wish to remark upon the informal language. "Sure sounds like him" is

292. Bultmann, *History*, p. 128. Whether or not he was right or wrong in his judgment, C. H. Dodd, *The Founder of Christianity* (London: Collins, 1971), p. 33, was offering a subjective impression when he wrote that "it remains that the first three gospels offer a body of sayings on the whole so consistent, so coherent, and withal so distinctive in manner, style and content, that no reasonable critic should doubt, whatever reservations he may have about individual sayings, that we find reflected here the thought of a single, unique teacher."
293. *The Five Gospels: The Search for the Authentic Words of Jesus*, ed. Robert W. Funk and Roy W. Hoover, and the Jesus Seminar (New York: Macmillan, 1993).

not the conclusion of a formal argument. This is rather the language of interpersonal relationships—and here some of the truth comes out. Despite their methodological deliberations, the members of the Jesus Seminar were, when voting, partly giving expression to personal convictions not wholly controlled by strict rational analysis. They rather employed, in the terminology of Cardinal Newman, their "illative sense," that is, they considered factors "too fine to avail separately, too subtle and circuitous to be convertible into syllogisms, too numerous and various for such conversion, even were they convertible." [294] How indeed could it have been otherwise?

All of us, prior to and apart from discussions of criteria, stratification, and so on, have some idea of what Jesus might have said or could have done. And this must affect what indices we use and how we use them. What are we really doing when we say, "That's Jesus!" or "There's been some mistake"? Few of us conduct research by establishing rules and then obeying them; our rules and methods are partly rationalizations after the fact. Harvey McArthur once wrote:

> It may be that the most creative scholars do not carry out research by establishing rules and then obeying them. When they encounter an item of evidence their total knowledge of the situation is brought into play, and suddenly this new item falls into place with a little click in one or another of the available slots. The rules of the game, or criteria, then serve as rationalizations for what has happened. For the outsider they serve also as a check on the plausibility of the almost unconscious decision made by the creative researcher.[295]

Most of us, after years of reading and studying the Synoptics and their relatives, somehow feel that we have come not just to know a collection of facts about another human being but rather have come to know Jesus in a sense somehow analogous to the way in which we know the people around us: we have formed an idea of the sort of person he must have been. Our unarticulated convictions in this matter have a lot to do with how we go about our business as historians of Jesus. For to know someone is to feel that we can predict what he or she would likely say or do in this or that situation. So we have to wonder, in times of candid reflection, to what extent our arguments are rationalizations of previously formed impressions. Are we not all, in the end, bringing not only our personal

294. John Henry Cardinal Newman, *An Essay in Aid of a Grammar of Assent*, ed. I. T. Kerr (Oxford: Clarendon, 1985), p. 187.
295. McArthur, "Burden of Proof," p. 119.

prejudices but also our interpersonal skills, or lack thereof, to the Jesus tradition and, whether consciously or not, somehow using them to fathom who Jesus must have been?

This is no easy business we are in. Sometimes a bereaved husband will convince himself that he has encountered his late wife in a seance. In like manner, New Testament scholars, wishing for one reason or another to say as much as possible about Jesus, may think they have found him when they have not. It is human nature to believe what we want to believe. Similarly, if people can be absolutely wrong about individuals close to them, as when a wife is unable to believe that her husband has been unfaithful, then obviously there is ample room for error in trying to say much about a man who died two thousand years ago, a man who can be only indirectly recognized. And, given the various portrayals of Jesus, quite a few of us must be wrong about quite a bit. What "sure sounds like Jesus" varies from book to book and article to article: we do not all have ears to hear, or at least to hear the same thing.

But it is precisely because we are so prone to error in judging the people around us, and must be even more prone to error when it comes to sizing up someone from another time and place, that we manufacture indices and discuss methodology. We wish, if not to escape our subjectivity and fallibility, at least to be self-critical as well as honorable with the evidence, so as to come as close as we can to an approximation of what Jesus was all about. Although this may sound a bit old-fashioned, ideally we are neither defense attorney nor prosecutor, that is, people predisposed to a particular outcome. Our goal should rather be to emulate the judge, whose hard business it is to look for the truth.

DETACHED NOTE

Some Common Features of Millenarianism

The preceding chapter refers to features that the pre-Easter Jesus movement shares with worldwide messianic and millenarian movements, including cargo cults. It is the purpose of this note to document, in incomplete fashion, those features outside the Jesus tradition.[1]

Although I cannot here consider at any length the theoretical and methodological problems of cross-cultural comparisons, I should perhaps preface my catalogue by briefly explaining why one may reject the skepticism of Bengt Holmberg, who speaks of "the circular reasoning specifically inherent in the attempt to explain the strongly apocalyptic early Christianity with the help of a set of characteristics, i.e., a model, found in strongly apocalyptic movements, which all stand under the influence of the Judaeo-Christian heritage."[2]

Not all millenarianism can by any means be traced to Judeo-Christian influence. Ceylonese millennialism was wholly indigenous and "took place in the Kandyan Provinces which were least subject to Christian intrusions."[3] Also indigeneous and pre-Christian were the Guarani millenarianism of Brazil[4] and several messianic movements in ancient

1. New Testament students interested in an introduction to millenarianism in connection with early Christianity may find helpful, beyond what follows, Dennis C. Duling, "Millennialism," in *The Social Sciences and New Testament Interpretation*, ed. Richard L. Rohrbaugh (Peabody, Mass.: Hendrickson, 1996), pp. 183–205.

2. Bengt Holmberg, *Sociology and the New Testament* (Minneapolis: Fortress, 1990), pp. 85–86. Cf. Jonathan Z. Smith, "Too Much Kingdom, Too Little Community," *Zygon* 13 (1978), pp. 127–28.

3. Kitsiri Malalgoda, "Millennialism in Relation to Buddhism," *Comparative Studies in Society and History* 12 (1970), pp. 424–41.

4. See Mircea Eliade, *The Quest: History and Meaning in Religion* (Chicago and London: University of Chicago, 1969), pp. 104–11, and the literature cited there.

China.[5] Charles F. Keyes has no difficulty at all accounting for Thai millenarian movements on the basis of purely Buddhist beliefs and political situations;[6] and the Buddhist traditions about Maitreya, which in Japan, Korea, and Vietnam have sometimes become millenarian, clearly have nothing to do with western influence.[7] We should, one would think, balk at asserting Christian influence when there is no clear evidence of such, even in those situations where a millenarian movement is not completely isolated from the Christian mission.[8] Kitsiri Malalgoda is probably wise to conjecture that "the absence of reliable or readily available data in relation to the more traditional ideologies [of non-Western peoples] has resulted in an over-emphasis of the Christian influences."[9]

Human psychology is such that the same convictions sometimes crop up independently in different cultures—e.g., the incest taboo, or the idea of a great deluge in primeval time, or the tragic expectation, so often found among the indigenous victims of colonialism, that their magic will protect them from the bullets of their oppressors. With regard to millenarianism in particular, it remains striking that so many movements, from various times and places, share so many features. Why should such movements, even if under Judeo-Christian or Islamic influence, select similar sets of eschatological symbols and recurrently behave in comparable ways? And are we to think, for instance, that the Christian tradition has really been responsible for so many millenarians destroying their means of livelihood? Is this something found in the Bible or the proclamation of missionaries? One understands why Robert H. Lowie could find precisely in millenarianism proof that diffusionist explanations of common beliefs and behaviors are not always correct.[10]

5. Anna K. Seidel, "The Image of the Perfect Ruler in Early Taoist Messianism: Lao-Tzu and Li Hung," *History of Religions* 9 (1969), pp. 216–47; idem, Taoist Messianism," *Numen* 31 (1984), pp. 161–74; also the entry under "millenarianism" in *The HarperCollins Dictionary of Religion*, ed. Jonathan Z. Smith (San Francisco: Harper San Francisco, 1995), p. 719.

6. "Millennialism, Theravada Buddhism, and Thai Society," *Journal of Asian Studies* 36 (1977), pp. 283–302.

7. See Alan Sponberg and Helen Hardacre, eds., *Maitreya, the Future Buddha* (Cambridge: Cambridge University Press, 1988).

8. For an illustration see the study of modern Japanese sects by Carmen Blacker, "Millenarian Aspects of the New Religions of Japan," in *Tradition and Modernization in Japan*, ed. Donald H. Shively (Princeton: University of Princeton, 1971), pp. 563–600.

9. "Millennialism in Relation to Buddhism," p. 439. Cf. Kenelm Burridge, "Millennialisms and the Recreation of History," in *Religion, Rebellion, Revolution: An Interdisciplinary and Cross-Cultural Collection of Essays*, ed. Bruce Lincoln (New York: St. Martin's, 1985), pp. 226–27.

10. "Le messianisme primitif: contribution a un problème d'ethnologie," *Diogenes* 19 (1957), pp. 1–15.

According to Bryan A. Wilson, despite the abundant evidence for the diffusion of ideas from the Judeo-Christian tradition into worldwide millenarianism, it is hard to suppose that eschatological enthusiasm was a unique product of this one tradition and its peculiar circumstances.[11] Is not the diffusionist theory, when applied to millenarianism, a secular descendant of the old view that all alleged messiahs must be inferior imitations of the one true Messiah? For Weston La Barre, "It is fatuously and absurdly ethnocentric to suppose that every native messiah is necessarily patterned on a European Christ, since many native messiahs have never heard of Jesus. The fact is not so much that all native messiahs derive historically from the only genuine Messiah as that Christ is an example of a very common figure in the world's cultures." [12] Surely it is better to concede that "the expectation of the return of deity . . . or of a culture hero is already a religious possibility in many cultures prior to the coming of the Europeans . . . . The coming of the Europeans has only intensified this original notion of return and renewal." [13]

For our purposes it is crucial to observe that, even were one inclined to assign all medieval and modern millenarianism to Judeo-Christian or Muslim influence, it remains that millenarian movements are attested in the pre-Christian period. See the analysis of Daniel and Maccabean times in Philip F. Esler, *The First Christians in their Social Worlds: Social-Scientific Approaches to New Testament Interpretation* (London and New York: Routledge, 1994), pp. 92–109. One also thinks of those who produced and read the Qumran scrolls; and maybe if we knew enough about earliest Zoroastrianism we would consider it too to be millenarian. In any event there was a native tradition of Jewish millenarianism by Jesus' time. So in using a millenarian model we are not just comparing Jesus and early Christianity with their spiritual descendants.

Some critics of comparative millenarian studies have objected that there are so many varieties of millenarian movements—some are pacifistic, some violent, some are sexually rigorous, some profligate, etc.—that to make generalizations about them is a hazardous enterprise. I concede that we may have some trouble defining "millenarianism," if by that is meant listing characteristics that invariably belong to it. But this is no

11. "Millennialism in Comparative Perspective," *Comparative Studies in Society and History* 6 (1963), p. 110.
12. "Materials for a History of Studies of Crisis Cults: A Bibliographic Essay," *Current Anthropology* 12 (1971), p. 18.
13. Charles H. Long, "Cargo Cults as Cultural Historical Phenomena," *JAAR* 42 (1974), p. 406.

different than the difficulty we have when we try to define "chair" in a way that fits all chairs, or "religion" in a way that fits all religions. All we can do, as Wittgenstein observed, is draw up a list of "family characteristics," things that tend to recur but may be absent from this or that instance of "chair" or "religion." This is just how common nouns work in the world. Wittgenstein spoke of "a complicated network of similarities overlapping and criss-crossing: sometimes overall similarities, sometimes similarities of detail."[14] The list offered below serves as just such a network of similarities that may be found among millenarian movements.

It may also be observed, as a practical matter, that millenarianism has, to judge by the twentieth-century's flood of publications on this topic, proven itself a valid area of study that has indeed shed light on phenomena from various times and divers places. Although one must be cautious with broad and simple generalizations and come to terms with the concrete and distinctive figures of each movement and resist blurring differences at the expense of commonalities—not all cargo cults are millenarian, for instance[15]—comparative studies remain cogent.[16]

I now turn to certain recurring attributes of millenarianism that recall what we find in the pre-Easter Jesus movement as outlined on pp. 61–64 above.

(1) Millenarian groups commonly appeal first of all to the disaffected or unfortunate in a period of social change that threatens traditional ways and symbolic universes.[17] Peter Worsley writes that millenarian movements "have found support at all levels of society at one time or another. But it is amongst people who feel themselves to be oppressed and who are longing for deliverance that they have been particularly welcomed: especially by the populations of colonial countries, by discontented peasants and by the jetsam of towns and cities of feudal civilizations."[18] One

14. See *Philosophical Investigations: The English Text of the Third Edition*, 2d ed. (New York: Macmillan, 1958), pp. 31ff.

15. See Garry W. Trompf, *Melanesian Religion* (Cambridge: Cambridge University Press, 1991), pp. 189–98.

16. Cf. Yonina Talmon, "Millenarian Movements," *Archives européenes de sociologie* 7 (1966), pp. 159–200.

17. See David F. Aberle, "A Note on Relative Deprivation Theory as applied to Millenarian and other Cult Movements," in *Millennial Dreams in Action: Studies in Revolutionary Religious Movements*, ed. Sylvia L. Thrupp (New York: Schocken, 1970), pp. 209–14, and Peter Worsley, *The Trumpet Shall Sound: A Study of "Cargo" Cults in Melanesia*, 2d ed. (New York: Schocken, 1968), especially the Introduction on pp. ix–lxix.

18. Ibid., p. 225. On relative deprivation and Palestinian messianic movements before and after Jesus see Sheldon R. Isenberg, "Millenarism in Greco-Roman Palestine," *Religion* 4 (1974), pp. 26–46.

understands why millenarian movements have so often emerged in times of aspiration for national independence. Daniel and the first edition of the *Testament of Moses* coincided with the Maccabean revolt, and the Ghost Dance, like Pacific cargo cults, envisaged the end of the white man's domination and the return of native sovereignty. Some theorists[19] have indeed argued that cargo cults are the first stirrings of nationalism. Others have thought that millenarians emerge in the wake of political insurrection.[20]

One should, it is prudent to add, refrain from offering simple, one-sided explanations for the rise of millenarian groups.[21] Reductionism should be avoided. Adela Yarbro Collins is no doubt correct to observe that "facts of background, temperament, and, to some degree, choice of theological perspective are . . . at least as important as aspects of the sociohistorical situation in producing an apocalyptic mentality."[22] Further, there are examples of millenarian groups that are seemingly not deprived but rather in power.[23]

One cannot predict the advent of millenarianism any more than one can predict tornados. All one can do is observe that, when certain conditions overtake certain individuals with certain mythologies or theological expectations, certain outcomes commonly, but not inevitably, ensue.[24] Brazilian millenarianism even offers an example of a movement that appears to have been motivated almost entirely by religion, in a context in which any sort of deprivation, relative or otherwise, seems irrelevant.[25]

(2) Millenarian groups typically interpret the present and near future as times of atypical or even unprecedented suffering and/or catastrophe.

19. E.g., the Marxist Worsley, *Trumpet.*

20. E.g., Norman Cohn, *The Pursuit of the Millennium: Revolutionary Millenarians and Mystical Anarchists of the Middle Ages,* rev. ed. (New York: Oxford, 1970). For further discussion see Michael Hill, *A Sociology of Religion* (New York: Basic, 1973), pp. 205–27.

21. Helpful here are Garry W. Trompf, "Mircea Eliade and the Interpretation of Cargo Cults," *Religious Traditions* 12 (1989), pp. 31–64, and Gershom G. Scholem, *Sabbatai Ṣevi: The Mystical Messiah 1626–1676* (Princeton: University Press, 1973), pp. 4–8.

22. *Crisis and Catharsis: The Power of the Apocalypse* (Philadelphia: Westminster, 1984), p. 105.

23. See Stephen L. Cook, *Prophecy and Apocalypticism: The Postexilic Social Setting* (Minneapolis: Fortress, 1995), especially pp. 55–84—although one wonders if his interpretation of biblical materials neglects the relative deprivation that Jewish priests and leaders experienced *vis-à-vis* the Persian empire; also, his mixing of millenarian movements which stand on opposite sides of the industrial revolution is perhaps questionable; see Ernest R. Sandeen, "The 'Little Tradition' and the Form of Modern Millenarianism," *The Annual Review of the Social Sciences of Religion* 4 (1980), pp. 165–81.

24. See further Maria Isaura Pereira de Queiroz, "Messianic Myths and Movements," *Diogenes* 90 (1975), pp. 78–99.

25. Rene Ribeiro, "Brazilian Messianic Movements," in Thrupp, *Millennial Dreams in Action,* pp. 55–69.

The motif is ubiquitous.[26] The Ghost Dance religion taught that the passage from the devastation of the present to the paradise of the future would come through floods, earthquakes, and landslides. So too the Earth Lodge Cult.[27] The Milne Bay Prophet Cult expected that a volcanic eruption and tidal wave would soon destroy all unbelievers.[28] The njuli movement of Borneo prophesied storms, earthquakes, floods, and (alternately) drought.[29] Similar expectations have appeared in both Chinese[30] and Japanese millenarianism[31] and elsewhere.[32] Jewish and Christian history repeatedly offer the same thing. According to Cohn, "by medieval Christians catastrophes were accepted as 'signals' for the Second Coming and the Last Judgment;[33] while for the Jews intensified persecution was traditionally expected to herald the coming of the messiah."[34] The so-

26. Cf. Michael Adas, *Prophets of Rebellion: Millenarian Protest Movements against the European Colonial Order* (Cambridge: University Press, 1987), p. 116; Michael Barkun, *Disaster and the Millennium* (New Haven: Yale, 1974); and Sylvia L. Thrupp, "Millennial Dreams in Action: A Report on the Conference Discussion," in Thrupp, *Millennial Dreams in Action*, p. 22.

27. Cora Du Bois, "The 1870 Ghost Dance," *Anthropological Records* 3/1 (1939), pp. 76–116.

28. Vittorio Lanternari, *The Religions of the Oppressed: A Study of Modern Messianic Cults* (New York: Knopf, 1963), p. 167.

29. Justus M. van der Krief, "Messianic Movements in the Celebes, Sumatra, and Borneo," in Thrupp, *Millennial Dreams in Action*, p. 111.

30. See Seidel, "Taoist Messianism," pp. 169–70; Richard Shek, "Chinese Millenarian Movements," in *The Encyclopedia of Religion*, ed. Mircea Eliade, vol. 9 (New York: Macmillan, 1987), pp. 533–34; and E. Zürcher, "'Prince Moonlight': Messianism and Eschatology in Early Medieval Chinese Buddhism," *T'oung Pao* 68 (1982), pp. 1–59.

31. Blacker, "Millenarian Aspects of the New Religions in Japan," pp. 585, 586, 588–89.

32. See Todd A. Diacon, "Peasants, Prophets, and the Power of a Millenarian Vision in Twentieth-Century Brazil," *Comparative Studies in Society and History* 32 (1990), p. 506; Mircea Eliade, "'Cargo-Cults' and Cosmic Regeneration," in Thrupp, *Millennial Dreams in Action*, pp. 139–43; Patrick Gesch, "The Cultivation of Surprise and Excess: The Encounter of Cultures in the Sepik of Papua New Guinea," in *Cargo Cults and Millenarian Movements: Transoceanic Comparisons of New Religious Movements*, ed. Garry W. Trompf (Berlin: Mouton de Gruyter, 1990), pp. 218–19; and Hue-Tam Ho Tai, *Millenarianism and Peasant Politics in Vietnam* (Cambridge: Harvard University Press, 1983), pp. 29, 123.

33. Compare already Cyril of Jerusalem, *Catech.* 15 and Eusebius, *H.E.* 6:7 (on the prophecies of a certain Jude). Cohn, *Pursuit*, pp. 42, 137–47, has data on Gregory of Tours and the flagellants. Bernard McGinn, *Apocalyptic Spirituality: Treatises and Letters of Lactantius, Adso of Montier-en-Der, Joachim of Fiore, the Franciscan Spirituals, Savonarola* (New York: Paulist, 1979), pp. 149–81, discusses the Franciscan Spirituals while James West Davidson, *The Logic of Millennial Thought: Eighteenth-Century New England* (New Haven: Yale, 1977), pp. 103–115, cites the early American sources which interpreted earthquakes as eschatological events.

34. "Medieval Millenarism: Its Bearing on the Comparative Study of Millenarian Movements," in Thrupp, *Millennial Dreams in Action*, p. 40.

called "birth pangs of the Messiah" were thought to be present by the Kabbalists of the late fifteenth century[35] and during the time of Sabbatai Ṣevi.[36] The same is already true in some intertestamental writings.[37] Scholem commented: "Messianic apocalypticism" is by nature "a theory of catastrophe," that is, it stresses the "cataclysmic element in the transition from every historical present to the Messianic future."[38] And according to R. J. Zwi Werblowsky, the "catastrophic element remained an essential feature of the dialectic of messianic utopia: ultimate salvation was accompanied, or preceded by destruction and by the terrors of the 'birth pangs' of the messianic age. In fact, this catastrophic aspect became so much part and parcel of the messianic complex that in later periods, the occurrence of particularly cruel persecution and suffering was frequently regarded as heralding the messianic redemption."[39] The generalization continues to be illustrated in contemporary Judaism.[40]

It is worth remembering that archaic myths, such as the Hindu myths about the Kali and Golden Age, invariably see the history of the world as one of decline and typically locate the decadent present before the coming of a new and better age.[41] Also relevant and related are the worldwide agricultural myths that recount how, every year, new life comes out of a dead world.[42]

(3) A divinely-wrought comprehensive righting of wrongs, constituting "a holistic solution," is regularly envisaged.[43] Hope casts itself not upon

35. See Gershom G. Scholem, *Major Trends in Jewish Mysticism* (New York: Schocken, 1961), pp. 246–47, and Isaiah Tishby, "Acute Apocalyptic Messianism," in *Essential Papers on Messianic Movements and Personalities in Jewish History*, ed. Marc Saperstein (New York: University Press, 1992), pp. 259–86.

36. See Scholem, *Sabbatai Ṣevi*, pp. 91–93, and Stephen Sharot, *Messianism, Mysticism, and Magic: A Sociological Analysis of Jewish Religious Movements* (Chapel Hill: University of North Carolina, 1982), p. 105.

37. Examples in my book, *The End of the Ages Has Come: An Early Interpretation of the Passion and Resurrection of Jesus* (Philadelphia: Fortress, 1985), pp. 6–22.

38. *The Messianic Idea in Judaism and Other Essays on Jewish Spirituality* (New York: Schocken, 1971), p. 7.

39. "Messianism in Jewish History," in Saperstein, *Essential Papers*, p. 39.

40. Aviezer Ravitzky, *Messianism, Zionism, and Jewish Religious Radicalism* (Chicago: University of Chicago Press, 1996), pp. 169–73, 195.

41. Harald A. T. Reiche, "The Archaic Heritage: Myths of Decline and End in Antiquity," in *Visions of Apocalypse: End or Rebirth?* ed. Saul Friedländer et al. (New York: Holmes and Meier, 1985), pp. 21–43, and *Encyclopedia of Religion and Ethics*, ed. James Hastings (New York: Charles Scribner's Sons, 1928), s.v. "Ages of the World," by various authors.

42. See Mircea Eliade, *The Myth of the Eternal Return or, Cosmos and History* (Princeton: Princeton University Press, 1971).

43. So Kenelm Burridge, *New Heaven, New Earth: A Study of Millenarian Activities* (New York: Schocken, 1969), p. 52. Cf. Norman Cohn, "Medieval Millenarism," in Thrupp,

an otherworldly afterlife but longs for "the metahistorical future in which the world will be inhabited by a humanity liberated from all the limitations of human existence, redeemed from pain and transience, from fallibility and sin, thus becoming at once perfectly good and perfectly happy. The world will be utterly, completely and irrevocably changed."[44]

Such change will, in the language of Acts 17:6, turn the world upside down: redemption will come through a reversal of current circumstances. According to Worsley, believers in the Mansren myth believed not only that "the order of society [was] to be inverted, but even the order of Nature itself. Yams, potatoes and other tubers would grow on trees like fruit, while coconuts and other fruit would grow like tubers. Sea-creatures would become land-creatures, and vice-versa."[45] The African American "Wilderness Worshipers" in the late nineteenth-century American South expected themselves to become white and whites to become black.[46] Hope for the reversal of skin colors also appears in cargo cults.[47] Patrick F. Gesch says that "the outlook" of the Mt. Rurun Movement in New Guinea "was for a world turned on its head: the birds would fly upside down, and all the coconuts would fall to the earth. . . . The night that came in the day bore antipodean significance."[48] And Lawrence E. Sullivan tells us that the leader of the Canudos messianic uprising in Brazil foretold that "the interior of the continent would become the seaboard and the seashore would become the interior."[49] Obviously "the idea of 'reversals' is common."[50]

Millennial Dreams in Action, p. 31 (salvation for a millenarian group is "total, in the sense that it is utterly to transform life on earth, so that the new dispensation will be no mere improvement on the present but perfection itself") and Yonina Talmon, "Millenarian Movements," *Archives européennes de sociologie* 7 (1966), p. 166 ("The millenarian conception of salvation is total in the sense that the new dispensation will bring about not mere improvement, but a complete transformation and perfection itself. . . . The believers will be liberated from all ills and limitations of human existence").

44. Yonina Talmon, "Pursuit of the Millennium: The Relation between Religious and Social Change," *Archives européenes de sociologie* 3 (1962), p. 130.

45. *The Trumpet Shall Sound*, pp. 136–37.

46. Wilson D. Wallis, *Messiahs: Christian and Pagan* (Boston: Gorham, 1918), p. 126.

47. Henri Desroche, *The Sociology of Hope* (London: Routledge & Kegan Paul, 1979), p. 71. See further the index on p. 299 of Worsley, *Trumpet*, s.v., "Reversal, of skins."

48. *Initiative and Initiation: A Cargo Cult-Type Movement in the Sepik Against Its Background in Traditional Village Religion*, Studia Instituti Anthropos 33 (St. Augustin: Anthropos-Institut, 1985), p. 67.

49. *Icanchu's Drum: An Orientation to Meaning in South American Religions* (New York: Macmillan, 1988), p. 556.

50. Burridge, *New Heaven, New Earth*, p. 50. See further Garry W. Trompf, *Payback: The Logic of Retribution in Melanesian Religions* (Cambridge: Cambridge University Press, 1994), especially pp. 169–74.

(4) Reversal will come soon. Cohn asserts that millenarian sects always picture deliverance as "imminent, in the sense that it is to come both soon and suddenly."[51] One must, however, qualify this assertion. Belief in the nearness of the end may be muted as time marches on, and a group may develop a scenario that foretells a long series of events yet to unfold before the end. One recalls 1QpHab. 7:7, which testifies that "the end-time will be prolonged," as well as the conflicting chronologies of Daniel 12 and Mk 24:14 (the good news must first be preached, and then the end will come).

(5) Millenarian movements are regularly revivalistic. They deepen the piety of the faithful and stir up religious faith among the indifferent. The agitation in cargo cults is matched by the agitation in Jewish messianic movements and the medieval groups examined by Cohn in *Pursuit of the Millennium*. In other words, "enthusiasm" is a regular concomitant of millenarianism. As I. C. Jarvie observed, a terrific release of emotional energy has characterized millenarian movements.[52]

In line with this, evangelism is a recurrent feature of millenarian movements. This is how they become *movements*. "Millenarism usually evokes exceptionally intense commitment and fervour and . . . expands swiftly almost as if by contagion, cross-cutting and breaking down local barriers."[53] People within a small group often feel constrained to convert others to their side. The psychology is obvious: the larger the company, the more confident the adherents. For documentation see Chapter 2 below, pp. 110–11.

(6) Millenarianism characteristically promotes egalitarianism. Examples are listed on p. 109 of chapter 2. To these one may add the Jjuli movement of Borneo[54] and the movement surrounding Augusto C. Sandino: the latter "envisgaed a universal commune where all things would be held in common."[55]

(7) Millenarian adherents tend to divide humanity into two camps, the saved and the unsaved. Already Dan 12:2 foresees that, of the human beings who sleep in the dust of the earth, some will awake to everlasting life, others to everlasting contempt. The Dead Sea Scrolls sort the world into

51. *Pursuit*, p. 15.

52. *The Revolution in Anthropology* (London: Routledge & Kegan Paul, 1964), p. 51. See further Barkun, *Disaster and the Millennium*, pp. 129–65; Norman Cohn, "The Ranters," *Encounter* 34 (1970), pp. 15–25; and Worsley, *Trumpet*, pp. 248–50.

53. Talmon, "Pursuit of the Millennium," p. 141.

54. See Lanternari, *Religions of the Oppressed*, pp. 215–16.

55. Marco A. Navarro-Génie, "Failed Prophecy and Revolutionary Violence: The Case of Augusto C. Sandino," at http://www.pagusmundi.com/sandino/failed.htm (6/30/97).

"the sons of light" and "the sons of darkness," and the Nicaraguan millenarian Augusto C. Sandino prophesied that "the chosen would be redeemed and they would remain in the earthly paradise forever while the others would be purged and banished to less evolved planets." Talmon offers this generalization: "A fundamental division separates the followers from non-followers. History is viewed as a struggle between saints and satans. . . . The adversaries are viewed as incarnate evil. They will either be wholly transformed or mercilessly destroyed." [56]

(8) The breaking of hallowed taboos associated with religious custom is typical. "Millenarism usually has a strong anti-traditional component and preparation for the millennium has often entailed a ritualised overthrow of traditional norms. Primitive millenarian movements have engaged in breaking of hallowed taboos and in a desecration of their most valued religious symbols, thus dissociating themselves from their traditional culture." [57] Examples from cargo cults and Amerindian movements are numerous.[58] According to Scholem, "There seems to be an intrinsic connection between active messianism and the courage for religious innovation. Messianic movements would often produce individuals with sufficient charismatic authority to challenge the established authority of rabbinic Judaism." [59] He adds: "Utopianism . . . threatens existing traditional patterns." [60]

(9) Millenarian movements have been described as nativistic because they emphasize the value of an indigenous cultural heritage or selected portions of it. Often that heritage is threatened by the domination of a foreign culture.[61] The generalization is obvious with regard to Amerindian messianic movements. It also well suits the appearance of Jewish apocalyptic during the time of Antiochus Epiphanes. Worsley objected that the use of "nativism" in connection with millenarian movements is problematic because they are forward looking.[62] But one can be oriented to a future that regains the best of the past—paradise regained. "Mille-

---

56. "Millenarian Movements," p. 168.
57. Talmon, "Pursuit of the Millennium," p. 130.
58. See the index of Worsley, *Trumpet*, s.v., "Reversal, of customs," and for Amerindians Fred W. Voget, "The American Indian in Transition: Reformation and Accommodation," *American Anthropologist* 58 (1956), pp. 250–52.
59. *Sabbatai Ṣevi*, p. 10.
60. Ibid., p. 12. See further his essay on "Redemption through Sin," in *The Messianic Idea*, pp. 78–141.
61. See Ralph Linton, "Nativistic Movements," *American Anthropologist* 45 (1943), pp. 230–40.
62. *The Trumpet Shall Sound*, pp. 272–76.

narian movements are forward looking not backwards looking movements, yet their vision of the future usually contains many reinterpreted elements of native tradition. It is precisely this combination of a radical revolutionary position with traditionalism which accounts for the widespread appeal of these movements."[63] "Nativism" in the sense used here is consistent with the reversal of customs and the undoing of taboos.

The "nativistic" orientation goes hand in hand with the communal dimension. "The aim of millenarian movements is not only the salvation of individual souls but the erection of a heavenly city for a chosen people. The millenarian message is directed to an already existing group or calls for a formation of new groups of elect."[64] "Millenarism involves both inclusion and exclusion: there are always God's people within and the ungodly without. . . . Only those who belong . . . will be redeemed and enjoy the new, happy life."[65] Cohn's definition of a millenarian movement includes this: salvation is depicted as "collective, in the sense that it is to be enjoyed by the faithful as a collectivity."[66] Here the task is not finding examples but counterexamples. Millenarianism is a group phenomenon.[67]

(10) In breaking with traditional customs and values, millenarian groups—like sectarian movements generally—often replace traditional familial and social bonds with fictive kin. Worsley writes that "the break with ancient custom" helps weld "devotees together in a new fraternity of people."[68] To illustrate he quotes J. Graham Miller: for the Naked Cult of Espiritu Santo "the function of the cult seems to be to break all existing ties, of whatever description, and unite people on the exclusive basis of the cult." In this way the sect "cut across all family ties and totem ties."[69] The Dead Sea Scrolls show us the same phenomenon in ancient Judaism. Having exiled themselves from the traditional cult in Jerusalem and even their own families, the Essenes created a new community of property and kin.

(11) Millenarian leaders regularly mediate the sacred through new

---

63. So Talmon, "Pursuit of the Millennium," p. 147.

64. So Talmon, ibid., p. 131.

65. Talmon, "Millenarism," in *International Encyclopedia of the Social Sciences*, ed. David L. Sills (New York: Macmillan, 1968), vol. 10, p. 351.

66. *Pursuit of the Millennium*, p. 15.

67. See further Bryan R. Wilson, *Magic and the Millennium: A Sociological Study of Religious Movements of Protest among Tribal and Third-World Peoples* (New York: Harper & Row, 1973), pp. 272–308.

68. *The Trumpet Shall Sound*, p. 248. Cf. p. 237, where he says that there are always "specific injunctions to love one another" and to "forget the narrow loyalties of the past."

69. "Naked Cult in Central West Santo," *Journal of the Polynesian Society* 57/4 (1948), p. 334.

channels. Cargo cultists usually turn away from the religion of Christian missionaries and find new ways of interacting with the deity. The community that produced the Dead Sea Scrolls created their own world in which access to God was made through channels other than those controlled by the Jerusalem establishment. Burridge makes this generalization about certain Christian enthusiasts: "Rites, liturgy, sacraments and the priesthood—the organized framework of a religious congregation— are deemed unnecessary. . . . [A] direct, personal and individual approach to the Divine Presence involves a new theology of Grace, quite opposed to the established and traditional view that Grace is mediated through, and secreted in, the institutions of an organized sacramental life." [70]

(12) Millenarianism involves intense commitment and unconditional loyalty.[71] The literature on cargo cults is full of prophets making demands that not only undo custom but put followers' well-being at risk—as when groups have burned crops, slaughtered animals, and abandoned property in view of an imminent end. According to John G. Strelan, after a cargo cult prophet is believed, "the villagers usually follow him in a series of actions: all ordinary work comes to an abrupt halt; pigs and chickens are slaughtered in a holocaust; savings are spent or thrown away; property and harvest are destroyed—all with the idea of hastening the arrival of the spirits of the dead with the cargo they will bring." [72] One recalls that the followers of Theudas forsook their possessions.[73] This illustrates perfectly the summary of Talmon: "the intense and total commitment required by millenarism is summoned forth by leaders who are considered to be set apart form ordinary men and endowed with supernatural power." [74]

(13) In line with this, millenarian movements more often than not coalesce around a charismatic leader.[75] In his researches, Cohn discovered

70. *New Heaven, New Earth*, p. 127.

71. Cf. Annemarie de Waal Malefijt, *Religion and Culture: An Introduction to the Anthropology of Religion* (New York: Macmillan, 1968), p. 340.

72. *Search for Salvation: Studies in the History and Theology of Cargo Cults* (Adelaide: Lutheran Publishing House, 1977), p. 51. For an instance from India see Stephen Fuchs, *Rebellious Prophets: A Study of Messianic Movements in Indian Religions* (London: Asia Publishing House, 1965), pp. 27–34.

73. Josephus, *Ant.* 20:97.

74. "Millenarism," p. 351.

75. See Adas, *Prophets of Rebellion*, especially pp. 112–21; Burridge, *New Heaven, New Earth*, pp. 10–14; Palle Christiansen, *The Melanesian Cargo Cult: Millenarianism as a Factor in Cultural Change* (Copenhagen: Akademisk, 1969), pp. 114–24; John G. Gager, *Kingdom and Community: The Social World of Early Christianity* (Englewood Cliffs: Prentice-Hall, 1975), pp. 28–32; and Maria Isaura Pereira de Queiroz, "Messiahs in Brazil," *Past and Present* 31 (1965), pp. 62–86.

that "a millenarian revolt never formed except round a prophet. . . ."[76] According to Burridge, in Melanesia cargo cults "the charismatic figure . . .
personifies the myth-dream, and is the channel through whom the contents of the myth-dream may be realized. He it is who articulates the myth-
dream; whose activities nourish and refine the content of the myth-dream;
who stands for the new man. . . . In a certain sense, if only temporarily, the
charismatic figure—a single individual—*is* the myth dream."[77]

Given that early Christians came to believe in Jesus' resurrection and
return, it is relevant to observe that millenarian movements sometimes
expect that a charismatic prophet who has died will return. Instances include the eighth-century Persian forerunner of the messiah, Abu-Isa;[78]
Yudghan, the successor of Abu-Isa;[79] a ninth-century Japanese prophet of
Maitreya;[80] the twelfth-century French messiah, Ibn Aryeh;[81] David Al-
roy, a twelfth-century Jewish messiah of North Persia;[82] various Islamic
Mahdīs;[83] Sabbatai Ṣevi;[84] the eighteenth-century Peruvian prophet Juan
Santos;[85] the nineteenth-century Munda Birsa;[86] Selivanov, the leader of
the notorious Skoptsy sect;[87] the Brazilian Padre Cicero;[88] the Brazilian
warrior messiah José Maria;[89] the African prophet André Matswa;[90]
John Frum, cargo messiah;[91] and Haile Selassie I according to Rastafari-
ans.[92] Relevant too are the cargo myths of the return of Mansren and the

76. "Medieval Millenarism," p. 38.

77. *Mambu: A Study of Melanesian Cargo Movements and Their Social and Ideological Background* (New York: Harper & Row, 1970), p. 276.

78. See Sharot, *Messianism, Mysticism, and Magic*, p. 53.

79. Sharot, ibid., p. 54.

80. Miyata Noboru, "Types of Maitreya Belief in Japan," in Sponberg and Hardacre,
Maitreya, p. 178.

81. Moses Maimonides, *Iggeres Teiman;* see the Eng. translation in Avraham Yaakov
Finkel, *The Essential Maimonides* (London: Jason Aronson, 1996), p. 47.

82. Israel Friedlaender, "Shiitic Influences in Jewish Sectarianism," in Saperstein,
Essential Papers, p. 123.

83. Friedlaender, ibid., p. 133.

84. Scholem, *Sabbatai Sevi*, pp. 919–24.

85. Sullivan, *Icanchu's Drum*, p. 570.

86. Fuchs, *Rebellious Prophets*, pp. 27–34.

87. Frederick C. Conybeare, *Russian Dissenters*, Harvard Theological Studies 10
(Cambridge, Mass.: Harvard University Press, 1921), pp. 364–65.

88. Maria Isaura Pereira de Queiroz, "Brazilian Messianic Movements: A Help or a
Hindrance to 'Participation'?" *International Institute for Labour Studies* 7 (1970), p. 102.

89. Sullivan, *Icanchu's Drum*, p. 557.

90. Lanternari, *Religions of the Oppressed*, pp. 11–14.

91. Edward Rice, *John Frum He Come* (New York: Doubleday, 1974).

92. Ernest Cashmore, *Rastman: The Rastafarian Movement in England* (London: Allen
& Unwin, 1979), pp. 13–37.

Manup-Kilibob Myth[93] as well as the Shiite speculations about the hidden twelfth Imam. For those speculations being associated with a particular individual see Fouad Ajami, *The Vanished Imam: Musa al Sadr and the Shia of Lebanon* (Ithaca: Cornell, 1986). I have been told that, when Rabbi Schneerson, the object of messianic speculation, died in 1994, his followers broke into three camps. One holds that his death proved he was not the Messiah. Another says that his death was only temporary and that he will soon return. Another believes he has only removed himself from view and will reveal himself shortly.[94]

(14) The central beliefs of millenarians are formulated as fresh revelation, and they are authenticated by a prophet's miracles. "A classical cargo movement usually begins with an announcement by a prophet or leader that he has had a dream or vision which has revealed to him information about the imminent return of the ancestor or ancestors."[95] Similarly, according to Scholem, in Spanish kabbalism there was "emphasis on the close connection between the approach of redemption and the increasing knowledge of kabbalistic mysteries."[96] On messiahs and miracles see the selection of illustrations in Wallis, *Messiahs*, pp. 197–206. Peter Lawrence has catalogued quite a few supernatural feats of the cargo prophet Yali.[97] And Adas, in summarizing the five millenarian movements studied in his book, *Prophets of Rebellion*, says that "Each of the five prophets studied [herein] in depth gained a considerable reputation as a healer. . . . Cures were closely linked to the prophets' revelations and to their alleged invulnerability and ability to predict the future."[98]

(15) Millenarian movements sometimes take a passive political stance in expectation of a divinely-wrought deliverance. Many such movements, to be sure, have been, on the contrary, militaristic (e.g., the Peasants' Revolt, the Fifth Monarchy Men, and the Taiping Rebellion); but there are also parallels to the pacifism of Jesus. According to Trompf, "Hard indeed is it to find a cargo movement . . . which does not have its butt of reprisal,

---

93. See Strelan, *Salvation*, pp. 14–15, 17, 22.

94. On the whole question see further La Barre, "Materials for a History of Studies of Crisis Cults," pp. 18–20.

95. Strelan, *Salvation*, p. 51. See further Voget, "American Indian in Transition," pp. 250–51.

96. *Sabbatai Ṣevi*, p. 17. On revelation in old Jewish and Christian apocalyptic literature see Christopher Rowland, *The Open Heaven: A Study of Apocalyptic in Judaism and Early Christianity* (New York: Crossroad, 1982).

97. *Road Belong Cargo: A Study of the Cargo Movement in the Southern Madang District New Guinea* (Manchester: Manchester University Press, 1964); see the index on p. 290.

98. *Prophets of Rebellion*, p. 120.

but the real inequalities in weaponry being what they have been under colonial regimens, most protests have been sensibly 'psychological' and therefore non-violent."[99] Often there is, in the words of Jeffrey Kaplan, nothing more than "rhetorical violence."[100] Talmon refers to "political nonparticipation" as one of the "frequent concomitants of millenarism."[101] Especially interesting for comparison with the Jesus tradition are the teachings of the prophet of the Ghost Dance of 1890, Wovoka. According to James Mooney, Wovoka said, "You must not fight. Do not harm anyone"—an imperative that included harming whites as well as fellow Amerindians; for Wovoka fighting "was bad and we must keep from it . . . we must all be friends with one another."[102] One recalls that those who wrote the Dead Sea Scrolls appear, despite the War Scroll, to have lived a peaceful existence in the desert for a long time.[103] Cohn observes that millenarian movements often arise when individuals cannot organize "for the purpose of defending and furthering their interests by secular means"; this implies a need for supernatural aid.[104] Bryan Wilson writes that "when warfare has failed, revolutionist orientations become more totally religious: reliance is now placed entirely on supernatural action."[105]

(16) Millenarian believers commonly expect a restored paradise which will return the ancestors. According to Vittorio Lanternari, "the religion of return is the essential kernel of messianism as such. Through it the era of salvation appears mythically as the reinstatement of the age of origins."[106] Adherents of the Prophet Dance,[107] of the Ghost Dance (both in 1870 and 1890), of the Milne Bay Prophet Cult,[108] of the German Wislin

---

99. "Mircea Eliade," p. 53. See further Desroche, *The Sociology of Hope*, pp. 96–97.

100. *Radical Religion in America: Millenarian Movements from the Far Right to the Children of Noah* (Syracuse: University Press, 1997), p. 55.

101. "Millenarism," p. 354.

102. *The Ghost Dance Religion and the Sioux Outbreak of 1890*, abridged ed., ed. Anthony F. Wallace (Chicago: University of Chicago Press, 1965), pp. 19, 26.

103. See David Daube, *Civil Disobedience in Antiquity* (Edinburgh: Edinburgh University Press, 1972).

104. "Medieval Millenarism," p. 41. See further Rene Ribeiro, "Brazilian Messianic Movements," in Thrupp, *Millennial Dreams in Action*, pp. 65–66, and Wilson, *Magic and the Millennium*, pp. 272–308.

105. *Magic and the Millennium*, p. 272.

106. "Messianism: Its Historical Origin and Morphology," *History of Religions* 2 (1962), p. 63.

107. See Leslie Spier, *The Prophet Dance of the Northwest and Its Derivatives: The Source of the Ghost Dance* (Menasha, Wis.: George Banta, 1935).

108. Worsley, *The Trumpet Shall Sound*, p. 52.

movement,[109] of the African cult of the Bashilele,[110] of the Vailala Madness,[111] of the Naked Cult of Espiritu Santo,[112] and of the njuli movement of Borneo[113] all expected their ancestors to return to earth to share a world of bliss.[114] This is also a recurrent feature of Jewish messianism, which looks forward to "the resurrection of the dead." And it probably goes back to old Zoroastrian doctrine.

(17) Millenarian movements sometimes insist on the possibility of experiencing the coming utopia as a present reality. The works of Burridge and Cohn both supply examples.[115] The fully realized eschatology of the Shakers emerged in a context of messianic expectation, and according to Hillel Schwartz, "For those who follow prophets toward a New World already marked out . . . the millennium begins in miniature [in their communities] as a sacred prologue."[116] On this phenomenon among some modern Jewish messianists see Joel Marcus, "Modern and Ancient Jewish Apocalypticism," *Journal of Religion* 76 (1996), pp. 18–23.

Sometimes unfulfilled eschatological prophecies are thought of as having been partially fulfilled. Adherents of the Vailala Madness claimed, after the years of enthusiasm had waned, that there had indeed been earthquakes, that the steamer of the dead had come near, that trees had tottered;[117] and when Jesus did not appear on 2 October 1844, as the Millerites hoped, some claimed the second coming had occurred; it was not, however, an earthly but a heavenly event.[118] These sorts of reinterpretations of prophecy can encourage forms of "realized eschatology," as probably happened in early Christianity.

(18) Millenarian movements often grow out of precursor movements. Examples of this phenomenon may be found in Burridge, *New Heaven,*

109. Worsley, ibid., pp. 94–95.

110. Lanternari, *Religions of the Oppressed*, p. 24.

111. Lanternari, ibid., pp. 80–83.

112. Lanternari, ibid., pp. 148–49.

113. Justus M. van der Kroef, "Messianic Movements in the Celebes, Sumatra, and Borneo," in Thrupp, *Millennial Dreams in Action*, pp. 110–11.

114. See further Trompf, "Cargo and Millennium," in Trompf, *Cargo Cults and Millenarian Movements*, pp. 49–52, 64–65.

115. Burridge, *New Heaven, New Earth*, pp. 79–80, 82; Cohn, *Pursuit of the Millennium*, pp. 174–76.

116. "Millenarianism: An Overview," in *The Encyclopedia of Religion*, ed. Mircea Eliade (New York: Macmillan, 1987), vol. 9, p. 525.

117. Worsley, *Trumpet*, pp. 90–91.

118. John N. Loughborough, *The Great Second Advent Movement* (Washington, D.C.: Review & Herald, 1905), pp. 185–97.

New Earth, pp. 87 (several examples), 98, 112 ("partial successes are taken as evidence of having proceeded along the right lines"); Desroche, *Sociology of Hope*, p. 74 (on the Brazilians João Maria and José Maria); and Strelan, *Search for Salvation*, pp. 22, 25 (on Pako and his successor Sanop and on the link between Yali and Mambu). The movement centered around the eighth-century Persian forerunner of the messiah, Abu-Isa, was followed by the movement centered around his successor, Yudghan. Perhaps the relationship between Jesus and John the Baptist is paralleled in the relationship between Jan Bockelson and Jan Matthys—when the latter was killed a charismatic vacuum was created which the former then filled[119]—and between the Bab and Bahā' Ullāh in the Baha'í faith. According to Wilson, "once charismatic leadership has occurred among a people it is capable of periodic recrudescence, and may, apparently, be reactivated without the experience of new processes of social change which appear to be the first stimulant of charismatic claims." [120]

(19) Any millenarian movement that survives has to come to terms with disappointed expectations, since the mythic dream or end never comes. This leads to the production of "secondary exegesis." [121] Already Dan 12:12 (which alludes to Hab 2:3: "If it seems to tarry, wait for it") and 1QpHab 7:6–13 embody pre-Christian exegetical attempts to come to terms with unrealized expectations.[122] Sullivan remarks that when the prophecies of the Guaraní did not materialize, some shamans explained that messenger birds with special instructions had been killed. Thus the ritual dancing had not achieved its object. Others claimed that the Guaraní had failed because they had eaten European foods.[123] Such after the fact rationalizations are almost inevitable: it is easier to deceive oneself than to admit self-deception.[124]

119. See further Michael Hill, *A Sociology of Religion* (New York: Basic, 1973), pp. 161–63.

120. *Magic and the Millennium*, p. 273.

121. Talmon, "Pursuit of the Millennium," p. 133.

122. See further pp. 98–101 herein; also my *End of the Ages*, pp. 242–47; James A. Beckford, *The Trumpet of Prophecy: A Sociological Study of Jehovah's Witnesses* (New York: John Wiley & Sons, 1975); and W. P. Zenner, "The Case of the Apostate Messiah," *Archives de Sociologie des Religions* 21 (1966), pp. 111–18.

123. *Icanchu's Drum*, p. 575.

124. See further Eric Anderson, "The Millerite Use of Prophecy: A Case Study of a 'Striking Fulfilment,'" in *The Disappointed: Millerism and Millenarianism in the Nineteenth Century*, ed. Ronald L. Numbers and Jonathan M. Butler (Bloomington and Indianapolis: 1987), pp. 78–91.

2

THE ESCHATOLOGY OF JESUS

STILL RATLOS AFTER
ALL THESE YEARS

Introduction

Many are disquieted when the experts disagree. Those not experts but who wish to defer to them will not know what to think. The experts themselves may be uncertain what conflict means. A lack of concord can signify that the methods of a field of study are defective, or, what may be true at the same time, that personal predispositions are unduly prejudicing some people's reasoning. There is also the unhappy possibility, common enough in the study of history, that the data are so ambiguous that contradictory interpretations are equally plausible.

How is it with study of the historical Jesus? That the experts cannot concur on some very important matters is clear enough. Many, for instance, confidently affirm that central to Jesus' teaching and activity was the conviction that God was soon to intervene in dramatic and publicly visible fashion and inaugurate a golden age, the eschatological order. Such are the heirs of Johannes Weiss and Albert Schweitzer, two one-time radicals now wholly domesticated within the house of New Testament studies. As we have seen, however, others inform us with equal assurance that Jesus was not much concerned with eschatological topics, that he was instead preoccupied with scattering abroad a subversive wisdom befitting experience of the present reign of God. These, by now a considerable company, sometimes hold themselves out to be harbingers of a new consensus.[1]

1. Marcus J. Borg, *Jesus, A New Vision: Spirit, Culture, and the Life of Discipleship* (San Francisco: Harper San Francisco, 1987), p. 14: "The majority of scholars no longer thinks that Jesus expected the end of the world in his generation." But one may doubt whether dissatisfaction with the eschatological Jesus is so deep and widespread as this claim implies.

Persuaded that the influence of those august names, Weiss and Schweitzer, has been bane, not blessing, they think themselves to have shorn the old opposition establishment of its former strength. Are they right?

The relevant data are indeed malleable, amenable to manifold explanations. Ancient and fragmentary traditions from contradictory sources that were written down only after a period of oral tradition cannot be taken at face value; and as soon as one begins the inevitable task of composing hypothetical tradition histories, the possibilities multiply. This is not an easy business. Success is hardly guaranteed.

It is nonetheless the burden of the ensuing pages to show, in further confirmation of chapter 1, that the by now venerable belief that Jesus was an eschatological or millenarian prophet is our best thesis, and that the contrary conviction, that he was an aphoristic sage who did not promulgate an imminent eschatology, is, although vigorously argued by a growing contingent, problematic. Although neither reconstruction can, in the strict sense, be either proved or falsified, the former is far more plausible than the latter. In my mind the millenarian Jesus is indeed almost, if not quite, clear to demonstration.

Our disagreement is not in this case a product of divergent or deficient historical-critical methods. Nor, as I shall seek to show, are the data so lamentably equivocal that one hypothesis is as good as another. Whether—or rather how—personal prejudices and religious convictions play their role here I shall not speculate. Given how hard it can be to fathom one's own motives, it would be both idle and inappropriate to attempt to divine the impulses of others. But, however one explains the scholarly dissonance, those who imagine that the Jesus tradition was originally bereft of eschatological urgency have almost certainly come to the wrong conclusion.

Marcus Borg against E. P. Sanders

E. P. Sanders is a prominent advocate of the view that Jesus believed in a God who would soon create a radically new world. In *Jesus and Judaism* Sanders has offered several reasons for so thinking. Prominently among them are the following: (1) Jesus' action in the Jerusalem temple, attested in all four canonical Gospels, is best explained against the eschatological expectation that God will raise a new temple.[2] (2) Jesus' selection or sep-

2. E. P. Sanders, *Jesus and Judaism* (Philadelphia: Fortress, 1985), pp. 61–90.

aration of twelve disciples should be interpreted in terms of restoration eschatology, the end-time reestablishment of Israel's twelve tribes.[3] (3) Jesus' position between John the Baptist, for whom the imminent judgment
was central, and the early church, which longed for the *parousia*, makes
most sense on the supposition that Jesus himself was much concerned
with eschatology.[4]

These arguments, especially the third, wield considerable force. But
Marcus Borg, who prefers to label Jesus an aphoristic sage rather than an
eschatological prophet, has recently disputed them. Borg, with clarity, but
not, I shall urge, persuasion equal to that of his opponent, counters
Sanders with these claims:[5] (1) We know neither that Jesus expected a
new temple to take the place of the old one nor that his act of overturning tables was an eschatological prophecy. (2) Even if he chose twelve disciples, "it would indicate that Jesus saw his mission as having to do with
'Israel,' but it need not imply the framework of imminent restoration eschatology."[6] (3) There was discontinuity between Jesus and John in several particulars, among which may have been eschatological convictions;
and the early church—whose eschatological enthusiasm has, in Borg's
view, probably been exaggerated—looked forward to the return of Jesus,
something to which Jesus himself, according to most modern scholarship,
did not look forward.

How strong is this rebuttal? Borg is proof that Sanders's arguments
will not convince everyone. But Cartesian doubt is one thing, reasonable
doubt another. The issue, to state the obvious, is not whether Sanders has
passed beyond all critical rejoinder, for no historian can do that. The past
holds few certainties. The pressing question is only whether Sanders's reconstruction of what took place, or something like it, is more probable
than competing reconstructions. And despite Borg's contentions to the
contrary, Sanders's basic thesis has not been undone.

Jesus and the temple. I begin with a concession. Although one presumes
it was otherwise for Jesus' first audience, for us at least Jesus' overturning

---

3. Ibid., pp. 95–106.
4. Ibid., pp. 91–95. This last argument is not new with Sanders. Sanders himself cites
its use by James D. G. Dunn, *Jesus and the Spirit* (Philadelphia: Westminster, 1975), p. 42.
Dunn in turn cites Klaus Koch, *The Rediscovery of Apocalyptic*, SBT 2/22 (London: SCM,
1972), p. 78. I have found it as early as B. Harvie Branscomb, *The Teachings of Jesus*
(Nashville: Cokesbury, 1931), pp. 131–33. No doubt it goes back beyond that.
5. Marcus J. Borg, *Jesus in Contemporary Scholarship* (Valley Forge: Trinity Press International, 1994), pp. 74–84.
6. Ibid., p. 76.

of the tables is equivocal.[7] About this Borg is right. Commentators have offered all sorts of explanations for it, and, it is only fair to say, recent work has raised a question mark over Sanders's claim that Jesus, whatever else he was doing, could not have been protesting certain practices.[8]

On the other hand, even if there are, as there seem to be, reasons to believe that Jesus' act was a protest against some activity of the priestly establishment, Sanders's main position is not thereby invalidated. For although current scholarship, following Sanders's statement of the problem, has tended to suppose that we should here choose between two competing theories—either Jesus enacted a prophecy of destruction or he was unhappy with some aspect of the temple business—these two theories are scarcely at odds. Protest against abuses and symbolic expression of judgment could readily have gone together. In Jeremiah, Ezekiel, Micah 3, and *1 Enoch* 83–90, criticism of priestly corruption is joined to expectation of the temple's destruction and/or hope for a new temple. It is possible, then, that Jesus indicated God's eschatological judgment upon the temple, and that he opposed, not the sacrificial system itself, but what he perceived to be inappropriate business proceedings,[9] which had made the sacred secular and had encouraged in the first place or confirmed in the second his expectation of judgment.

Although Sanders prefers, when possible, to ground his judgments about Jesus in the few facts we know about him instead of in the sayings attributed to him, the facts in the present case do not take us far enough. The turning over of tables in the temple is, as just indicated, less an illuminating episode than an episode that needs to be illuminated. So it is inevitable that we look for sayings of Jesus regarding the temple.

Mk 13:2; Lk 19:44; Acts 6:14; and *Gos. Thom.* 71 attribute to him a prophecy of the temple's destruction. Although some deny that it goes back to Jesus,[10] the arguments on the other side—here Borg[11] and Sanders[12] concur—persuade.[13] Not only did other Jewish prophets fore-

7. The following discussion assumes a historical event behind Mk 11:15–18 par. But for doubt see George Wesley Buchanan, "Symbolic Money-Changers in the Temple," *NTS* 37 (1991), pp. 280–89.

8. Craig Evans, "Jesus' Action in the Temple," *CBQ* 51 (1989), pp. 237–70.

9. Although this could have been neither money-changing itself (a necessity) nor the selling of animals (legislated by the Bible).

10. E.g. Jürgen Becker, *Jesus von Nazaret* (Berlin: Walter de Gruyter, 1996), pp. 403–407.

11. Marcus Borg, *Conflict, Holiness and Politics in the Teachings of Jesus* (Lewiston: Edwin Mellen, 1984), pp. 177–91.

12. Sanders, *Jesus and Judaism*, pp. 71–76.

tell the temple's doom,[14] but the temple was burned, and a forecast after the event might have reflected this circumstance.[15]

More controversial is the proposition that Jesus also spoke of a new temple being rebuilt.[16] But the sources that preserve this prophecy[17] show that its interpretation was the subject of troubled reflection. In Jn 2:13–22 Jesus' saying is misapprehended by his audience to refer to the physical shrine in Jerusalem, and we are further told that the disciples understood the prophecy to pertain to the resurrection only *ex eventu*. In Mt 26:61 and 27:40 (but not the Markan parallels) Jesus is quoted as saying no more than that he is "able" to destroy the temple and rebuild it, not that he will. In Mk 14:58 and 15:29 false witnesses and hostile passersby, but not Jesus, utter the words. Luke omits them entirely.

The tradition also betrays a series of sometimes subtle but nonetheless detectable tendentious reinterpretations. In Jn 2:13–22 "the Jews" believe that Jesus is speaking about the Jerusalem temple, but the evangelist insists that Jesus' words instead refer to his own body. In Mk 14:53–65 false witnesses quote Jesus' prediction against him and obviously give it a literal reference. Mark's editorial work, however, hints that, for the evangelist, the saying is a forecast of the new community that the risen Jesus will build.[18] The evangelist Matthew, who omits the antithesis between a temple made with hands and one not made with hands, may, to the contrary, construe the saying as does John. In his Gospel, it may well be, it has to do, not with the temple (so the false witnesses and passersby) or with the church (so Mark), but with Jesus' death and resurrection.[19] *Gos.*

13. See further Gerd Theissen, "Die Tempelweissagung Jesu," *TZ* 32 (1976), pp. 144–58.

14. Full documentation in C. A. Evans, "Predictions of the Destruction of the Herodian Temple in the Pseudepigrapha, Qumran Scrolls, and Related Texts," *JSP* 10 (1992), pp. 89–147.

15. See Mt 22:6–7; *T. Mos.* 6:9; *T. Jud.* 23:3; *2 Bar.* 7:1; 80:3; *Sib. Orac.* 4:126; 5:399; *Apoc. Abr.* 27:3; Chrysostom, *Hom. on Mt.* 75.3.

16. Doubts in J. Schlosser, "La parole de Jésus sur la fin du Temple," *NTS* 36 (1990), pp. 398–414.

17. Mk 14:58; 15:29; Jn 2:19; *Gos. Thom.* 71.

18. Donald Juel, *Messiah and Temple*, SBLDS 31 (Missoula: Scholars Press, 1977), pp. 143–57. For the argument that Paul also knew the saying and interpreted it similarly see J. P. M. Sweet, "A House Not Made with Hands," in *Templum Amicitiae: Essays on the Second Temple Presented to Ernst Bammel*, ed. William Horbury, JSNT 48 (Sheffield: JSOT, 1991), pp. 368–90.

19. W. D. Davies and Dale C. Allison, Jr., *A Critical and Exegetical Commentary on the Gospel according to Saint Matthew*, 3 vols. (Edinburgh: T. & T. Clark, 1988, 1991, 1997), vol. 3, p. 526.

Thom. 71 offers yet another reading, one fostered through a rewriting: "I shall de[stroy this] house and no one will be able to build it [again]." This appears to be a post-70 reading: Jesus predicted the destruction of the temple (which happened) but did not say anything about rebuilding it (which did not happen).

This is not the place to issue many conjectures about the tradition history behind Mk 14:58 and its relatives. The pertinent point is that our early sources protest too robustly when they go out of their way to stress that Jesus never prophesied the rebuilding of the Jerusalem temple. The prophecy, as we have seen, is not only given conflicting interpretations, but in two sources it is put on the lips of unreliable outsiders (Matthew, Mark), in another it is rewritten (*Gospel of Thomas*), in another it is misunderstood (John), and in another it is omitted altogether (Luke). That it was unusually troublesome is manifest. When the tradition struggles this much with a saying one is prodded to infer that it goes back to something Jesus said—something which, because so well known, generally disallowed, even though Luke managed it, discreet silence.[20] Mk 14:58 par. appears to be an example of what we find so often in millenarian movements, namely, a prediction modified—in this case in several different directions—in the light of seemingly disconfirming events.

If Jesus did indeed prophesy the temple's demise and replacement, one must back Sanders, not Borg. For such a prophecy coheres with the expectation preserved in *1 En.* 90:28–29 and 11QTemple 29:8–10, passages that anticipate the end and renewal of Jerusalem's temple.[21] Borg himself concedes: "If we were confident that Jesus expected a new temple that would physically replace the old one, then we could say that Jesus

20. Perhaps Mark and Matthew are correct in linking Jesus' condemnation with his words about the temple. If so, then there is a good chance that knowledge of those words was widespread, and perhaps the fact that outsiders know them in Matthew, Mark, and John is a sign that non-Christians later used them as polemic against Christians, to show that Jesus was a false prophet. However that may be, although (with the possible exception of Mark) all of the sources that attest to our saying were composed after 70, the prophecy must have been known before that time. For the prediction of rebuilding, problematic after 70, was not invented after that date; and since this prophecy presupposes the prophecy of destruction, both must have circulated together before 70.

21. See also Tob 13:16–18; 14:5; *Jub.* 1:27; 4QFlor 1:1–3; *4 Ezra* 10:54; *Sib. Or.* 5:414–33; *Tg. on Isa* 53:5. I leave aside here the difficult question of whether such a prophecy was originally formulated with Jesus as subject ("I will destroy . . . I will rebuild") or with the divine passive. But it may be observed that Jewish tradition was well acquainted with the idea of a human being building the temple: 2 Sam 7:10–14 (David's son); Zech 6:7 (the man whose name is "Branch"); *Sib. Or.* 5:422 ("a blessed man" who comes "from the expanses of heaven").

was operating within the framework of restoration eschatology."[22] One cannot but agree. It follows that those who find an authentic saying behind the dual prediction in Mk 14:58 par. should interpret Jesus' action in the temple as does Sanders, which in turn means that Jesus was an eschatological prophet.

Jesus and the Twelve. Some deny that Jesus chose twelve disciples. Those who think otherwise—they have the better of the argument[23]—must ask what sense to give to that choice. Sanders, like others before him, finds a connection with restoration eschatology: Jesus hoped for the ingathering of the twelve tribes. Borg, however, claims that the choice of twelve simply implies that Jesus associated his mission with Israel.

This, with all due respect, seems to me a strangely deficient rebuttal. Most of the twelve tribes had disappeared into the mists centuries before Jesus, and he could not possibly have thought of himself as ministering to them. So if his appointment of a group of twelve was intended to put people in mind of all Israel,[24] what was the point? It is hard to avoid thinking that Jesus shared the expectation, so widely attested, of the eschatological restoration of the twelve lost, or rather hidden, tribes.[25] The later Jewish messiah, Sabbatai Ṣevi, whose movement thrived amid rumors of the imminent return of the ten tribes, chose twelve rabbinic scholars to represent restored Israel.[26]

Fortifying the eschatological interpretation of Jesus' election of a group of twelve are the many texts which link bodies of twelve with eschatological events. In 1QM 2:1–3 we read that, on the day of battle with the Kittim, there will be twelve chief priests and twelve chiefs of the Levites. 4QpIsa^d frag. 1 mentions "the heads of the tribes of Israel at the end of days." According to *T. Jud.* 25:1–2, the twelve sons of Israel will rise and wield the scepter in Israel. *T. Benj.* 10:7 offers the same picture: "each of us over our tribe." The twenty-four elders of Revelation are most likely,

---

22. Borg, *Jesus in Contemporary Scholarship*, p. 76.

23. See John P. Meier, "The Circle of the Twelve: Did It Exist during Jesus' Public Ministry?" *JBL* 116 (1997), pp. 635–72; R. P. Meye, *Jesus and the Twelve* (Grand Rapids: Eerdmans, 1968), pp. 192–209; and Sanders, *Jesus and Judaism*, pp. 98–106.

24. Examples from the Bible of twelve things or people representing the twelve tribes are many and include Exod 24:4; 28:21; Num 17:2, 6; Joshua 4; 1 Kgs 18:31; Ezek 48:31.

25. See Isa 27:12–13; 43:5–6; Hos 11:11; 2 Macc 1:27; 2:18; Bar 4:37; 5:5; *Ps. Sol.* 8:28; 11:2–3; *1 En.* 57:1; 11QTemple 57:5–6; *4 Ezra* 13:32–50; *2 Bar.* 78:1–7; *Sib. Or.* 2:170–73; *T. Jos.* 19:3–8 (Arm.); *m. Sanh.* 10:3.

26. Gershom Scholem, *Sabbatai Sevi: The Mystical Messiah* (Princeton: Princeton University Press, 1973), p. 222.

if we may follow the modern commentaries, the twelve apostles and the twelve tribal angels reigning together in eschatological glory (see 21:12).

The Synoptic tradition itself invites us to connect the number twelve with eschatology. Q 22:28–30 promises Jesus' followers that they will "rule over" or "judge" the twelve tribes of Israel. This assumes that the twelve tribes will soon come home to the land.[27]

Even if one doubts that Jesus himself authored Q 22:28–30, his appointment of a special group of twelve, presumably for missionary work, almost inevitably turns one's thoughts to eschatological expectation. Again Sanders appears to be right.

The Baptist and the Church. In disputing that the Baptist's eschatological outlook implicates Jesus in a similar view, Borg raises the possibility that John did not have such an outlook: the tradition may mislead us in this particular. Because, however, Borg himself is prudently "not very persuaded of this,"[28] and because in this he is with the majority,[29] we can quickly quit this point and go on to the next.

Borg perceives significant differences between John and Jesus. There is, for instance, a "strong emphasis upon an imminent judgment and the consequent need for repentance in the preaching of John," but these things are not as prominent in the words of Jesus.[30] Borg in fact goes so far as to say that "the affirmation of substantial continuity" between John and Jesus "is questionable."[31]

What shall we say to this? Regarding imminent judgment and repentance, the Jesus tradition is full of both. Q, for instance, contains many units which, so far from referring to the signs of the times as wholly propitious for those within Israel, rather explicitly or implicitly proclaim the divine judgment: Q 6:37–38 (judge not so you will not be judged), 6:49 (the house that falls to storm); 10:12–15 (warnings and woes upon those who reject the disciples and upon Chorazin, Bethsaida and Capernaum); 11:31–32 (judgment upon "this generation"), 11:50 (the blood of all the prophets required of "this generation"); 12:9 (denial at the judgment of those who have denied Jesus), 12:10 (no forgiveness for those who blaspheme the Holy Spirit), 12:46 (judgment of the unfaithful servant); 13:27 (banishment from the kingdom), 13:28–29 (weeping and gnash-

27. See further below, pp. 141–45.
28. Borg, *Jesus and Contemporary Scholarship*, p. 77.
29. Even the Jesus Seminar has voted that "the historical JB, in all probability, was an apocalyptic preacher." See W. Barnes Tatum, *John the Baptist and Jesus: A Report of the Jesus Seminar* (Sonoma: Polebridge, 1994), p. 167.
30. Borg, *Jesus and Contemporary Scholarship*, p. 77.
31. Ibid., p. 78.

ing of teeth), 13:30 (the first will be last), 13:35 (Jerusalem and/or the temple forsaken); 14:41 (the exalted will be humbled); 17:2 (warning against causing a little one to stumble); 17:27–30 (the day of the Son of man will be like the time when Noah entered the ark and the flood came), 17:33 (those who save their lives will lose them), 17:34–35 (one will be taken, another left). These Q texts and the many similar ones in Mark, M, and L[32] would seem to speak for themselves, and to speak volumes. This material reflects the conviction that God's judgment is coming, and that it is coming soon. Is all of it incongruent with Jesus' proclamation?[33] Surely here is a theme that is so much a part of the tradition that, were one to deny it to Jesus, the very possibility of the modern quest would fall into disrepute for the reason that the sources are too untrustworthy.

As for "repent" (μετανοέω) and "repentance" (μετανοία), these are more than faintly inscribed upon our sources. One or the other appears on Jesus' lips in Q 10:13–15 (Tyre and Sidon would have repented long ago) and 11:32 (the Ninevites repented at Jonah's preaching) as well as in Lk 13:3–5 (unless you repent you will perish); 15:7 (joy over one repentant sinner; is this from Q?), 15:10 (joy in heaven over one sinner repenting); and 16:30 (repentance of relatives in the parable of the rich man and Lazarus). Again one wonders whether all of this material can so easily be shoved into the post-Easter period,[34] and why Mk 1:15 ("repent

32. See p. 46, n. 142 herein.
33. See further Becker, *Jesus von Nazaret*, pp. 58–99. Recently David Seeley, "Futuristic Eschatology and Social Formation in Q," in *Reimagining Christian Origins*, ed. Elizabeth A. Castelli and Hal Taussig (Valley Forge: Trinity Press International, 1996), pp. 144–53, has argued that Q fails to connect futuristic eschatology and the ethics of social formation, which implies that the original community behind Q had no futuristic eschatology—a thesis consistent with a nonmillenarian Jesus. But there are difficulties. (1) There is no link between futuristic eschatology and foundational proclamation in the missionary discourse only if all future sense is emptied from 10:9. (2) Seeley plays down or passes over the ties between eschatology and ethics in the Sermon on the Plain (6:47–49 is often given an eschatological sense), in the Lord's Prayer (in 11:2–4 forgiveness and dependence upon God for daily need cannot be dissociated from the petition, "thy kingdom come"), in the tradition about ravens and lilies (on the eschatology of 12:22–31 see C. M. Tuckett, "Q, Prayer and the Kingdom," *JTS* 40 [1989], pp. 367–76), and in 12:51–53 (where the fundamental circumstance of familial division is related to Mic 7:6 understood as a prophecy of the latter days; see my article, "Q 12:51–53 and Mk 9:11–13 and the Messianic Woes," in *Authenticating the Words of Jesus*, ed. Craig Evans and Bruce Chilton [Leiden: E. J. Brill, forthcoming, 1998]). (3) Q is insider literature that assumes much and so leaves much out of account (e.g., there is nothing at all about communal rituals). Seeley himself acknowledges that his critics can accuse him of an argument from silence.
34. For arguments for the authenticity of Q 10:13–15 see Davies and Allison, *Matthew*, vol. 2, pp. 270–71, and Ulrich Luz, *Das Evangelium nach Matthäus (Mt 8–17)*, EKK 1/2 (Zurich and Neukirchen-Vluyn: Benziger and Neukirchener, 1990), p. 192 (although he excludes 10:15). For Q 11:32 see Franz Mussner, "Wege zum Selbstbewusstsein Jesu," *BZ* 12

and believe") and 6:12 (the disciples are to preach repentance), even if redactional, cannot hold authentic memory. Moreover, the idea of repentance itself, if broadly defined, is often present when the vocabulary— μετανοέω, μετανοία—is not. The moral exhortation implies the need for reform, and the Jesus tradition is full moral exhortation. Announcements of judgment, so plentiful as we have seen, likewise imply the need for amending one's ways.

If one is dissuaded that Jesus spoke little of a repentance made requisite by the coming judgment,[35] one additionally has to ask what likely follows from Jesus' baptism. This is, on its face, a very compelling sign that Jesus followed in the way of John. Did not the former submit to the latter's baptism because the former believed what the latter taught? So if the Baptist averred that repentance was required and that judgment was coming, must not Jesus have thought this too? The argument is all the stronger if John's Gospel is right in asserting that Jesus himself baptized (3:22). Maybe John was, after all, Jesus' spiritual father.

We are beckoned to this conclusion by the handful of sayings about the Baptist that the tradition attributes to Jesus. In Q 7:26 Jesus says that John is a prophet and more than a prophet. In Q 7:27 Jesus makes John out to be the fulfillment of a prophetic oracle. In Q 7:28 Jesus declares John to have been the greatest among those born of women. In Q 7:33–34 Jesus tells the parable of children in the marketplace, a parable that aligns his ministry with that of John. In Q 16:16 Jesus sees in John the turn of the aeons. In Mk 11:27–33 Jesus implies that the authority of John was from heaven. Most have rightly thought that Jesus fashioned one or more of these tributes,[36] and there is in none of them a distancing of Jesus from John's eschatology.

I freely admit that there were differences between Jesus and John. Q 7:31–35 may imply (although I shall have occasion to qualify this in the subsequent chapter) that John was more ascetic than Jesus, something also reflected in Mk 2:18 (John's disciples fast voluntarily but Jesus' do not). Again, some of Jesus' words have been taken to mean that God's reign is not just coming but has already arrived or begun to arrive, an idea

---

(1968), pp. 169–71. Lk 13:1–5 has frequently been attributed to Jesus; cf. Becker, *Jesus von Nazaret*, pp. 63–65.

35. See further N. T. Wright, *Jesus and the Victory of God* (Minneapolis: Fortress, 1996), pp. 246–58. He rightly understands repentance in the Jesus tradition to be a part of the eschatological scenario: at the last, Israel repents.

36. Compare Tatum, *John*, p. 155, reporting that the Jesus Seminar has voted in favor of (and so colors red) the proposition that "Jesus identified JB as a great figure."

not found in John's proclamation (in which "reign [of God]" is unattested).[37] But Jesus' "eschatology in the process of realization" may simply show that he took himself to be further along the eschatological time line than John. It certainly does not demonstrate that Jesus had abandoned John's eschatological framework.[38]

It is of interest that, despite the manifest desire of early Christians to maintain the superiority of their master over John, the New Testament assimilates the two figures. Matthew, for example, has them say the same things,[39] and Luke gives them similar nativity stories.[40] Moreover, the popular pre-Markan legend behind Mk 6:14–29 has Herod interpret Jesus as John returned from the dead; and Jesus himself, in Q 7:31–35, sees "this generation" as united in its comparable opposition to himself and the Baptist. If John and Jesus were really as different as some now make out, and if Jesus' proclamation finally veered away altogether from John's eschatological direction, would early Christian literature so often associate the two and liken them one to another? Is it not more natural to suppose that the frequent parallelism between John and Jesus is not just a literary or theological phenomenon but also a remembrance of the widely known fact that the two men, notwithstanding differences, preached closely related messages?

Borg appeals to John Dominic Crossan as one who "accepts that John was Jesus' mentor and that John had an apocalyptic eschatology," but also holds that Jesus went on to produce a "radically different" message.[41] Crossan's view is based in part upon his reading of Q 7:28//Gos. Thom. 46, a saying he attributes to Jesus. This unit says that the least in the kingdom is greater than John, which Crossan reads as a sort of criticism. Now because Crossan also accepts the authenticity of Q 7:24–26, where Jesus praises John, he concludes that "Jesus changed his view of John's mission and message. John's vision of awaiting the apocalyptic God, the Coming One, as a repentant sinner, which Jesus had originally accepted and even defended in the crisis of John's death, was no longer deemed adequate."[42]

37. For a full review of the discussion see John P. Meier, *A Marginal Jew: Rethinking the Historical Jesus*, 2 vols. (New York: Doubleday, 1994), vol. 2, pp. 398–506. But are not the surviving materials about John so meager as to make it imprudent to argue from silence?

38. Belief in an imminent redemption and in the presence of salvation need not be antagonistic convictions but can rather be two sides of the same eschatological enthusiasm; see Joel Marcus, "Modern and Ancient Jewish Apocalypticism," *JR* 76 (1996), pp. 18–23.

39. Compare 3:2 with 4:17, 3:7 with 12:34 and 23:33, and 3:10 with 7:19.

40. Lk 1:26–38 (on Jesus) echoes 1:5–23 (on John).

41. Borg, *Jesus in Contemporary Scholarship*, p. 77.

42. John Dominic Crossan, *The Historical Jesus: The Life of a Mediterranean Jewish Peasant* (San Francisco: Harper & Row, 1991), p. 238.

Although the example of Aristotle departing from Plato reminds us that students need not adhere to their teachers, I must express reservations. The first problem is that many have attributed Q 7:28b not to Jesus but to the early church.[43] The second is that, even if Jesus uttered Q 7:28b, it scarcely disengages him from John's eschatology. If Jesus uttered the saying before John died, then it probably meant that the least in the kingdom (when it comes) will be greater than the greatest (John the Baptist) is now.[44] If Jesus uttered it after John died, then it probably meant that those now alive, who experience the presence of God's reign, are the most blessed and privileged of all, even more blessed and privileged than the Baptist, of revered memory.[45] In either instance John's eschatological proclamation is not overturned. On the contrary, in both cases it is John's greatness that makes him an appropriate foil for declaring the surpassing greatness of the kingdom.[46] So Borg's invocation of Crossan is not compelling.

With regard to the continuity Sanders sees between Jesus and early Christianity on the question of eschatology, Borg offers two rejoinders. First, the church expected Jesus' return, an expectation not often credited to Jesus; so "the eschatological expectation of the early movement was not simply a continuation of something going back to Jesus."[47] Second, Borg doubts the centrality of eschatology in earliest Christianity. "Most of us know of Christian groups today for whom the imminent expectation of the second coming and the final judgment is central. What we know about the early Christian movement, generally speaking, does not sound like what we associate with these groups."[48]

To take the latter point first: Borg is quite aware that one might discern tension in the argument that, although the eschatological orientation of earliest Christianity has often been exaggerated, it is precisely the church that drafted so much of the eschatological sentiments now found in the Synoptics. Why, if the church was not caught up in eschatological enthu-

43. So, e.g., Martin Dibelius, *Die urchristliche Überlieferung von Johannes dem Täufer*, FRLANT 15 (Göttingen: Vandenhoeck & Ruprecht, 1911), pp. 12–15, and Luz, *Matthäus*, vol. 2, p. 176.

44. J. C. O'Neill, *Jesus the Messiah: Six Lectures on the Ministry of Jesus* (London: Cochrane, 1980), pp. 10–11.

45. Jacques Schlosser, *Le Règne de Dieu dans les Dits de Jésus*, 2 vols., EB (Paris: J. Gabalda, 1980), vol. 1, 161–67.

46. See further Joan E. Taylor, *The Immerser: John the Baptist within Second Temple Judaism* (Grand Rapids: Eerdmans, 1997), pp. 302–304.

47. Borg, *Jesus in Contemporary Scholarship*, p. 78.

48. Ibid., p. 78

siasm, did it transform Jesus from an aphoristic sage into an eschatological prophet? Is it plausible to play down the eschatological character of the early community while blaming the church for inserting into the tradition the apocalyptic Son of man sayings, Mark 13, the prophecies that announce a near end (Mk 9:1; 13:30), etc.? Ernst Käsemann, one recalls, saved Jesus from apocalyptic eschatology only by stressing the fervently apocalyptic character of the earliest Christian community.[49]

To relax the tension his reconstruction creates, Borg could, although he does not, appeal to recent studies that have proposed that Q passed through two stages, the first of which was characterized by a lesser interest in things eschatological.[50] This might strengthen his conviction that the very earliest Christianity was not focused on eschatological expectation, that eschatological enthusiasm entered only at a later stage. But the current tendency to divine an eschatologically subdued stratum behind the Q known to Matthew and Luke has, despite its welcome among many, already been subjected to severe and, in my judgment, nearly decisive criticism.[51] It does not take prophetic powers to see that its popularity will probably last only for a season.

Borg, however, takes another and more prudent path out of the problem created by a nonapocalyptic Jesus and an apocalyptic early Christianity. He suggests that it was not in fact the very earliest Christianity that altered the Jesus tradition. Rather, events in the 40s and 60s wrought an influx of eschatological and even apocalyptic ideas into the church. This is the revivification of a hypothesis that has been around in one form or another for a very long time. B. H. Streeter, Ernst von Dobschütz, C. H. Dodd, John A. T. Robinson, and C. L. Mearns, among others, have all contended that the church borrowed more and more from Jewish apocalyptic as time went on.[52] There is an initial plausibility in the suggestion

49. Ernst Käsemann, *New Testament Questions of Today* (Philadelphia: Fortress, 1969), pp. 82–107.

50. John S. Kloppenborg, *The Formation of Q: Trajectories in Ancient Wisdom Collections* (Philadelphia: Fortress, 1987). For Borg's doubts about Kloppenborg's theory see *Jesus in Contemporary Scholarship*, p. 123, n. 50.

51. E.g., C. M. Tuckett, *Q and the History of Early Christianity: Studies on Q* (Edinburgh: T. & T. Clark, 1996), pp. 41–82.

52. B. H. Streeter, "Professor Burkitt and the Parables of the Kingdom," *The Interpreter* 7 (1910–11), pp. 241–47; idem, "Synoptic Criticism and the Eschatological Problem," in *Oxford Studies in the Synoptic Problem*, ed. W. Sanday (Oxford: Clarendon, 1911), pp. 425–36; Ernst von Dobschütz, *The Eschatology of the Gospels* (London: Hodder & Stoughton, 1910); C. H. Dodd, *The Apostolic Preaching and Its Developments* (Chicago: Willett, Clark & Co., 1937), 53–64; John A. T. Robinson, *Jesus and His Coming* (Philadelphia: Westminster, 1979); C. L. Mearns, "Early Eschatological Development in Paul: The

that first the Caligula crisis and then the political unrest in the 60s led to increased speculation about eschatological subjects. The composition of Mark 13 has often, and I think rightly, been associated with one episode or the other,[53] and the commentaries routinely link Caligula's attempt to set up a statue of himself as Jupiter in the Jerusalem temple with the eschatological materials in 2 Thessalonians 2.

Borg's hypothesis nonetheless falters, for his characterization of earliest Christianity—Christianity in the 30s—is without persuasion. Borg contrasts what we know of movements dominated by eschatological expectation with earliest Christianity. This last, he says, "seems by and large to have been a community with a strong experiential sense of the Spirit of God, quite egalitarian, and to a considerable degree boundary-shattering and culturally subversive."[54] Unless I misunderstand, there appears to be implicit here a dubious dichotomy. Borg, in saying that the earliest Christianity was typified not so much by its eschatological beliefs as by its sense of the Spirit, its egalitarianism, and its "boundary-shattering and culturally subversive" nature, seemingly exhibits a curious oversight. Surely many early Christians, in accordance with Jewish expectation, interpreted the coming of the Spirit as an eschatological sign.[55] And their egalitarian proclivities as well as antagonism to many cultural conventions harmo-

---

Evidence of I and II Thessalonians," *NTS* 27 (1981), pp. 137–57. But for precisely the opposite thesis—that the influence of apocalyptic eschatology diminished with time—see Willoughby C. Allen, "Mr. Streeter and the Eschatology of the Gospels," *The Interpreter* 7 (1910–11), pp. 359–64, and Paul J. Achtemeier, "An Apocalyptic Shift in Early Christian Tradition: Reflections on Some Canonical Evidence," *CBQ* 45 (1983), pp. 231–48. This second view accords with the transition from the earlier Pauline epistles (e.g., 1 Thessalonians) to the later Paulines and those produced by his circle (e.g., Ephesians): apocalyptic language recedes as time moves forward. This is also the usual pattern within millenarian movements.

53. For an attempt to associate the origin of Mark 13 with the Caligula crisis see Gerd Theissen, *The Gospels in Context: Social and Political History in the Synoptic Tradition* (Minneapolis: Fortress, 1991), pp. 125–65; also N. H. Taylor, "Palestinian Christianity and the Caligula Crisis. Part II. The Markan Eschatological Discourse," *JSNT* 62 (1996), pp. 13–41. On the possible connections with the Jewish War see Joel Marcus, "The Jewish War and the *Sitz im Leben* of Mark," *JBL* 113 (1992), pp. 441–62.

54. Borg, *Jesus in Contemporary Scholarship*, p. 78

55. Compare Hans Conzelmann, *An Outline of the Theology of the New Testament* (New York: Harper & Row, 1969), pp. 37–38, and note the remarks of Benjamin D. Sommer, "Did Prophecy Cease? Evaluating a Reevaluation," *JBL* 115 (1996), pp. 36–39. Pertinent texts include Isa 32:15; 34:16; 44:3–4; 61:1; Ezek 11:19; 36:25–27; 37:1–14; Joel 2:28–29; Zech 2:10; 1QS 4:21–22; 4Q521 fr. 2; *1 En.* 49:3; 62:2; *Ps. Sol.* 17:37; *T. Jud.* 24:3; *T. Levi* 18:11; Mt 3:11; 12:28; Acts 2:17; Rom 8:23–24; *Tg.* on Isa 42:1–4; *t. Soṭa* 13:2.

THE ESCHATOLOGY OF JESUS • 109

nize perfectly with eschatological enthusiasm, which longs for God to overturn present circumstances. These are indeed regular features of messianic or millenarian movements, the necessary correlates of belief in imminent eschatological reversal.[56] One thinks of the "astonishing democratization of the formerly exclusive sacerdotal office"[57] in Isa 61:6 ("you shall be called priests of the Lord");[58] of the equality of all people in *Sibylline Oracles* 8;[59] of the egalitarianism and revolutionary spirit of the followers of Joachim of Fiore; of John Ball (d. 1381), who believed that Adam and Eve were equal in Eden and that equality would obtain between man and woman in the future; of the antinomianism and mass prophecy of the Sabbatian movement; of the communism of the Münsterites, who abandoned private property; of the Ranters, who hoped for an age without individual ownership and class distinctions;[60] of the "proclaimed equality of all men and the liberation of all women" in the Taiping Rebellion;[61] of the communal living and abolition of status distinctions in the cargo cult on the island of Espiritu Santo;[62] and of Gershom Scholem's generalization about Jewish messianism: "There is an anarchic element in the very nature of Messianic utopianism: the dissolution of old ties which lose their meaning in the new context of Messianic freedom. The total novelty for which utopianism hopes enters thus into a momen-

56. Norman Cohn's *The Pursuit of the Millennium: Revolutionary Millenarians and Mystical Anarchists of the Middle Ages*, rev. ed. (New York: Oxford University Press, 1970), discusses several movements under the rubric, "the egalitarian millennium" (chapters 10–13). Egalitarianism was already a part of certain strands of old Zoroastrian eschatology; see Bruce Lincoln, "'The Earth becomes Flat'—A Study of Apocalyptic Imagery," *Comparative Studies in Society and History* 25 (1983), pp. 136–53.

57. Paul D. Hanson, *The Dawn of Apocalyptic: The Historical and Sociological Roots of Jewish Apocalyptic Eschatology*, rev. ed. (Philadelphia: Fortress, 1979), p. 68.

58. Also interesting is Joel 2:28–29, which envisages the spirit coming upon everyone, including "menservants and maidservants."

59. *Sib. Or.* 8:110–21: "No one is slave there, no lord, no tyrant, no kings, no leaders who are very arrogant. . . . The age will be common to all."

60. Norman Cohn, "The Ranters," *Encounter* 34 (1970), pp. 20–24.

61. Richard Shek, "Millenarianism: Chinese Millenarian Movements," in *The Encyclopedia of Religion*, ed. Mircea Eliade (New York: Macmillan, 1987), vol. 9, p. 535. He continues: "To be sure there was the inevitable discrepancy between theory and practice. Yet this Taiping ideal was unequivocally enunciated and applied to concrete situations in the form of policy promulgations such as the land tenure system. This system provided equitable land redistribution, going so far as to observe no distinction between the sexes in land allotment."

62. Peter Worsley, *The Trumpet Shall Sound: A Study of "Cargo" Cults in Melanesia* (New York: Schocken, 1968), pp. 148–49. For another illustration from a cargo cult see John G. Strelan, *Search for Salvation: Studies in the History and Theology of Cargo Cults* (Adelaide: Lutheran Publishing House, 1977), p. 44 (on the Story Cult of West New Britain).

tous tension with the world of bonds and laws which is the world of *Halakah.*[63]

Eschatology is, among other things, an expression of dissatisfaction with the present, and millenarian cults typically foster meaningful solidarity between individuals who feel powerless or alienated from the structures of society.[64] Despite its hierarchy, the eschatological community behind the Dead Sea Scrolls was to "eat in common, pray in common, and deliberate in common" (1QS 6:2–3). What Borg finds in earliest Christianity—egalitarianism and the shattering or subversion of convention—is just what one expects to find in a movement possessed by eschatological convictions.[65]

The truth is that Bultmann's statement that "the earliest Church[66] regarded itself as the Congregation of the end of days"[67] remains overwhelmingly probable. Almost everything we known about early Christianity brands it as an eschatological movement. In addition to the features Borg highlights, we know, for instance, that many early Christians constructed their theology out of the Jewish Bible, in which they found prophecies that had come to pass in their midst.[68] This focus upon fulfillment, with its close parallel in the scrolls from Qumran, necessarily reflects their conviction that "the ends of the ages have come" (1 Cor 10:11). We also know that early Christianity witnessed a missionary explosion. Here too eschatology offers itself as at least partial explanation. For the apocalyptic expectations of the few often encourage the proselytization of the many; this is how large millenarian movements are sometimes so quickly produced. Certainly the New Testament itself joins es-

63. Gershom Scholem, *The Messianic Idea in Judaism and Other Essays on Jewish Spirituality* (New York: Schocken, 1971), p. 19.

64. Compare Peter Worsley's remarks regarding millenarian movements: *The Trumpet Shall Sound*, pp. 243–54. According to Annemarie de Waal Malefijt, *Religion and Culture* (New York: Macmillan, 1968), p. 331, "If it is true that millenarian movements expect a better future in this world, it follows that dissatisfaction with existing conditions will favor the rise of such movements."

65. See further Victor Turner, *The Ritual Process: Structure and Anti-Structure* (Ithaca: Cornell University Press, 1969), pp. 111–12, 153–54, and John J. Gager, *Kingdom and Community: The Social World of Early Christianity* (Englewood Cliffs: Prentice-Hall, 1975), pp. 32–36.

66. I take him to be writing of the Palestinian community in the 30s.

67. *Theology of the New Testament*, vol. 1 (New York: Charles Scribner & Sons, 1951), p. 37.

68. C. H. Dodd, *According to the Scriptures: The Sub-structure of New Testament Theology* (London: Fontana, 1965); Donald Juel, *Messianic Exegesis: Christological Interpretation of the Old Testament in Early Christianity* (Philadelphia: Fortress, 1988).

chatology and mission (Mk 13:10).[69] Again, soon after Easter, Christians acknowledged Jesus to be the "Messiah." They did not, as far as we know, confess, "Jesus is a sage" or "Jesus is a wise teacher." Their fundamental christological confession had eschatological content: the Messiah had come—a belief that entailed that the consummation was unfolding.

There is also the further fact that many if not all of the early Christians practiced baptism. Why? And what did the rite mean? Surely Bultmann was right again: "The meaning of baptism can hardly have been different from that of John's baptism, which Jesus and his first 'disciples' had received. That is, baptism in conjunction with repentance was a bath of purification (closely connected with repentance) for the coming Reign of God. . . ."[70]

Weighing next Borg's comment that early Christians expected the return of Jesus, something Jesus himself did not expect, one may grant that Jesus did not predict his resurrection followed by an interim period followed by his *parousia*. But can we dismiss the possibility that belief in Jesus' return grew out of the post-Easter identification of Jesus with the Son of man, about whom Jesus himself spoke as though he were another, preexistent figure?[71] And, to entertain another possibility, are the odds

69. See Oscar Cullmann, "Eschatology and Missions in the New Testament," in *The Background of the New Testament and Its Eschatology*, ed. W. D. Davies and D. Daube (Cambridge: Cambridge University Press, 1964), pp. 409–21; also Gager, *Kingdom and Community*, pp. 37–49 (although his focus upon cognitive dissonance does not, as far as I can see, explain the missionary activities of John the Baptist and the historical Jesus), and Johannes Munck, *Paul and the Salvation of Mankind* (London: SCM, 1959). For more general observations see Reinaldo L. Román, "Christian Themes: Mainstream Traditions and Millenarian Violence," in *Millennialism and Violence*, ed. Michael Barkun (London: Frank Cass, 1996), pp. 72–75. For concrete instances of the close connection that can obtain between evangelism and eschatological expectation, see John Carey, "Saint Patrick, the Druids, and the End of the World," *History of Religions* 36 (1996), pp. 42–53; Bernard McGinn, "The End of the World and the Beginning of Christendom," in *Apocalypse Theory and the Ends of the World*, ed. Malcolm Bull (Oxford: Blackwell, 1995), pp. 66–70; Marco A. Navarro-Génie, "Failed Prophecy and Revolutionary Violence: The Case of Augusto C. Sandino," Online. 30 June 1997. Available, URL: http://www.pagusmundi.com/sandino/failed.htm; Hue-Tam Ho Tai, *Millenarianism and Peasant Politics in Vietnam* (Cambridge: Harvard University Press, 1983), p. 18; and E. Zücher, "'Prince Moonlight': Messianism and Eschatology in Early Medieval Chinese Buddhism," *T'oung Pao* 68 (1982), pp. 52, 54.

70. Bultmann, *Theology*, vol. 1, p. 39. See further Adela Yarbro Collins, *Cosmology and Eschatology in Jewish and Christian Apocalypticism*, JSJS 50 (Leiden: E. J. Brill, 1996), pp. 213–38.

71. See Adela Yarbro Collins, "The Apocalyptic Son of Man Sayings," in *The Future of Early Christianity*, ed. Birger A. Pearson (Minneapolis: Fortress, 1991), pp. 220–28.

really so staggeringly high against the thought that Jesus, as Joachim Jeremias argued, anticipated eschatological vindication, which he sometimes associated with resurrection and other times with the imagery of Dan 7:14, and that the post-Easter church introduced the necessary adjustments in the light of its faith in the resurrection?[72] The point is simply that one can, and many have, envisage scenarios in which Jesus did not exactly speak of his own return as the Son of man and yet said things that later encouraged belief in his *parousia*. Certainly it is obvious that even if he never said, "I will come again," Jesus could still have been an eschatological or millenarian prophet.

Perhaps the most telling fact against Borg's reconstruction is the primitive preaching of Jesus' resurrection, whose import I have briefly considered in chapter 1. Borg himself concedes that resurrection is an eschatological concept. So one must ask him why some early followers of Jesus, in the aftermath of his ministry, interpreted his vindication in eschatological terms. Borg suggests that belief in the return of Jesus soon followed from belief in the resurrection. What, however, effected belief in the resurrection? "God raised Jesus from the dead" is an interpretive statement. What is the satisfactory explanation for it if the earliest Christians did not come to their Easter experiences already filled with eschatological expectations? Put otherwise, and to revert to the earlier discussion, when were those expectations fashioned, if not before the close of Jesus' earthly tenure?[73] Hans Conzelmann once made this appropriate generalization: "Continuity is in itself historically more probable than the assertion of a discontinuity that can scarcely explain the origin of the categories of expression for the community's faith."[74]

The earliest Christians must have owed a considerable debt to Jesus of Nazareth. While his death and resurrection together required the rethinking of much, they surely did not require the rethinking of everything. And, since we cannot avoid supposing that the earliest post-Easter leaders had been followers of the pre-Easter Jesus, we have to do with a sociological continuity that must have involved ideological continuity. The circumstance is corroborated by the wholly justified habit of historians of

---

72. Joachim Jeremias, "Eine neue Schau der Zukunftsaussagen Jesu," *Theologischer Blätter* 20 (1941), pp. 216–22. Compare C. K. Barrett, *Jesus and the Gospel Tradition* (London: SPCK, 1967), pp. 77–86, and Ben F. Meyer, *The Aims of Jesus* (London: SCM, 1979), pp. 202–209.

73. Compare Walter Schmithals, "Jesus und die Apokalyptik," in *Jesus Christus in Historie und Theologie*, ed. Georg Strecker (Tübingen: Mohr-Siebeck, 1975), pp. 67–68.

74. Hans Conzelmann, "Present and Future in the Synoptic Tradition," *Journal for Theology and the Church* 5 (1968), p. 29.

explaining a host of particulars about early Christianity by referring to Jesus. Why did Christians oppose divorce? Why did they so often call God "Father"? Why were they so little concerned with the details of Pharisaic halakah? Why did they exhibit a strong missionary impulse? Why did they stress the imperative to love others? Why did they abandon the common belief that descent from Abraham and the keeping of Torah were necessary and sufficient for salvation? The same answer is usually returned to all of these questions as well as to many others: in these particulars the church was following Jesus. So to contend, as E. P. Sanders does, that Jesus was an eschatological prophet and that the early church expected history's culmination in the near future, is simply to offer the same answer— the church was following Jesus—to one more question: why did the primitive community have such a strong eschatological orientation?

The Case against Marcus Borg

The result of our several observations is that Borg's criticisms of Sanders are far from fatal: they do not erase our image of Jesus as an eschatological prophet. What then of Borg's positive case for an alternative Jesus, for envisaging Jesus as a noneschatological, aphoristic sage?

Wisdom. Borg urges that wisdom is central to the Jesus tradition, that Jesus was a teacher of subversive wisdom, that Jesus' words reflect a "mentality deeply aware of the conventions that dominate people's lives, animating, preoccupying, and ensnaring them," and that the combination of literal eschatology and world-subversive wisdom is "possible" but "improbable."[75] This seems to be a version of the so-called criterion of coherence or consistency. He adds:

> In making this judgment, I am of course making a judgment about what is a possible or probable combination in a first-century Jewish mind. We have often been rightly cautioned about presuming what is possible or probable for a person to think in a time and place so far removed from us. But scholars who take the opposite point of view— that such a combination is possible or probable—are involved in the same kind of judgment. Such judgments seem unavoidable when one moves beyond collecting and analyzing data to imaging a sense of the whole.[76]

75. Borg, *Jesus in Contemporary Scholarship*, pp. 82–83.
76. Ibid., p. 83. This is a new variant of the old complaint that, as Jesus' moral instruction does not harmonize with apocalyptic eschatology, there must be something wrong with the idea that he advanced or was heavily influenced by an apocalyptic eschatology. See

Borg rightly cautions us about our ability to decide what sorts of con-tradictions could exist within an ancient mind, and that we are nonethe-less forced to decide just this. But here Borg makes the wrong decision. Why can we not think that Jesus' subversive wisdom and the threat of im-minent judgment went hand in hand because they functioned similarly, namely, to deny the validity of the status quo? More importantly, Borg does not cite a single wisdom saying to establish his point but rather ex-presses a general impression and draws a sweeping inference. Is this be-cause there is no one logion that is obviously or even implicitly at odds with an eschatological orientation?

Even if such a saying did exist, what would it mean? Anyone can walk into a so-called Christian bookstore and find shelves of books announc-ing that the end is near. The very same bookstore will also feature books concerned with long-term issues, such as what the future holds for our children. Not only are such books found in one place and often read by the same people, but, strange as it may seem, some of each come from the same publishers and even the same authors.[77] This appears irrational to those of us in the academy, but the real world does not submit to reason. The Lubavitcher Rebbe, Menachem Schneerson, was announcing the im-minence of the Messiah's coming while simultaneously denouncing Pales-tinian autonomy because it would eventually lead to a Palestinian state.[78]

---

already Francis Greenwood Peabody, "New Testament Eschatology and New Testament Ethics," in *Transactions of the Third International Congress for the History of Religions*, 2 vols. (Oxford: Clarendon, 1907), vol. 2, pp. 305–12. But the complaint, which regularly in-volves a misunderstanding of Albert Schweitzer's position, is without merit; see Richard H. Hiers, *Jesus and the Future* (Atlanta: John Knox, 1981), pp. 50–61. Also relevant is D. S. Russell, *The Method and Message of Jewish Apocalyptic* (London: SCM, 1964), pp. 100–103, and the literature cited there.

77. One may refer to the books of the well-known American TV evangelist Pat Robert-son. See further Timothy Weber, *Living in the Shadow of the Second Coming: American Premillennialism, 1875–1982*, rev. ed. (Chicago: University of Chicago Press, 1987).

78. Marcus, "Modern and Ancient Jewish Apocalypticism," p. 19, n. 82. For another example of what seems to us a blatant contradiction in the use of eschatological language see Garry Trompf, "The Cargo and the Millennium on Both Sides of the Pacific," in *Cargo Cults and Millenarian Movements: Transoceanic Comparisons of New Religious Move-ments*, ed. G. W. Trompf (Berlin: Mouton de Gruyter, 1990), pp. 49–52: the modern Cali-fornian sectarians gathered around Norman Paulsen have believed the second coming of Jesus to be an inner reality, and yet they have simultaneously expected it to come after a fu-ture catastrophe. On p. 61 Trompf offers that "if one hopes for a radically better cosmos in the future it is not illogical to be found trying to create the best one can out of the present one; if one dreams that the future holds eventual (and thus including material, this-worldly) blessing, then taking steps practically expressive of one's dreams' realization can be seen as premonitorily. . .appropriate."

The seeming contradiction between near expectation and long-term perspective or a "mentality deeply aware of the conventions that dominate people's lives" does not just characterize contemporary Christian fundamentalists or modern orthodox Jews looking for the Messiah. The sources that Borg excavates—Q, Mark, Matthew, Luke—all contain the very same incongruity. Why could the writers of these books tolerate a tension that Jesus could not? Does Borg think that Jesus must have been more consistent than the tradents of the tradition, or more reasonable than others who have preached a near end, or more rational than Christians and Jews of today? Again, can we not find related tensions in the authentic Paulines, in James, in the *Didache*, and in the *Testaments of the Twelve Patriarchs*—and later in Mohammed, St. Francis, and Martin Luther?

We are in truth here dealing not with something exceptional but with something typical: eschatological thinking is not (maybe about this Albert Schweitzer was wrong) *Konsequent* or consistent about anything.[79] Jesus the first-century eschatological prophet was not a systematic thinker akin to Aristotle. His parables, warnings, and imperatives appealed first to religious devotion and feeling, not to the intellect. And his poetic mind roamed in a mythological world closely related to that of the Dead Sea Scrolls, a world alive with fabulous stories such as those in *Ahikar* and fantastic images such as those in Daniel.[80] That world did not celebrate logical consistency as a virtue.

The Son of man. Borg stresses the importance of the Son of man sayings in modern scholarship for establishing the eschatological character of Jesus' message. He also emphasizes that recent study has tended to doubt that any of the "apocalyptic Son of man" sayings go back to Jesus. In reply it may be said that some important scholars remain convinced that Jesus himself composed at least a few of those sayings,[81] and further

79. On this see Rudolf Otto, *The Kingdom of God and the Son of Man*, rev. ed. (London: Lutterworth, 1943), pp. 62–63, and C. C. McCown, "The Eschatology of Jesus Reconsidered," *JR* 16 (1936), pp. 30–46.

80. Suggestive here are the brief remarks of Charles W. Jones, "The Millennial Dream as Poetry," in *Millennial Dreams in Action: Studies in Revolutionary Religious Movements*, ed. Sylvian L. Thrupp (New York: Schocken, 1970), pp. 208–209. One guesses that Jesus' success as a teacher was partly due to his ability to create speech that was, in Jones' words, "poetically satisfying."

81. According to Borg, *Jesus in Contemporary Scholarship*, p. 8, since the late 60s it has become "increasingly accepted that the coming Son of Man sayings were not authentic." But in order to be fair it should be added that there is hardly here a consensus. Those who still believe that Jesus spoke of the coming Son of man include Becker, *Jesus von Nazaret*, pp. 249–67; David R. Catchpole, "The Angelic Son of Man in Luke 12:8," *NovT* 24

that the case for Jesus' status as eschatological prophet has been made quite apart from verdicts about the place of the Son of man in the teaching of Jesus.[82]

Borg supports his dismissal of the "apocalyptic Son of man" sayings by appealing to Crossan's analysis of them.[83] Crossan finds that the Jesus tradition contains eighteen complexes in which the "apocalyptic Son of Man" appears. Six of these complexes have plural attestation, but in none of them is the phrase, "(the) Son of man," itself plurally attested. Borg infers: "the phrase 'Son of man' in an apocalyptic context is not firmly grounded in the earliest layers of the tradition," which is consistent with the supposition that the coming Son of man sayings do not go back to Jesus.[84]

Is this so? One can do anything with statistics, and perhaps, in the present instance, the desire to cast suspicion upon the "apocalyptic Son of man" sayings has led to reading the evidence in a way that makes it corroborate that initial suspicion. Certainly the evidence can be read in another way. Crossan's eighteen complexes are as follows:

First stratum (30–60 C.E.)

1. Jesus' apocalyptic return, attested in 1 Thess 4:13–18; *Did.* 16: 6–8; Mt 24:30a (M); Mk 13:24–27 = Mt 24:29, 30b-31 = Lk 21: 25–38; Rev 1:7, 13; 14:14; Jn 19:37. "The Son of man" appears only in Mk 13:24–27 par.[85]

. 2. Before the angels, attested in Lk 12:8–9 = Mt 10:32–33; *2 Clem.* 3:2; Mk 8:38 = Mt 16:27 = Lk 9:26; Rev 3:5; 2 Tim 2:12b. "The Son of man" appears only in Mk 8:38 par. (but see below).

3. Knowing the danger, attested in 1 Thess 5:2; 2 Pet 3:10; *Gos. Thom.* 21:3; *Gos. Thom.* 103; Lk 12:39–40 = Mt 24:43–44; Rev 3: 3b; 16:15a. "The Son of man" appears only in Lk 12:39–40 par. (Q).

4. Revealed to James, attested in 1 Cor 15:7a; *Gos. Thom.* 12; *Gos. Heb.* 7.

5. Request for a sign, attested in Lk 11:29–30 = Mt 12:38–40; Mt

---

(1982), pp. 255–65; John Collins, "The Second Coming," *Chicago Studies* 34 (1995), pp. 262–74; Adela Yarbro Collins, "Apocalyptic Son of Man Sayings"; V. Hampel, *Menschensohn und historischer Jesu* (Neukirchen-Vluyn: Neukirchener, 1990); Luz, *Matthäus*, vol. 1, p. 124; Marius Reiser, *Jesus and Judgment* (Minneapolis: Fortress, 1997); and E. P. Sanders, *The Historical Figure of Jesus* (London: Penguin, 1993), pp. 247–48.

82. See my article, "A Plea for thoroughgoing Eschatology," *JBL* 113 (1994), pp. 651–68.

83. Borg, *Jesus in Contemporary Scholarhsip*, pp. 84–86. See Crossan, *Jesus*, pp. 238–55, 454–56.

84. Borg, *Jesus in Contemporary Scholarship*, p. 85.

85. But since Mt 24:30a ("then will appear the sign of the Son of man in heaven") is listed as independent of Mark, might we not have here plural attestation of "Son of man"?

16:4a; *Gos. Naz.* 11; Mk 8:11–13 = Mt 16:1, 4b = Lk 11:16. "The Son of man" is attested only in Lk 11:29–30 par. (Q).

6. On twelve thrones, attested in Lk 22:28–30 = Mt 19:28 (Q, but "the Son of man" appears only in Matthew).

7. As with lightning, attested in Lk 17:24 = Mt 24:27 (Q).

8. As with Noah, attested in Lk 17:26–27 = Mt 24:37–39a (Q).

9. As with Lot, attested in Lk 17:28–30 = Mt 24:39b (Q).

Second stratum (60–80 C.E.)

10. The unknown time, attested in Mk 13:33–37; Mt 24:42; 25:13; Lk 12:35–38; 21:34–36; *Did.* 16:1 ("the Son of man" appears only in Lk 21:34–36).

11. Some standing here, attested in Mk 9:1 = Mt 16:28 = Lk 9:27.

12. Priest's question, attested in Mk 14:53, 60–65 = Mt 26:57, 62–68 = Lk 22:54a, 63–71.

Third stratum (80–120 C.E.)

13. Planted weeds explained, attested in Mt 13:36–43a.

14. Cities of Israel, attested in Mt 10:23.

15. The last judgment, attested in Mt 25:31.

16. Days are coming, attested in Lk 17:22.

17. The unjust judge, attested in Lk 18:1–8.

Fourth stratum (120–150 C.E.)

18. The heavens opened, attested in Acts 7:55–56.

We know from what Matthew and Luke have done to Mark that "the Son of man" was both added to and subtracted from the tradition. Mt 16:21 omits the title from Mk 8:31 just as Lk 22:22b drops it from Mk 14:21b. But Mt 16:13 and 28 feature redactional additions to Mark, and Lk 22:48 inserts the phrase into Mk 14:45. All this is not surprising, for a similar fluctuation appears with the other Christological titles.[86] We also know that, for whatever reason, early Christian epistles never refer to Jesus as "the Son of man," so its absence from 1 Thess 4:13–18 (complex 1), 2 Tim 2:12b (complex 2), and 1 Thess 5:2 (complex 3) presumably tells us little or nothing about those complexes in particular; we rather have to do here with a global epistolary phenomenon, whatever its explanation.[87] Thus our question is not whether "the Son of man" is

---

86. E.g., Matthew adds "Son of God" to Mk 15:30 and 32 (see Mt 27:40, 43) whereas Luke omits it from Mk 15:39 (see Lk 22:47); Matthew adds "Lord" to Mk 1:40 (see Mt 8:2) whereas Luke omits it from Mk 5:19 (see Lk 8:39); Matthew adds "Christ" to Mk 8:30 and 15:9 (see Mt 16:20; 27:17) but omits it from Mk 9:41 (see Mt 10:42).

87. Was the title avoided because, outside a Jewish milieu, it could only be understood as referring to the humanity of Jesus (compare the patristic interpretation from Ignatius, *Eph.* 20:2, on)? Or do we conclude that the expression was never confessional and so was confined to the Jesus tradition, where Jesus' habit of speaking was remembered?

consistently attested in a particular complex but how often it appears, to the best of our ability, to be attested in the earliest source for or version of that complex. Crossan himself admits that in his complex 5. Request for a Sign, the use of "the Son of man" in Q is earlier than its absence from Mark.[88] Others have argued the same for other complexes.[89]

Crossan's claim that the "apocalyptic Son of man" is never independently attested in more than one source within his six plurally attested complexes can be queried. For it is true only if one believes that Mt 10:32–33 (which does not have "the Son of man") more or less reproduces Q. For the Lukan parallel, Lk 12:8–9 ("the Son of man also will acknowledge"), indeed has the expression, and many have forwarded robust reasons for surmising that the use of "the Son of man" in Lk 12:8–9 comes from Q, not from Luke under Markan influence.[90]

Aside from this difficulty, if, as Borg thinks, the lack of plural attestation for the "apocalyptic Son of man" in any of Crossan's complexes really means that the expression is not firmly grounded in the earliest tradition, is Borg equally prepared to jettison the so-called earthly Son of man sayings from the earliest stage? The problem here is that, of Crossan's ten "earthly Son of man" complexes, only one features plural attestation (Q 9:58//Gos. Thom. 86). Crossan nonetheless considers at least five of these to be authentic. Surely, however, one must be consistent. Either the lack of plural attestation means something or it does not. If one thinks it does and thus refrains, for this reason, from tracing any of the "apocalyptic Son of man sayings" to Jesus, does not consistency demand that we likewise deny that Jesus spoke (except maybe once) of the "earthly Son of man"? If, on the other hand, the lack of plural attestation is not a sound argument, then Borg's sally is feeble.

88. Crossan, Jesus, pp. 251–53.

89. See especially Frederick Houk Borsch, The Christian and Gnostic Son of Man, SBT 2/14 (London: SCM, 1970), pp. 8–27. In this he argues, against Joachim Jeremias, "Die älteste Schicht der Menschensohn-Logien," ZNW 58 (1967), pp. 159–72, that when a tradition is attested with and without "the Son of man," the version with the expression is usually earlier.

90. A. J. B. Higgins, "'Menschensohn' oder 'ich' in Q: Lk 12,8-9/Mt 10,32–33?" in Jesus und der Menschensohn, ed. Rudolf Pesch and Rudolf Schnackenburg (Freiburg: Herder, 1975), pp. 117–23; Henk Jan de Jonge, "The Sayings on Confessing and Denying Jesus in Q 12:8–9 and Mark 8:38," in Sayings of Jesus: Canonical and Non-Canonical: Essays in Honour of Tjitze Baarda, ed. William L. Petersen, Johan S. Vos, and Henk J. de Jonge, NovTSup 89 (Leiden: Brill, 1997), pp. 105–21; Rudolf Pesch, "Über die Autorität Jesu: Eine Rückfrage anhand des Bekenner- und Verleugnerspruchs Lk 12,8f par.," in Die Kirche des Anfangs, ed. Rudolf Schnackenburg, Josef Ernst, and Joachim Wanke (Freiburg: Herder, 1978), pp. 25–55; Anton Vögtle, Die "Gretchenfrage" des Menschensohnproblems, QD 152 (Freiburg: Herder, 1994), pp. 14–21. See also the tradition-history suggested on pp. 28–29 herein.

As Crossan himself notes, there are complexes wherein only one unit has "the Son of man" but other units allude to Dan 7:13. For example, if Mk 13:24–27 refers to Jesus as the Son of man coming on the clouds of heaven, the parallel in 1 Thess 4:13–18 uses the phrase "in the clouds" (compare Dan 7:13) with reference to the *parousia*.[91] So too Rev 1:7 (compare 1:13; 14:14).[92] Crossan takes this to imply that the employment of imagery from Dan 7:13 eventually led to the titular use of "the Son of man." But one could just as plausibly surmise that Dan 7:13 and "the Son of man" were firmly associated with complex 1 from its inception. The absence of "the Son of man" in 1 Thess 4:13–18 and its replacement with "Lord" might then be put down to (1) Paul's failure ever to use "the Son of man" and (2) the apostle's habitual use of "Lord" for Jesus.[93]

Fully half of Crossan's "apocalyptic Son of man" sayings are from his first stratum. Only one is from the latest. Furthermore, five or six instances come from Q. So the chief impression of Crossan's display of the data is that the farther from the beginning we get, the fewer the texts about the apocalyptic Son of man. This is consistent with—although admittedly it does not prove—the hypothesis that speech about the "apocalyptic Son of man" goes back to Jesus himself.

In the end Crossan's data scarcely establish that Jesus did not compose any "apocalyptic Son of man" sayings. Crossan has to go beyond his statistics and insist that contributors to both the Q tradition and Mark independently added the expression to received materials; that is, he has to reconstruct tradition histories, which are always fragile things. But is the common independent creation of "apocalyptic Son of man" sayings obviously more credible than the supposition that such sayings are independently attested in Mark and Q because they were there at the tradition's nativity, with Jesus himself?

This is not the place to enter further into discussion of this mired topic, and my immediate purpose is not to sway readers that they should accept (as I do) the authenticity of one or more of the "apocalyptic Son of man sayings." I wish merely to emphasize that Borg's appeal to Crossan's sta-

---

91. Despite Maurice Casey, *Son of Man: The Interpretation and Influence of Daniel 7* (London: SPCK, 1979), pp. 153–54, most commentators have related 1 Thess 4:17 to Dan 7:13. Compare B. Rigaux, *Les Épitres aux Thessaloniciens*, EB (Paris: J. Gabalda, 1956), pp. 546–47.

92. See Adela Yarbro Collins, *Cosmology and Eschatology*, pp. 159–97.

93. Compare Sanders, *Historical Figure*, p. 182: "After Jesus' death and resurrection, the early Christians concluded that his references to the coming of the Son of Man were a cryptic way of saying that he himself would return, and accordingly they changed 'the Son of man will come' to 'the Lord will come (or return).'"

tistics does not settle anything one way or the other, and, further, that the discussion about the "apocalyptic Son of man" is not closed. On this matter we may pontificate only that there can be no pontification.

Kingdom of God. Borg emphasizes that only some sayings about the kingdom speak of its coming as imminent. He also contends, probably rightly, that Mark's Gospel has greatly influenced how modern scholarship has appraised these sayings. Mk 1:15 and 9:1 imply that the end is near, and Mark 13 contains a "little apocalypse." Borg, however, contends that Mk 1:15, which is now often seen as redactional, tells us about Mark, not Jesus,[94] and it is "of a piece" with 9:1 and chapter 13. So we have in all this material the reflection of Mark's theology: "The author of Mark, writing around the year 70, thought that the eschaton was imminent."[95] Mark "may represent an intensification of eschatological expectation triggered by the Jewish war of rebellion against Rome in the years 66–70, and the threat (and actuality) of the temple's destruction that those years brought."[96] Borg goes on to ask some questions:

> Without Mark 1:15, would we think of the kingdom of God as *the* central theme of Jesus' message? We would see it as *a* central theme, yes; but as *the* central theme? And without Mark 1:15 and 9:1, would we think of imminence as central to Jesus' teaching about the kingdom? And, more broadly, without the coming Son of man sayings and without Mark's reading of the kingdom, would we think of the heart of Jesus' message as the need for repentance because the eschaton was imminent?[97]

My own judgment is that we should, notwithstanding Borg's inclination, return a hearty "yes" to each of his queries. Would we, without Mk 1:15, think of the kingdom of God as the central theme of Jesus' message? Yes, because (1) "kingdom of God" runs throughout every source and stage of the Jesus tradition, including the earliest, Q,[98] (2) the Q missionary discourse makes the kingdom the sole theme of the disciples' proclamation (Q 10:9), and (3) the tradition says explicitly that the subject of Jesus' parables is the kingdom.[99] Would we, without Mk 1:15 and 9:1,

94. But even if Mk 1:15 is redactional, it remains that Mark thought it an appropriate summary of the message of Jesus as he knew it in his tradition.

95. Borg, *Jesus in Contemporary Scholarship*, p. 87. This appears to be a retraction of his earlier judgment: "Mark's programmatic advance summary of the ministry of Jesus" is "likely to be an authentic saying of Jesus" (*Conflict, Holiness and Politics*, pp. 257–58).

96. *Jesus in Contemporary Scholarship*, p. 87. Compare Marcus (see n. 53).

97. Ibid., p. 87.

98. It appears at least ten times in the text of the International Q Project.

99. See, e.g., Q 13:18–21; 14:16 (?); Mk 4:30; Mt 13:24, 47; 18:23; 22:2; *Gos. Thom.* 57.

think of imminence as central to the logia about the kingdom? Yes, because (1) Mk 1:15 and 9:1 are not the only kingdom sayings that can be given the sense of imminence,[100] (2) imminence appears in other parts of the tradition,[101] and (3) Jewish texts hope for the imminent arrival of the kingdom.[102] Finally, would we, without the Son of man sayings and Mark's "reading of the kingdom," believe that, at the heart of Jesus' message, was the need for repentance in the face of the world's sunset? Yes, because (1) "repent" and "repentance" appear outside of Mark,[103] (2) the Jesus tradition is full of moral imperatives that demand change in behavior, that is, in the broad sense of the word, "repentance,"[104] and (3) Jesus acclaimed John the Baptist, whose central demand was seemingly repentance in the face of imminent judgment.[105]

Having declined to interpret "kingdom" within the context of imminent eschatological expectation, Borg suggests that kingdom language has the following "resonances or nuances of meaning."[106] The kingdom is associated sometimes with (1) God's power, other times with (2) God's presence, and other times with (3) life under God's kingship. Sometimes

100. See, e.g., Q 10:9, and on this the still useful discussions of Kenneth W. Clark, "'Realized Eschatology,'" *JBL* 59 (1940), pp. 367–83, and R. H. Fuller, *The Mission and Achievement of Jesus*, SBT 1/12 (London: SCM, 1954), pp. 20–25. Lk 19:11 plainly says that the disciples themselves "supposed that the kingdom of God was to appear immediately," and many exegetes have also found imminence in Q 11:2 (the Lord's Prayer) and in Mk 14:25 (which can be taken to mean that "the next Feast will be the Messianic Feast"; so F. C. Burkitt, "The Parable of the Wicked Husbandmen," in *Transactions of the Third International Congress for the History of Religions*, vol. 2, p. 326; compare Barry S. Crawford, "Near Expectation in the Sayings of Jesus," *JBL* 101 [1982], p. 234: "a bold declaration that the Kingdom is imminent").

101. E.g., Q 11:50–51 (the blood of all the prophets will be required of "this generation"); 12:39–40 (the thief in the night); Mt 10:23 ("you will not have gone through all the towns of Israel before the Son of man comes"); and Lk 18:1–8 (the parable of the unjust judge, who does not delay but quickly grants justice).

102. See, e.g., *T. Mos.* 10:1 ("his [God's] kingdom shall appear throughout his creation" follows a historical review which ends in the reader's present) and the Kaddish Prayer ("May he establish his kingdom in your lifetime and in your days, and in the lifetime of the whole house of Israel, speedily and at a near time"). The Qumran texts which speak of a future kingdom (e.g., 4Q521 and 1QSb 4:25–26) were presumably composed with the hope of an imminent redemption in view. So too Daniel 7–12.

103. See pp. 102–104 herein.

104. If it were not so, could Mark really have reduced the missionary message of the twelve to "people should repent" (6:12)?

105. Compare Benjamin W. Bacon, "Jewish Eschatology and the Teaching of Jesus," *The Biblical World* 34 (1909), p. 18: "Even if we had not a host of sayings recording Jesus' warnings of impending doom upon Israel, we might be sure from his deep veneration for John the Baptist that he accepted and sympathized with the essence of the Baptist's message, Repent for the Judge is at hand."

106. Borg, *Jesus in Contemporary Scholarship*, p. 87. Compare the related analysis of Sanders, *Jesus and Judaism*, pp. 141–50.

the kingdom is (4) a reality one can be in or out of, other times (5) a political metaphor, yet other times (6) an ideal state.

There is nothing wrong with any of this, which rather represents a helpful sorting of the material. But there is also nothing here to disturb those who identify the kingdom as essentially an eschatological idea. On the contrary, each of Borg's "resonances or nuances" can be readily linked with Jesus' eschatological nostalgia for perfection. Indeed, one can, if so inclined, as I am, subordinate Borg's first five categories to his sixth. If the kingdom is indeed (6) "an ideal state," that is, the eschatological state when God's will is done on earth as in heaven, this would explain why (5) the kingdom is also a political metaphor (when the ideal comes Rome will be gone), why (4) it is something one can be in or out of (some will enter, others will not enter), why (3) it is associated with God's kingship (God will then be universally recognized as king), why (2) it is linked with the divine presence (in the end God will be, as Rom 15:28 puts it, all in all), and, finally, why (1) it is bound up with God's power (the ideal only comes because of God's might and only after a great struggle against evil).

The Case against Stephen Patterson

The millenarian Jesus is, as I read the evidence, none the worse for Borg's critical assault. The brave attempt to take the hill from Sanders and the rest of those bred and faithful to the general results of Weiss and Schweitzer has failed. But Borg is not a solitary voice in the wilderness; he is not the only one calling us to repent of our old eschatological ways. In an article entitled, "The End of Apocalypse: Rethinking the Historical Jesus," [107] Stephen J. Patterson has, like Borg, happily heralded what he calls "the collapse of the apocalyptic hypothesis." He finds four pegs upon which to hang his case that the real Jesus little resembled Schweitzer's Jesus, who should now rest in peace. Since Patterson's arguments add to those of Borg, and since they represent so well and so clearly the opinions of many, I should like, however briefly, to review them in turn.

He begins with Q. Patterson follows John Kloppenborg and those who believe that Q passed through at least two stages, the first of which was a wisdom document focused on Jesus' words. Only at a secondary stage were apocalyptic sayings, including the apocalyptic Son of man sayings, added. As noted already, however, this hypothesis, although popular in

---

107. Stephen J. Patterson, "The End of Apocalypse," *Theology Today* 52 (1995), pp. 29–58.

certain circles, is hardly a firm result of criticism. The number of its adherents is not sufficient to permit us to speak fairly of a consensus as to
how Q came into being or subsequently evolved. There is also the difficulty that even Kloppenborg's Q^1 contains sayings which seem to presuppose the final judgment to be at hand.[108]

But even were we to grant that Kloppenborg has indeed found the
truth, one wants to know why Q^1 should be credited as a more reliable
witness to Jesus than Paul, who assigns the apocalyptic material in 1 Thess
4:15–17 to "the word of the Lord." If Jesus really was not a millenarian
prophet, how can it be that Kloppenborg's Q^2, Paul, and Mark all contain
traditions that make him out to be such? Why does not Patterson entertain the possibility that the witness of Kloppenborg's Q^1 is tendentious
and less helpful than the combined testimony of three other early witnesses? Recently Kloppenborg himself has remarked that items belonging
only to his Q^2, including the pronouncements of judgment, may well have
been known to the community even at his Q^1 stage and could even go
back to Jesus, for "one must presume a basic continuity in eschatological
outlook between Q^1 and Q^2 in spite of the changes in idiom." [109]

Perhaps Patterson follows another course because of the *Gospel of
Thomas*, which supplies him with his second strategic strike against
Schweitzer's camp. *Thomas*, although according to Patterson independent of the Synoptics, overlaps with them so that we may speak of a common tradition. But

> there is one element profoundly absent from it [the common tradition]:
> apocalypticism. Most of Thomas's parallels to Q are to Kloppenborg's

108. Q 6:20–23, for instance, which draws upon the prophetic Isaiah 61, contrasts
present misery—the addressees are poor, hungry, and sad—with the future happiness of the
kingdom of God. What else but the last judgment, which brings eschatological reversal, can
here be in mind? For additional examples and discussion see C. M. Tuckett, "A Cynic Q?"
Bib 70 (1989), pp. 349–76; also Helmut Koester, "The Sayings of Q and Their Image of
Jesus," in Petersen, Vos, and de Jonge, *Sayings of Jesus*, pp. 137–54. Koester concludes that
"the image of Jesus that is accessible through the most original version of Q is that of an
eschatological prophet."

109. John Kloppenborg, "The Sayings Gospel Q and the Question of the Historical
Jesus," *HTR* 89 (1996), p. 337. On this subject see further C. M. Tuckett, "On the
Stratification of Q," *Semeia* 55 (1992), pp. 213–22. On p. 214 he writes: "One must remember that theories of different stages in the development of Q concern the growth of a
single body of tradition in Christian history. In distinguishing different layers within Q, one
is not distinguishing two quite separate strands of Christian tradition which never had contact with each other. . . . Rather one is envisaging a process whereby an earlier tradition is
adopted and positively evaluated, so that the older tradition is re-'published,' albeit with further additions and possible redactional alterations. A priori one would therefore expect a
firm measure of continuity between the different levels."

early, wisdom stratum in Q (Q¹). There are a few parallels to sayings from the later apocalyptic stratum (Q²), but where there are parallels to Q², in each case tradition-historical analysis shows that the Q saying has been secondarily "apocalypticized." [110] This is also true of the Thomas-Mark parallels. When Mark's version of a saying or parable is framed to reflect apocalyptic concerns, such framing can without exception be shown to be secondary. [111]

Several assertions are here involved. Not all of them can be fairly evaluated without exploring in detail the credible tradition-histories of various complexes. I shall spare readers the tedium of such an exercise and content myself with three observations:

1. It is no secret that, in Helmut Koester's words, "the *Gospel of Thomas* presupposes, and criticizes, a tradition of the eschatological sayings of Jesus." [112] How then could we expect *Thomas* to contain such sayings or many parallels to Kloppenborg's Q²? The failure of *Thomas* to give us apocalyptic traditions may tell us more about *Thomas* than the early contours of the Jesus tradition. [113]

2. Patterson's claim that sayings in Q or Mark have been secondarily "apocalypticized" is problematic to the extent that the inference depends upon parallels in *Thomas*. For, to repeat, *Thomas* deliberately revised the tradition in order to move away from apocalyptic. To illustrate the point: Patterson seems to be wrong in holding that *Thomas* 16 (a house divided) is more primitive than Q 12:51–53, with its eschatological use of Mic 7:6, [114] or that *Thomas* 103 (the thief) preserves the original nonapocalyptic form of Q 12:39. [115]

3. Why should we confine ourselves to studying the overlaps between *Thomas* and Q or between *Thomas* and Mark? Why not also examine the parallels between Q and Paul, between Q and Mark, between Mark and Paul, between Mark and M, between Mark and L, etc? When this larger

110. See further Patterson's article, "Wisdom in Q and *Thomas*," in *Search of Wisdom: Essays in Memory of John G. Gammie*, ed. Leo G. Perdue, Bernard Brandon Scott, and William Johnston Wiseman (Louisville: Westminster/John Knox, 1993), pp. 187–221.

111. Patterson, "End of Apocalypse," p. 37.

112. Helmut Koester, "Jesus the Victim," *JBL* 111 (1992), p. 7, n. 16.

113. Koester himself, however, in "One Jesus and Four Primitive Gospels," in *Trajectories through Early Christianity*, by James M. Robinson and Helmut Koester (Philadelphia: Fortress, 1971), pp. 169–75, argues to the contrary that *Thomas*'s eschatology is "an interpretation and elaboration of Jesus' most original proclamation." See further Koester's *Ancient Christian Gospels: Their History and Development* (Philadelphia: Trinity Press International, 1990), pp. 86–95.

114. See my article, "Q 12:51–53 and Mk 9:9–13 and the Messianic Woes."

115. Does not Paul's apocalyptic application (1 Thess 5:4) argue for the antiquity of the apocalyptic form?

task is undertaken, we discover that, in our early sources, the apocalyptic tendency appears again and again—in Q, Paul, Mark, M, and L. The exceptions are *Thomas*, which consciously spurns imminent apocalyptic expectation, and Kloppenborg's Q[1], which is a hypothetical reconstruction many of us reject.

The full demonstration of these contentions cannot be undertaken here. But one can appeal to two recent studies of the overlaps between Mark and Q, an article by Benedict T. Viviano[116] and a book by Werner Zager.[117] Both conclude that, to judge by the common traditions in these sources, Jesus had a strong eschatological hope that was bound up with belief in the final judgment, conceived as imminent. Consider also the following overlaps between Paul and the Jesus tradition, which are consistent with the strongly eschatological character of the pre-Pauline tradition:

Paul and Mark

- 1 Cor 11:23–26 and Mk 14:22–25: these two variants of the last supper agree in referring to a (new) covenant—an eschatological concept in Judaism—and refer to the eschatological consummation (1 Cor 11:26; Mk 14:25).
- 1 Thess 4:15–17 and Mk 13:24–27: both passages use the imagery of Dan 7:13–14 to refer to Jesus' eschatological return.

Paul and Q

- 1 Thess 5:13 and Q 12:39: the Lord will come like a thief in the night.[118]
- 1 Thess 2:14–16 and Q 11:47–51: Paul and Q here share a common tradition which associated the killing of the prophets with the persecution of the faithful and link this last to the eschatological judgment that will fall upon the present generation.[119]

---

116. Benedict T. Viviano, "The Historical Jesus in the Doubly Attested Sayings: An Experiment," *RevBib* 103 (1996), pp. 367–410. See especially pp. 406–407.

117. Werner Zager, *Gottesherrschaft und Endgericht in der Verkündigung Jesu: Eine Untersuchung zur markinischen Jesusüberlieferung einschliesslich der Q-Parallelen*, BZNW 82 (Berlin: Walter de Gruyter, 1996).

118. On this parallel see further C.-P. März, "Das Gleichnis vom Dieb: Überlegungen zur Verbindung von Lk 12,39 par Mt 24,43 und 1 Thess 5,2.4," in *The Four Gospels 1992: Festschrift Frans Neirynck*, 3 vols., ed. F. Van Segbroeck et al., BETL 100 (Leuven: University Press, 1992), vol. 1, pp. 633–48. März demonstrates that Paul's use of "night," "watch," and "drunk" in 1 Thess 5:2–6 reveals a knowledge of the eschatological material that in Q surrounded the simile of the thief.

119. See my *The Jesus Tradition in Q* (Valley Forge: Trinity Press International, 1997), pp. 57–60.

Paul and M

- 1 Thess 4:15–17 and Mt 24:30: the *parousia* will be accompanied by the sound of a trumpet.

The early testimony of Paul, so far from adding to Patterson's case, subtracts from it.

What, then, of the parallels between Q and *Thomas*? Patterson inventories these in this way: (1) "There are a number of sayings and parables that have not been recast by the respective hermeneutical tendencies at work in each trajectory (apocalypticism in Q, Gnosticism in *Thomas*)." [120] (2) Some of *Thomas*'s sayings appear in Kloppenborg's Q^2, but if removed from their Q contexts they do not show an apocalyptic understanding of the world.[121] (3) A few of the apocalyptic sayings in Q^2 have a non-apocalyptic form in Thomas.[122] (4) Several sayings with a Gnostic cast in *Thomas* have a non-Gnostic form in Q.[123] (5) Some sayings are apocalyptic in Q and Gnostic in *Thomas*.[124]

What does Patterson infer from this inventory? Among other things he contends that "the apocalypticism of the Q trajectory and the esotericism of the *Thomas* trajectory have had little or no impact" upon the first category, which is the largest.[125] This is said to verify the view that the earliest tradition was neither apocalyptic nor Gnostic. The inference is further bolstered by categories 2–5, which are again said to imply the existence of an early tradition that was only later moved in two different directions, one of them being apocalypticism.

The problem with Patterson's conclusion is simply that it does not follow from the data, which he otherwise helpfully sorts. It is consistent with that data but is not demanded by them. The truth is that Patterson's interesting analysis is no stumbling block for those of us who think that in the earliest tradition Jesus was a millenarian prophet. To show this all one

120. Patterson, "Wisdom in Q and Thomas," p. 194. He cites *Thomas* 6:3//Q 12:2; *Thomas* 14//Q 10:8–9; *Thomas* 20//Q 13:18–19; and twenty-four additional texts.

121. Patterson cites *Thomas* 24//Q 11:33–36 (the eye as lamp); *Thomas* 39//Q 11:52 (the keys of knowledge); *Thomas* 44//Q 12:10 (blaspheme against the Holy Spirit); *Thomas* 46//Q 7:28 (none greater than John); *Thomas* 64//Q 14:15–24 (the great supper); *Thomas* 78//Q 7:24–26 (going out to see John); *Thomas* 89//Q 11:39–41 (washing the outside).

122. *Thomas* 10//Q 12:49 (fire on the earth); *Thomas* 16//Q 12:51–53 (a house divided); *Thomas* 35//Q 11:21–22 (binding the strong man); *Thomas* 41//Q 19:26 (have and receive); *Thomas* 91//Q 12:56 (reading the time); *Thomas* 103//Q 12:39 (the thief).

123. *Thomas* 2; 92//Q 11:9–10 (seek and find); *Thomas* 5//Q 12:2 (hidden and revealed); *Thomas* 69//Q 6:22–23 (blessed are the persecuted); *Thomas* 101//Q 14:26–27.

124. *Thomas* 4//Q 13:30 (first and last); *Thomas* 21//Q 12:39 (the thief); *Thomas* 61//Q 17:34 (one taken, one left); *Thomas* 61//Q 10:22a (revelation of Father to Son).

125. Patterson, "Wisdom in Q and *Thomas*," p. 196.

has to do is to consider an alternative approach to the phenomena as Patterson outlines them.

Category 5 consists of sayings that are apocalyptic in Q but Gnostic in *Thomas*. One can in each of these cases regard *Thomas* as secondary, for if one believes that Christianity began as a messianic movement and only later gained Gnostic devotees, presumption will naturally favor the Q form over *Thomas*. Category 4, with sayings that are Gnostic in *Thomas* but not Q, is subject to the same appraisal. This is all the more true because *Thomas* has doublets in this category: the sayings that are Gnostic in *Thomas* but not Gnostic in Q also have non-Gnostic forms in *Thomas*. This has been thought to imply the use of a written non-Gnostic source.[126] Q, on the other hand, does not have nonapocalyptic doublets to its apocalyptic complexes.

As for category 3, sayings that are apocalyptic in Q but not *Thomas*, once more a ready explanation is that *Thomas* consistently lacks the apocalyptic cast because of its later theological tendencies, which eclipsed the apocalyptic orientation of the original tradition, still preserved in Q. This analysis, moreover, is consistent with the circumstance that some of these sayings are attested within an apocalyptic context outside of *Thomas* and Q.[127]

Category 2 consists of materials that have an apocalyptic cast in Q (but not *Thomas*) only by virtue of their present context. But surely this does not establish that they once had a nonapocalyptic cast. Maybe the way they are construed in Q is how they were construed before Q. Certainly Patterson has not demonstrated the contrary.

Finally, concerning Patterson's first category—units that show neither an apocalyptic nor Gnostic orientation—many modern exegetes have found in some of these units, when considered in isolation, an intense eschatological expectation.[128] It is, moreover, no objection to a millenarian Jesus that some sayings in the tradition neither explicitly nor implicitly pertain to eschatology. Holy men were, in Jesus' era, expected to be versatile, to be able to do many things and address multiple concerns.[129]

---

126. Compare G. Quispel, review of Bentley Layton, ed., *Nag Hammadi Codex II, 2–7* (Leiden: E. J. Brill, 1989), in *VC* 45 (1991), p. 84.

127. *Thomas* 103//Q12:39//1 Thess 5:2//Rev 3:3; 16:15 (the thief); *Thomas* 35//Q 11:21-22//Mk 3:27 (binding the strong man); *Thomas* 41//Q 19:26//Mk 4:25 (have and receive).

128. E.g., Q 6:20–22 (the beatitudes); 10:2 (the harvest); 12:2 (hidden and revealed); 12:33–34 (treasure in heaven); 13:18–19 (the mustard seed), 20–21 (the leaven). See further Tuckett, *Q and the History of Early Christianity*, pp. 139–63.

129. Graham Anderson, *Sage, Saint and Sophist: Holy Men and Their Associates in the Early Roman Empire* (London: Routledge, 1994), pp. 70–72.

That Jesus was an eschatological prophet with an apocalyptic scenario and yet also a teacher of wisdom who sometimes addressed everyday matters cannot startle. One thinks of Paul, who believed that "salvation is nearer to us than when we first believed" (Rom 13:12) and yet could write many things that have no obvious connection with eschatology.

I now pass on to Patterson's third major argument, which is that the students of Bultmann—he names Ernst Käsemann, Philip Vielhauer, and Hans Conzelmann—came, against their teacher's judgment, to reject the authenticity of all the apocalyptic Son of man sayings. Whence, it is implied, we might do well to do likewise. I have already, when discussing Borg, traveled a way down the road of the evidence on this vexed subject and said what needs to be said, which is that, despite the overwhelming volume of pertinent learned literature, any claim here is precarious. We have not reached any assured results. Certainly we have not come to the day when historians of Jesus can bid the Son of man, apocalyptic or not, a fond farewell. So one might do better to find a point of view without entering this titular—or is it nontitular?—quagmire.

Patterson's fourth and final argument against the apocalyptic Jesus has to do with the modern North American discussion of the parables, which he thinks—no doubt correctly—has helped move many away from the traditional consensus. For the notion that Jesus' parables are "language events in which the reign of God becomes a present reality,"[130] a notion that now commends itself to many, need not be associated with an imminent eschatological judgment. Indeed, many think the two things at odds, irreconcilable.

But here everything depends upon one's frame of reference, upon what chapter 1 refers to as one's paradigm. As N. T. Wright remarks, "Scholarly interpretation of the parables tends always—and surely rightly—to be a function of a particular view of Jesus' career (and/or of the nature and purpose of the gospels), rather than a free-standing entity."[131] The history of the interpretation of the parables shows that they are unusually pliable things; they can be poured into various interpretive molds. The church fathers and medieval theologians read them as allegories.[132] Adolf Jülicher took them to be moral lessons.[133] C. H. Dodd construed them in terms of "realized eschatology."[134] Joachim Jeremias readily interpreted

130. Patterson, "End of Apocalypse," p. 41.
131. N. T. Wright, *Jesus and the Victory of God* (Minneapolis: Fortress, 1996), p. 175.
132. S. L. Wailes, *Medieval Allegories of Jesus' Parables* (Berkeley: University of California, 1987).
133. *Die Gleichnisreden Jesu*, 2 vols. (Tübingen: J. C. B. Mohr, 1888, 1899).
134. C. H. Dodd, *The Parables of the Kingdom*, rev. ed. (London: Collins, 1961).

them as expressions of an imminent eschatological expectation.[135] That others have come to still different ways of reading them, including non-eschatological ways, is scarcely astonishing. So would it not be unwise to seek the historical Jesus via one's interpretation of the parables? Should we not, if at all possible, rather interpret the parables in accord with what we have established about Jesus on other grounds? Those of us who accept the eschatological paradigm shared by Schweitzer and Sanders will obviously find much in Jeremias's reading of the parables congenial. Those such as Patterson, who do not accept that paradigm, will naturally prefer to look elsewhere. But that the debate over what sort of eschatology Jesus may or may not have held will be decided by what we make of the parables seems most doubtful.

Some Particulars

When evaluating the proposal, which has held and probably still holds the field, that Jesus was a millenarian prophet, one confronts those who, seemingly eager to consign such a one to an earlier scholarship, say that he was instead an aphoristic sage whose wisdom sayings are inconsistent with an imminent eschatology. If, however, as argued above, the two things can be held together, it is clear what we should think. There are very good grounds to believe that Jesus' proclamation reverberated with eschatological themes. Those who have sought to kindle into a blaze their heap of doubts about an eschatological Jesus have failed to burn up anything. Our excursion among their arguments has revealed that the non-millenarian Jesus is, in the pejorative sense of the term, apocryphal. At the same time, there are—here Borg and Patterson are undeceived—reasons to believe that Jesus was a purveyor of subversive wisdom. So why play down one side of the tradition at the expense of the other, or play the sage against the prophet? Should we not rather decide that Jesus was an eschatological prophet who sometimes expressed himself as an aphoristic sage?

Despite recent disputants to the contrary, Jesus and those who enjoyed his company shared an eschatological vision, one that was not peripheral to what they were all about. It rather permeated their thoughts, reinforced their imperatives, and energized their activities. We can accordingly quit examination of the contentions of Borg and Patterson and advance to ask about the particulars of that vision. The interpolator of Mal 4:5-6 hoped that Elijah would return for a ministry of reconciliation.

135. Joachim Jeremias, *The Parables of Jesus*, 2d rev. ed. (New York: Charles Scribner's Sons, 1971).

The author of the Qumran War Scroll expected to fight in a real Armageddon. Paul thought that the resurrected saints would meet their Lord in the air. What did Jesus expect?

For at least two reasons we can only return very incomplete answers. First, although Jesus lived out of an eschatological hope, he was not, all would agree, a cartographer of future states. According to the extant evidence, eschatology was for him not a subject for recondite curiosity but part of his native religious language, the mythology within which he articulated demand, warning, and consolation. So if we expect to wring from the sources a detailed outline of things to come, that is try to create an apocalpypse according to Jesus, we shall be disappointed.[136] Indeed, perhaps we should ask whether Jesus was like members of the Rodeador millenarian movement in Brazil, who were unable "to express their conception of the new era at all clearly; their hopes and ideas were vague and dreamlike."[137] Did Jesus' thoughts similarly remain undeveloped on certain matters?[138]

Second, we must honor the fact that Jesus always took much for granted. Certain eschatological expectations were, to judge from the literary remains, widespread in the first century.[139] So he could communicate with his contemporaries by alluding to those expectations, or to the well-known texts that supported them. In other words, there was little need to spell out the minutiae of an eschatological scenario, for he shared so much with so many of his contemporaries. When he spoke about the resurrection, for instance, he had no need to tell people what it was, just

136. The lack of detail in Jesus' eschatological prophecies partly explains why some scholars resist associating him with the eschatology of the major Jewish apocalypses—*1 Enoch, 4 Ezra, 2 Baruch*. The latter show speculative interests foreign to the Jesus tradition.

137. René Ribeiro, "Brazilian Messianic Movements," in Millennial *Dreams in Action: Studies in Revolutionary Religious Movements*, ed. Sylvia L. Thrupp (New York: Schocken, 1970), p. 66. Similarly, B. R. Wilson, *Sects and Society: A Sociological Study of the Elim Tabernacle, Christian Science, and the Christadelphians* (Berkeley: University of California Press, 1961), p. 318, says that "the Elimite has, usually, only a vague and general idea of what things shall come to pass, and the details are of little moment. . . ."

138. Compare Christoph Burchard, "Jesus of Nazareth," in *Christian Beginnings: Word and Community from Jesus to Post-Apostolic Times*, ed. Jürgen Becker (Louisville: Westminster/John Knox, 1993), p. 37: "Jesus does not seem to have clarified in detail—perhaps not even to himself—how all of that [his future expectation] was to take place. . . . In general, his contemporaries did not do it either. . . ."

139. Several expectations appear frequently enough to give us a measure of assurance that they were widespread among the people; see the survey in Emil Schürer, *The History of the Jewish People in the Age of Jesus Christ*, vol. 2, rev. and ed. Geza Vermes, Fergus Millar, and Matthew Black (Edinburgh: T. & T. Clark, 1979), pp. 514–54; also E. P. Sanders, *Judaism: Practice and Belief 63 B.C.E.—66 C.E.* (London: SCM, and Philadelphia: Trinity Press International, 1992), pp. 279–303.

as, when he referred to angels, he had no need to explain to his audience what they were. The sayings of Jesus presuppose the eschatological ideas that belonged to Jewish folklore. This means that we should beware of inferring too much from things left unsaid. It also means that we must discover his eschatology primarily by investigating what his sayings presuppose and imply. Such, at any rate, is the task of the remainder of this chapter.

The Final Judgment

As observed in chapter 1, the theme of reversal runs throughout the sayings of Jesus. The following three texts are particularly interesting:

> For all who exalt themselves
>   will be humbled,
> and those who humble themselves
>   will be exalted (Q 14:11; compare Mt 23:12; Lk 18:14)

> Those who try to make their life secure
>   will lose it,
> but those who lose their life
>   will keep it (Q 17:33; compare Mk 8:35)

> Many who are first
>   will be last
> and the last
>   will be first (Mk 10:31; compare Gos. Thom. 4)

Rudolf Bultmann affirmed that "here if anywhere we can find what is characteristic of the preaching of Jesus."[140] Surely he was correct. There is, admittedly, no sign that the early church wrestled with these sayings; nor would it be difficult to concoct a post-Easter setting for them. A sectarian community, feeling itself oppressed, could readily have manufactured words which prophesy its vindication and foretell its opponents' loss of status.

On the other hand, real evidence of a community origin is lacking, and Q 14:11; 17:33; and Mk 10:31 cohere with the paradigm of Jesus as eschatological prophet and illustrate his message of eschatological reversal. They also exhibit a confluence of formal features characteristic of Jesus—

140. Rudolf Bultmann, *History of the Synoptic Tradition* (New York: Harper & Row, 1963), p 105.

antithetical parallelism, the divine passive (at least in Q 14:11), aphoristic formulation, and unexpected or paradoxical content.[141] Our three sayings, moreover, exhibit the phenomenon of intertextual linkage.[142] We have here three units from two different sources that say similar things by means of exactly the same chiastic structure, one that Jesus borrowed from his Jewish tradition, as we shall find. Consider the following analysis:

Honor now	For all who exalt themselves Those who try to make their life secure Many who are first
Shame then	will be humbled will lose it will be last
Shame now	and those who humble themselves but those who lose their life and the last
Honor then	will be exalted will keep it will be first [143]

If we believe that these three sayings originated with Jesus, what was he talking about? Unlike Prov 29:23 ("A person's pride will bring humiliation, but one who is lowly in spirit will obtain honor"), it seems doubtful that our aphorisms were born of optimistic experience or appealed to it. It is true that, in biblical texts, God opposes the proud but gives grace to the humble.[144] Proverbial wisdom, however, knows the sad truth to be

141. See above, pp. 49–50. Relevant here is William A. Beardslee's idea of an anti-proverb; see his article, "Saving One's Life by Losing It," *JAAR* 47 (1977), pp. 57–72.

142. On this see pp. 53–57 herein.

143. Compare the related structures in Q 19:26//Mk 4:25:

Honor now	To everyone who has
Honor then	will more be given
Shame now	but from the one who has not
Shame then	even what that one has will be taken away

and in Mt 20:16//Lk 13:30 (Q?; compare *Teach. Silv.* 104:21–24):

Shame now	The last
Honor then	will be first
Honor now	and the first
Shame then	will be last

144. James 4:6 and 1 Pet 5:5, quoting Prov 3:34. Compare Job 22:29; Ezek 21:26.

that the rich get richer and the poor get poorer. In contrast to this truism, the sentiments of Q and Mark are implausible as generalizations about experience. Like Lk 6:20 and 24, which bless the poor and censure the rich, they say that those on top will not be on top forever, and that those on the bottom will not always be on the bottom. What could be the justification for this sort of improbable proposition?

The closest Greek parallel to our three Synoptic sayings seems to be Diogenes Laertius, *Vit. phil.* 1:69: "He is humbling the proud and exalting the humble." The subject of this sentence is the divinity Zeus. In like fashion God does the humbling and exalting in Ps 18:27 ("For you deliver a humble people, but the haughty eyes you bring down"); *b. 'Erub.* 13b ("He who humbles himself the Holy One, blessed be he, raises up, and whoever exalts himself the Holy One, blessed be he, humbles"); and *Ahiqar* 60 (Lindenberger: "If [y]ou wis[h] to be [exalted], my son, [humble yourself before Šamaš], who humbles the [exalted] and [exalts the humble]"). Matters are the same in Q 14:11; 17:33; and Mk 10:31. If the first become last and the last first, this can only be God's doing.

But when will God do this, and how? Our sayings do not envisage God working through good people, who slowly make the world a better place to live. Nor do they refer to a past event, as do 1 Sam 2:4 and 5 (compare Lk 1:52–53):

Honor then	The bows of the mighty
	Those who were full
Shame now	are broken
	have hired themselves out for bread
Shame then	but the feeble
	but those who were hungry
Honor now	gird on strength
	are fat with spoil

The sayings of Jesus instead use the future tense—"will be exalted," "will keep it," "will be first." What is envisaged is the final judgment, a staple of Jewish eschatology in the Hellenistic period and ever since.[145] Wrongs will be righted once and for all at the consummation. As *T. Jud.* 25:4 has it:

145. P. Volz, *Jüdische Eschatologie von Daniel bis Akiba* (Tübingen and Leipzig: Mohr-Siebeck, 1903), pp. 257–70, and Marius Reiser, *Jesus and Judgment* (Minneapolis: Fortress, 1997), Part 1.

And those who died in sorrow
   will be raised in joy;
and those who died in poverty for the Lord's sake
   shall be made rich;
those who died on account of the Lord
   shall be awakened to life

In *b. Pes.* 50a Rabbi Joseph ben Joshua catches a glimpse of the next world. He beholds that it is "topsy-turvy" (*hāpûk*), for "those who are on top here are at the bottom there, and those who are at the bottom here are on the top there." This has the same chiastic arrangement as Q 14:11; 17:33; and Mk 10:31:

Honor now	Those who are on top here
Shame then	are on the bottom there
Shame now	and those who are at the bottom here
Honor then	are on the top there [146]

These words portray the future world on the far side of judgment. Jesus' sayings do the same thing.

Additional logia in the Jesus tradition refer to or presuppose the common idea of a final judgment.[147] These corroborate my analysis of Q 14:11; 17:33; and Mk 10:31. With the exception, however, of Mt 25:31–46, which may owe as much to the influence of *1 Enoch* upon Matthew or his tradition as to Jesus, none of these logia contains vivid details. This does not wreck the conclusion that Jesus believed in the great assize but discloses only that he could take the expectation, in its broad essentials, for granted.

How did the judgment function in Jesus' proclamation? One assumes that his millenarian message resonated especially with people whose perceived material welfare, cultural values, or social status had, for one reason or another, become problematic. In other words, we may suppose that for him and those around him belief in the final judgment was part of an attempt to come to terms with experience of anomie and evil in a world they believed to have been created and sustained by a good and powerful God.

It does not take a philosopher to feel the problem of evil. The book of

146. Compare also *b. B. Bat.* 10b: In the future world things are upside down: "the upper [is] below and the lower [is] above." Upper and lower no doubt refer respectively to the honored and the despised.

147. See above, p. 46.

Job shows one theodicean tactic—things are beyond our comprehension. The Jesus tradition, for the most, proffers another. It inspires the imagination to behold, beyond the tardy operations of providence in the mundane present, the great judgment. It focuses the eyes of the mind on God's subsequent verdict, when the good will be rewarded and the bad punished. It anticipates the time when today's losers will be winners, when the honor of the dishonored will be established again, when inadequate recompense will become abundant reward. This vision of retributive justice (compare Mt 18:23–35), unmerited favor (compare Mt 20:1–15), and a perfected future hardly solves the philosophical issues. But it does something no less important: it draws the sting of injustice by insisting upon its temporary character.

This, however, is an obvious generality, and it is possible to be a bit more specific. The sayings in the Jesus tradition about judgment are naturally sorted into at least three categories, each of which has a different aim. Some function primarily as exhortation, others as consolation, still others as rebuke. Sayings that forecast that the humble will be exalted and that those who lose their lives will find them serve partly as exhortation. For they are invitations to self-abasement, a theme otherwise well attested in the Jesus tradition.[148] Jesus may have composed such sayings for his fellow itinerants, from whom he demanded great sacrifices and unconditional obedience.

A second category is designed to bring consolation. To tell the poor, the hungry, and those who mourn (Q 6:20–22) that God will reverse their present circumstances is to offer encouragement. Again, this is something we can imagine Jesus doing for his immediate followers. But equally we can imagine him cheering Galilean peasants with promises of better things to come. Difficulties can be endured more readily, and God can continue to be trusted, if there is faith that someday all will be made good.

Jesus appears to have used the traditional image of an eschatological judgment for yet a third end. If he told the unresponsive citizens of Chorazin and Bethsaida that it would go better for the people of Tyre and Sidon than for them at the judgment (Q 10:13–14), he was making a threat. So too when he solemnly warned about the sin against the Holy Spirit (Q 12:10; Mk 3:29), or when he warned against a sin so heinous that it would have been better for its perpetrators to have a great millstone hung about their necks and be cast into the sea (Mk 9:42). If, as the tradition indicates, sayings such as these really were sometimes addressed to

---

148. See further the following chapter, including the discussion of Mk 9:43–48.

people who had not thrown their lot in with Jesus, one assumes that the purpose was to create the sort of unease that might lead to repentance. But words of woe and condemnation, if heard by Jesus' followers, would also have functioned as a way of defining and building up a group or community.[149] For they make clear that there are outsiders as well as insiders and illuminate the basis for the distinction.

One final point regarding eschatological judgment. The Hebrew Bible has very little to say about life after death, and only one text depicts the great, postmortem judgment that inaugurates the everlasting kingdom of God. That text is Daniel 7. Even Third Isaiah, which some have dubbed "apocalyptic" or "protoapocalyptic," still sees death existing in the golden age. For, after God creates "new heavens and a new earth," we read that "one who dies at a hundred years will be considered a youth, and one who falls short of a hundred will be considered accursed" (65:20). In Jesus' teaching, however, the world after the judgment is, as we shall see in the next chapter, the world of eternal life, the deathless life of the angels. This means that his eschatology is not like that of the old Hebrew prophets but akin to that found in Daniel and later apocalyptic literature. Like his belief in demons and angels, then, Jesus' focus on the final assize marks him as a citizen of the Hellenistic period. So too with the next belief to be considered.

The Resurrection of the Dead

Millenarian movements, when imagining the paradisiacal future, regularly hope for the return of the ancestors,[150] and in Jewish sources the final judgment is often linked with the resurrection of the dead. This last undoes the evil of death and so restores the meaning that death steals away. In Dan 12:2 the dead are raised precisely in order to inherit everlasting life or everlasting contempt. In *4 Ezra* 7:31–44, immediately after the earth gives up those asleep in it, the Most High takes the seat of judgment. Did Jesus envision something similar?

Chapter 1 has already argued that the defense of the resurrection in Mk 12:18–27 reflects the thought of Jesus. Here we must consider the origin of a second complex, namely, Q 11:31–32. According to this passage, "the queen of the south will be raised at the judgment with this generation and will condemn it," and "the people of Nineveh will be raised

---

149. See on this Ben F. Meyer, "Jesus and the Remnant of Israel," *JBL* 84 (1965), pp. 123–30. His formulation, "open remnant," seems applicable to Jesus.

150. See above, pp. 92–93.

at the judgment with this generation and will condemn it." The future tenses, the use of "at the judgment," the natural meaning of "will be raised" when followed by "at the judgment,"[151] the eschatological associations of "this generation" elsewhere in the Jesus tradition,[152] the idea that the last generation will be especially wicked,[153] and the gathering together of people from different times and places leave little doubt that Q 11:31–32 envisions resurrection at the final judgment. But who composed the saying?

Bultmann rightly observed that "if one regards the saying for itself, there is no need to take it as a community formulation."[154] He went on, however, to observe that Q 11:31–32 has a parallel in Q 10:13–15 (the woes against Chorazin, Bethsaida, Capernaum), and he then claimed that, because the latter is a community formulation, the former is also. One problem with this reasoning is that, while the parallels are real enough (see below), Q 10:13–15 is not a community formulation.[155]

Norman Perrin, unlike Bultmann, thought that Jesus authored Q 11: 31–32:

> The double saying has no earlier history in the tradition; the point at issue is the question of repentance in face of a challenge, certainly a major concern of the message of the historical Jesus; the reference to the queen of the South and the men of Nineveh are vividly apposite and absolutely in accord with Jesus' use of unlikely good examples in his

151. Although "will stand/rise in the judgment" occurs in Ps 1:5 without eschatological sense, later the phrase gained such meaning; see *m. Sanh.* 10:3, 4 and the targum on Ps 1:1 (which substitutes "in the great day" for "in the judgment). One is, however, unpersuaded by Joachim Schaper, *Eschatology in the Greek Psalter*, WUNT 2/76 (Tübingen: Mohr-Siebeck, 1995), pp. 46–47, that the Septuagint already sees in Ps 1:5 a reference to the resurrection of the just.

152. E. Lövestam, *Jesus and 'this Generation.' A New Testament Study*, CBNT 25 (Stockholm: Almqvist & Wicksell, 1995).

153. See, e.g., 1QpHab 2:5–10; 2 Tim 3:1–5; *Sib. Or.* 4:152–61; *m. Soṭa* 9:15; and Lactantius, *Div. inst.* 7:18. The idea that wickedness increases as the golden age approaches is a commonplace in the history of religions; it appears, e.g., in the Iranian sources, *Jāmāsp Nāmak* 62, 68, 69, and *Zand ī Wahman Yašt* 4:21 ("During that most evil time a bird will have more reverence than the religious Iranian") as well as in the *Oracles of Hystaspes* according to Lactantius, *Div. inst.* 7:15. See further Mircea Eliade, *The Myth of the Eternal Return or, Cosmos and History* (Princeton: Bollingen, 1971), pp. 112–30. On p. 118 he writes: "To bear the burden of being contemporary with a disastrous period by becoming conscious of the position it occupies in the descending trajectory of the cosmic cycle is an attitude that was especially to demonstrate its effectiveness in the twilight of Greco-Oriental civilization."

154. Bultmann, *History*, p. 113.

155. See Becker, *Jesus von Nazaret*, pp. 78–80, and Davies and Allison, *Matthew*, vol. 2, pp. 270–71.

comparisons (the Good Samaritan); and the element of warning in the sayings coheres with a major aspect of the message of the parables.[156]

To these respectable arguments we can add that nowhere else in early Christianity do we hear anything about the queen of the South, and that the Ninevites are not elsewhere met until *1 Clem.* 7:7.

We may also, reverting to Bultmann's point, observe the strong intertextual linkage between Q 11:31–32 and the woes in Q 10:13–14. Both complexes

a. refer to a Gentile pair from the past (Tyre and Sidon in Q 10:13–14; the queen of the South and the Ninevites in Q 11:31–32)

b. speak of their repentance or positive response (in Q 10:13–14 Tyre and Sidon "would have repented long ago"; in Q 11:31–32 the queen of the South visited Solomon, and the Ninevites "repented at the preaching of Jonah")

c. implicitly contrast this Gentile repentance with the failure of Jesus' audience (in Q 10:13–14 Chorazin and Bethsaida obviously have not repented; in Q 11:31–32 Jesus' hearers obviously have not sought wisdom or repented)

d. mention the final judgment (Q 10:13–14: "It shall be more tolerable in the day of judgment"; Q 11:31–32: "will be raised at the judgment")

Despite these agreements, it does not appear that either unit was modeled upon the other. I infer that one person authored them both. Since Q 10:13–14 probably goes back to Jesus (see n. 155), we may turn Bultmann's reasoning on its head and affirm that Q 11:31–32 does likewise.

At least one text from Mark and another one from Q, then, inform us that Jesus, like the Pharisees but unlike the Sadducees, looked forward to the resurrection of the dead. If further proof were required, it is supplied by the fact that some of Jesus' followers, shortly after his death, claimed that God had raised him from the dead. As argued elsewhere in this book, the best explanation for their interpretation of events is that they and he went up to Jerusalem expecting the resurrection to take place soon.

Ancient Jewish sources are not at one on who would be raised. Some thought that only the righteous would be resurrected.[157] But, probably

---

156. Norman Perrin, *Rediscovering the Teaching of Jesus* (New York: Harper & Row, 1967), p. 195. Compare the verdict of Becker, *Jesus von Nazaret*, pp. 81–82.

157. See, e.g., *Psalms of Solomon* 3; *1 Enoch* 83–90; Josephus, *Bell.* 2:163; *2 Bar.* 30:1–5.

under Iranian influence, a universal resurrection appears in *Sib. Or.* 4: 179-90; *T. Benj.* 10:8; and *4 Ezra* 7:32. The same view is also put forward in Jn 5:28-29 (attributed to Jesus) and Acts 24:15.[158] What did Jesus think?

In Lk 14:12-14 Jesus says that, when one gives a dinner, one should not invite friends or relatives but the poor, the crippled, the lame, and the blind, people who cannot repay those who benefit them, for then "you will be repaid at the resurrection of the righteous." This could be taken to mean that the unrighteous will not be resurrected. But Luke probably did not understand the words in this way, because he elsewhere has Paul express hope "that there will be a resurrection of both the righteous and the unrighteous" (Acts 24:15). It was quite possible to believe in a "resurrection of life" and yet also speak of "the resurrection of condemnation" (Jn 5:29). Beyond that, we cannot with any confidence assign Lk 14:12-14 to Jesus.[159]

More promising is Q 12:5. Matthew's version, which refers to God "who can destroy both soul and body in hell" (10:28), more likely preserves Q than does Luke's Hellenized version ("who, after he has killed, has power to cast into hell").[160] It is also often thought to come from Jesus.[161] If so, we seemingly have reason to believe not only that, for Jesus, resurrection was unequivocally corporeal but also that he held the view attributed to him in Jn 5:28-29, namely, that there will be a resurrection of the just and the unjust. For the destruction of a body in hell assumes that an individual has been raised from the dead, condemned at the judgment, and then cast bodily into the place of punishment.

The inference is confirmed by Q 11:31-32. This last, as we have seen, says that "the queen of the south will be raised at the judgment with this generation and will condemn it," and "that the people of Nineveh will be raised at the judgment with this generation and will condemn it." Here seemingly it is not just righteous Gentiles who are resurrected but also the impious "generation" that has failed to respond appropriately to Jesus. That generation is raised only to be condemned.

The Jesus tradition offers very few hints as to how Jesus might have

158. It is also presupposed by Mt 5:29-30, which speaks of "your whole body" going to hell.

159. It is not Lukan redaction: J. Jeremias, *Die Sprache des Lukasevangeliums*, MeyerK (Göttingen: Vandenhoeck & Ruprecht, 1980), pp. 238-39. Beyond this one hesitates to say anything.

160. Compare Joachim Gnilka, *Das Matthäusevangelium I. Teil*, HTKNT I/1 (Freiburg: Herder, 1986), pp. 384-85.

161. See, e.g., Ulrich Luz, *Das Evangelium nach Matthäus (Mt 8-17)*, EKKNT I/2 (Neukirchen Vluyn: Neukirchener, 1990), p. 124.

envisaged the resurrected state. Mk 9:43–48, where he says it is better to enter life maimed, lame, or with one eye than to be thrown into hell whole, might be taken to imply that the body is raised exactly as it was buried.[162] That is, if a limb has been cut off, then it will be missing at the resurrection. Just such a thought is expressed in *Eccl. Rab.* 1:4: People are raised as they were buried, so the blind will be blind, the lame will be lame, the deaf will be deaf.[163] The antiquity of this belief is confirmed by *2 Bar.* 50:2: "The earth will surely give back the dead at that time; it receives them now in order to keep them, not changing anything in their form. But as it has received them so it will give them back. And as I have delivered them to it so it will raise them."

Although I have defended just such an interpretation of Mk 9:43–48 and its Matthean parallels in previous publications, I now realize and so confess that it probably reads too much into the text. The passage, it now seems to me, makes no explicit reference to the resurrection, and the meaning is more likely to be, "It is better for you to enter life [having been in the present world] maimed/lame/with one eye than to have two hands/feet/eyes [in this life] and go to hell." Moreover, even if Jesus did expect bodies to arise just as they departed, we may assume, in view of Mk 12:18–27, which prophesies that the saints will be "like angels in heaven," that he did not expect a resumption of mundane existence.[164] Even though the authors of *2 Baruch* and *Ecclesiastes Rabbah* imagined that bodies will come out of their graves just as they went into them, they also supposed that, shortly after the resurrection, the righteous will be healed and transformed. Such a conviction was probably common. One recalls not only 2 Macc 7:10–11, where a martyr professes his belief that if his tongue and hands are cut off, God will give them back to him again, but also the north wall of the Dura-Europos synagogue, which depicts body parts being reassembled at the resurrection. These texts are in line with the later Jewish interpretations of Ezekiel 37: the old vision of bones coming together was widely taken to depict the literal restoration of human bodies into perfect wholes at the general resurrection.[165] We may associate this conviction with Jesus.

That Jesus hoped for resurrection tells us nothing about his view of the

---

162. On the authenticity of this text see Chapter 3, pp. 187–88.

163. Attributed to R. Levi and R. Jacob of Gebal in the name of R. Ḥanina.

164. Compare Jacques Schlosser, "Die Vollendung des Heils in der Sicht Jesu," in *Weltgericht und Weltvollendung: Zukunftsbilder im Neuen Testament,* ed. Hans-Josef Klauck, QD 150 (Freiburg: Herder, 1994), pp. 74–78.

165. Harald Riesenfeld, *The Resurrection in Ezekiel XXXVII and in the Dura-Europos Paintings,* Uppsala Universitets Årsskrift 11 (Uppsala: Almqvist & Wiksell, 1948).

so-called interim state, the period between death and resurrection. Given his hope that the resurrection would take place soon, he, perhaps like some of Paul's converts in Thessalonica, may never have reflected much on this subject. On the other hand, many Jews who believed in the resurrection also believed in a blessed interim state,[166] and the possibility that Jesus shared their belief is raised by Lk 16:19–31, the tale of the rich man and Lazarus. While it is unwise to read much into the details of what amounts to a parable, one does wonder whether Jesus would have told the tale if the notion of a disembodied existence was uncongenial to him.

The Restoration of Israel

R. Akiba, according to *m. Sanh.* 10:3, taught that the ten tribes shall not return again: they are lost forever. R. Eliezer, however, is supposed to have retorted with this: "Like as the day grows dark and then grows light, so also after darkness is fallen upon the ten tribes shall light hereafter shine upon them." Many sources indicate that R. Eliezer's opinion was prevalent at the turn of the era.[167] We may, moreover, assume that those who held it took it no less literally than the German Jews who, in 1096, started for Palestine and expected to be met on their way by the ten lost tribes, who were thought to live beyond the distant mountains.[168] The expectation should not be spiritualized or turned into a metaphor.

At least three reasons indicate that Jesus' eschatological scenario, so far from being, against all historical plausibility, "*stripped* not only of all nationalistic features but also of all *materialistic* features,"[169] included the return of the lost tribes. The first has already been considered (pp. 101–102). There Jesus' selection of a group of twelve was explained as a probable prophetic sign. By associating himself with such a group he likely expressed the conviction that the eschatological salvation of Israel would include the lost tribes, who were believed to be living in distant exile.[170]

166. See, e.g., 2 Macc 7:9 and 36; *1 En.* 22:1–14; 60:8 and 62:15; *4 Ezra* 7:32, 76–101. Paul may also be cited here.

167. See Isa. 27:12–13; 43:5–6; Hos. 11:11; 2 Macc. 1:27; 2:18; Bar. 4:37; 5:5; *Ps. Sol.* 8:28; 11:2–3; *1 En.* 57:1; 11QTemple 57:5–6; *4 Ezra* 13:32–50; *2 Bar.* 78:1–7; *Sib. Or.* 2:170–73; *T. Jos.* 19:3–8 (Arm.).

168. See David Kaufmann, "A Hitherto Unknown Messianic Movement," *JQR* 10 (1897–98), pp. 139–51.

169. J. Jeremias, *New Testament Theology: The Proclamation of Jesus* (New York: Charles Scribner's Sons, 1971), p. 248.

170. On beliefs about the lost tribes see the evidence cited by Montague Rhodes James, *The Lost Apocrypha of the Old Testament: Their Titles and Fragments* (London: SPCK, 1920), pp. 103–106.

The second reason is Q 22:28–30, where Jesus promises his followers that they will "sit on thrones judging the twelve tribes of Israel." The word here translated "judging," and any Semitic equivalent that might lie behind it, almost certainly means not "condemning" but "ruling." [171] So the promise visualizes Jesus' followers governing Israel, including the tribes scattered abroad. The disciples, then, will be like the phylarchs under Moses. A similar expectation reappears in *T. Jud.* 25:1–2 (where Judah and his brothers will, after the resurrection, wield their scepter in Israel) and *T. Benj.* 10:7 (where Benjamin says, "Then shall we also be raised, each of us over our tribe").

While the meaning of Q 22:28–30 seems clear, can we attribute it to Jesus?[172] Reverting to the discussion of indices of authenticity in Chapter 1, the following points may be made.

1. Q 22:28–30 concerns itself with the coming age and so is compatible with the paradigm of Jesus as eschatological prophet.

2. The saying has caused Christians puzzlement, for it would seem to include Judas. The apologetically motivated commentators are quick to say that Judas did not "follow" Jesus to the end (e.g., Theophylact, *Comm. on Mt.* ad loc.), or that his place was taken by Matthias (Acts 1: 15–26). That only Q preserves our saying may be a sign that it was felt troublesome from earliest times.

3. It is not clear we can concoct a persuasive narrative explaining its emergence in the post-Easter period. Not only must one deal with the problem, just noted, of the presence of Judas among Jesus' immediate followers, but, to judge from Paul and Acts, the twelve (explicitly mentioned in Matthew's version of the saying, 19:28) do not appear to have played much of a role in the post-Easter period. So an exalted assertion about them, if that is what our saying originally was, is perhaps unexpected after the crucifixion.

4. Although Q 22:28–30 does not contain any of the formal features, listed above, that are characteristic of Jesus, it does show interesting links with another complex that could have pre-Easter roots, namely, Mk 10: 35–40.[173] The Markan complex has the sons of Zebedee asking Jesus to

171. Davies and Allison, *Matthew*, vol. 3, pp. 55–56, and Richard A. Horsley, *Jesus and the Spiral of Violence: Jewish Resistance in Roman Palestine* (Minneapolis: Fortress, 1993), pp. 203–206.

172. Horsley, ibid., pp. 199–208; Meier, "Circle of the Twelve," pp. 653–59; and Sanders, *Jesus and Judaism*, pp. 98–106, think it authentic. Philip Sellew, "The Last Supper Discourse in Luke 22:21–38," *Forum* 3/3 (1987), pp. 83–88, does not.

173. On this complex see Davies and Allison, *Matthew*, vol. 3, pp. 85–86.

let them sit in glory at his right and his left. It shares with Q 22:28–30 four features:

- In both units a small group around Jesus is involved in eschatological rule (compare also probably Lk 12:32); this contrasts with other scenes in the tradition, in which Jesus alone is the eschatological authority (e.g., Mt 25:31–46).
- In both passages eschatological rule is represented by sitting on thrones; this is explicit in Q 19:28 and implicit in Mk 10:35–40 ("sit at your right and left").
- In Matthew's version of Q 22:28–30 the small group with eschatological rule is identified as the twelve (there are twelve thrones). The same idea seems to be implicit from Luke's context. In Mk 10: 35–40 two among the twelve are asking for special places while the other ten express resentment (10:41). So Mk 10:35–40 is about which of the twelve are to have the highest seats of authority and presupposes that the twelve will rule in the eschatological kingdom.
- In both texts Jesus himself, despite not being the sole eschatological ruler, is the central figure. In Mark he sits on a throne with people at his right and left. In Mt 19:28 he sits on the throne of his glory. In Lk 22:28–30 he speaks of "my kingdom." Whatever exactly Q said, it was obviously something that made plain that Jesus would stand above those near him.

The preceding observations are far from conclusive. The arguments on the other side, however, are no less so. The upshot is that Q 22:28–30 *could* reflect something that Jesus said.

A third and better reason for surmising that Jesus expected the return of the lost tribes is Q 13:28–29, which speaks of many coming from east and west and reclining with Abraham, Isaac, and Jacob in the kingdom of God.[174] Throughout much of exegetical history this saying has been spiritualized into a prophecy of the church. Even today it appears in liturgies of the Lord's Supper. Joachim Jeremias, however, argued that it envisages the eschatological sojourn of the Gentiles to Zion. His case has seemed compelling to most, and it harmonizes with Q 11:31–32, which foresees the resurrection of the Queen of Sheba and the Ninevites. Here pious Gentiles share in eschatological salvation.

---

174. In addition to what follows see my *The Jesus Tradition in Q*, pp. 179–92.

Jeremias and the majority are, however, almost certainly wrong. Several commentators have sensed that, if we ignore the Matthean setting for the saying, the prophecy is more plausibly construed as having to do with the eschatological gathering of Israel.[175] Not only does the Q context have nothing at all to do with Gentiles, but the phrase "east and west" repeatedly occurs in Jewish texts in connection with prophecies of the return of Jews to the holy land.[176] By contrast, as far as my researches extend, not a single ancient text uses "east and west" in connection with the eschatological arrival of Gentiles, an event that accordingly affords an inadequate explanation of Q 13:28–29.

When one asks how the return of the lost tribes might have functioned in Jesus' proclamation, two things may be conjectured. First, the notion was perhaps a fictional way of enlarging group membership. We always feel more confident when others agree with us: the more numbers the more security. Now if, as the tradition indicates, Jesus and his itinerants at some point came to be truly disappointed in the Galilean response to their activities,[177] they must have sought theological explanations for their lack of success. In such a situation it would have been encouraging to believe that there were others out there, however far away, who would soon join their cause—so many others that they would indeed swell to become the majority in Israel. Even if Chorazin and Bethsaida had not repented, surely the disciples could count on ruling over the hidden tribes when they returned. Here cognitive dissonance would be lessened by imagining that one's unreceptive audience would soon be replaced by a more amicable group. Thought of the return of the righteous dead at the general resurrection could have served the same purpose.

Second, Q 13:28–29 presupposes, in accord with traditional expectation, that Israel will be the eschatological center of the world. The people from east and west obviously come up to Palestine and Zion. Nonetheless, certain members of Jesus' audience, dwellers in Israel, will be expelled from the kingdom and gnash their teeth. So Q 13:28–29 offers a new twist on an old theme and seems as much rebuke as encouragement. It implies that the land will not be a safe haven or guarantee of salvation in the eschatological crisis.[178] In our saying it is those outside the borders

175. Note, e.g., Sanders, *Jesus and Judaism*, pp. 119–120.
176. E.g., Deut 30:4 LXX; Zech 8:7–8; Bar 4:4; 5:5; *Ps. Sol.* 11:2; *1 En.* 57:1. While Mt 8:11–12 uses "east and "west," Luke 13:28–29 uses the longer expression, "from east and west and north and south." This phrase too was traditionally associated with Israel's return: Ps 107:2–3; Isa 43:5–6; Zech 2:6 LXX; *Ps. Sol.* 11:2–3.
177. Is this why they went to Jerusalem—to find a better audience?
178. Contrast *2 Bar.* 29:2; 71:1; *4 Ezra* 9:7–8; and *b. Ketub.* 111a.

of Israel who are redeemed whereas those inside, or at least some of them, fall under judgment. Jesus apparently used the restoration of the exiles to threaten those close to hand who had not supported his cause. One is reminded of Jer 24:1–10 and Ezekiel 11. In these place exiles return to the land while those already there stand condemned.

The Great Tribulation

Well-nigh all worldwide mythology puts human beings closer to the end, when things are bad, than the beginning, when things are good.[179] It also commonly depicts destruction before new creation.[180] Millenarian movements may be included in the generalizations. "Terrible tribulations. . . are the birth pangs of salvation. The new dispensation is born out of unprecedented cataclysms, disastrous upheavals and bloody calamities."[181] This generalization holds for Jewish messianism throughout the ages— the rabbis spoke of the "birth pains of the Messiah"—as well as for early Christianity. And several of the ancient Jewish apocalypses contain detailed depictions of the trials and tribulations of the end times.[182] Already Dan 12:1 prophesies "a time of anguish, such as has never occurred since the nations first came into existence." Even the Stoics expected a cataclysm at the end of the present world cycle.[183]

It is hardly a surprise, then, that Jesus also held this expectation. When he looked into the future he saw what others before and after him did— not just the golden age but its prelude, the final cataclysm. Yet just as he thought of the kingdom as already manifesting itself, so too did he think

179. See in general Eliade, *Cosmos and History*, pp. 112–30, and for a particular example H. C. Warren, *Buddhism in Transition* (New York: Atheneum, 1968), pp. 482–85. For this idea in pagan and Jewish texts in the Hellenistic and Roman periods see Marco Frenschkowski, *Offenbarung und Epiphanie*, vol. 1, WUNT 2/79 (Tübingen: Mohr-Siebeck, 1995).

180. According to Jonathan Z. Smith, "Ages of the World," in *The Encyclopedia of Religion*, ed. Mircea Eliade (New York: Macmillan, 1987), vol. 1, p. 128, the "notion of a worldwide, catastrophic winter that will destroy terrestrial life is an archaic Indo-European motif." The entire article (on pp. 128–33) is instructive.

181. Yonina Talmon, "Millenarian Movements," *Archives européenes de sociologie* 7 (1966), p. 167.

182. E.g., *1 Enoch, 4 Ezra, 2 Baruch*, and the *Apocalypse of Abraham*. Here one may detect a debt perhaps to Zoroastrian tradition; see John R. Hinnells, "The Zoroastrian Doctrine of Salvation in the Roman World: A Study of the Oracle of Hystaspes," in *Man and His Salvation: Studies in Memory of S. G. F. Brandon*, ed. Eric J. Sharpe and John R. Hinnells (Manchester: Manchester University Press, 1973), pp. 125–48.

183. Texts in H. F. von Arnim, ed., *Stoicorum veterum fragmenta* (Stuttgart: B. G. Teubner, 1964), pp. 27–33.

of the painful eschatological necessity as a present experience. This is the best explanation for his comment, surely authentic, that "The law and the prophets were until John; from then the kingdom of God has suffered violence and violent men take it by force" (Q 16:16).[184] Eschatological violence is not confined to the future but belongs to the here and now. Similarly, Q 12:51–53 ("Do you think that I came to give peace on the earth? I did not come to give peace but a sword. For I came to divide a man against father and daughter against mother and a daughter-in-law against mother-in-law") draws upon Mic 7:6, a text used to characterize the discord of the latter days.[185] For Jesus the tension between his followers and their families belonged to the messianic woes.

Jesus did not proclaim that eschatological peace had arrived but rather that the eschatological sword had been drawn. He was living in the darkness between the eve of the old era and the dawn of the new. Maybe Elijah, in the person of John the Baptist, had come to turn the hearts of children to their parents (Mal 4:5–6), but, if so, he had been murdered (Mk 9:9–13).[186] So "this generation" remained an evil and adulterous generation—as the last generation was expected to be. Lambs were in the midst of wolves (Q 10:3), and all were facing the trying and purifying fires of judgment (Mk 9:49; Lk 12:49–50).[187] It was opportune to ask for deliverance from the time of trial (Q 11:4; compare Rev 3:10).[188]

Q 12:51–53 and 16:16 show us that Jesus used the concept of eschatological tribulation to make sense of misfortunes around him. The expectation offered a theological framework within which to interpret unhappy circumstances. No doubt the premature death of John the Baptist, especially if construed as a harbinger of things to come, was traumatic for Jesus and his company. But placing that death at the turn of the ages and making it part of the climactic struggle between good and evil brought it

---

184. So Norman Perrin, *Jesus and the Language of the Kingdom* (Philadelphia: Fortress, 1976), p. 46. Compare Richard H. Hiers, *The Kingdom of God in the Synoptic Tradition* (Gainesville: University of Florida Press, 1970), pp. 36–42, and G. R. Beasley-Murray, *Jesus and the Kingdom of God* (Grand Rapids: Eerdmans, 1986), pp. 95–96.

185. For interpretation and authenticity see my article, "Q 12:51–53 and Mk 9:11–13 and the Messianic Woes."

186. On Mk 9:11–13 see further ibid.

187. Compare James D. G. Dunn, "The Birth of a Metaphor—Baptized in Spirit (Part I)," *ExpT* 89 (1978), p. 138, and Vincent Taylor, *The Gospel according to St. Mark*, 2d ed. (New York: St. Martin's, 1966), p. 413.

188. For the eschatological interpretation of this line from the Lord's Prayer see Raymond E. Brown, *New Testament Essays* (New York: Doubleday, 1968), pp. 314–19, and Joachim Jeremias, *New Testament Theology: The Proclamation of Jesus* (New York: Charles Scribner's Sons, 1971), pp. 201–202.

into accord with prophetic necessity. Indeed, the martyrdom of such a one as John may have been taken as added evidence that the end was near.

Another point can be made. When Jesus called people to abandon their work and families he was asking them to do things both difficult and against custom. That those who responded experienced both doubt and guilt is certain. But such guilt and doubt would be easier to live with if conflict, including familial conflict, was a prophesied and so necessary part of the eschatological scenario.

Imminence

If Deut 18:21–22 is anything to go by, biblical prophecies were, as a rule, sufficiently short-term that their truth or falsity could be judged by a prophet's contemporaries. In line with this, Jesus did not speak of a golden age which might just as well come later as sooner. For him salvation was close at hand. His generation, upon whom the eschatological tribulation had come, would be the last generation. This is implicit in the analysis so far. Additional features of the tradition do nothing but confirm this result: the sands of time had run out.

Like other millenarian prophets,[189] Jesus, for example, depicted the present as a period of unprecedented divine disclosure. This is the testimony of Q 10:21 ("you have hidden these things from the wise and the intelligent and have revealed them to infants"),[190] 23 ("Blessed are the eyes that see what you see. For I tell you that many prophets and kings desired to see what you see but did not see it, and to hear what you hear, but did not hear it);[191] and Mk 4:11 ("To you has been given the secret of the kingdom of God, but for those outside, everything is in parables").[192] Now, many Jews believed that the latter days would bring special knowledge to the elect.[193] It is altogether natural to think that this is the back-

189. See above, p. 91.

190. Bultmann, *History*, p. 160: this is "in my opinion, a saying originally Aramaic. I also think it possible that it comes from a lost Jewish writing. . . . It is different from the sayings of Jesus; yet, on the other hand, I see no compelling reason for denying it to him." Compare Luz, *Matthäus*, vol. 2, pp. 199–200.

191. Few would disagree with Bultmann, *History*, p. 126, who regarded this as from Jesus and (on p. 109) rightly asserted that Jesus must have been speaking of "the Messianic age, for it has been this that the pious of the past have longed to see." Compare Becker, *Jesus von Nazaret*, pp. 135–36.

192. On this see especially Bruce D. Chilton, *A Galilean Rabbi and His Bible: Jesus' Use of the Interpreted Scripture of His Time* (Wilmington: Michael Glazier, 1984), pp. 90–97.

193. See Jer 31:34; Hab 2:14; CD 3:13–14; 1QpHab 11:1; *1 En.* 51:3; 90:6; 93 + 91:12–17; 104:12–13; Dan 12:9–12; *T. Jud.* 18:3, 5.

ground to the sayings just cited. When Jesus sought to satisfy the universal desire to understand the true nature of one's situation, to know one's meaningful place in the cosmos, he crafted an eschatological scenario and construed it as revelatory.

Jesus also composed parables of harvest—the parable of the sower (Mk 4:2–9; Gos. Thom. 9), the parable of the scattered seed (Mk 4:26–29), the parable of the tares (Mt 13:24–30; Gos. Thom. 57)—and said that "the harvest is plentiful" (Q 10:2; compare Jn 4:35–38). This matters because Jewish tradition used the images of threshing, winnowing, and harvesting in prophecies of judgment,[194] and in apocalyptic literature the same images are associated with the eschatological consummation. 4 Ezra can, without adding explanation, even call the end "the time of threshing" (4:30, 39).[195] John the Baptist also used harvest imagery within an eschatological context (Q 3:17). There is no reason to suppose it was otherwise with Jesus. For him the eschatological harvest was ripe.

A related point, too often neglected, is that, among sayings usually thought to declare the kingdom present, we find not reference to a changeless reality but rather the language of advent. According to Q 10: 9, the kingdom has come or has come near. Similar are Q 11:20 ("upon you has come the kingdom of God") and Mk 1:15 ("The kingdom of God has come near"). Whatever else these statements mean, they imply the temporal character of the kingdom. Presumably there was a time when the kingdom of God had not come upon people. Does this make sense if Jesus proclaimed an "always available divine dominion"?[196] Heikki Räisänen has observed that, "If the kingdom has 'arrived' with Jesus, it can hardly have been there all along."[197] The use of temporal verbs with the kingdom reflects Jesus' belief that something new and unprecedented had happened. So once more we are impelled to think in terms of an unfolding eschatological scenario.

In addition to the observations already made, the Synoptics contain

194. E.g., Isa 41:14–16; Jer 15:7; 51:33; Hos 6:11; Joel 3:13; Mic 4:12–13. The significance of this was already seen by Schweitzer, The Quest of the Historical Jesus (New York: Macmillan), pp. 362–63.

195. Note also Rev 14:14–16 and 2 Bar. 70:2.

196. So Crossan, Jesus, p. 292.

197. "Exorcisms and the Kingdom: Is Q 11:20 a Saying of the Historical Jesus?" in Symbols and Strata: Essays on the Sayings Gospel Q, ed. Risto Uro (Helsinki: The Finnish Exegetical Society; Göttingen: Vandenhoeck & Ruprecht, 1996), p. 140. He goes on: "Q 11:20 does not speak of God's eternal, unchanging kingship, but of something novel, of a change in the situation."

statements that explicitly make the eschatological kingdom of God temporally near:

> Amen, I say to you, there are some standing here who will not taste death until they see that the kingdom of God has come with power. (Mk 9:1)

> Amen, I say to you, this generation will not pass away until all these things have taken place. (Mk 13:30)

> When they persecute you in one town, flee to the next; for amen, I say to you, you will not have gone through all the towns of Israel before the Son of man comes. (Mt 10:23)[198]

It has been popular in the last few decades to dismiss these sayings as the product of some unknown Christian prophet(s).[199] This is a possibility one cannot refute. But it must be added that there is no real evidence for this common conviction. The sayings could just as well go back to a word or words of Jesus.[200]

All three texts are structurally related. They consist of:

(a) "Amen" +
　(b) "I say to you" +
　　(c) statement about what will not happen +
　　　(d) temporal conjunction +
　　　　(e) statement about the consummation

I suspect that we are actually dealing here with three variants of one saying, and that there is another variant in Jn 8:51–52.[201] Elements (a), (b), and (d) do not vary significantly. Concerning (e), one has no difficulty imagining that a saying about the kingdom (Mk 9:1) became one about the Son of man (Mt 10:23) or vice versa, or further that either could, as part of the conclusion to Mark 13, be turned into the more general "all these things have taken place."

Even element (c) does not vary much. Both Mk 9:1 and 13:30 refer to death ("not taste death," "not pass away"), and Mt 10:23 has to do with persecution and flight—perhaps flight in order to avoid death. The

198. On the unity of this saying see Davies and Allison, *Matthew*, vol. 2, p. 189.
199. Crawford, "Near Expectation in the Sayings of Jesus," is typical.
200. Compare Luz, *Matthäus*, vol. 2, pp. 107–108, and 488.
201. On this last see Barnabas Lindars, "Discourse and Tradition: The Use of the Sayings of Jesus in the Discourses of the Fourth Gospel," *JSNT* 13 (1981), pp. 95–96.

original composition may have referred to those who would "stand" (compare Mk 9:1), that is, endure the tribulations of the end (compare Mk 13:13, 20).[202] One can easily envisage such a word being turned into several different things—into a prophecy partially fulfilled in the transfiguration (Mk 9:1), into a word relevant for the period immediately after the Jewish war (Mk 13:30), into consolation for the continuing Christian mission (Mt 10:23), and into a promise of eternal life for those who keep Jesus' word (Jn 8:51–52).

Although Schweitzer was almost surely wrong to argue that the Matthean missionary discourse preserved the original context of the original composition, he may have been right to see in Mt 10:23 something that Jesus said to his disciples. Eschatological enthusiasm is always difficult to maintain for any length of time. Doubts come easily and rapidly. So strategies must be devised to keep hope alive and well. Perhaps, as Schweitzer conjectured, Jesus and those around him already experienced the delay of the end and so a saying about living to see the fullness of time had a purpose even before Easter. Certainly the woes upon the cities in Galilee (Q 10:13–15) show us that certain high hopes or expectations of Jesus fell to the ground. As C. J. Cadoux, in a book that has passed into undeserved oblivion, commented fifty years ago: if he "meant what he said, and was not simply indulging in meaningless stage-play or unintelligent fatalism, he was expressing real and passionate disappointment. No feasible alternative view is possible. If these utterances do not evince a most poignant sense of frustration, they mean nothing."[203] Although in this matter we can do little more than speculate, one would hardly be surprised to learn that frustration in his missionary work raised for Jesus questions about his initial eschatological expectations.

Whatever one makes of Mk 9:1; 13:30; and Mt 10:23, one must come to terms with the parables that advise people to watch for the coming of the Lord or the Son of man,[204] with the pronouncements of escha-

---

202. See further Davies and Allison, *Matthew*, vol. 2, p. 189 (which argues that the "some" and "here" of Mk 9:1 are secondary), and J. C. O'Neil, "Did Jesus Teach that His Death Would Be Vicarious as well as Typical?" in *Suffering and Martyrdom in the New Testament*, ed. William Horbury and Brian McNeil (Cambridge: Cambridge University Press, 1981), pp. 9–27.

203. C. J. Cadoux, *The Historic Mission of Jesus: A Constructive Re-Examination of the Eschatological Teaching in the Synoptic Gospels* (New York: Harper & Brothers, n.d.), p. 192.

204. E.g., Q:12:39–40 = *Gos. Thom.* 91; Lk 12:35–38 (Q?); Mt 25:1–13.

tological woes on contemporaries,[205] and with the miscellaneous complexes that either announce or presuppose that the final fulfillment of God's saving work is nigh.[206] Those who dissociate Jesus from imminent eschatological expectation need to show us not only that *all* of this material comes from the church but additionally that it misrepresents what Jesus was all about. They have not done so.

Like the author of *Testament of Moses*, a book that probably attained its present form in his lifetime, Jesus expected to see God's kingdom appear throughout the whole creation. If the Kaddish prayer was already known in his day, he could have prayed it whole-heartedly: "May he establish his kingdom in your lifetime and in your days, and in the lifetime of the whole house of Israel, speedily and at a near time." He certainly did pray, "Your kingdom come" (Q 11:2).

Imminence is, for us moderns, the most difficult aspect of the Jesus tradition to appreciate, and it is safe to suppose that this is one reason Schweitzer's construction of the past and its relatives have been, from his day to ours, received with something other than hearty hallelujahs. We may have grown comfortable with the fact that all language about the end must, like all language about the beginning, be mythological. Revelation 21–22 is the analogue of Genesis 1–3. Nevertheless, what was near to many in the first century has become far off for us. Further, to wax mythological when imagining the divine future is one thing; to live as though that mythological future were coming tomorrow is another. But as historians we must not confuse our convictions with Jesus' creed. And regarding the latter, eschatological imminence was part and parcel.

When we inquire how imminence functioned for Jesus and his hearers, the answer seems obvious. Attention tends to focus on what is nearby, not on what is far away. Those who have been told that they have only weeks or months to live will think about death much more than those who believe death to be distant. In like manner, the kingdom of God will inevitably receive more attention if it is perceived not as creeping towards us at a petty pace, nor as reserved exclusively for the dead, but rather as coming anon. So when Jesus proclaimed that the judgment, the resurrection, and the restoration of Israel were at hand, he was communicating, among other things, that they were too important to ignore, that in fact they mattered above all else. In this way he hoped to turn his hearers into eschatological actors, into conscious participants in the end-time drama.

205. E.g., Q 6:24–26; 10:12–15; Mk 13:17.
206. E.g., Mk 1:15; 13:28–29, 33, 37; Lk 18:1–8; 21:34–36.

The Language of Millenarian Eschatology

The immediate future was, for Jesus, not mundane but rather some sort of supernaturally wrought state. But what did he mean when he spoke, as he probably did, of "the Son of man"? Did he live with the expectation that not just dispersed Israel but righteous Gentiles would go up to Zion? What prophetic texts, if any, were particularly important for him? Did he ever change his mind about any of his eschatological convictions? Did he think that the end could be hastened through repentance, or perhaps delayed through the same? Did he, as Mark tells us, really identify the Baptist with Elijah?

These are all interesting and important issues that need not be prudently eschewed. Probably some of them can be answered with a decent measure of assurance, or at least with more than vague surmises. At this juncture, however, I shall not further fill out the details of Jesus' eschatological vision. I rather wish to anticipate the rejoinder that my more or less prosaic reading of the evidence is misleading. I have already sought to repel the objections of those who exclude Jesus from the error of imminent eschatological expectation by excising large portions from the tradition. Here I should like instead to counter what I take to be the misguided ingenuity of four prominent scholars who have willed the same end through a different means, namely, by interpreting our sources in a nonmillenarian manner.

C. H. Dodd, in *The Parables of the Kingdom* and elsewhere, famously urged that Jesus had a "realized eschatology." That is, the kingdom of God, Jesus' name for the transcendent order in which there is no before or after, had manifested itself in the crisis of his ministry. Further, Jesus expected vindication after death, which he variously spoke of as resurrection, the coming of the Son of man, and the rebuilding of the temple. But the church, before too much time rolled by, came to long for the future coming of the Son of man, now conceived of as Jesus' return. In this way eschatology ceased to be realized. The change of outlook was such that the church eventually ended up with Revelation, an apocalypse, as its scriptural finale.

T. F. Glasson achieved a similar result by claiming that Jesus accepted the distinction, attested in *4 Ezra* 7:27–31, the book of Revelation, and some rabbinic sources, between an earthly messianic kingdom and the supramundane age to come. Jesus anticipated a first fulfillment, a temporary messianic reign of considerable although unspecified duration, and beyond that the resurrection, the final fulfillment, a new heaven, and a new earth. Jesus' expectation of an impermanent kingdom can, moreover, be fairly identified with the post-Easter era. In other words, Jesus' prophecies for the near future found their fulfillment in his fate and in the church.[207]

G. B. Caird provided yet another way of discounting Schweitzer's admirers and delivering Jesus from eschatological fallacy. Caird argued that, although the biblical writers believed literally that the world would someday come to an end, they regularly used end-of-the-world language metaphorically to refer to what they well knew was not the end of the world. Caird then declared that the Synoptic passages that scholars have taken to imply an imminent consummation have a metaphorical sense: they do not contemplate the world's end in the near future.[208] N. T. Wright, arguing that first-century Jews would have known a good metaphor when they came across one, has recently endorsed Caird's general approach.[209]

I shall not here lodge at length my individual complaints about Dodd, Glasson, Caird, and Wright—scholars from whom, I am happy to acknowledge, I have otherwise learned much.[210] I rather wish to explain why, despite their general agreement with each other when it comes to eschatology, a different view of things is preferable—a view which plainly recognizes, reluctantly but without equivocation, that what Jesus foretold can be identified neither with his earthly mission nor with post-Easter history. In other words, subsequent events neither confirmed nor conformed to Jesus' eschatological vision.

1. My first observation is not controversial but nonetheless merits considerable emphasis. It is this: the notion of a blissful, trouble-free age to come, which makes amends for all previous deficiencies, appears in much world mythology and religion and was certainly part of Jesus' Jewish tradition.[211] Moreover, this golden age, for which the last two thousand

---

207. T. F. Glasson, *Jesus and the End of the World* (Edinburgh: Saint Andrew, 1980).

208. G. B. Caird, *The Language and Imagery of the Bible* (Philadelphia: Westminster, 1980), pp. 243–71.

209. N. T. Wright, *The New Testament and the People of God* (Minneapolis: Fortress, 1992), pp. 280–338, and *Jesus and the Victory of God*, especially pp. 320–68.

210. For my evaluation of Glasson see "A Millennial Kingdom in the Teaching of Jesus?" *IBS* 7 (1985), pp. 46–52. I have criticized Caird in *The End of the Ages*, pp. 84–90. Some of the problems with Wright are considered in "Jesus and the Victory of Apocalyptic," in *N. T. Wright's Jesus and the Victory of God: A Critical Assessment*, ed. Carey Newman (Downers Grove: InterVarsity, forthcoming 1998).

211. Mircea Eliade, *Myth and Reality* (New York: Harper & Row, 1963), pp. 54–74. Already the end of the Akkadian *Uruk Prophecy* seems to foretell a golden age, and pre-Christian Germanic myth told of earth and sky someday perishing, after which the earth would once again emerge from the sea to witness, for a time, freedom from evil.

years of human misery seem a most implausible candidate, has often been thought to be imminent. "In every age and in every corner of the globe, small groups of people have become unalterably convinced that the processes of history are coming to an end."[212] Recurrently, when a people's social world has disintegrated, they have longed for another world, or for their present world to be recreated. It is particularly significant for our purposes that, "in the second century B.C. and later, many [in the Graeco-Roman world] were saying that the last age had nearly run its course and the great change was at hand."[213]

The expectation of supernatural renewal in the offing is one of the central energizing elements in all millenarian movements, which typically "expect imminent, total, ultimate, this worldly collective salvation."[214] To say that Jesus spoke of and behaved as though the end were really at hand, therefore, is simply to put him into a well-known category.

By "end" is not meant the cessation of the space-time universe—although that possibility should not be excluded. The Stoics believed in a literal end,[215] and the *Oracle of Hystaspes* prophesied that, 6000 years after creation, "everything ought to come to a halt."[216] *1 En.* 91:16 foresees that "the first heaven shall depart and pass away; a new heaven shall appear,"[217] and *2 En.* 65:7(A) prophesies that "time (periods) will perish."[218] *LAB* 3:10 says that someday "the world will cease, and death will be abolished," and "there will be another earth and another heaven, an everlasting dwelling place." According to 2 Pet 3:10–13, the day of the Lord—which can be hastened by godly living—will come like a thief, "and then the heavens will pass away with a loud noise, and the elements will be dissolved with fire, and earth and everything that is done on it will be disclosed." And then there are the Jewish *Sibylline Oracles*, which, in more than one place, plainly tell that the world will be burned up with fire.[219]

212. Jeffrey Kaplan, *Radical Religion in America: Millenarian Movements from the Far Right to the Children of Noah* (Syracuse: Syracuse University Press, 1997), p. 165.

213. T. Francis Glasson, *Greek Influence in Jewish Eschatology* (London: SPCK, 1961), p. 76. See further F. Gerald Downing, "Common Strands in Pagan, Jewish and Christian Eschatologies in the First Century," *TZ* 51 (1995), pp. 196–211.

214. Yonina Talmon, "Millenarian Movements," *Archives européenes de sociologie* 7 (1966), p. 159.

215. Arnim, *Stoicorum*, pp. 27–33.

216. See Hinnells, "The Zoroastrian Doctrine of Salvation in the Roman World," p. 128, citing Aristokritos, *Theosophy*.

217. See also 45:4–5; 69:29; 72:1.

218. Compare *2 En.* 65:10 (J): "everything corruptible will perish."

219. *Sib. Or.* 2:196–210; 3:75–90; 4:171–92.

But most millenarian movements, whether ancient, medieval, or modern, have expected not the utter destruction and replacement of this world but rather a revolutionary change.[220] For medieval messianic Jews, for the cargo cultists of Melanesia,[221] and for the Amerindian participants in the Ghost Dance, for instance, the dead were going to come back to live on their old land, not in some supraterrestrial locale. Soo too already the book of Daniel. And Jesus, who probably drew no distinction between a millennial kingdom and the eternal world to come,[222] and whose eschatology probably contained, to use Scholem's categories, elements of both restorative and utopian-catastrophic messianism, may similarly have looked for a time "free from old age, death, decomposition and corruption. . .when the dead shall rise, when immortality shall come to the living, when the world shall be perfectly renewed."[223] These words, from a Zoroastrian source, appear to envision not another earth but this earth made new—a revised, second edition with the earlier deficiencies corrected.[224] The story of the flood in Genesis is analogous: this world is first

---

220. Compare Richard Landes, "Lest the Millennium Be Fulfilled: Apocalyptic Expectations and the Pattern of Western Chronography 100–800 C.E.," in *The Use and Abuse of Eschatology in the Middle Ages*, ed. Werner Verbeke, Daniel Verhelst, and Andries Welkenhuysen (Leuven: Leuven University Press, 1988), p. 207. According to Bryan Wilson, "Millennialism in Comparative Perspective," *Comparative Studies in Society and History* 6 (1963), pp. 94–95, "new religious movements" tend, in reaction to "institutionalized religion," which usually "organize the attainment of transcendental goals," to seek "this-worldly goals." Relevant is Gregory Tillett's study of some modern adventist cults: "Esoteric Adventism; Three Esoteric Christian Adventist Movements of the First Half of the Twentieth Century," in Trompf, *Cargo Cults and Millenarian Movements*, pp. 143–77.

221. I. C. Jarvie, "On the Explanation of Cargo Cults," *Archives européenes de sociologie* 7 (1966) 299–312.

222. This is why the attempt to decide whether Jesus anticipated an "earthly" or "heavenly" fulfillment is so difficult; see Schlosser, "Die Vollendung des Heils in der Sicht Jesu."

223. *Bahman-Yašt* 19:14, 89, quoted in Eliade, *Eternal Return*, p. 124.

224. Compare the generalization, regarding five millenarian movements, of Michael Adas, *Prophets of Rebellion: Millenarian Protest Movements against the European Colonial Order* (Cambridge: Cambridge University Press, 1987), p. 115: "The adherents of these movements anticipated far more profound transformations than the destruction of the colonial order. Victory over the agents of colonialism was merely a preliminary, but necessary, stage in the establishment of a new order that would be radically different from any that had gone before. Although there was often an appeal to past golden ages and honored precedents as a means of lending legitimacy to millennial prophecies, the coming age of salvation would be beyond time and history and yet represent the culmination of both. It would be free of sin, suffering, and social injustice. The promised kingdom of peace and bliss would be terrestrial in Norman Cohn's sense that it would come in the here-and-now rather than after death, but it was clearly envisioned as a blend of material and spiritual, of this world and the supernatural."

destroyed before it—the same world—is recreated. Presumably the biblical prophecies of a desert in bloom (Isa 35:1–2), unprecedented fertility (Amos 9:13–15), and the taming of wild animals (Isa 11:6–9) are already moving in this direction.[225] Whether this be so or not, maybe the best conclusion with regard to Jesus is that the differences between heaven and earth became, in his imagination, indistinct in the eschaton, that is, the two things in effect merged and became one. "Heaven on earth," we might say.

It is true that, occasionally in Jewish tradition, the messianic kingdom does not reach much beyond present possibilities. Maimonides thought of the messianic age in rather mundane terms,[226] and one can find in the Babylonian Talmud the notion that "there is no difference between this world and the days of the Messiah except [that in the latter there will be no] subjection to the nations" (b. Ber. 34b). Most Jewish messianism, however, has wanted much more. In medieval Jewry "not only the Jewish masses but most Jewish scholars conceived the millennium as an entirely new world,"[227] and often in the Talmud "descriptions of life after death, the messianic age, and the new world after the messianic age overlapped considerably."[228] We have something similar in many of the old Jewish apocalypses[229] as well as in the Jesus tradition, where the immediate future involves resurrection to an angelic life.

Perhaps it is not out of place to cite Martin Buber's story in which a zaddik, in response to claims about the Messiah's arrival, opens his window, sniffs the air, and then declares, "The Messiah has not come."[230]

---

225. In private correspondence Don Gowan has commented: "Isaiah 11 expresses the same conviction as Genesis 1 and 9: that in the world as God intended it to be there would be no killing. That is not the world we know, so the belief is projected both into the beginning and the end. I think the prophet must have meant peace among the animals to be taken literally. Otherwise, he was just writing a platitude: God does not like killing. He says more than that: God does something about it." Even the great allegorist Philo took the prophecies of the reconciliation of animals (Isa 11:6–9; 35:1–2; Amos 9:13–15) literally: De praem. 85–88. See on this Peder Borgen, Philo of Alexandria: An Exegete for His Time, NovTSup 86 (Leiden: Brill, 1997), pp. 262–64.

226. Marcel Poorthuis, "Messianism between Reason and Delusion: Maimonides and the Messiah," in Messianism through History, ed. Wim Beuken, Seán Freyne, and Anton Weiler (London: SCM, 1993), pp. 57–68.

227. Stephen Sharot, Messianism, Mysticism, and Magic: A Sociological Analysis of Jewish Religious Movements (Chapel Hill: University of North Carolina Press, 1982), p. 47.

228. Ibid., p. 48.

229. D. S. Russell, The Method and Message of Jewish Apocalyptic 200 B.C.–A.D. 100 (Philadelphia: Westminster, 1964), pp. 285–303.

230. Menachem Kellner, "Messianic Postures in Israel Today," in Saperstein, ed., Essential Papers, p. 510.

This anecdote vividly depicts the conviction that, when the redeemer finally comes, everything will be different.

2. Caird, taking up where Dodd left off,[231] has argued that modern readers sometimes find literal meaning where they should instead find metaphor. It is true that the Tanak can use poetic hyperbole to depict historical events. But should we assume that the way some older texts used language is the way in which everyone else later on used language? Does not the apocalyptic literature of the Hellenistic period present us with some things truly new? If the resurrection in Ezekiel 37 was, in the author's intention, a metaphor for the resuscitation of Israel, by the time we come to the walls of the Dura-Europos synagogue the text is clearly being read as a prophecy of the saints literally exiting their tombs at the consummation. Most biblical scholars hold that certain words and images came later to mean things that they once did not mean: hermeneutics was not forever fixed.[232] Not only, to illustrate again, was there was an increase in the use of cosmic imagery after the Babylonian exile, but, as we shall see, literal interpretation of it is, in later sources, sometimes unavoidable.

If we leave aside obviously symbolic prophecies in a visionary context (for example *4 Ezra* 11–12 and the phantasmagoric maze that is John's Revelation), surely I will not be alone in my sentiment that eschatological language often held a strongly literal component. The Qumran War Scroll is ostensibly a prophecy of a real eschatological battle complete with fighting angels. Papias (in Eusebius, *H.E.* 3:39:12), Justin Martyr (*Dialogue* 80),[233] Irenaeus (e.g., *Adv. haer.* 5:32–36), Tertullian (*Adv. Marc.* 3:24), the Montanists (Epiphanius, *Pan.* 49:1:2–3), and Lactantius (*Div. inst.* 7:24–26) all believed, because they read their Bible literally, in a rather worldly millennium involving a transformation of the natural world. Commodian expected the ten lost tribes to return to the land (*Carm. apol.* 941–46). Rabbinic texts contain the conviction that bones

231. On p. 81 of *Parables*, Dodd asks whether we must assume that apocalyptic writers "always intended their visions of the end, unlike their visions of coming events within history, to be taken with the strictest literalness, or does a consciously symbolic element still persist?" He goes on: "It is at least open to the reader to take the traditional apocalyptic imagery as a series of symbols standing for realities which the human mind cannot directly apprehend, and as such capable of various interpretation and re-interpretation as the lessons of history or a deepening understanding of the ways of God demand."

232. Instructive here is J. Vermeylen, *Du prophète Isaïe à l'apocalyptique. Isaïe, I–XXXV, miroir d'un demi-millenaire d'expérience religieuse en Israel*, EB, 2 vols. (Paris: J. Gabalda, 1977–78).

233. Justin says that he shares his opinion with many Christians.

will roll through underground tunnels before being reassembled for the resurrection on the Mount of Olives (b. Ketub. 111a).

Just how literal the ancients could be about some things is brought home by a passage in Aristobulus. He is commenting on Exod 19:16–18 ("On the morning of the third day there was thunder and lightning, and a blast of a trumpet so loud that all the people who were in the camp trembled. . . . Now Mount Sinai was wrapped in smoke, because the Lord had descended upon it in fire; the smoke went up like the smoke of a kiln, while the whole mountain shook violently"). Now Exod 19:16–18 seems to us moderns to invite a nonliteral reading. It is, however, fascinating to learn that a hellenized Jew of Alexandria who applied Stoic allegorical method to biblical exegesis took it quite literally. The following words of Aristobulus, preserved in Eusebius, Praep. ev. 10:8, deserve to be quoted at length:[234]

> In the book of the Law, it is said that at the time when God was giving the law, a divine descent took place, so that all might see the active power of God. This descent is manifest; and anyone who wants to preserve what is said about God would explain these accounts in the following way. It is declared that "the mountain was alight with fire," as our law code says, because of God's descent. There were the voices of trumpets and the fire blazing beyond all power to resist it. And the number of the entire throng was no less than a million, not counting those outside the prescribed age. They were called to assembly from all around the mountain (the circuit of the mountain took no less than five days) and the blazing fire was observed by them from every vantage point, as they were encamped around it. As a result, the descent was not local, for God is everywhere. And as for the force of the fire, which is exceedingly marvelous because it consumes everything, he showed that it burned irresistibly and actually consumed nothing, which would not have happened unless a divine power had been in it. For, though the place burned furiously, the fire consumed none of the things growing on the mountain, but the fresh green of all the plants remained untouched by the fire. The voices of the trumpets sounded more vehemently together with the lightning-like illumination of the fire, although there were no such instruments ready at hand, nor anyone playing them, but everything came to be by divine provision.[235]

234. I quote from the edition of Carl R. Holladay, Fragments from Hellenistic Jewish Authors, Volume III: Aristobulus, TT 39/PS 13 (Atlanta: Scholars Press, 1995), pp. 142–47.

235. Compare the variant of this passage of Aristobulus preserved by Clement of Alexandria, Strom. 6.3.32.

Surely we have to wonder whether, in a world where even an allegorist could find literal events in the fire and trumpet and earthquake of Exod 19:16–18, readers of apocalyptic prophecies might not have expected literal fire, literal trumpets, and literal earthquakes?[236]

Most of us have known many moderns who take their eschatology straight, with as little symbolism as possible. It suffices to recall Hal Lindsey's *The Late, Great Planet Earth* and its onetime popularity. Now do we really have suitable reasons, other than saving our theology, for holding that, when the Jesus tradition speaks about the Son of man coming on the clouds of heaven, this was not meant literally? Why imagine instead that this was just a picturesque way of saying something about Jesus' vindication after death, or of prophesying the judgment of Jerusalem in 70 C.E.? In a world wherein many, it appears, were credulous enough to be taken in by the transparent forgeries of the pseudepigrapha, should we really expect refined hermeneutics? If Plutarch could report the literal sound of a trumpet from heaven (*Sulla* 7),[237] and if Aristobulus could discuss what sort of noise the supernatural trumpets at Sinai made (Eusebius, *Praep. ev.* 8:10), is it manifest that we should reckon the trumpet of Mt 24:31 and 1 Thess 4:16 to be a metaphor?[238] *Sib. Or.* 4:174 also refers to an end-time trumpet. It heralds the conflagration of the world and belongs to a passage that can otherwise be taken at face value (compare *Apoc. Abr.* 31:1).

In this particular case we know what one very early Christian, and an unusually sophisticated one at that, made of such language. In 1 Thess 4:13–18, Paul passes on tradition closely related to Mk 13:24-27// Mt 24:29, 30b-31//Lk 21:25–38 as well as Mt 24:30a.[239] The apostle writes about the coming of the Lord Jesus, who will meet the saints in the clouds. The Synoptic Jesus similarly speaks of the Son of man coming on

236. Although I cannot discuss the issue further here, Aristobulus has led me to recant my formerly metaphorical interpretation of the accounts of the giving of the law in *LAB* 11:5; *4 Ezra* 3:18–19; and *b. Zeb.* 116a; see Allison, *End*, p. 89 (cited with approval by Wright, *Jesus and the Victory of God*, 321, n. 2).

237. "The most striking phenomenon of all was when the sound of a trumpet rang out from a perfectly clear and cloudless sky with a shrill, prolonged, and dismal note so loud that people were driven half crazy with terror."

238. One also cannot interpret the heavenly trumpets of *Par. Jer.* 3:2 and 4:1 as metaphorical, although here we are dealing with a narrative whose fictional character was probably assumed by the listeners (compare *LAE* 47:1).

239. See Allan J. McNicol, *Jesus' Directions for the Future: A Source and Redaction-History Study of the Use of the Eschatological Traditions in Paul and in the Synoptic Accounts of Jesus' Last Eschatological Discourse*, New Gospel Studies 9 (Macon: Mercer University Press, 1996).

clouds and of the elect being gathered to him. The point for us is that 1 Thess 4:13–18 does not readily lend itself to being understood as metaphorical language. One has difficulty imagining that Paul was not referring to literal clouds in the atmosphere, or that his first readers might have given his words figurative sense. So an appeal to metaphor when pursuing the meaning of the closely related Mk 13:24–27 par. seems equally out of place. Paul did not interpret the tradition behind Mk 13:24–27 as does N. T. Wright, that is, as a symbolic prophecy of Jerusalem's destruction.[240] The apostle rather construed it as have millenarian Christians down through the centuries: Paul expected Jesus to come on the clouds. Some words of Shirley Jackson Case are apropos: "Imagine the shock to Mark had he been told that this expectation was already realized in the appearances of Jesus after the resurrection, or in the ecstatic experiences of the disciples at Pentecost, or in the salvation of the individual Christians at death."[241]

Consider Mk 13:24:

> The sun will be darkened,
>   and the moon will not give its light,
>   and the stars will be falling from heaven,
>   and the powers in the heavens will be shaken

Some commentators think that this free combination of Isa 13:10 and 34:4, which has numerous parallels in apocalyptic literature,[242] is poetry, not literal description.[243] Perhaps they are right. But I have my doubts.[244]

240. See *Jesus and the Victory of God*, pp. 360–65, which does not discuss 1 Thess 4:13–18 in this connection. I fancy that had Wright stood amid Noah's audience and been warned of the flood about to pour forth upon the earth, our exegete might have commended the righteous herald for his apt metaphor but would, to his own fatality, not have bothered to check the weather.

241. Shirley Jackson Case, *The Millennial Hope: A Phase of War-Time Thinking* (Chicago: University of Chicago Press, 1918), p. 216.

242. See *1 En.* 80:4; Rev 6:12–13; *Sib. Or.* 2:194, 200–202; 3:81–93, 796–83; 5:344–50; 7:125; 8:190–92, 341; *T. Levi* 4:1; *4 Ezra* 5:4–5; *T. Mos.* 10:5; *Apoc. Elijah* 5:7; also Isa 13:10; 24:21, 23; Jer 4:23; Ezek 32:7–8; Joel 2:10, 30–31; Amos 5:20; Zeph 1:15; Hag 2:6, 21; *Barn.* 15:8 *b. Sanh.* 99a.

243. See further Wright, *Jesus and the Victory of God*, pp. 354–56, citing Isa 13:10; 14:12–15; 34:4; Ezek 32:7; Joel 2:10. For myself, however, I wonder whether some of these texts only appear nonliteral to us after the fact because we associate them with historical events that in the event were (against the prophets' expectations) unaccompanied by cosmic signs. Does Wright's analysis assume that the prophets must always have been accurate prognosticators?

244. Compare Ferdinand Hahn, "Die Rede von der Parusie des Menschensohnes Markus 13," in *Jesus und der Menschensohn: Für Anton Vögtle*, ed. Rudolf Pesch and Rudolf Schnackenburg (Freiburg: Herder, 1975), pp. 265–66.

Maybe such a reading unduly extends the range of metaphorical language. Maybe Calvin, ad loc., was right to be a literalist here ("How the sun must be obscured we cannot guess today, but the event itself will reveal"). Maybe Mk 13:24 should be taken to mean what it says, just like *Sib. Or.* 2:200–202: "But the heavenly luminaries will crash together, also into an utterly desolate form. For all the stars will fall together on the sea." Certainly other dramatic events prophesied in Mark 13—wars, famines, earthquakes—must, as the consensus of the commentaries indicates, be intended as literally as Exodus intends the plagues,[245] or as literally as the list of portents Josephus associates with the Jewish War.[246]

Many ancient texts, both within the Bible and without, recount episodes of a literal, supernatural darkness.[247] Others tell of heavenly portents that cannot be construed as purely picturesque speech. In Joshua 10, the sun really stands still.[248] In 3 Macc 6:18–19, awe-inspiring angels appear in the heavens and confuse and stop the army of Ptolemy. In Josephus, *Bell.* 6:289, a star "resembling a sword" hangs over Jerusalem as a portent of its destruction. In Tertullian, *Adv. Marc.* 3:24, we read of a vision of a heavenly city suspended in the morning sky for forty days. In Eusebius, *V.C.* 1:28, Constantine sees "the trophy of a cross of light in the heavens, above the sun, and an inscription, 'Conquer by this,' attached to it." Obviously real heavenly portents were commonly enough believed to have happened. Why then suppose that Mk 13:24 is less prosaic than, let us say, *1 En.* 70:6, which foretells that one day the stars "will change their courses and their activities, and will not appear at the times which have been prescribed for them," or that it is less realistic than *Barn.* 15:8, which says that when the Son of God abolishes the time of the lawless one, God "will change the sun and the moon and the stars," or that it is less literal than Lactantius, *Div. inst.* 7:24, where we are told that, during the millennium, the moon will shine like the sun and the sun will be seven times brighter than it is now? According to Seneca, *Quaest. nat.* 3:29, Berosus, the Babylonian astrologer, foretold that "the world

---

245. In *Apocalypse of Abraham* 30–31 the end-time woes are ten plagues that recapitulate what happened in Egypt.

246. See *Bell.* 6:288–300: a star, a comet, a light at midnight around the temple altar, a cow giving birth to a lamb, the opening of its own accord of the eastern gate of the inner court of the temple, armies in the clouds, a voice in the temple.

247. E.g., Philo *apud* Eusebius, *Praep. ev.* 8:14 (395d) (eclipses "are indications either of the death of kings or of the destruction of cities"); Plutarch, *Caes.* 69 (darkness at the death of Julius Caesar); Dio Cassius 56.29.3 (darkness at the death of Augustus); Josephus, *Ant.* 17:167 (an eclipse when Matthias died); Ambrose, *De Obitu Theod. Orat.* 1 (darkness at the death of Theodosius I).

248. While one might construe Josh 10:12–13a as poetry, 10:13b demands a literal reading.

will burn when all the planets that now move in different courses come together in Cancer, so that they all stand in a straight line in the same sign. . . ." Here again changes in the heavens cannot be metaphor, and this is the sort of language one finds again and again in millenarian prophecy. As Lawrence Sullivan has written, "In nearly all millennial visions, the sky tumbles to earth, or the sun, moon, stars. . .plummet from above."[249]

We should further not forget that the ancients identified the heavenly lights with living beings;[250] so Mk 13:24 might depict the fall of evil beings, "the spiritual forces of wickedness in the heavenly places" (Eph 6:12) or, alternatively, of the heavenly hosts who come down to do battle against evil (compare T. Levi 3.1–3). In this case we could compare the equation of falling stars with demons in T. Sol. 20:16: this is not symbolism but an ancient interpretation of meteors.[251]

This last fact reminds us that, sometimes unconsciously, the findings of modern science move us to find metaphor where the ancients could have found real events. We distinguish between stars, those massive bodies of energy removed from us by unimaginable distances, and meteors, those relatively small celestial bodies that usually burn up as they enter earth's atmosphere. But to the prescientific naked eye, a meteor looks just like a star, save it is hurtling downward. One presumes, then, that Mark's first readers, unenlightened by Renaissance science, would have had no reason to think twice about what they called "stars" falling from the sky: they saw it happen all the time. (Even today we preserve the old habit of speaking of meteors as "falling stars.") So for them Mk 13:24 was just foretelling that someday all the stars would behave as some do now: some fall now, all will fall then. At the end the sky will become a meteor shower writ large. It is only a scientific conception of the night sky that makes this thought incredible.[252]

W. D. Davies, after observing that Sabbatai Ṣevi carved up the world into geographical sections for his followers to rule, went on to write:

Much modern discussion of the meaning of apocalyptic language which overmuch spiritualizes it must be regarded as misguided. For ex-

---

249. *Icanchu's Drum: An Orientation to Meaning in South American Religions* (New York: Macmillan, 1988), p. 675. For illustrations see pp. 560, 562–63.

250. D. C. Allison, "What Was the Star that Guided the Magi?" *BR* 9/6 (1993), pp. 20–24, 63.

251. For the crash of demonic stars from the sky see *1 En.* 86:1–3; 88:1–3; 90:24; Rev 12:4; *Apoc. Elijah* 4:11; compare Isa 14:12.

252. Bruce J. Malina, "Jesus as Astral Prophet," *BTB* 27 (1997), pp. 83–98, duly appreciates the literal aspects of ancient language about the sky.

ample, to understand the term "kingdom of God" as used in early Christianity, as nonpolitical and nonterrestrial, is unjustifiable, if it be taken to have been so used universally. Whatever their limitations, in their tenacious insistence on a literal understanding of the messianic prophecies chiliastic movements are doubtless true to much in . . . early Christianity. There was a literal dimension to apocalyptic language which must not be evaded. . . .[253]

Did the early Christians or Jesus himself use eschatological language any less realistically than have so many others? Why should we suppose that their expectations were so very different from those of Mohammed, who wrote about an earthquake ushering in the judgment, about the splitting apart of the moon, and about the falling of extinguished stars to the ground?[254] Or unlike the Xhosa of South Africa, who, in the middle of the nineteenth century, thought that the new age would be heralded by two suns, a great darkness, and a violent gale?[255] Or unlike the Vietnamese followers of the twentieth-century millenarian prophet, Huynh Phu So, who expected disaster of every sort: fire, floods, epidemics, animal attacks, starvation, war, smoke, deforestation, and sun and moon changing places?[256] Or unlike Augusto C. Sandino, who "envisaged a new deluge where the Pacific and the Atlantic Oceans would meet covering everything but the volcanic peaks over Nicaraguan territory" and then a "world conflagration"?[257] Maybe, as Robert Carroll has argued with reference to the Hebrew Bible prophets, "the need to treat the language as symbolic only arises because of the failure of the predictions in the first place."[258] This suggestion must be taken seriously.

One must, to be sure, be cautious here. English folklore holds that some people have, in accord with their belief in eschatological reversal, had themselves buried head down so that they will be right side up on the

253. W. D. Davies, *Jewish and Pauline Studies* (Philadelphia: Fortress, 1984), p. 267.

254. See Tor Andrae, *Mohammed: The Man and His Faith* (New York: Harper & Row, 1960), pp. 54–55. The Ḥadith, moreover, envisages a literal descent of Jesus from heaven: *Kanz al-'Ummāl* 7:2939. David Flusser, "Salvation Present and Future," *Numen* 16 (1969), p. 140, refers to twentieth-century Moslems who, expecting the eschatological climax in the near future, "actually looked for signs in the skies on fine summer evenings."

255. Bryan R. Wilson, *Magic and the Millennium: A Sociological Study of Religious Movements of Protest among Tribal and Third-World Peoples* (New York: Harper & Row, 1973), p. 239.

256. Tai, *Millenarianism*, p. 123.

257. Navarro-Génie, "Failed Prophecy and Revolutionary Violence: The Case of Augusto C. Sandino," at http://www.pagusmundi.com/sandino/failed.htm (6/30/97).

258. *When Prophecy Fails: Cognitive Dissonance in the Prophetic Traditions of the Old Testament* (New York: Seabury, 1979), p. 66.

last day.[259] We can all concur that this is bad hermeneutics, an example of the literal swallowing the figurative. Similarly, to return to the ancient world, one can wholly agree with Wright that 2 *Baruch* 36–37 is a parable that is not a lesson about forestry and viticulture.[260] But one can hardly infer from the appearance of parabolic language in one part of a book that it contains nothing beside parables. Consider *2 Bar.* 29:5: When the Messiah comes, the earth will "yield fruits ten thousandfold. And one vine will be a thousand branches, and one branch will produce a thousand clusters, and one cluster will produce a thousand grapes, and one grape will produce a cor of wine." It would be inane to interpret this without imagination. Prosaic exactitude is not what this text is about. And yet, at the same time, it would be unwise to reduce the language to metaphor. *2 Bar.* 29:5 foretells, in hyperbolic language, a time of unprecedented, supernatural fertility. The physical world will itself be different (compare Zech 14:6–7: "On that day there shall not be either cold or frost. And there shall be continuous day [it is known to the Lord], not day and not night, for at evening time there shall be light").

Most eschatological language functions as both sign and symbol; that is, it has a literal referent—it denotes—and a symbolic dimension—it connotes.[261] There is nothing remarkable about this. A restored '57 Chevy is simultaneously a literal, functioning transport and a symbol of a particular period of American popular culture. When Theudas, probably making himself out to be the eschatological prophet like Moses, promised his followers that he was going to part the Jordan River so that they could pass through (Josephus, *Ant.* 20:97–99), he was doing two things. He was, on the one hand, inviting people to go down to the river, to follow him literally. He was, on the other hand, evoking a world of hoary, salvific memories and so casting symbolic shadows all about. In like fashion, when the Jesus tradition envisions the Son of man coming on the clouds or foretells the general resurrection, we should, even if this puts us in the disagreeable company of modern fundamentalists, think of the redeemer literally flying upon the clouds and of the redeemed literally coming forth from their graves—and also of all that those events represent: the vindication of Jesus, the triumph of believers, the judgment of the wicked, the fulfillment of prophecy, etc. The literal and the symbolic need not be sundered.

---

259. Jacqueline Simpson, "The World Upside Down Shall Be: A Note on the Folklore of Doomsday," *Journal of American Folklore* 91 (1978), pp. 559–67.

260. Wright, *New Testament and the People of God*, pp. 281–82.

261. Helpful here is John J. Collins, "The Symbolism of Transcendence in Jewish Apocalyptic," *Papers of the Chicago Society of Biblical Research* 19 (1974), pp. 5–22.

3. That many ancient Jews took their eschatology more or less literally seemingly follows from their struggles with unfulfilled prophecy. Already one can divine in the Hebrew Bible signs of the cognitive dissonance that trailed upon the failure of forecasts.[262] Isaiah 56–66 presumably projects hope onto the future because the expectant oracles of Isaiah 40–55 had not come to fulfillment.[263] Dan 12:12—"Happy are those who persevere and attain the one thousand three hundred thirty-five days"—was probably imposed upon its predecessor, Dan 12:11—"From the time that the regular burnt offering is taken away and the abomination that desolates is set up, there shall be one thousand two hundred ninety days"—when the latter came to grief against the facts.[264] Outside the Bible one recalls the wrestling with eschatological delay in 1QpHab 7:6–14[265] and the continual reinterpretations of Daniel's seventy weeks of years.[266] One reason the rabbis discouraged messianic speculation was that expectations had been dashed again and again. This also explains the later skepticism of Maimonides. Now if, as Caird and Wright suppose, eschatological prophecies were naturally construed as metaphors, whence all the anxiety and disenchantment? If oracles about the Day of the Lord were poetic ways of predicting judgment and good fortune, woe and vindication, of proclaiming cosmic significance or the hand of God, would it not have been relatively easy to construe them, no matter what came, as fulfilled? Good days and bad times are always around us, and it is as easy to espy God behind everything as it is to see the devil everywhere. How could one ever falsify a metaphorical prophecy?

The question is the more pressing because early Christian literature testifies that believers were troubled by the failure of prophecies in the Jesus tradition to come true. This should be a particularly difficult problem for the view of Caird and Wright. Lk 19:11 and Acts 1:6 dissociate

---

262. See Carroll, *Failure of Prophecy*, passim; also his article, "Eschatological Delay in the Prophetic Tradition?" *ZAW* 94 (1982), pp. 47–58.

263. Carroll, *Failure of Prophecy*, pp. 150–56. On pp. 180–82, however, he observes that Ezra and the Chronicler saw the postexilic community in the land as the fulfillment of prophecy.

264. John J. Collins, *Daniel: A Commentary on the Book of Daniel*, Hermeneia (Minneapolis: Fortress, 1993), pp. 400–401.

265. See A. Strobel, *Untersuchungen zum eschatologischen Verzögerungsproblem auf Grund der spätjüdisch-urchristlichen Geschichte von Habakuk 2:2ff.*, NovTSup 2 (Leiden: E. J. Brill, 1961), pp. 7–19.

266. William Adler, "The Apocalyptic Survey of History Adapted by Christians: Daniel's Prophecy of 70 Weeks," in *The Jewish Apocalyptic Heritage in Early Christianity*, ed. James C. VanderKam and William Adler, CRINT III/4 (Assen: Van Gorcum; Minneapolis: Fortress, 1996), pp. 201–38.

Jesus, but not his disciples, from a mistaken belief in a near end (compare also Lk 24:21 and Acts 1:6). It does not take much detective work to see behind the tendentious notice the unhappy suspicion—perhaps a suspicion made explicit by detractors—that Jesus did in fact erroneously hail the end as near.

Similarly, Jn 21:22–23 reflects consternation that the Beloved Disciple has died although Jesus has not yet returned: "The rumor spread among the brothers that the disciple would not die. Yet Jesus did not say to him that he would not die, but, 'If it is my will that he remain until I come, what is that to you?'" Obviously some such saying as Mk 9:1, interpreted to mean that not all of Jesus' disciples will die before the consummation, is in the background.[267]

The prediction of the eschatological destruction and rebuilding of the temple is also relevant. As we have found, this forecast was reinterpreted in several ways, all of which have in common the attempt to avoid attributing to Jesus a false prophecy.[268]

Clearly the sources betray the tacit awareness that Jesus and those around him erroneously hoped for a near end. This fact has far-reaching consequences. Jesus' prophecies were not originally construed as metaphors fulfilled in his ministry or in the time thereafter. That came only with subsequent, apologetical exegesis.

One might reject this conclusion by saying, as does Lk 19:11, that Jesus' followers did not really grasp his intention. Ethelbert Stauffer took this route. Like others who have offered us a more theologically convenient Jesus, Stauffer asserted that the disciples did not understand their master's message. For they "were wholly children of their time, furiously tossed upon the waves of Jewish political and apocalyptic messianism."[269] This conceit is, however, nothing but unpersuasive apologetics in Luke,

267. See the commentaries on John. That Mk 9:1 or something like it was known to the Johannine community also appears from 8:51–52.

268. See above, pp. 98–101.

269. Ethelbert Stauffer, *Jesus and His Story* (New York: Alfred P. Knopf, 1959), pp. 156–57. Compare C. H. Dodd, *The Founder of Christianity* (New York: Macmillan, 1970), p. 123 (Jesus' reporters "understandably anxious to find his words relevant to their own urgent preoccupations, have given them a twist away from their original intention"); Robert Funk, *Honest to Jesus: Jesus for a New Millennium* (New York: Macmillan, 1996), p. 164 ("We can understand the intrusion of the standard apocalyptic hope back into his [Jesus'] gospel at the hands of his disciples, some of whom had formerly been followers of the Baptist: they had not understood the subtleties of Jesus' position, they had not captured the intensity of his vision, and so reverted to the standard, orthodox scenario once Jesus had departed from the scene"); Donald A. Hagner, *Matthew 14–28*, WBC 33B (Dallas: Word, 1996), p. 711 (Jesus spoke of the temple's end, not of the *parousia*, as imminent; but the

and nothing less in modern scholars. We can no more admire this white-wash than we can believe the rabbinic texts that tendentiously explain sectarianism by positing that the disciples of Antigonus of Socho and other rabbis misapprehended their masters' teaching.[270] We should give credit where credit is due, not exonerate Jesus by blaming his followers. It makes little sense to imagine that Jesus' disciples or those who initially passed on the tradition about him missed the truth but that Luke, writing over a generation after the events he describes, found it, or that modern scholars, removed by the further distance of two millennia, can nonethe-less work around the misunderstandings of Jesus' contemporaries and get back to the facts.

4. The interpretations of Dodd, Glasson, Caird, and Wright are sever-ally illustrations of a phenomenon well known to sociologists of religion. Any millenarian movement that survives must, in due season, come to terms with disappointed expectations since the mythic dream or end never comes. So adherents, as one of several strategies, produce "sec-ondary exegesis"[271] in the face of cognitive dissonance.[272] As Carroll has put it, "dissonance gives rise to hermeneutics. That is, the experience of dissonance forced individuals or groups to reinterpret their basic material or the contemporary events so as to avoid dissonance."[273]

Recently, members of a Bahá'í sect known as Bahá'í's Under the Provisions of the Covenant circulated a prophecy predicting for 1991 massive earthquakes and a meteor striking the earth. When nothing came to pass, their leader explained that there had been a "spiritual

---

disciples could not separate the two events and so wrongly imputed imminence to the lat-ter). According to Wright, *Jesus and the Victory of God*, p. 318, "Jesus knew that his fol-lowers would be muddled and ambiguous."

Interestingly enough, this sort of scapegoating is common outside the academy. Readers may remember that John Lennon's infamous statement about the Beatles being more popu-lar than Jesus Christ was immediately followed by this: "Jesus was all right, but his disciples were thick and ordinary. It's them twisting it that ruins it for me." I remember my father reg-ularly saying the same sort of thing.

270. See Albert I. Baumgarten, "Rabbinic Literature as a Source for the History of Jew-ish Sectarianism in the Second Temple Period," *DSD* 2/1 (1995), pp. 52–53. Note also *t. Ḥag.* 2:9: controversy arose in Israel only after the disciples of Shammai and Hillel did not adequately serve their masters.

271. Talmon, "Pursuit of the Millennium," p. 133.

272. The classic work on cognitive dissonance within a millenarian group is Leon Festinger, Henry W. Riecken, and Stanley Schachter, *When Prophecy Fails: A Social and Psychological Study of a Modern Group that Predicted the Destruction of the World* (New York: Harper & Row, 1964); see especially the introduction, pp. 3–32.

273. *Failure of Prophecy*, p. 110.

earthquake"[274] created by the apostasy of an important member, and that "everything happens on the spiritual plane before it manifests in the physical plane." Earlier, when forecasts that Halley's comet would crash in 1986 failed to materialize, the same leader had this to say: "The spiritual fulfillment did take place. A spiritual stone hit the earth. This stone is the message of the messiahship that only the Bahá'í understand."[275]

Let me offer another example, this one also from the Bahá'í faith but from a much earlier time. When the Bab failed to fulfill literally the prophecies concerning the 12th Imám, his followers offered figurative reinterpretations: "They regarded the sovereignty of the Promised One, like that of the Galilean 'Man of Sorrows,' as a mystical sovereignty; His glory as spiritual, not earthly glory; His conquests as conquests over the cities of men's hearts. . . ."[276] One cannot but think of John's Gospel.

What we find in John's Gospel, namely, the spiritualization of eschatology, a spiritualization nourished by history's failure to halt its normal course, is simply the continuation of a natural process that started long before John. The placement of Mk 9:1 before the transfiguration, and the addition of "hereafter" and "from now on" to Mt 26:64 and Lk 22:69 respectively, are attempts to give eschatological prophecies new applications. Handed on without a context, the plain sense of these texts no doubt became, after the passage of time, embarrassing. The kingdom of God did not soon come, and no one saw the Son of man upon the clouds of heaven. Thus there arose the need to find for these expectations some sort of fulfillment in events that had already transpired. Mk 9:1; Mt 26:64; and Lk 22:69 offer prime examples of "secondary exegesis," of the desire to displace doubt by contriving the fulfillment of unfulfilled expectations. The early and unexpected interpretation of the death and vindication of Jesus in eschatological categories is yet another illustration. For this view of things was undoubtedly fostered by a desire to show that Jesus' imminent eschatological expectation was not false; rather it had begun to be realized in his own fate. I do not have space to do justice to this important subject here, but I have elsewhere given a full account of it.[277]

274. Compare Wright, *Jesus and the Victory of God*, p. 362: Mk 13:24ff. is really a way of saying that what these verses envisage will be "earth-shattering."

275. See Robert W. Balch, John Domitrovich, Barbara Lynn Mahnke, and Vanessa Morrison, "Fifteen Years of Failed Prophecy: Coping with Cognitive Dissonance in a Baha'i Sect," in *Millennium, Messiahs, and Mayhem: Contemporary Apocalyptic Movements*, ed. Thomas Robbins and Susan J. Palmer (New York and London: Routledge, 1997), pp. 78–79.

276. J. E. Esslemont, *Bahá'u'lláh and the New Era* (Wilmette, Ill.: Bahá'í Publishing Trust, 1950), pp. 20–21.

277. See my *End of the Ages*, passim. There I document several early Christian strategies for coping with eschatological disappointment.

THE ESCHATOLOGY OF JESUS • 169

The process of reinterpretation continued with Origen and Augustine and, in time, led to the total dismissal of millenarian expectation by the great patristic authorities.[278] From one point of view, one might think that Dodd, Glasson, Caird, and Wright have just composed new lyrics to a very old theological melody, that they have, whether intentionally or not, turned critical history into a subordinate minister to the needs of Christian doctrine.[279] However that may be, beginning with Origen, most of the church fathers disparaged chiliasm and literal eschatological expectations as "judaizing."[280] They were right—not to disparage, but to make the association with Judaism. For the literal interpretation corresponds to the original intention of the texts, which were forged within the Jewish tradition, a tradition that so often anticipated a literal messianic kingdom in Jerusalem. In other words, the prophecies of a millennium or golden age were originally taken at more or less face value, and this continued to be the case through much of the second century.[281] But as Christianity became an almost wholly Gentile phenomenon and the elapse of the years saw the fires of eschatological enthusiasm die down, things changed. Eventually the fathers, like the rationalist Maimonides after them, and like some New Testament scholars today, came to regard eschatological prophecy as "merely a parable and a figure of speech" (*Mishneh Torah* 14).

Concluding Observations

Graham Allan has written that

> millennial movements are attempts to interpret and order situations in which a group of individuals feel that their total worth is being denied.

---

278. See Hans Bietenhard, "The Millennial Hope in the Early Church," *SJT* 6 (1953), pp. 12–30.

279. Wright, *Jesus and the Victory of God*, p. 342, rightly foresees that "the scholarly are likely to accuse me of pious trickery, getting round the problem that Jesus seems to have been mistaken." He goes on, of course, to insist that his interpretation best fits the first-century understanding of apocalyptic language.

280. Origen, *De prin.* 2:11:2; Basil, *Ep.* 263:4. Compare Eusebius, *H.E.* 7:24: Nepos "taught that the promises given to the saints in the Scriptures should be understood more as the Jews understood them, and supposed that there would be a certain millennium of sensual luxury on this earth."

281. Jean Daniélou, *The Theology of Jewish Christianity* (London: Darton, Longman & Todd, 1964), pp. 377–404. When Charles E. Hill, *Regnum Caelorum: Patterns of Future Hope in Early Christianity* (Clarendon: Oxford, 1992), argues, against the usual view, that millennialism was not clearly the predominant view in the second-century church, he has in mind an earthly kingdom of limited duration. But did not some think of the kingdom as both earthly and eternal?

The assumptions they make about the social world no longer seem to match reality. Their usual frame of reference no longer accounts for or explains the world as they are now experiencing it. Consequently they need to re-interpret the situation using a new frame of reference and making new assumptions about reality. Paradoxically though, these new assumptions cannot be "new" at all if they are to be accepted as satisfactory interpretations of the present. Rather they must be modifications and re-emphases of traditional cultural patterns.[282]

This generalization in its entirety probably holds for the pre-Easter Jesus movement. Here, however, I wish to comment only on the final two sentences. Millenarian movements do not commence by creating truly new eschatological doctrines. They typically take up traditional convictions and apply them to the present. This does not mean that nothing new will come out of such movements. But their initial appeal makes use of "traditional cultural patterns." Millenarian groups recurrently reinterpret, with reference to their contemporary situation, conventional expectations. In the words of Tord Olsson, they effect "the revitalization of mythic material."[283]

This is what happened with Jesus. The final judgment, the resurrection of the dead, the restoration of Israel, and the great tribulation were scarcely new ideas. They were rather part of Jesus' Jewish heritage, part of an archetypically compelling eschatological scenario, part of the "little tradition" that came to him through the institutions of his village life.[284] What he did with them was twofold. First, like others before and after him, he made them overwhelmingly relevant to his own time and place

282. Graham Allan, "A Theory of Millennialism: The Irvingite Movement as an Illustration," *The British Journal of Sociology* 25 (1974), p. 309.

283. Tord Olsson, "The Apocalyptic Activity: The Case of Jāmāp Nāmag," in Hellholm, *Apocalypticism in the Mediterranean World* (Tübingen: Mohr-Siebeck, 1979), p. 29. See further Maria Isaura Pereira de Queiroz, "Messianic Myths and Movements," *Diogenes* 90 (1975), pp. 78–99, and Tai, *Millenarianism*, p. 29. According to Mircea Eliade, *Mephistopheles and the Androgyne: Studies in Religious Myth and Symbol* (New York: Sheed and Ward, 1965), p. 137, cargo cult leaders "have merely resumed, amplified, revalorised and charged with prophetic and millenary power the traditional religious theme that the Cosmos renews itself periodically, or to be more exact that it is symbolically re-created every year." Even if these words are exaggeration—see G.W. Trompf, *Melanesian Religion* (Cambridge: Cambridge University Press, 1991), pp. 198–201—the main point, that millenarian visions revise tradition, remains valid.

284. On the concept of "great tradition" and "little tradition" see Robert Redfield, *Peasant Society and Culture* (Chicago: University of Chicago Press, 1956). On the application to millenarism see Ernest R. Sandeen, "The 'Little Tradition' and the Form of Modern Millenarianism," *The Annual Review of the Social Sciences of Religion* 4 (1980), pp. 165–81.

through the notion of imminence. Nearness was designed to make people attend to the one thing needful.

Second, his association of eschatological expectations with events and persons around him gave traditional myths a fresh and inventive application. Although this chapter has fastened upon what Jesus shared with his contemporaries rather than points of originality, it remains true that he went beyond tradition when he associated the coming of the kingdom with John the Baptist (Q 16:16; Mk 9:11–13) and linked the judgment with response to himself and his itinerants (Q 10:13–15; 12:8–9). The upshot of this and other innovations,[285] of Jesus' improvisation on Jewish eschatology, was the creation of a new religious identity based on a novel interpretation of the world in the light of Jewish tradition. To some extent, then, Jesus was a transformer as well as a tradent of culture, and no doubt whatever success he enjoyed derived as much from his creative ability to relate, in novel fashion, conventional symbols directly to his audience's situation as from their political, economic, and social circumstances.[286] Jesus' millenarian eschatology was, then, the revised religious story that became the context of his followers' experience. That story, with its belief in the impossible and its hope in a transcendent reality, freed imaginations to pass creatively beyond the mundane so that those who believed could, despite difficult times and "little faith," find the meaning of their existence.

285. For example, Jesus seems to have muted the element of vengeance in his eschatological language; see Riches, *Transformation*.

286. For this formulation I am indebted to Robin M. Wright and Jonathan D. Hill, "History, Ritual, and Myth: Nineteenth Century Millenarian Movements in the Northwest Amazon," *Ethnohistory* 33 (1986), p. 32.

3

JESUS AS
MILLENARIAN ASCETIC

DELETING A CONSENSUS

Current Opinion

"Asceticism," which may be defined as "the practice of the denial of the physical or psychological desires in order to attain a spiritual ideal or goal,"[1] is not a word we usually associate with Jesus. Modern scholars, typically on the basis of Mk 2:18–20[2] and Q 7:31–35,[3] routinely assert, in the words of John Dominic Crossan, that whereas "John lived an apocalyptic asceticism. . . Jesus did just the opposite."[4] According to Robert Funk, "as a follower of John, Jesus would have become an ascetic"; but Jesus "soon rejected the options offered by the Baptist. He returned to

1. So Arthur Vööbus in *Encyclopaedia Britannica*, 15th ed., s.v. "Asceticism." Compare Walter O. Kaelber, "Asceticism," in *The Encyclopedia of Religion*, ed. Mircea Eliade (New York: Macmillan, 1987), vol. 1, p. 441: "Although the modern word *asceticism* has eluded any universally accepted definition, the term, when used in a religious context, may be defended as a voluntary, sustained, and at least partially systematic program of self-discipline and self-denial in which immediate, sensual, or profane gratification are renounced in order to attain a higher spiritual state or a more thorough absorption in the sacred." There is a wealth of comparative material in the old *Encyclopaedia of Religion and Ethics*, ed. James Hastings (Edinburgh: T. & T. Clark, 1924), s.v., "Asceticism" (by various authors).
2. "As long as the bridegroom is with them they cannot fast." Compare *Gos. Thom.* 104.
3. Here the Son of man (= Jesus), in contrast to John, has come "eating and drinking."
4. John Dominic Crossan, *The Historical Jesus: The Life of a Mediterranean Jewish Peasant* (San Francisco: Harper San Francisco, 1991), p. 260. Compare Johannes Leipoldt, *Griechische Philosophie und frühchristliche Askese*, Berichte über die Verhandlungen der Sächsischen Akademie der Wissenschaften zu Leipzig, Philologisch-historische Klasse 106/4 (Berlin: Akademie Verläg, 1961), pp. 31–32, and Bernhard Lohse, *Askese und Mönchtum in der Antike und in der alten Kirche* (Munich: R. Oldenbourg, 1969), pp. 115–16.

hellenized Galilee and feasted rather than fasted. His rule was not merely to simplify, simplify, like Henry David Thoreau, but to celebrate, celebrate, celebrate." Jesus was indeed "the proverbial party animal."[5]

Although many would regard this last formulation as extreme—where does Jesus "party" in any modern sense of the word?—the scholarly wisdom now has it that Jesus "was anything but an ascetic."[6] If he accepted the hospitality of the well-to-do,[7] if he moved in the company of women,[8] and if he did not flee from the world,[9] then how could it be otherwise?

Often, however, things are not what they seem to be. The reference in Q 7:31–35[10] to Jesus "eating and drinking"—a phrase denoting carefree excess[11]—presumably adopts the polemical language of Jesus' adversaries. Jesus, like Paul after him, was wont to take up his opponents' abuse, imaginatively remake it, and then hand it back to them. So perhaps the "eating and drinking" of Q 7:31–35 should not be reckoned an objective description of circumstances any more than the Synoptics' polemic against the Pharisees.[12] Those who make so much of Q 7:31–35 always neglect to remind us that Jesus himself, in Q 17:26–30, uses "eating and drinking" with a pejorative sense: "Just as it was in the [proverbially wicked] days of Noah, so too it will be in the days of the Son of man. They were eating and drinking," etc. (note also Q 12:45).

5. Robert W. Funk, *Honest to Jesus: Jesus for a New Millennium* (San Francisco: Harper San Francisco, 1996), p. 203. Klaus Berger, *Wer war Jesus wirklich?* (Stuttgart: Quell, 1995), pp. 28–35, similarly argues that Jesus at one time lived as a Nazarite but later gave it up.

6. So Robert L. Webb, "John the Baptist and His Relationship to Jesus," in *Studying the Historical Jesus: Evaluations of the State of Current Research*, NTTS 19, ed. Bruce Chilton and Craig A. Evans (Leiden: E. J. Brill, 1994), p. 226. This conviction also appears in more popular works; see, e.g., Uta Ranke-Heinemann, *Women, Sexuality and the Catholic Church* (New York: Penguin, 1990), pp. 43–44. Compare already Adolf Harnack, *What Is Christianity?* (New York: Harper & Brothers, 1957), pp. 87–88. An apparent exception to the consensus is Wayne A. Meeks, *The Moral World of the First Christians* (Philadelphia: Westminster, 1986), pp. 104–105: "Many of the sayings of Jesus seem to demand an ascetic detachment" from an "exploitative society." Earlier, Joseph Klausner, *Jesus of Nazareth: His Life, Times, and Teaching* (New York: Menorah, 1925), p. 405, spoke of Jesus' "extremist ascetic ethical system."

7. So at least Mk 2:15–17 and Lk 19:1–10.

8. C. Ricci, *Mary Magdalene and Many Others* (Minneapolis: Fortress, 1994).

9. There is no need to document that the tradition not only puts Jesus in houses and cities but in the company of disreputable individuals.

10. I here assume both the unity and authenticity of the Q unit; compare Ulrich Luz, *Das Evangelium nach Matthäus, 2. Teilband Mt 8–17*, EKK I/2 (Neukirchen: Neukirchener, 1990), p. 184. But an origin with the community would make my case even easier.

11. Isa 22:13; Mt 24:38, 49; 1 Cor 15:32.

12. J. Blinzler, Εἰσὶν "εὐνοῦχοι," *ZNW* 48 (1957), pp. 254–70. Note Mk 2:17; Q 7:31–35; 11:19; Mt 19:12; 21:31. See further James M. Robinson, "Galilean Upstarts: A Sot's Cynical Disciples?" in Petersen, Vos, and de Jonge, *Sayings of Jesus*, pp. 223–49.

Beyond this, Mk 2:18–20[13] is not a blanket denial of the legitimacy of all fasting. Were it otherwise, Jesus would here prove himself an antinomian, for the Torah itself prescribes fasting for the day of atonement.[14] The passage from Mark presumably tells us little more than that Jesus, unlike the Pharisees and the followers of John, did not set aside fixed days every week for fasting. One should, moreover, not neglect that Q tells a story in which Jesus fasts (Q 4:1–13),[15] that Mark at one point may associate Jesus with Nazirite tradition,[16] and that M attributes its instructions for fasting to Jesus (Mt 6:16–18). All this sits a bit uneasily beside the proposal that Jesus either abandoned fasting altogether or (as the *Gospel of Thomas* would have it) actually opposed the practice.[17] I recall that when the seventeenth-century Jewish Messiah, Sabbatai Ṣevi, sought to turn "the sorrow of the fast into the rejoicing of gladness" (note Mk 2:18–19), he abolished the abstinence commemorating the destruction of the temple and Jewish exile—but he did not set aside all fasting. On the contrary, his followers continued the regular Monday and Thursday fasts.[18] Probably in like fashion Jesus' celebration of the presence of the kingdom did not exclude other, more solemn sorts of behavior.

But there is an even weightier point to consider. In at least two respects the Jesus tradition clearly moves in ascetic directions. There is no ques-

---

13. Most assume that this unit rests upon something Jesus said; compare Crossan, *Historical Jesus*, pp. 259–60.

14. Lev 16:29–31; 23:32; Num 29:7–11; compare Philo, *Spec. leg.* 2:195; *m. Yoma* 8:1.

15. On the problem of historical memory in this complex see my article, "Behind the Temptations of Jesus: Q 4:1–13 and Mk 1:12–13," in *Authenticating the Deeds of Jesus*, ed. Bruce Chilton and Craig A. Evans (Leiden: E. J. Brill, forthcoming).

16. See Frans Mussner, "Ein Wortspiel in Mk 1,24?" *BZ* 4 (1960), pp. 285–86. Jesus seems to be a sort of Nazirite in Matthew's infancy narrative; compare Raymond E. Brown, *The Birth of the Messiah: A Commentary on the Infancy Narratives in Matthew and Luke* (New York: Doubleday, 1977), pp. 210–11, 223–25. For additional possible links between Jesus and the Nazirite tradition see Klaus Berger, "Jesus als Nasoräer/Nasiräer," *NovT* 38 (1996), pp. 323–35.

17. Ulrich Luz, *Matthew 1–7: A Commentary* (Minneapolis: Augsburg, 1989), p. 355, in raising the possibility that both Mt 6:16–18 and Mk 2:19 go back to Jesus, has offered that "Matt. 6:16–18 could be a general instruction to the people, Mark 2:19a could refer to the special situation of the disciples. Or Mark 2:19a could have in mind the praxis of the disciples as a group while Matt. 6:16–18 speaks of the private fasting of the individual." While I doubt that Matt. 6:16–18 goes back to Jesus, Luz's comments do show that the implications of Mk 2:19 are not unequivocal. Perhaps we should wonder whether it is wise to interpret what may have been little more than an on-the-spot riposte as though it were a well-considered statement of fixed principle. And surely J. Behm, *TDNT* 4 (1964), p. 932, n. 59, was right when he asserted that "it is going too far to conclude from the practice of the disciples in Mk. 2:18 that non-fasting was for Jesus a form of life."

18. Gershom Scholem, *Sabbatai Ṣevi: The Mystical Messiah*, Bollingen Series 93 (Princeton: Princeton University Press, 1973), p. 414.

tion about this with regard to wealth.[19] Jesus asked at least some individuals to give away all their money and goods.[20] He sent out itinerants with less than the bare essentials for survival and told them not to worry about food and clothing.[21] And he himself abandoned work and family and had no place to lay his head.[22]

In addition to reporting that Jesus demanded and embodied rigorous self-denial with regard to what Q calls mammon, the tradition about him assumes that he was unmarried.[23] It further contains complexes which either promote celibacy or caution against sexual desire. It is the first purpose of this chapter to investigate these complexes. The conclusion will be that, whatever Jesus taught with regard to fasting, his teaching and behavior in other respects reflects a type of asceticism, and further that this circumstance should be related to his eschatological convictions.

Sexual Desire in the Jesus Tradition

Four complexes fall initially to be considered:

1. Mt 19:10–12 concludes with this sentence: "For there are eunuchs who have been so from birth, and there are eunuchs who have been made eunuchs by others, and there are eunuchs who have made themselves eunuchs for the sake of the kingdom of heaven. Let anyone accept this who can." These words are sometimes construed, in their Matthean context, as recommending that those who have separated from a spouse should not remarry.[24] The more likely interpretation is that Mt 19:10–12 is about life-long celibacy: some people have the self-imposed discipline to remain unmarried and to refrain from sexual intercourse throughout their lives.[25] Whatever interpretation one follows, the text obviously com-

---

19. Compare Peter Nagel, *Die Motivierung der Askese in der alten Kirche und der Ursprung des Mönchtums*, TU 95 (Berlin: Akademie, 1966), pp. 6–7.

20. See, e.g., Mk 10:17–27. The demand is probably implicit in Mk 1:16–20; 2:14; and Q 9:57–60.

21. See, e.g., Q 10:1–12 and 12:22–31.

22. Note especially Q 9:58. Lk 8:1–3 says that certain women provided for Jesus and his disciples out of their resources; and Jn 13:29 refers to a "common purse."

23. There is no reason to question this, notwithstanding Stephen Twycross, "Was Jesus Married?" *ExpT* 107 (1996), p. 334. Paul, in 1 Cor 9:5, refers to the female companions of important men. He surely would also have named Jesus in this connection if he had known he was married. Note further the loud silence of Mk 3:31–35 and 6:3 par.

24. So Q. Quesnell, "'Made themselves Eunuchs for the Kingdom of Heaven' (Mt 19:12)," *CBQ* 30 (1968), pp. 335–58.

25. See W. D. Davies and Dale C. Allison, Jr., *A Critical and Exegetical Commentary on the Gospel according to Saint Matthew*, 3 vols., ICC (Edinburgh: T. & T. Clark, 1988,

176 + JESUS OF NAZARETH

mends the personal sacrifice of sexual activity—probably not literal castration[26]—when it is "for the sake of the kingdom of heaven." Although
Kurt Niederwimmer may exaggerate when he speaks, with regard to Mt
19:12, of a "truly comprehensive sexual asceticism,"[27] the verse certainly
does teach that sex is not necessary for all, and that in certain circumstances abstinence will accord with the divine will.

2. In Mt 5:27–28 we read: "You have heard that it was said, 'You
shall not commit adultery.' But I say to you that everyone who looks at a
woman with lust has already committed adultery with her in his heart."
This sets a fence around the Torah: if there is no lust in the heart there is
not going to be adultery. The prohibition, which has good Jewish and pagan parallels,[28] could have to do specifically with a man lusting after another man's wife, for the Greek word translated above as "woman" may
here mean "wife," and the subject of the Hebrew Bible citation is adultery. Nonetheless, it would seem odd to narrow the scope of the imperative—as though it censures unlawful lust toward a married woman but
not lust toward an unmarried woman, prostitute or not. Fornication was
not, in the first century, a second-class sin but rather in the same category
as adultery (note Mt 15:19).

Mt 5:27–28 probably does not, one should nonetheless add, condemn
the sexual impulse as such. Matthew's construction (πρὸς τὸ ἐπιθυμῆσαι)
implies that what is condemned is not the entrance of a thought but let-

---

1991, 1997), vol. 3, pp. 19–24, and Joachim Gnilka, *Das Matthäusevangelium*, 2 vols.,
HTKNT I/1, 2 (Freiburg: Herder, 1986, 1988), vol. 2, pp. 154–56.

26. For the reasons see T. W. Manson, *The Sayings of Jesus* (London: SCM, 1949),
pp. 215–16. This is true even though literal castration is well attested in the history of religion; see Dario M. Cosi, "Castration," in Eliade, *Encyclopedia of Religion* (New York:
Macmillan, 1987), vol. 2, pp. 109–12. Note also Philo, *Quod det. pot. ins.* 175–76: "Those
who are not utterly ignorant would choose to be blinded rather than see unfitting things,
and to be deprived of hearing rather than listen to harmful words, and to have their tongues
cut out to save them from uttering anything that should not be divulged. . . . It is better to
be made a eunuch than to be mad after illicit unions."

27. Kurt Niederwimmer, *Askese und Mysterium: Über Ehe, Ehescheidung und Ehe-
verzicht in den Anfängen des christlichen Glaubens*, FRLANT 113 (Göttingen: Vandenhoeck & Ruprecht, 1975), p. 53.

28. In the *Testament of Issachar*, the patriarch, at the end of his life, boasts, "I have not
had intercourse with any woman other than my wife, nor was I promiscuous by lustful
look" (7:2). In the *Mekilta* of R. Simeon we read that one should not commit adultery
"either with the eye or with the heart" (111). R. Simeon ben Lakish is recorded as saying,
"Even he who visualizes himself in the act of adultery is called an adulterer" (*Leviticus Rab.*
23:12). The Stoic philosopher Epictetus congratulated himself with these words: "Today,
when I saw a beautiful woman, I did not say to myself, Oh, that I could possess her . . . nor
did I go on to fancy her in my arms" (Arrian, *Diss.* 2:18).

ting it incite to wrongful passion (compare the use of the related expressions in Mt 6:1 and 23:5). One might translate: "Everyone looking upon a woman *in order to* lust after her. . . ." This makes the problem not the appearance of desire but what one does with it.[29] Still, Matthew's verses regard sexual desire as a potentially dangerous thing, as something one must seek to control. Sensual pleasure is to be constrained. There must be some sort of abstinence on the part of the imagination.

3. In Mk 12:18–27, Jesus affirms that, in their resurrected state, "(Men) neither marry nor are (women) given in marriage." The justification for this is brief: they will be "like angels in heaven." The meaning appears to be related to the sentiment in the rabbinic source, *b. Ber.* 17a: "In the world to come there is no . . . propagation."[30] No doubt the belief was widespread. Its appearance in the Jesus tradition should not surprise, for in messianic movements generally, "the new reign is often thought of as being one where there will no longer be 'men nor women.'"[31] The reason is obvious. The fixed roles of men and women are always symbols of the old order of things, so altering those roles becomes a sign of the new order.[32]

In first-century Judaism, sex was largely thought of as serving the purpose of procreation, not pleasure,[33] and angels (usually conceived of as male)[34] were thought of as deathless. It followed that intercourse for the

29. Compare Evagrius, *Praktikos* 6, on evil thoughts: "It is not in our power to determine whether we are disturbed by these thoughts, but it is up to us to decide if they are to linger within us or not and whether or not they are to stir up our passions."

30. Compare *Midr. Ps.* on Ps 146:7 (there will be no intercourse in the age to come, because the presence of the *Shekinah* will be constant) and the commentary on this by W. D. Davies, *The Setting of the Sermon on the Mount* (Cambridge: Cambridge University Press, 1966), pp. 163–65. The opposite view is, however, also met with; see *y. Qidd.* 4:12(66d) (compare the view of Cerinthus according to Eusebius, *H.E.* 3:28). The Zoroastrian work, the *Bundahishn*, teaches that intercourse will take place in the coming golden age but that no children will be born; see R. C. Zaehner, *The Teachings of the Magi: A Compendium of Zoroastrian Beliefs* (New York: Macmillan, 1956), p. 149.

31. Henri Desroche, *The Sociology of Hope* (London: Routledge & Kegan Paul, 1979), p. 91. This seems to be a part of Pauline thought; see J. Louis Martyn, "Apocalyptic Antinomies in Paul's Letter to the Galatians," *NTS* 31 (1985), pp. 410–24.

32. Ted Daniels, *Millennialism: An International Bibliography* (New York and London: Garland, 1992), p. xiii, observes that, when human beings envisage paradise, "joyous sex is free for everyone, or else no one wants it any more, which amounts to the same time."

33. Full documentation in Dale C. Allison, Jr., "Divorce, Celibacy, and Joseph," *JSNT* 49 (1993), pp. 3–10.

34. Recall the male names for the angels—Michael, Gabriel, Raphael, Uriel, etc.—and 1 Cor 11:2–16, where unveiled females (but not males) evidently tempt the angels. *Jub.* 15:27 informs us that the angels were born circumcised. According to an old interpretation of the myth in Gen 6:2, the wicked angels engaged in sexual intercourse with human females (*1 Enoch* 6–7, etc.).

angels was unnecessary and would only have been self-indulgence. So too, according to Mark's argument, shall it for the saints in the world to come. They, having become deathless like the holy ones in heaven,[35] will no longer need to reproduce. Intercourse will be no more. The saints, like the good angels who "restrained themselves" (2 Bar. 56:14) when the bad angels fell (Gen 6:2), will forever be chaste.

The chief point for us is that Mk 12:25 can envision human nature apart from, or without any use of, its sexual component. Christian monasticism saw this plainly. Our text became not only inspiration for imagining the Christian life to be an imitation of the angels[36] but also, and in particular, the exhortation to asceticism was often supported by appeal to the precedent of the heavenly hosts.[37] Virginity especially was espoused as in accord with the angelic standard.[38]

4. Mk 9:42–48 contains a series of sayings warning against sins of the hand, foot, and eye: "If your hand causes you to stumble, cut it off; it is better for you to enter life maimed than to have two hands and to go to hell, to the unquenchable fire," etc. The commentators are nearly united in finding here little more than vivid illustrations of the principle of self-denial. "The aim is to impress indelibly upon us that the kingdom of God is worth any sacrifice."[39] Or, as Alfred Plummer, commenting on the Matthean parallel in 18:8–9, put it, "We sacrifice even the most valuable of our limbs, in order to avoid the death of the body by incurable disease.

35. The thought that eschatological destiny will be angelic is well-attested: Wisd 5:5 (assuming that "sons of God" = angels); 4QSb 4:25; 4Q511 fr. 35; 1 En. 104:1–6; 2 Bar. 51:5, 10; Acts 6:15; T. Isaac 4:43–48, etc. Also relevant are those texts which promise the saints that they will become stars or like stars (e.g., Dan 12:2–3; 1 En. 104:2–7; 4 Macc 17:5; 2 Bar. 51:10; LAB 33:5; As. Mos. 10:9; CIJ 2:43–44, no. 788), for stars were typically thought of as angels; see my article, "What Was the Star that Guided the Magi?" BR 9/6 (1993), pp. 20–24, 63, and Alan Scott, Origen and the Life of the Stars: A History of an Idea (Oxford: Clarendon, 1991).

36. See Nagel, Motivierung, pp. 34–48. This is in continuity with Jewish tradition; see 1 Sam 29:9; 2 Sam 14:17; 19:27; Jub. 30:18; Philo, Sacr. Abel 1:5; Hist. Rech. 7:11; Prayer of Jacob; Prayer of Joseph; Tg. Neofiti on Gen 32:29; b. Hag. 16a.

37. Ps.-Ephrem, Herm. hom. 129; Theodoret of Cyrrhus, Graec. affect. 91–92; Evagrius Ponticus, Or. 39, 113, 142; Babai, Ep. ad Cyr. 1; Evagrius Scholasticus, H.E. 1.13; Leontius of Neapolis, Vit. Sym. 1; Jacob of Serug, Hom. Sym. (ed. Bedjan), p. 660; Nicephorus of Constantinople, Antirr. 2:6.

38. Clement of Alexandria, Paed. 2:10; Methodius of Olympus, Symp. 8:2; Gregory of Nazianzus, Orat. 37:10–11; John Climacus, Scal. 15; Mark the Ascetic in Philokalia 1 (ed. Palmer et al.), p. 153.

39. D. E. Nineham, Saint Mark, Westminster Pelican Commentaries (Philadelphia: Westminster, 1977), p. 255. Helmut Koester, "Mark 9:43–47 and Quintilian 8.3.75," HTR 71 (1978), pp. 151–53, however, thinks the verses were "originally designed as a rule for the community: members of the Christian church who give offense should be excluded."

We ought to be ready to sacrifice things of still greater value, in order to avoid the death of the soul. . . ."[40] This, however, probably reads too little into the text.

The earliest surviving interpreter of Mark's sequence is Matthew. He places it immediately after 5:27–28, the verses on lust which we have already examined. In other words, he appears to give the complex a sexual application: plucking out the eye and cutting off the hand are ways of avoiding sexual sin. The point is not missed by Justin Martyr, who introduces Mt 5:29 under the remark, "Concerning chastity, he [Jesus] uttered such sentiments as these." Other early interpreters also maintain a sexual reference.[41]

A remarkable talmudic parallel sets us in the same direction. According to *m. Nid.* 2:1, "the hand that oftentimes makes examination [of the private parts] is, among women, praiseworthy [because it is necessary to determine menstrual uncleanness]; but among men—let it be cut off!" The commentary on this in *b. Nid.* 13b includes the following:

> Have we here learned a law as in the case where R. Huna [really] cut off someone's hand [see *b. Sanh.* 58b]? Or is it merely an execration? Come and hear what was taught: R. Tarfon said, "If his hand touched the membrum let his hand be cut off upon his belly." "But," they said to him, "would not his belly be split?" He said, "It is preferable that his belly shall be split rather than that he should go down into the pit of destruction."

The parallels between these sentences and Mk 9:43 are several.[42] In both the hand that sins should be cut off. In both this act of mutilation is preferable to going to "the pit of destruction" or "Gehenna." And in both the thought is expressed in the so-called "Tobspruch" or "better . . . than" form.[43]

It is possible, in view of the great distance in time between Mark and the Babylonian Talmud, that we should refrain from making anything much of the parallel. Two other options, however, seem more plausible.

40. Alfred Plummer, *An Exegetical Commentary on the Gospel according to St. Matthew* (New York: Charles Scribner's Sons, 1910), p. 250.

41. E.g., *Ps.-Clem. Rec.* 7:37; Clement of Alexandria, *Paed.* 3:11. Sextus, *Sent.* 273, may also be relevant: here the cutting off of limbs is in the service of "self-control."

42. In addition to what follows see especially Will Deming, "Mark 9.42–10.12, Matthew 5.27–32, and *b. Nid.* 13b: A First Century Discussion of Male Sexuality," *NTS* 36 (1990), pp. 130–41.

43. On this form see G. F. Snyder, "The *Tobspruch* in the New Testament," *NTS* 23 (1976), pp. 117–20.

One is that here rabbinic tradition was influenced by Christian tradition.[44] In this case the application in the Talmud would establish what we already know from patristic texts, that at least some people in antiquity gave Jesus' words about cutting off bodily members a sexual sense.

The other possibility is the serious prospect that Mk 9:43 and *b. Nid.* 13b are so close because they independently reflect a traditional saying or sentiment.[45] In this last case the application in the rabbinic text to sexual behavior (the context in the Talmud is a discussion of masturbation) would invite us to infer that Mk 9:42–48 originally concerned sexual sin. This was the view of George Foot Moore.[46]

If one supposes that Mk 9:42–48 originally had to do with sexual sins, it is easy to explain the references to eye, hand, and foot. An injunction to pluck out the eyes, understood as a figurative way of demanding one guard the eyes from lust, falls in line with many old texts. In Job 31:1 we read, "I have made a covenant with my eyes; how then could I look upon a virgin?" Ben Sira warns, "Turn away your eyes from a shapely woman, and do not look intently at beauty belonging to another; many have been misled by a woman's beauty, and by it passion is kindled like a fire" (Ecclus 9:8). The *Testament of Reuben* speaks of the spirit of seeing, "which comes with desire" (2:4–6). Ancient Jewish and Christian literature is filled with expressions such as "lustful eyes" (1QS 1:6), "eye brimming with adultery" (2 Pet 2:14), and "the desire of the eyes" (1 Jn 2:16). Ephraem, *Comm. Diat.* 6:8, could say simply, "the eye is lust." Getting rid of this sort of eye would make perfect sense.

With regard to cutting off the hand, in both *m. Nid.* 2:1 and *b. Nid.*

---

44. Herbert W. Basser, "The Meaning of 'Shtuth,' Gen. R. 11 in Reference to Matthew 5.29–30 and 18.8–9," *NTS* 31 (1985), pp. 148–51, has argued that at least *Gen. Rab.* 11:7 shows knowledge of the Synoptic saying.

45. There are also some interesting non-Jewish parallels. See Hildebrecht Hommel, "Herrnworte im Lichte sokratischer Überlieferung," in *Sebasmata: Studien zur antiken Religionsgeschichte und zum frühen Christentum, Band II*, WUNT 32 (Tübingen: Mohr-Siebeck, 1984), pp. 51–75, and Johannes Schattenmann, "Jesus und Pythagoras," *Kairos* 21 (1979), pp. 215–20. These parallels suggest that, if indeed a Jewish tradition is behind the Synoptics and its talmudic relatives, then that tradition may owe something to Hellenistic sources.

46. See *Judaism in the First Centuries of the Christian Era* (New York: Schocken, 1971), vol. 2, p. 268. So too Deming, "Mark 9.42–10.12," who observes that, if *b. Ned.* 13b and the Synoptics have in common warnings about eye and hand, the former also condemns those who play with children (pederasty) whereas the latter censures those who scandalize "little ones." I also owe to Deming the observation that σκανδαλίζω has a sexual sense in *Ps. Sol.* 16:7. Although Niederwimmer, *Askese*, pp. 29–33, does not examine the rabbinic parallels in detail, he concurs that our complex originally had to do with sexual sins.

13b the hand that is cut off is the hand that touches the male member;[47] and already Deut 25:11–12 has this to say: "If men get into a fight with one another, and the wife of one intervenes to rescue her husband from the grip of his opponents by reaching out and seizing his genitals, you shall cut off her hand; show no pity" (compare Philo, *Spec. leg.* 3:175). The Talmud more than once expresses serious concern with the issue of a man touching his sexual member with his hands, even when only urinating (*b. Šabb.* 41a, 43a; *b. Nid.* 13a). Clearly Mk 9:43 could have been formulated with sexual sin in view.

Concerning the cutting off of the "foot," we could have here a well-known euphemism for the male sex organ, as in Exod 4:25; Deut 28:57; 2 Kgs 18:27 *Qere* ("water of their feet"); Ruth 3:7; Isa 6:2; 7:20; and Ezek 16:25.[48] And if one equates "foot" with the sex organ in Mk 9:45, the verse would then become the equivalent of Mt 19:12, where those who make themselves eunuchs are commended.[49] The other possibility is that "foot" and "feet" are here used of sexual sins because they walk the path that leads to the house of illicit union, as in Proverbs 5–6.[50]

Although I am proposing that Mk 9:42–48 was first formulated with sexual sins in view, this must be differentiated from a literal interpretation. It is true that the excision of body parts was known,[51] and there are, as noted already, history-of-religion parallels to amputation for religious reasons. One recalls the tale of the Zen student Hui-k'o, who cut off his arm to prove his religious sincerity. Yet it is unlikely that Mk 9:42–48 envisages physical amputation any more than it seriously envisions mutilated resurrection bodies. In Ps 137:5 the speaker says, "If I forget you, O Jerusalem, let my right hand wither." Prov 10:31 speaks of the tongue

---

47. *b. Nid.* 13b construes Isa 1:15 ("your hands are full of blood") to refer to "those that commit masturbation with their hands." The story of the Lord's displeasure with Onan in Gen 38:9–10 was widely understood to prohibit masturbation; compare *b. Nid.* 13a. On the seemingly universal condemnation of masturbation in old Jewish sources see David Feldman, *Marital Relations, Birth Control and Abortion in Jewish Law* (New York: Schocken, 1968), pp. 109–31, 144–68. One should perhaps note that the Jesus tradition alludes to the story of Onan in Mk 12:19 par.

48. "Hand" is only rarely used in this way; see Isa 57:8.

49. I do not, however, wish to follow Schattenmann, "Jesus und Pythagoras," in conjecturing that Mt 19:11–12 originally belonged with the material in 5:29-30//Mk 9:43–48.

50. See Robert H. Gundry, *Mark: A Commentary on His Apology for the Cross* (Grand Rapids: Eerdmans, 1993), pp. 524–25. Compare Prov 7:11 and *Sent. Syr. Menander* 2:45.

51. See, e.g., Deut 25:11–12; Judg 16:21; Josephus, *Vita* 171–73, 177; *Bell.* 2:642–44; *b. Pes.* 57b; *b. Sanh.* 58b.

of the wicked being cut off, and Joel 2:13 calls to repentance with the phrase, "tear your heart." Mk 9:42–48, in accord with the earliest interpretations,[52] probably employs the same sort of figurative hyperbole as these Hebrew Bible texts. One is reminded of Col 3:5, where the writer commands readers to "put to death (your) members on the earth." This figurative imperative is followed by a list of sexual sins: "immorality, impurity, passion, evil desire. . . ."[53]

The Origin of the Complexes

We have looked at two and maybe three complexes that demand restraint with regard to sexual desire and another that envisages perfected human nature as doing without its sexual component.[54] Their ascetic tendency is manifest. The next question before us then becomes, How many of these texts go back to something that Jesus might have said?

In chapter 1 I gave reasons for believing that Mk 12:18–27 preserves teaching from Jesus.[55] What then of Mt 19:12?[56] The arguments that

---

52. See Sextus, *Sent.* 12–13; *Ps.-Clem. Rec.* 7:37; Origen, *Comm. on Mt.* 15:1.

53. For the possibility that Col 3:5 alludes to the tradition behind Mk 9:43–48 see David Wenham, *Paul: Follower of Jesus or Founder of Christianity?* (Grand Rapids: Eerdmans, 1995), pp. 274–75.

54. I have passed over Jesus' prohibition of divorce (Q 16:18; Mk 10:11–12), which equates remarriage with adultery. It may be relevant that this passage disallows the experience of multiple sexual partners, and that CD 4:21 thinks of marrying two women in one lifetime as an act of lust or fornication. I have also passed over Q 17:27 (people in the days of Noah were heedlessly eating, drinking, marrying, and being given in marriage) because, against J. Massingberd Ford, *A Trilogy on Wisdom and Celibacy* (Notre Dame: Notre Dame University Press, 1967), p. 100, I am unsure about its "ascetic savor."

55. See also J.-G. Mudiso Mbâ Mundla, *Jesus und die Führer Israels: Studien zu den sog. Jerusalemer Streitgesprächen*, NTAbh 17 (Münster: Aschendorff, 1984), pp. 71–109. After his exhaustive discussion, O. Schwankl, *Die Sadduzäerfrage (Mk 12.18–27 parr.): Eine exegetisch-theologische Studie zur Auferstehungserwartung*, BBB 66 (Frankfurt am Main: Athenäum, 1987), pp. 466–587, concludes that our pericope coheres with other teachings of Jesus. Although Joachim Gnilka, *Das Evangelium nach Markus (Mk 8,27–16,20)*, EKKNT II/2 (Neukirchen/Vluyn: Neukirchener, 1979), pp. 156–57, 160–61, follows Rudolf Bultmann, *History of the Synoptic Tradition*, rev. ed. (New York: Harper & Row, 1963), p. 26, in supposing that vv. 26–27 are secondary and from the "hellenistic-Jewish Christian tradition," he also holds that the kernel of 12:18–25 can be accepted as historical reminiscence. W. Weiss, *"Eine neue Lehre in Vollmacht." Die Streit- und Schulgespräche des Markus-Evangelium*, BZNW 52 (Berlin: Walter de Gruyter, 1989), pp. 234–48, however, finds the primitive tradition in 12:(19)20–23, 24a, 25 and attributes it to the Hellenistic Jewish Christian community.

56. For an origin with Jesus see Blinzler, "Εἰσὶν εὐνοῦχοι," and Gnilka, *Matthäusevangelium*, vol. 2, pp. 156–57. Against an origin with Jesus is Niederwimmer, *Askese*, p. 57.

have been brought against its authenticity are several. The logion, which does not appear in Q or Mark, has only single attestation. Moreover, had Paul known it he would not, it is sometimes said, have written what he did in 1 Cor 7:25, "Now concerning virgins, I have no command of the Lord." Finally, Mt 19:12 has been thought redactional.[57]

These objections, however, do not carry conviction. Regarding the alleged Matthean origin, the variant in Justin, *1 Apol.* 15.4, could be independent of Matthew.[58] Even if it is not, sometimes, as observed in chapter 1, sayings are singly attested because the church found them difficult. In the present instance, Mt 19:12 is cryptic and has often proved embarrassing because of the ever-present possibility of a literal explication. Further, "eunuch" would likely have called up unpleasant images and associations that some preferred to avoid.[59] One can imagine that if Paul, Mark, or Luke knew our saying he might have found it more a distraction than an aid.

What is to be said on the other side, that is, in favor of authenticity? Reverting to the five indices proposed in chapter 1, three intimate that Jesus himself composed Mt 19:12. First, the saying is illuminated by what we otherwise know about him. In the Talmud eunuchs are sometimes the butt of contemptuous taunts or disparaging jokes (e.g., *b. Sanh.* 152a), and in *b. Yeb.* 80b we learn that "eunuch" could be derisively directed at single men. Now since many Jews frowned upon the unmarried state,[60] it seems plausible enough that Mt 19:12 was originally an apologetical counter, a response to the jeer that Jesus was a eunuch.[61] In other words,

57. So Robert H. Gundry, *Matthew: A Commentary on His Literary and Theological Art* (Grand Rapids: Eerdmans, 1982), pp. 381–83.

58. So Joseph Blinzler, "Justinus Apol. I 15,4 und Matthäus 19,10–12," in *Mélanges Bibliques en hommage au R. P. Béda Rigaux,* ed. A. Descamps and R. P. André de Halleux (Gembloux: Duculot, 1970), pp. 45–55.

59. The word "eunuch" had decidedly unappealing connotations in first-century Judaism—despite the tradition that Daniel was a eunuch (Josephus, *Ant.* 10:186; *Liv. Proph. Dan.* 2; *b. Sanh.* 93b) and despite the prophecy of Isa 56:3–5, which foretells the acceptance of eunuchs into the congregation of Israel at the final redemption (Wisd 3:14; Acts 8:26–40). The Hebrew Bible contains several prohibitions having to do with eunuchs (Lev 21:20; 22:24; Deut 23:1). These associate eunuchs with bastards, Ammonites, and Moabites (compare Philo, *Migr. Abr.* 69; Josephus, *Ant.* 4:291; *Ps.-Phoc.* 187). See further Louis M. Epstein, *Sex Laws and Customs in Judaism* (New York: Bloch, 1948), pp. 138–41. Tertullian, *De monog.* 7, wrote that eunuchs were "ignominious in olden days." For an example of negative sentiment about eunuchs outside Judaism see Diogenes, *Ep.* 11.

60. Only a single rabbi, a certain Simeon Ben Azzai (2d century C.E.), is known to have been celibate (*t. Yeb.* 8:7). Rabbinic Judaism taught that procreation is a duty, that the unmarried state is blameworthy (compare *b. Yeb.* 61b–64b; *Mek.* on Exod. 21:10).

61. So Blinzler, "Εἰσὶν εὐνοῦχοι," and F. J. Moloney, "Matthew 19:3–12 and Celi-

Mt 19:12 harmonizes (a) with Jesus being unmarried, (b) with his often being slandered, and (c) with his habit of taking up such slander and employing it for his own purposes.

Second, the Christian tradition has struggled with our saying. The reason, as already observed, is that a literal application has always been near to hand. Origen is far from being the sole Christian to have castrated himself in obedience to Mt 19:12.[62]

Third, the index of intertextual linkage is helpful. Mt 19:12 exhibits a pattern typical of the wisdom tradition: the first two lines relate concrete facts about the everyday world and serve to introduce or illustrate the third line, which proclaims a truth—much less concrete—from the moral or religious sphere.[63] In the present instance, Matthew's maxim mentions three types of eunuchs. The first two are taken for granted: they are known entities.[64] They thus serve to illustrate the third type, which is novel.

This is significant because the very same proverbial pattern appears in several Q texts that are generally reckoned dominical. In Q 9:58 Jesus speaks first about foxes that have their holes, then second about birds that have their nests, and then third about "the Son of man" who has nowhere to lay his head. Similarly, in Q 12:54–55 Jesus speaks initially about people being able in the morning to foresee good weather, then about their being able in the evening to predict a storm, then about their inability to read the spiritual signs of the times. Yet a fourth instance of this form appears in Q 11:11–13, where we read about a father who does not

---

bacy," *JSNT* 2 (1979), pp. 42–60. Aphraates, *Dem.* 18, shows us that some Jews later mocked Christian virgins.

62. For such (mis)interpretation and attacks against it see Justin, *1 Apol.* 29; *Acts of John* 53–54; Eusebius, *H.E.* 6:8 (the story of Origen castrating himself out of youthful zeal; compare Jerome, *Ep.* 84:8; Epiphanius, *Pan.* 64:3:9–13); *Mart. Pal.* 7; First Council of Nicaea, canon 1 (those who have castrated themselves cannot be priests); *Apostolic Canons* 23; Epiphanius, *De fide* 13; *Pan.* 58; Cyril of Scythopolis, *V. Sabae* 41(131); also the remarks of Henry Chadwick, "Enkrateia," *RAC* 5 (1960), pp. 357–58.

63. Compare R. Yaron, "The Climactic Tricolon," *JJS* 37 (1986), pp. 153–59. Examples include Prov 17:3; 20:15; 27:3; 30:33; *Ahiqar* 21 (Lindenberger).

64. According to the rabbis there were two sorts of eunuchs, those of human device and those of nature's making (compare *m. Zab.* 2:1; *m. Yeb.* 8:4; *b. Yeb.* 75a, 79b). The first type was spoken of as being *sěrîs 'ādām*, literally "eunuch of man," that is, a male who had either been literally castrated or who had, sometime after birth, lost the power to reproduce, whether through a disease, an injury, or some other debilitating factor. The second type was spoken of as being *sěrîs ḥammâ*, literally "eunuch of the sun," that is, from the first seeing of the sun, a eunuch by birth, a male born with defective male organs or one who had otherwise been rendered impotent by the circumstances of his birth (*b. Yeb.* 79b, 80a; compare Eusebius, *H.E.* 7:32).

give his son a stone when asked for a loaf of bread, then of a father who does not give his son a snake when he asks for a fish, and finally of God the Father who gives good gifts from heaven to those who ask him.[65]

To the structural link with other texts one may add that, given the pejorative connotations of "eunuch," the commendation of "eunuchs for the sake of the kingdom of heaven" would no doubt have sounded very strange. This matters because we know that Jesus sometimes made a point by commending unusual behavior or unexpected persons. Lk 16:1–9 holds up a dishonest steward for emulation. *Gos. Thom.* 98 does the same thing with an assassin, Lk 10:29–37 the same thing with a Samaritan.

If there are, then, good reasons to hold to the authenticity not only of Mk 12:18–27 but also of Mt 19:12, what of Mt 5:27–28, the injunction against lust? The question cannot be answered without at the same time considering the very closely related 5:21–22, which reads, "You have heard that it was said to those of old, 'You shall not kill.' But I say to you that everyone who is angry with a brother shall be liable to the council." Mt 5:21–22 and 27–28 stand or fall together. Both consist of (1) "You have heard that it was said (to those of old)" + (2) a quotation from the Decalogue (the prohibition of murder, the prohibition of adultery) + (3) "But I say to you" + (4) an equation of an internal disposition (anger, lust) with sin.

Some now consider Matthew's six misnamed "antitheses" (5:21–48) to be redactional creations. We know, however, that even if Matthew himself created the "You have heard . . . but I say to you" form, the basic *material* in most of the contrasts was, as may be inferred from comparison with other sources, pre-Matthean.[66] This means that the question of the origin of "Everyone who looks upon a woman in order to lust after her has already committed adultery against her in his heart" need not be determined by one's judgment on the derivation of "You have heard . . . but I say to you."

Beyond this, my own work has led me to doubt that we should attribute all six instances of this construction to Matthean redaction. While the evangelist probably was responsible for the contrasts in 5:31–32 (do not divorce), 38–39 (turn the other cheek), and 43–44 (love your enemy), Bultmann had good reasons for claiming that these three instances

---

65. It seems likely that the originating structure behind Q 12:24–28 also exhibited the same pattern. First there were the words about ravens, then the words about lilies, then the words about human beings and faith.

66. Compare Mt 5:31–32 with Q 16:18; Mt 5:33–37 with Jas 5:12; Mt 5:38–42 with Q 6:29–30; and Mt 5:43–48 with Q 6:35.

were "moulded on the [pre-Matthean] pattern of the antithetical forms in vv. 21f., 27f., 33–37."[67] He observed, among other things, that in 5: 21–22 (do not be angry), 5:27–28 (do not look to lust), and 5:33–37 (do not swear) "the antithesis was plainly never an isolated saying, for it is only intelligible in relation to the thesis, and does not have the form of a mashal." Moreover, "in distinction from the three secondary formulations, these three passages [5:21–22, 27–28, 33–37] are all alike in putting the thesis in the form of a prohibition (οὐ φονεύσεις, οὐ μοιξεύσεις, οὐκ ἐπιορκήσεις). . . ."[68] This last observation is particularly convincing because, while it shows that the first, second, and fourth of the six units belong together, Matthean redaction makes 5:21–26 + 27–30 + 31–32, that is, the first three units, one triadic section and 5:33–37 + 38–42 + 43–48, the last three units, a second triadic section.[69] So the pattern Bultmann uncovers is not the pattern Matthew imposed. This inconcinnity directs us to pre-Matthean tradition. When one adds that outside of chapter 5 Matthew never used either ἐγὼ δὲ λέγω or ἀρχαῖος, one may infer that Mt 5:21–22 and 27–28 were traditional formulations.

But do they go back to Jesus? In Crossan's inventory they receive a negative sign. Bultmann leaves the question open: we cannot determine whether or not Jesus composed them.[70] Gnilka and Luz affirm the basic authenticity of both complexes.[71] Who is right?

Mt 5:21–22 and 27–28 fall in line with two of the major themes of the Jesus tradition, namely, the focus upon intention and the making of difficult demands. There are, moreover, firm intertextual links with two logia regularly assigned to Jesus, these being Mk 7:15 ("There is nothing outside a person that by going in can defile, but the things that come out are what defile")[72] and Gos. Thom. 89 ("Why do you wash the outside of the cup? Do you not understand that he who made the inside is also he who made the outside?").[73] These latter two texts together "insist that the

---

67. Bultmann, History, p. 135. Compare Gnilka, Matthäusevangelium, vol. 1, pp. 152–53, and Luz, Matthew 1–7, pp. 274–76.

68. Ibid.

69. Dale C. Allison, Jr., "The Structure of the Sermon on the Mount," JBL 106/3 (1987), pp. 432–33.

70. Bultmann, History, p. 147.

71. Gnilka, Matthäusevangelium, vol. 1, pp. 157–58, 163; Luz, Matthew, vol. 1, pp. 276–79, 281, 291. Niederwimmer, Askese, p. 26, also believes that the content of 5:28 goes back to Jesus.

72. Compare Gos. Thom. 14. For authenticity and interpretation see Davies and Allison, Matthew, vol. 2, pp. 527–30.

73. Compare Q 11:39–41. For critical analysis and history of the tradition see Davies and Allison, Matthew, vol. 3, pp. 296–99.

inside and what comes from inside are more important than the outside and what comes from outside in." [74] What matters for our purposes is that Mk 7:15 and *Gos. Thom.* 89 are structurally related to Mt 5:21-22 and 27-28. In all four instances (a) reference is initially made to an accepted teaching or practice—murder is wrong (Mt 5:21), adultery is wrong (Mt 5:27), food can defile (Mk 7:15), dishes should be washed (*Gos. Thom.* 89). In each case (b) Jesus relativizes the traditional teaching or practice by turning attention to something more fundamental (anger, lust, speech, internal cleanness). And in each saying (c) that which is more fundamental is one's inner condition as opposed to an outward activity or circumstance. The inference that the common sequence of thought testifies to a common origin with Jesus seems plausible. That is, if there is good reason to think that Mk 7:15 and *Gos. Thom.* 89 originated with Jesus, then it seems a good bet that Mt 5:21-22 and 27-28 did also.

The triadic Mk 9:43-48 is the last text whose origin we need to consider. Probably most scholars have traced it to Jesus.[75] B. Harvie Branscomb, without elaborating, wrote that "the sharpness of the alternatives set out, as well as the form of expression, seem characteristic of Jesus' thought." [76] This seems to be a routine judgment. According to Gnilka, for instance, the shocking character and vivid imagery point to Jesus.[77]

While their justification is inadequate, the verdict of Branscomb and Gnilka is probably right.[78] Not only does the eschatological motivation—one must act so as to avoid hell and enter the kingdom—fit Jesus' prophetic call to repentance, but Mk 9:43-48 contains four themes that run throughout the Jesus tradition—kingdom of God, future reward, future judgment, difficult demands. Moreover, the hyperbolic exaggeration must be reckoned characteristic of Jesus, and the complex has proved

---

74. Crossan, *Historical Jesus*, p. 262.

75. According to Bultmann, *History*, p. 86, the double saying in Mt 5:29-30 is original; the saying about the foot is secondary. This is also the judgment of Joachim Gnilka, *Das Evangelium nach Markus (Mk 8,27—16,20)*, EKK II/2 (Zurich: Benziger/Neukirchener, 1979), pp. 63-64. For my analysis it does not much matter whether the original unit had two or three members.

76. B. Harvie Branscomb, *The Gospel of Mark*, Moffatt New Testament Commentary (New York: Harper & Row, n.d.), p. 173.

77. Gnilka, *Matthäusevangelium*, vol. 1, p. 164.

78. In addition to what follows see especially Werner Zager, *Gottesherrschaft und Endgericht in der Verkündigung Jesu: Eine Untersuchung zur markinischen Jesusüberlieferung einschließlich der Q-Parallelen*, BZNW 82 (Berlin: Walter de Gruyter, 1996), pp. 210-13.

problematic for Christians. As with Mt 19:12, most commentators have always been quick to insist that Christians should not seriously entertain mutilating themselves.

Renunciation and Eschatology

Having introduced several complexes with ascetical tendencies and argued that they are probable testimonies to Jesus' own teaching, the next step in the argument is to observe that these complexes are all, in one way or another, linked with eschatology.

In Mk 9:43–48 the imperatives to do away with hand, foot, and eye are plainly motivated by eschatological promise and warning: if amputation is necessary for entering life, then it is better to take such drastic action than to go to the hell of fire. Here the command to control sexual desire is grounded in one's eschatological destiny.

Matters are a bit different in Mt 19:12, the word about eunuchs. Jesus commends those who are eunuchs "for the sake of (διά) the kingdom of heaven." "For the sake of" could be given final sense: one becomes a eunuch in order to enter the kingdom. This would make for an exact parallel with Mk 9:43–48. It seems preferable, however, to find here causal meaning. "For the sake of the kingdom" is a way of saying that some people have made themselves eunuchs because the approach of the kingdom requires of them a service that they might otherwise not be able to fulfill. Jesus and other celibates like him—were John the Baptist and/or some of Jesus' disciples originally within the saying's purview?—have chosen their uncommon condition because, as heralds and servants of the approaching order, it is their primary duty to prepare people for its coming. There can be no time for marriage and children, no time for those consuming responsibilities. This is why, when Jesus calls others to the full-time job of fishing for people, he calls them to abandon their jobs, families, and money.[79]

One is reminded of Paul's self-defense in 1 Cor 7 and 9. In these chapters Paul defends his single state on the ground that the obligations and worries of married life would detract him from his appointed task. The situation is the same in Mt 19:12. Among those preparing Israel for the kingdom's coming are people who have renounced marriage for themselves in order to dedicate themselves utterly to the one thing needful.

79. Q 9:59–60; 14:26; Mk 1:16–20; 2:14; 10:17–22.

What about Mk 12:18–27, in which Jesus defends the resurrection of the dead? This complex is not about life in the present but life in the eschatological future. This makes it different from Mt 19:12 and Mk 9: 43–48, which focus upon things one might do now before the coming of the kingdom. The three texts can, however, be read as mutually reinforcing. For an unmarried and celibate individual who believed that perfected human nature would be angelic and so not need its sexual component would surely find in the eschatological scenario of Mk 12:18–27 encouragement in the hard task of being continent in the here and now. Indeed, such an individual might, as did so many Christian celibates later on, interpret his or her forswearing of sex in terms of realized eschatology: if one can make do without intercourse then this might be understood as one way of making present an eschatological circumstance.

When we turn to Mt 5:27–28, we find no explicit association with eschatology. There appears, however, to be an implicit association. "You have heard that it was said" introduces Moses. "But I say to you" introduces Jesus. It is not the case that one authority contradicts the other, for those who refrain from anger and lust will scarcely commit murder or adultery. At the same time, the formula goes out of its way to emphasize that Jesus is taking us beyond Moses and asking for something more— and this implicitly highlights the limitations of the Torah.

Can anything account for the focus upon one's internal state as opposed to one's external deeds and simultaneously explain the reason for stressing a contrast with Moses? The answer presumably lies in eschatology. Jer 31:31–34 foresees a time when God will make a new covenant with the house of Israel and the house of Judah. That covenant will be different from the old one made in Egypt. For God will then put the law within them and will write it on their hearts (compare Ezek 11:19–20). This is likely the prophetic background of Mt 5:27–28 (as well as of 21–22), which on this view illustrate the fact that sometimes "good arguments can be brought forward for the eschatological implications of the wisdom sayings." [80] Jesus' focus upon intention was a way of sowing the law in human hearts; and his formula, "You have heard . . . But I say to you," was a way of declaring that something new was happening. If so, Mt 5:21–22 and 27–28 were, on his lips, every bit as eschatological as complexes that refer to the kingdom of God or the Danielic Son of man.

---

80. The line is from Helmut Koester, "Redirecting the Quest for the Historical Jesus," *Harvard Divinity Bulletin* 23/1 (1993), p. 10.

Whether or not one accepts this interpretation of Mt 5:27–28, the link in the Jesus tradition between eschatology, on the one hand, and reservation toward sexual desire, on the other, does plainly appear in Mt 19:12; Mk 12:18–27; and (assuming a sexual interpretation) Mk 9:43–48. This circumstance might have been anticipated. For although a variety of factors may encourage asceticism, one such factor is eschatological expectation. When the present world order is negated, it is natural to withdraw from it. The psychology, while far from inevitable,[81] is natural, and it is more than confirmed by comparative materials. Karl Suso Frank has remarked, with reference to early Christianity, that "the conviction that the end of the world was near always fostered asceticism."[82] Peter Worsely makes the even broader generalization that "sexual asceticism . . . [is] common in millenarian movements."[83]

Paul supplies an example.[84] In 1 Cor 7:25–32 the apostle argues that it is well for people to remain as they are. The married should stay married, and the single should stay single. What reason does he give? "In view of the present [or: impending] distress [ἐνεστῶσαν ἀνάγκην] it is well for you to remain as you are" (7:26). The word translated here by "distress" elsewhere has eschatological sense (e.g., Zeph 1:15 LXX; Lk 21:23); and the connotation of "the present distress" becomes evident in 1 Cor 7: 28–31: "Are you bound to a wife? Do not seek to be free. Are you free from a wife? Do not seek a wife. But if you marry, you do not sin, and if a virgin marries, she does not sin. Yet those who marry will experience tribulation (θλῖψιν)[85] in the flesh, and I would spare you that. I mean,

81. Eschatology can also encourage antinomianism. This is a different way of separating oneself from the normal course of things. Although Sabbatai Ṣevi began as a severe ascetic, his followers eventually experimented with libertine sexuality. Sabbatianism was "not so much the direct product of the Kabbalah as its dialectical negation, in which the urge toward sexual renunciation was turned into its opposite. Only with the coming of the messianic age might the sensual, now liberated from evil materiality, be indulged in all its antinomian possibilities." So David Biale, *Eros and the Jews: From Biblical Israel to Contemporary America* (New York: HarperCollins, 1992), pp. 119–20.

82. Karl Suso Frank, *With Greater Liberty: A Short History of Christian Monasticism and Religious Orders* (Kalamazoo: Cistercian, 1993), p. 30.

83. Peter Worsely, *The Trumpet Shall Sound: A Study of "Cargo" Cults in Melanesia*, 2d ed. (New York: Schocken, 1968), p. 251. Compare Yonina Talmon, "Pursuit of the Millennium: The Relation between Religious and Social Change," *Archives européenes de sociologie* 3 (1962), p. 136: "Sexual aberrations in the form of either extreme asceticism or sexual excess are very common. . . ."

84. On the millenarian character of Pauline Christianity see Wayne A. Meeks, *The First Urban Christians: The Social World of the Apostle Paul* (New Haven: Yale University Press, 1983), pp. 171–80.

85. For this word with eschatological meaning see Dan 12:1; Hab 3:16; Zeph 1:15; Acts 14:22; Col 1:24; Rev 7:14.

brothers and sisters, that the appointed time has grown short: from now on, let even those who have wives be as though they had none. . . . For the present form of the world is passing away." Heinrich Schlier comments: "With the awareness of the shortening of the time, Paul obviously sees the afflictions of the last time breaking into the present, and his advice is designed to lessen the related *thlipsis* for his community."[86] Paul tells the unmarried to stay unmarried because the woes of end are entering the present (compare *2 Bar.* 10:13–14). The final time of trouble will prove to be especially arduous for the married (as in Mk 13:17 and Lk 23:29), so one should not now undertake to be married.[87] Thus Paul's eschatological outlook makes him favor celibacy.[88]

The association between eschatology and celibacy in Paul is not anomalous. One suspects that eschatological enthusiasm was also part of the impulse behind Essene asceticism. To judge from Philo, Josephus, and Pliny, at least some of the Essenes did not marry.[89] Josephus adds that they also "despise[d] riches" (*Bell.* 2:122),[90] took "just enough food and

---

86. Heinrich Schlier, in *TDNT* 3 (1965), p. 145. See further Will Deming, *Paul on Marriage and Celibacy: The Hellenistic Background of 1 Corinthians 7*, SNTSMS 83 (Cambridge: Cambridge University Press, 1995), pp. 177–97 (he argues for integration of apocalyptic and Stoic elements in 1 Corinthians 7); Franzjosef Froitzheim, *Christologie und Eschatologie bei Paulus* (Würzburg: Echter-Seelsorge, 1978), pp. 18–28; and Vincent L. Wimbush, *Paul: The Worldly Ascetic* (Macon: Mercer, 1987) (Wimbush rightly recognizes the influence of an apocalyptic tradition in 1 Corinthians 7 but wrongly argues that Paul distances himself from it).

87. Had some of the Corinthians embraced celibacy for eschatological reasons? Such is the view of Peter Brown, *The Body and Society: Men, Women, and Sexual Renunciation in Early Christianity* (New York: Columbia University Press, 1988), p. 53. See further Judith M. Gundry-Volf, "The Corinthian Sexual Ascetics (1 Cor 7)," in *The Corinthian Correspondence*, ed. Reimund Bieringer, BETL 125 (Leuven: Peeters, 1996), 519–41. She briefly reviews opinion on this subject.

88. This is not to say that other factors also could not have played a role; see David L. Balch, "1 Cor 7:32–35 and Stoic Debates about Marriage, Anxiety, and Distraction," *JBL* 102 (1983), pp. 429–39.

89. Philo, in Eusebius, *Praep. ev.* 380d (8.11); Josephus, *Bell.* 2.120; *Ant.* 18.21; Pliny, *N.H.* 5.15.73. The Dead Sea Scrolls, on the other hand, at points presuppose marriage (e.g., 1QSa 1:4, 9–12). Maybe there was diversity within the movement, or maybe members lived as married couples until a certain age, after which they became celibates (an idea common in the history of religions; recall the stages of life in the Laws of Manu). Matthew Black, "The Tradition of Hasideaean-Essene Asceticism: Its Origin and Influence," in *Aspects du Judéo-Christianisme: Colloque de Strasbourg 23–25 avril 1964* (Paris: Presses Universitaires de France, 1965), p. 31, suggests that the Therapeutae entered their state of renunciation only late in life. See further Joseph M. Baumgarten, "The Qumran-Essene Restraints on Marriage," in *Archaeology and History in the Dead Sea Scrolls*, ed. Lawrence H. Schiffmann (Sheffield: JSOT, 1990), pp. 13–24.

90. This judgment is confirmed by the Qumran materials; see T. S. Beall, *Josephus'*

drink for satisfaction" (*Bell.* 2:133), and "turn[ed] aside from pleasures as an evil, and regard[ed] self-control (ἐγϰϱάτεια) and not succumbing to the passions as a virtue" (*Bell.* 2:120). In line with this, the astrological physiognomy, 4Q186, depicts a son of light as thin and lean, a son of darkness as thick and fat. Certainly the Essene's desert location, their simple dress, and avoidance of luxuries (such as oil) were part of an ascetical program.

We do not expect to learn from Philo, Josephus, or Pliny about a possible eschatological motivation for all this. But the Dead Sea Scrolls, most of which were composed or copied by Essenes,[91] tell us that eschatological expectation was at the heart of what they were all about.[92] Surely their sexual renunciation, like their renunciation of property, was encouraged by their eschatological convictions. Probably, as Frank Moore Cross argued,[93] the expectation of soon participating in an eschatological holy war (see 1QM) was a major factor in their sexual abstinence.[94] Steven Fraade has written:

> The Qumran group understood itself to be living in the last days of the present age, awaiting a final battle between itself ("the sons of light") and the forces of darkness, in which the latter would be destroyed and the world would be restored to the rule of God's spirit, messianically embodied. Thus, their disciplined way of life was intended to ensure their constant preparedness, individually and communally, for that

Description of the Essenes Illustrated by the Dead Sea Scrolls, SNTSMS 58 (Cambridge: Cambridge University Press, 1988), pp. 43–44.

91. The identification of the Dead Sea sect with Essenes remains likely; see Joseph A. Fitzmyer, "The Qumran Community: Essene or Sadducean?," *HeyJ* 36/4 (1995), pp. 467–76. But for another view see Lena Cansdale, *Qumran and the Essenes: A Re-Evaluation of the Evidence*, TSAJ 60 (Tübingen: J. C. B. Mohr [Paul Siebeck], 1997).

92. John J. Collins, *Apocalypticism in the Dead Sea Scrolls* (London: Routledge, 1997).

93. Frank Moore Cross, *The Ancient Library of Qumran*, 3d. ed. (Minneapolis: Fortress, 1995), pp. 82–84.

94. See further the cogent argument of Black, "Hasideaean-Essene Asceticism," pp. 19–32. 1QM 7:3–4 excludes women from the camp of the forty-year eschatological war. Black refers to Deut 23:10–11 (compare Lev 15:16–17); 1 Sam 21:4–5; and 2 Sam 11:11 and remarks that "the prohibition of marital intercourse for those engaged in war is widespread among primitive peoples. . . . This practice was not wholly obsolete among the Arabs as late as the second century of Islam, and during blood-feuds among the Bedouin it was customary to abstain from wine and unguents as well as sexual relations" (pp. 20–21). Robert Murray, "The Exhortation to Candidates for Ascetical Vows at Baptism in the Ancient Syriac Church," *NTS* 21 (1974), pp. 60–70, observes that Syrian Christians could relate their celibacy to the holy war tradition.

seismic event, for which they would provide the ranks of pure, holy warriors.[95]

Matters must have been much the same with John the Baptist. Christian tradition assumes that he was unmarried; and certainly everything else we know about him points to asceticism.[96] Q 7:24–25 tells us that John dwelt in the wilderness. So does Mk 1:2–8, which adds that he was clothed with camel's hair and ate locusts and honey. Further, Mk 2:18 presupposes that John's followers fasted, and with this Q 7:33 agrees: "John came neither eating or drinking."

If John's asceticism is plain, so too is his eschatological focus. Mark 1:2–8 associates him with eschatological prophecies (v. 2) and relates that he foretold a messianic figure (v. 7). According to Q 3:7–17, John warned of the coming wrath, called people to repent, and spoke of the fires of judgment. So as with Jesus, Paul, and the Dead Sea Scrolls, we see asceticism and eschatology side by side.[97]

In line with this, ascetical tendencies sometimes appear in apocalyptic texts from ancient times. Abstinence and acts of self-abnegation are referred to as part of preparation for visionary experiences in, for instance, Dan 9:3 (fasting, sackcloth, ashes); 10:2–3 (no meat or wine or anointing);[98] 4 *Ezra* 5:13 (prayer, weeping, fasting), 20 (fasting, mourning, and weeping); 6:31 (prayer and fasting), 35 (weeping and fasting); 2 *Bar.* 9:2 (rending garments, weeping, mourning, fasting); 20:5 (fasting); *Mart. Isa.* 2:7–11 (poverty, vegetarianism, isolationism); and *Apoc. Abr.* 9:7 (abstinence from certain foods and wine and anointing with oil).[99] More-

95. Steven Fraade, "Ascetical Aspects of Ancient Judaism," in *Jewish Spirituality: From the Bible through the Middle Ages*, ed. Arthur Green (New York: Crossroad, 1986), p. 267. See further Anton Steiner, "Warum lebten die Essener asketisch?" *BZ* 15 (1971), pp. 1–28. Steiner also stresses the importance of the Essenes' desire to recapitulate the experience of Israel at Sinai (in the desert the people were continent to receive revelation: Exod 19:9–15) and of their priestly orientation.

96. See further Joan E. Taylor, *The Immerser: John the Baptist within Second Temple Judaism* (Grand Rapids: Eerdmans, 1997), pp. 32–42.

97. The generalization might hold for other baptist movements of the period if we knew more about them. Elkesai, for example, announced that an eschatological war would blaze up three years after the Parthian War (C.E. 114–116; see Hippolytus, *Ref.* 9:11), and Mani's asceticism was partly inherited from a Jewish-Christian baptist sect; see Albert Henrichs, "Mani and the Babylonian Baptists," *Harvard Studies in Classical Philology* 77 (1973), pp. 23–59.

98. On the ascetical piety of Daniel see Jürgen C. H. Lebram, "The Piety of the Jewish Apocalyptists," in *Apocalypticism in the Mediterranean World and the Near East*, ed. David Hellholm (Tübingen: Mohr-Siebeck, 1983), pp. 171–210.

99. In some of these texts we also have to do with rites of mourning.

over, Rev 14:4 identifies the 144,000 who have been redeemed as those "who have not defiled themselves with women, for they are virgins; they follow the lamb wherever he goes." Even if one does not take this literally, surely the language implies an ascetical view of things.[100] Such a view also appears in *1 En.* 108:8–9: "Those who love God have loved neither gold nor silver, nor all the good things which are in the world, but have given over their bodies to suffering—who from the time of their very being have not longed after earthly food, and who regarded themselves as a passing breath."

What we find in Paul and elsewhere in ancient literature appears throughout the history of Jewish messianism. That is, the distancing of oneself from the normal course of the world through the giving away of possessions, fasting, or other ascetic acts often appears when the end is perceived to be near. The eighth-century followers of Severus, a Gentile convert to Judaism, who led a messianic movement in Syria, gave all their possessions to him.[101] Those who gathered around Abu-Isa, the eighth-century Persian prophet who preached the imminence of the Messiah, fasted often, quit eating meat, shunned alcohol, and (curiously enough for students of the Jesus tradition) prohibited divorce.[102] The same was true of the followers of Yudgan. The "spirit of self-abnegation which was regarded as the only attitude befitting the unfortunate condition of the Jews in the exile found a particularly favorable soil" among the Yudganiyya, who believed the redemption to be near.[103] The millennial movement in Salonika in 1096 saw people quit work, fast, and give alms for repentance.[104] The same things happened when, in 1295, two messianic prophets in Avila and Ayllon announced the imminent coming of God's kingdom,[105] as well as in 1500, when the followers of Ines, the Maiden of

---

100. See further Georg Kretschmar, "Ein Beitrag zur Frage nach dem Ursprung frühchristlicher Askese," *ZTK* 61 (1964), pp. 62–63. Compare Black, "Hasidaean-Essene Asceticism," p. 30. For a survey of unconvincing attempts to escape the obvious meaning of the language see George Wesley Buchanan, *The Book of Revelation: Its Introduction and Prophecy*, Mellen Biblical Commentary, New Testament 22 (Lewiston: Mellen, 1993), pp. 349–61.

101. Stephen Sharot, *Messianism, Mysticism, and Magic: A Sociological Analysis of Jewish Religious Movements* (Chapel Hill: University of North Carolina Press, 1982), p. 53.

102. See ibid., p. 54

103. Israel Friedlaender, "Shiitic Influences in Jewish Sectarianism," in *Essential Papers on Messianic Movements and Personalities in Jewish History*, ed. Marc Saperstein (New York: University Press, 1992), p. 141.

104. Sharot, *Messianism*, p. 55.

105. Ibid., p. 62.

Herrara, believed the Messiah to be at the gates.[106] Nathan of Gaza, Sabbatai Ṣevi's interpreter, issued detailed instructions for fasting. These were "ascetic exercises born of messianic enthusiasm and not of sorrow."[107] The hasidic ascetic, Yossel of Kleck, like others of his kind, sought to hasten the coming of the Messiah through such austerities as fasting, rolling in the snow, and going without sleep.[108] Altogether it seems evident that, as R. J. Zwi Werblowsky has said, in Judaism "asceticism can easily combine with . . . messianic fervor."[109]

Asceticism also appears as a regular concomitant of worldwide millenarism throughout history.[110] The Franciscan Spirituals of the thirteenth century, who thought that a new world order was in the offing, were not just celibate but "rigorous ascetics who had broken away from the main body of the Franciscan order over the issue of absolute poverty."[111] The fourteenth-century flagellants, whose asceticism is notorious, were self-mortifying chiliasts who interpreted the Black Death as the messianic woes and "lived in a world of millenarian phantasy."[112] Medieval China knew a "kind of millenarian faith, that was probably limited to small groups of fanatic adventists who by fasting, repentance and prayer prepared themselves for the coming of the Lord."[113] The Shakers, who believed that the Messiah had returned and that the millennium had

106. Ibid., p. 77.

107. Scholem, *Sabbatai Ṣevi*, p. 414. Compare pp. 292–93, 356.

108. S. Maimon, *An Autobiography* (London: Alexander Gardner, 1988), p. 134.

109. "The Safed Revival and Its Aftermath," in *Jewish Spirituality: From the Sixteenth-Century Revival to the Present*, ed. Arthur Green (New York: Crossroad, 1987), p. 12. He goes on to observe that regularly in Jewish thought "the Messiah will appear only after Israel has atoned for all its sins. . . ."

110. In addition to what follows see Reinaldo L. Román, "Christian Themes: Mainstream Traditions and Millenarian Violence," in *Millennialism and Violence*, ed. Michael Barkun (London: Frank Cass, 1996), pp. 51–82. Lawrence E. Sullivan, *Icanchu's Drum: An Orientation to Meaning in South American Religions* (New York: Macmillan, 1988), p. 554, observes that "arduous restrictions" are typical of messianic movements in the Chaco. Hillel Schwarz, "The End of the Beginning: Millenarian Studies, 1969–1975," *RSR* 2/3 (1976), p. 6, suggests that millenarian activities, which involve saying good-bye to the old as well as hello to the new, can be related to "the process of bereavement."

111. Norman Cohn, "Medieval Millenarism: Its Bearing on the Comparative Study of Millenarian Movements," in *Millennial Dreams in Action: Studies in Revolutionary Religious Movements*, ed. Sylvia L. Thrupp (New York: Schocken, 1970), p. 35.

112. Norman Cohn, *The Pursuit of the Millennium: Revolutionary Millenarians and Mystical Anarchists of the Middle Ages*, rev. ed. (New York: Oxford, 1970), p. 136.

113. E. Zürcher, "'Prince Moonlight': Messianism and Eschatology in Early Medieval Chinese Buddhism," *T'oung Pao* 68 (1982), p. 44. See further pp. 48, 50.

begun, chose the path of celibacy.[114] The infamous Skoptsy sect, which practiced mutilation of the sexual organs, had an eschatological theology which anticipated a millennium centered in Moscow.[115] The nineteenth-century Brazilian Catholic priest Father Cicero and his enthusiastic followers combined intense apocalyptic expectation and ascetic living.[116] Some nineteenth-century Andalusian peasants, as part of their anarchist millenarianism, which sought the rejection of all tradition, refused drink, smoking, meat, and even marriage, at least until the coming of the new era.[117] Participants in the Taipang rebellion, with its strange mixture of pagan and Christian eschatology, were enjoined to give up not only opium and liquor but also tobacco, and their leaders insisted upon separation of the sexes.[118] Early in the twentieth century the Burkan cult of Mongolia proclaimed the coming restoration of the Mongolian empire and demanded that its adherents give up tobacco and money.[119] In the middle of our century in Japan a female proponent of Mioshi, who called herself Ogami-Sama (the Great Venerable Goddess), combined Buddhist asceticism with the belief that she had come to save the world before its near end. More recently we have had the notorious Heaven's Gate cult; before committing suicide as a way of participating in a science fiction eschatology involving a comet and UFOs, several male devotees had themselves castrated.[120]

The lesson from all these examples is that enthusiastic eschatology and the self-discipline of abstinence, including sexual continence, have often gone together.[121] When one believes that the world is about to go dra-

114. On the fully realized eschatology of official Shaker doctrine see *An Early View of the Shakers: Benson John Lossing and the "Harper's" Article of July 1857*, ed. Don Gittard (Hanover: University Press of New England, 1989), pp. 41–44. Some early adherents, however, continued to hope for the near end of the world; see Priscilla J. Bremer, *Shaker Communities, Shaker Lives* (Hanover: University Press of New England, 1986), p. 15.

115. Frederick Conybeare, *Russian Dissenters*, Harvard Theological Studies 10 (New York: Russell & Russell, 1962), pp. 363–70.

116. René Ribeiro, "Brazilian Messianic Movements," in Thrupp, *Millennial Dreams*, pp. 66–68.

117. E. J. Hobsbawm, *Primitive Rebels: Studies in Archaic Forms of Social Movement in the 19th and 20th Centuries* (New York: W. W. Norton, 1959), pp. 83–84.

118. Vittorio Lanternari, *The Religions of the Oppressed: A Study of Modern Messianic Cults* (New York: Knopf, 1963), pp. 232–36. See now the full treatment in Jonathan D. Spence, *God's Chinese Son: The Taiping Heavenly Kingdom of Hong Xiuquan* (New York: Norton, 1996). For sexual separation see pp. 120–22, 150–51, 184, 225.

119. Lanternari, *Religions of the Oppressed*, pp. 227–28.

120. Ibid., 223–24. See Rodney Perkins and Forrest Jackson, *Cosmic Suicide: The Tragedy and Transcendence of Heaven's Gate* (Dallas: Pentaradial, 1997).

121. Montanism may supply yet another illustration of this circumstance, for it exhibited ascetic tendencies. See Eusebius, *H.E.* 5:18, and Kurt Aland, "Bemerkungen zum

matically, one may let go of the world in dramatic ways; and to cease having sexual intercourse is one means of stopping the world.[122] This is why
the *Gospel of the Egyptians* could teach that continence would hasten the
end.[123] So to find ascetic elements in the Jesus tradition, where there is so
much eschatology, is in no way surprising. We have here a relative of what
we find in the Christian appendix to *4 Ezra*:

> The [final] calamities draw near and are not delayed. . . . Prepare for
> battle, and in the midst of the calamities be like strangers on the earth.
> Let him that sells be like one who will flee; let him that buys be like one
> who will lose; let him that does business be like one who will not make
> a profit; and let him that builds a house be like one who will not live
> in it; let him that sows be like one who will not reap; so also him that
> prunes the vines, like one who will not gather the grapes; them that
> marry, like those who will have no children; and them that do not
> marry, like those that are widowed. . . . (*4 Ezra* 16:37–44)[124]

The Functions of Jesus' Eschatological Asceticism

While the preceding materials permit some instructive generalizations, it
will be helpful if we can situate Jesus' eschatological asceticism more precisely within his own time and place. The following observations are intended to be a tentative, small first step in this direction.

We may begin with the well-known fact that an ascetic attitude had
taken hold of many in the Hellenistic world when Jesus came on the

---

Montanismus und zur frühchristlichen Eschatologie," in *Kirchengeschichtliche Entwürfe:
Alte Kirche, Reformation und Luthertum Pietismus und Erweckungsbewegung* (Gütersloh:
Gerd Mohn, 1979), pp. 126–27, and Nagel, *Motivierung*, pp. 21–25. Some recent schol-
arship, however, has challenged the millenarian character of Montanism; see, e.g., Christine
Trevett, *Montanism: Gender, Authority and the New Prophecy* (Cambridge: Cambridge
University Press, 1996).

122. Compare the protest of a Persian governor against Christian asceticism as quoted
in Brown, *Body and Society*, p. 429: "If you listen to them [your Christian guides], you will
never go near your wives again, and the end of the world will soon be upon you." Note also
2 Clement 12, where the coming of the kingdom is said to depend upon males not thinking
of sisters as females and females not thinking of brothers as males.

123. See the fragments preserved in Clement of Alexandria, *Strom.* 3:45, 63, and 64,
and the comments of T. H. C. van Eijk, "Marriage and Virginity, Death and Immortality,"
in *Epektasis: Mélanges patristiques offerts au Cardinal Jean Daniélou* (Paris: Beauchesne,
1972), pp. 215–16. On p. 235 he observes that "the end of marriage is also the end of time."

124. For discussion of this passage (and of its relationship to 1 Cor 7:29–31) see Wolf-
gang Schrage, "Die Stellung zur Welt bei Paulus, Epiktet und in der Apokalyptik," *ZTK* 61
(1964), pp. 125–54.

scene[125]—and Judaism must be included within the generalization.[126] According to Steven D. Fraade, one can discern in the extant literature composed between 200 B.C.E. and 200 C.E. "first, an increasing preoccupation, among individuals and religious groups, with the dichotomy of this-worldly life and otherworldly demands and hopes; and, second, an increasing resort to ascetic practices as responses to that tension."[127] When one reckons with what we know of the Essenes, the Therapeutae,[128] Bannus the hermit,[129] and John the Baptist,[130] it is not too much to say that there was, by Jesus' time, an established tradition of asceticism.[131] As Peter Brown has written:

> When Jesus of Nazareth preached in Galilee and Judaea after 30 A.D., the options open to him and to his followers were already clearly mapped out on the landscape of Palestine. Toward the Dead Sea, the wilderness of Judaea harbored sizable settlements of disaffected males. Ascetic figures whose prophetic calling had long been associated, in Jewish folklore, with sexual abstinence, continued to emerge from the desert to preach repentance to the nearby cities. One such [was] John the Baptist. . . .[132]

125. Here one may recall the Greek admiration for Spartan discipline, the Platonic dualism of spirit and matter, the detachment and control of the Stoics, and the self-sufficiency of the Cynics. See further E. R. Dodds, *Pagan and Christian in an Age of Anxiety* (New York: Norton, 1965), 11–36; André-Jean Festugière, *Personal Religion among the Greeks* (Berkeley: University of California Press, 1954), especially pp. 53–67; Leipoldt, *Griechische Philosophie und Frühchristliche Askese*; Lohse, *Askese*, pp. 17–78; Anthony Meredith, "Asceticism—Christian and Greek," *JTS* 27 (1976), pp. 313–32; Joseph Ward Swain, *The Hellenic Origins of Christian Asceticism* (New York: n.p., 1916); I. G. Whitchurch, *The Philosophical Bases of Asceticism in the Platonic Writings and in Pre-Platonic Tradition* (New York: Longmans, Green & Co., 1923); and Vincent L. Wimbush, ed., *Ascetic Behavior in Greco-Roman Antiquity: A Sourcebook* (Minneapolis: Fortress, 1990).

126. Already the Hebrew Bible contains texts that could later have been read so as to encourage asceticism. The Nazirites and Rechabites, for instance, took vows of abstinence from intoxicating drink (Numbers 6; Jeremiah 35); Daniel and his companions ate vegetables and water instead of the king's food (Daniel 1); and the prophets opposed the luxurious lives of city dwellers (e.g., Amos 3:15).

127. Steven Fraade, "Ascetical Aspects," p. 261.

128. See Emil Schürer, *The History of the Jewish People in the Age of Jesus Christ (175 B.C.–A.D. 135)*, vol. 2, rev. and ed. Geza Vermes, Fergus Millar, and Matthew Black (Edinburgh: T. & T. Clark, 1979), pp. 591–97.

129. Josephus, *Vita* 11, is our only source for this character, who "dwelt in the wilderness, wearing only such clothing as trees provided, feeding on such things as grew of themselves, and using frequent ablutions of cold water, by day and night, for purity's sake. . . ."

130. We must also reckon with the continuing presence of Nazirites. 1 Macc 3:49 refers to Nazirites in Jerusalem during Maccabean times. Note Acts 21:24 and see further Steven D. Fraade, "The Nazirite in Ancient Judaism," in Wimbush, *Ascetic Behavior*, pp. 213–23.

131. Note also Lk 2:37: Anna "never left the temple but worshiped there with fasting and prayer night and day."

132. Peter Brown, *Body and Society*, pp. 40–41.

Even the normally this-worldly rabbinic literature of later times now and then betrays an ascetic disposition or reveals awareness of such.[133] Not only does it contain many warnings against men looking at women,[134] but *b. Ned.* 20b favorably remembers Rabbi Eliezer as one who engaged in intercourse with as much modesty and speed as possible ("he uncovers a handbreadth and covers a handbreadth . . . it is as though he were compelled by a demon"). According to *ARN A 5*, the Sadducees had a tradition that the Pharisees afflicted themselves in this world; and according to *ARN A 28*, Rabbi Judah the Prince said, "Whoever accepts the pleasures of this world is denied the pleasures of the world to come. And whoever does not accept the pleasure of this world is granted the pleasures of the world to come." In *b. Ta'an.* 11a R. Eleazar says that if a Nazirite "who denied himself wine only is termed 'Holy,' how much more so he who denies himself enjoyment of ever so many things." Morton Smith may have exaggerated only a little when he claimed that, in Jesus' day, "the hellenized Palestinian Jewish population expected asceticism of holy men."[135]

The growing sympathy for asceticism coincided with a growing suspicion of the sexual impulse (although one should not forget that already Genesis 3 and 6 closely associate the entrance of sin into the world with sexual themes). Many morally serious Jews, under Greco-Roman influence,[136] came to believe that the exclusive purpose of sex was procreation,

133. But there are also many expressions of opposition to asceticism. David Halivni, "On the Supposed Anti-Asceticism or Anti-Nazritism of Simeon the Just," *JQR* 58 (1968), p. 244, cites *b. Ta'an.* 11a and the end of tractate *y. Qiddušin* as examples.

134. See, e.g., *b. 'Abod. Zar.* 20a–b; *ARN* 2, 4b; *b. B. Bat.* 16a- b; *b. Ned.* 20a; and the discussion in A. Büchler, *Types of Jewish-Palestinian Piety from 70 B.C.E. to 70 C.E.* (New York: KTAV, 1978), pp. 42–55.

135. Morton Smith, "Messiahs: Robbers, Jurists, Prophets, and Magicians," in Saperstein, *Essential Papers*, p. 81, n. 11. For the argument that rabbinic sources suggest an evolution away from an early, Palestinian view on sexuality which was akin to the asceticism of the Stoics see Daniel Boyarin, "'Behold Israel according to the Flesh': On Anthropology and Sexuality in Late Antique Judaisms," *Yale Journal of Criticism* 2 (1992), pp. 26–57.

136. See Iamblichus, *Vit. Pyth.* 31 ("The Pythagoreans forbade entirely intercourse that was unnatural, or resulting from wanton insolence, allowing only for the natural and temperate forms, which occur in the cause of chaste and recognized procreation of children"); Musonius Rufus, frag. 12 (in Stobaeus, *Anth.* 4.22.90); Clitarcus, *Sent.* 70; Seneca, as quoted by Jerome, *C. Jovinian* 1:49; Pliny, *Nat. hist.* 7:11.42 ("Few pregnant animals copulate, except women"); Lucan, *De bello civ.* 2 (for Cato "the sole purpose of love was offspring"); Dio Chrysostom, *Orat.* 7:133–37; Maximus of Tyre, *Disc.* 36; Hierocles, *On Marriage* 4.22; *Sentences of Sextus* 231–32 ("Every unrestrained husband commits adultery with his wife. Do nothing for the sake of mere sensual pleasure"; compare 239: "Let the marriage of believers be a struggle for self-control"); Plutarch, *Mor.* 144B ("sowing seed from which they are unwilling to have any offspring"). Discussion in Robin Lane Fox, *Pagans and Christians* (New York: Knopf, 1989), pp. 336–374; David Halpern, John J. Winkler, and Froma Zeitlin, eds., *Before Sexuality: The Construction of Erotic Experience in the Ancient Greek World* (Princeton: Princeton University Press, 1990); Aline Rousselle,

and that sex for enjoyment was questionable.[137] Philo spoke of men who "behave unchastely, not with the wives of others, but with their own" (*Spec. leg.* 3:2, 9). What he meant is clear from *Jos.* 43: "the end we seek in wedlock is not pleasure but the begetting of lawful children."[138] That Philo's view was shared by other Jews appears from Wisd 3:13 (the barren woman should not have intercourse, for its only rationale could be pleasure); *T. Iss.* 2:1–5 (Rachel is commended because she desired children but not sexual gratification); 3:5 ("pleasure with a woman never came to my mind"); *T. Benj.* 8:2 ("the person who is pure with love does not look on a woman for the purpose of having sexual relations"); and Tob 8:4–8 (the pious Tobit does not remarry but remains a widow who fasts). Josephus wrote that the "Essenes [or rather one group of Essenes] have no intercourse with them [women] during pregnancy, thus showing that their motive in marrying is not self-indulgence but the procreation of children."[139] While one might pass this off as apologetic for cultured readers, it may be observed that *Pseudo-Phocylides*, a book filled with conventional wisdom, offers as exhortation, without any explanation, this sentence: "Do not lay your hand upon your wife when she is pregnant" (186).[140] Surely Daniel Boyarin is right: "For Israel by the first century sexuality had become thoroughly anxiety-ridden and guilty as well. Many Jews of the first century had a sense that they were commanded by God to do that which God himself considered sinful."[141]

Porneia: On Desire and the Body in Antiquity (Oxford: Basil Blackwell, 1988); and P. Veyne, "La Famille et l'amour sous le Haut-Empire romain," *Annales* 33/1 (1978), pp. 35–63. For the belief, professed by several (but not all) physicians, that sexual intercourse is injurious to health, see the texts and discussion in Brown, *Body and Society*, pp. 17–25, and Dale B. Martin, *The Corinthian Body* (New Haven: Yale University Press, 1995), pp. 200–205. According to Diogenes Laertius, *Vit. Pyth.* 6, sex is "pernicious at every season, and is never good for the health."

137. This is true even of many later rabbis, despite frequent assertions to the contrary; see Biale, *Eros and the Jews*, pp. 33–59. He makes much of the close connection between the evil *yetzer* and the sexual impulse. Biale also observes, on pp. 28–31, that the levitical prohibition against intercourse during menstruation may have been associated with the conviction that women were then sterile. If so, this already may reflect the belief that intercourse without the possibility of conception is wrong.

138. Note also Philo's comments in *Abr.* 137 and *Spec. leg.* 3.20(113) and see further Richard A. Baer, Jr., *Philo's Use of the Categories Male and Female*, ALGHJ 3 (Leiden: E. J. Brill, 1970), pp. 94–95.

139. *Bell.* 2:161. Syriac sources report the same thing; see Dionysius Bar Salibi, *Against the Jew* 1.

140. Compare Josephus, *C. Ap.* 2:202 ("none who has intercourse with a woman who is with child can be considered pure"), and *Hist. Rech.* 11.6–8 (the Rechabites couple only once in their lives).

141. Daniel Boyarin, *A Radical Jew: Paul and the Politics of Identity* (Berkeley: University of California Press, 1994), p. 159.

If it is true that ascetical practices as well as reservation towards sexual intercourse were part of the Judaism of Jesus' day, it is also true that such practices and such reservation were often intensified in an eschatological context—which is precisely what happened with Jesus. His asceticism was not, from what we can tell, an attempt to free the soul from the body in order to gain either transcendent knowledge [142] or salvation. [143] Neither was his abstinence motivated by a Stoical quest to control the emotions nor by a religious longing to atone for or guard from sin. [144] We also have insufficient evidence that he sought through the diminution of desire to cultivate spiritual powers (the goal of certain celibates of Sūfism) or to gain something akin to ritual purity. [145] Jesus' asceticism, including his sexual continence, was rather part and parcel of his eschatological expectation. Let me clarify.

1. *Asceticism as dedication to an eschatological mission.* One of the conventional reasons given for the celibacy of Roman Catholic priests is that some matters require full attention, and marriage and its attendant responsibilities will, it is thought, take too much from those dedicated to

142. But Berger, *Wer war Jesus wirklich?* p. 27, raises the possibility that Jesus thought his singleness a condition of "intensive contact" with "the heavenly world." On the connection between asceticism and visionary experiences see Rudolph Arbesmann, "Fasting and Prophecy in Pagan and Christian Antiquity," *Traditio* 7 (1949), pp. 1–71, and Violet MacDermot, *The Cult of the Seer in the Ancient Middle East* (Berkeley: University of California Press, 1971). One wonders whether *1 En.* 83:2 and 85:3, which tell us that Enoch had visions before he was married, reflect the conviction that sexual activity inhibits visionary abilities. Note also Acts 21:9 (Philip's four daughters had the gift of prophecy and were virgins) and *Acts of Paul and Thecla* 4 (God speaks to the continent). Already the Pentateuch says that Israel at Sinai refrained from intercourse for three days (Exod 19:10, 15); and tradition held that Moses fasted when he was receiving revelation on Sinai (Exod 34:28; Deut 9:9; etc.). Tradition also attributed chastity to him: Philo, *Vit. Mos.* 2:68–69 (Moses renounced intercourse "to hold himself always in readiness to receive oracular messages"); the targumim on Num. 12:1–2; *Sipre Num.* § 99; *ARN* A 2; *b. Šabb.* 87a; *Deut. Rab.* 11:10; *Exod. Rab.* 46:3; *Cant. Rab.* 4:4; Louis Ginzberg, *The Legends of the Jews*, 7 vols. (Philadelphia: Jewish Publication Society, 1937–66), vol. 2, p. 316; vol. 3, pp. 107, 258; vol. 6, pp. 90 (with additional references). We really have to do here with a worldwide phenomenon, for everywhere the Shaman prepares for communicating with the other world by engaging in ascetic disciplines.

143. In the *Acts of Paul and Thecla* continence does not follow from the nearness of the end but is rather a condition of reward at the resurrection; see chapter 12. In chapter 5 Paul preaches "continence and resurrection."

144. But for ascetic practices atoning for or guarding from sin see *Ps. Sol.* 5:8 (fasting atones for sin); *T. Jud.* 15:4 (avoidance of wine and meat and merriment help prevent sexual sin); *T. Jos.* 3:4; 4:7–8 (fasting helps avoid sexual sin); *T. Sim.* 3:4 (fasting helps prevent envy); *Apoc. Elijah* 1:13–22 (fasting is a curb for the passions). *b. Ned.* 9b recounts the story of a young man taking a Nazirite vow and shaving his head in order to curb his lust.

145. For sex as a source of impurity see Lev 15:16–18; 1 Sam 21:5–6; 1QM 7:3–7; 11QTemple 45–7; CD 12:1–2; *m. Zabim*; etc.

the ministry of souls and other spiritual duties. This sort of argument appears often in religious history. Ben Azzai's motivation for being celibate was his all-consuming passion and dedication to Torah: "What shall I do, seeing that my soul is in love with the Torah; the world can be carried on by others."[146] Tertullian thought that when a man "abstains from a woman" he can "think spiritual thoughts."[147] Origen, according to Eusebius, *H.E.* 6:8, castrated himself for the sake of his all-important studies. Already we find Paul arguing in 1 Cor 7:32–35 that the married man is "divided" in his interests: "The unmarried man is anxious about the affairs of the Lord; but the married man is anxious about the affairs of the world. . . ." And long before Paul there was the tradition that the Hebrews abstained from sex before battle—no doubt a sign of single-minded service to Yahweh.[148]

Jesus' asceticism was, in the first instance, of like kind. That is, his urgent eschatological mission was sufficiently important and consuming as to disallow family entanglements. This is, after all, and as argued above, the plain meaning of Mt 19:12. The eunuchs that Jesus defended were those who, as heralds of the coming kingdom, had as little time for marriage as they did for business. To leave all for the sake of the grand cause was to leave behind the world and its attendant affairs once and for all.[149] If the discipline of the Spartans was to prepare for war, and if the exercises of the Greek athlete were to prepare him for the athletic contest, then the asceticism of the pre-Easter Jesus movement was similarly a strategy devised to meet a specific goal. The missionary endeavor to restore Israel in the face of judgment demanded complete dedication. In other words, the proclamation of the coming kingdom required sacrificing a normal course of life.[150]

---

146. *b. Yeb.* 63b. Biale, *Eros and the Jews*, pp. 53–57, compiles evidence (note especially *b. Ketub.* 62b-63a) to show that the custom of abstaining from intercourse for long periods of time for the sake of study was probably common among rabbis. Also helpful here is Harvey McArthur, "Celibacy in Judaism at the Time of Christian Beginnings," *AUSS* 25 (1987), pp. 163–81.

147. *De exh. cast.* 10:1. *T. Naph.* 8:9 says that "there is a time for having intercourse with one's wife, and a time to abstain for the purpose of prayer." If one thinks in terms of such a dichotomy, might it not follow that, if one wishes to spend as much time as possible in prayer, one should give up sex?

148. Compare 1 Sam 21:4; 2 Sam 11:11. The female mystic, Rabia al-Adawiya, supplies a famous example from Islam of chastity in the service of the spiritual life.

149. So also Q 14:26. Compare Brown, *Body*, p. 42: "The intensity of their mission" rendered the "eunuchs for the sake of the kingdom of heaven" "ineligible for marriage."

150. Geza Vermes, *Jesus the Jew* (Philadelphia: Fortress, 1981), pp. 99–102, speaks of Jesus' "prophetic celibacy." Meeks, *Moral World*, p. 105, refers to the asceticism of itinerant missionaries as "not the means of their salvation" but "the means for their mission."

When Jesus called people to be itinerants, he may well have expected them to give up their marriages just as he expected them to give up their businesses and money. Maybe indeed we should envisage around him a little brotherhood of wandering male celibates, something akin to a Pythagorean brotherhood.[151] If such had been the case, Jesus and his followers must have expected their break with family life to be permanent because the consummation was near. Perhaps it was only after the end delayed, and only in the post-Easter period, that Peter and others returned to their wives and kin (1 Cor 9:5).

2. *Asceticism as distance from the present world order.* There is a sort of dualism in both first-century Jewish thought and the Jesus tradition.[152] Although much less radical than Plato's dualism, "it does presuppose a 'spirit' that links humans with God and a 'body' that links them with the earth and animals, and it favors the former over the latter."[153] Such dualism is only accentuated when attended by the conviction that the world of present experience is soon to be replaced by another. This is why, in Kenneth Kirk's words, "both apocalyptic and asceticism are *dualist* in tone, and . . . it is natural therefore to expect to find them in conjunction."[154] If this world is passing away, and if its passing away is a good thing, then one cannot cling to it. Indeed, one can only express attachment to the better future by detaching oneself from the ephemeral present. If the social order is no longer going to exist, then its existing obligations are of comparatively little moment: one's business can no longer be business as usual.[155] To borrow an example from Q: the evil generation

151. Compare George W. Buchanan, *Jesus: The King and His Kingdom* (Macon: Mercer, 1983), pp. 183–90. Mt 5:27–28 and 19:12 preserve an androcentric perspective: men are being addressed. On the other hand, Lk 8:2–3 raises the possibility that women were among Jesus' itinerant followers. If so, then they were also presumably called to celibacy. But John Dominic Crossan, "Jesus and the Kingdom: Itinerants and Householders in Earliest Christianity," in *Jesus at 2000*, ed. Marcus J. Borg (Boulder: Westview, 1997), pp. 39–40, associates the "two by two" of Mk 6:7 with 1 Cor 9:5 ("Do we not have the right to be accompanied by a believing wife") and suggests that we should envisage itinerants with their wives.

152. See especially Robert H. Gundry, *Sōma in Biblical Tradition*, SNTSMS 29 (Cambridge: Cambridge University Press, 1976). Note Q 12:4–5.

153. Fraade, "Ascetical Aspects," p. 262.

154. Kenneth Kirk, *The Vision of God: The Christian Doctrine of the* Summum Bonum, 2d ed. (London: Longmans, Green and Co., 1932), p. 58. Kirk, however, went on to argue against grounding Jesus' rigorism in eschatology.

155. Compare Henry Chadwick, *The Early Church* (London: Penguin, 1967), p. 175, on primitive Christian asceticism: "Detachment from vanity fair was easier to those who expected the end of the world in the imminent future than to those who expected the historical process to roll on and who possessed some modest property to pass on to their children."

of Noah's day declared its stupidity by carrying on with its mundane affairs when divine disaster was about to rain down upon the earth (Q 17: 26–27).

Religious celibacy frequently reflects estrangement from the normal structures of society. This is why it so often appears, as it does in the Jesus tradition and in later Christian monasticism, beside renunciations of family and work in the world. We have no difficulty understanding why Jesus and his followers—like so many millenarian enthusiasts after them—let go of their possessions, their businesses, their families.[156] They did not need this world when they were soon to enter another, and they certainly did not have to worry about extending their community into the future through raising children. Their eschatological dualism—the present order will be eclipsed by another order—encouraged detachment from this world. As Gerd Theissen once said of the early Christian wandering charismatics, their "vivid eschatological expectations . . . went along with their role as outsiders: they lived as those who expected the end of the world. The more they detached themselves from this world in their everyday actions, the more they kept destroying this world in their mythical fantasies. . . ."[157]

"The driving force of asceticism is," Henry Chadwick has remarked, "a renunciation of success in the world"[158]—and there is nothing more

156. Millenarians often leave off work; for examples see Stephen Fuchs, *Rebellious Prophets: A Study of Messianic Movements in Indian Religions* (London: Asia Publishing House, 1965), pp. 27–34 (the followers of the Munda Bursa); Lanternari, *Religions of the Oppressed*, p. 24 (the African cult of the Bashilele); John G. Strelan, *Search for Salvation: Studies in the History and Theology of Cargo Cults* (Adelaide: Lutheran Publishing House, 1977), p. 51 (a generalization about cargo cults); and Wilson D. Wallis, *Messiahs: Christian and Pagan* (Boston: Gorham, 1918), p. 128 (the South African outbreak of 1856–57). It seems likely enough that some of Paul's Thessalonian converts gave up work (2 Thess 3: 6–12) because they thought the end was near or had come; see Robert Jewett, *The Thessalonian Correspondence: Pauline Rhetoric and Millenarian Piety* (Philadelphia: Fortress, 1986), especially pp. 173–74, and M. J. J. Menken, "Paradise Regained or Still Lost? Eschatology and Disorderly Behaviour in 2 Thessalonians," *NTS* 38 (1992), pp. 271–89. But for another view note R. Russell, "The Idle in 2 Thess 3:6–12: An Eschatological or a Social Problem?" *NTS* 34 (1988), pp. 105–19.

Maybe, if Acts 2:44–45 and 4:34–37 preserve some historical memory, the sharing of all in common in the primitive Jerusalem community was motivated by an eschatological utopianism.

157. Gerd Theissen, *Sociology of Early Palestinian Christianity* (Philadelphia: Fortress, 1978), pp. 16–17.

158. Henry Chadwick, "The Ascetic Ideal in the History of the Church," in *Monks, Hermits and the Ascetic Tradition*, ed. W. J. Sheils (London: Basil Blackwell, 1985), p. 2.

characteristic in the sayings of Jesus than rejection of success in the world. Jesus commended minimal dress (Q 10:4–11; Mk 6:7–13) and rejected ostentation (Q 7:24–27; Gos. Thom. 78). He anticipated a radical reversal of current circumstances, so that the first will be last, the last first (Q 13:30; Mk 10:31; Gos. Thom. 4). He blessed the destitute, the hungry, and mourners (Q 6:20–23; Gos. Thom. 54, 69). And he declared that those who save their lives will lose them while those who lose their lives will save them (Q 17:33; Mk 8:35). All this reveals a deep alienation from the world as it is,[159] the sort of alienation that typically coincides with an ascetical way of life.[160] Jesus marginalized himself in order to marginalize the world.

3. *Asceticism as rhetorical persuasion.* According to Stephen D. O'Leary, "When a prophet or prophetic interpreter proposes that the world is coming to an end, or that a period of millennial peace is about to begin, he or she is offering an argumentative claim—a statement that is designed to gain the adherence of an audience and that must be supported by reasons and proofs."[161] If the controversy narratives tell us anything about Jesus, then he sought to persuade people to his view of things. Actions, however, can speak louder than words, and Jesus also used his actions to persuade. He undoubtedly, for instance, understood his ministry of exorcism and healing to vindicate his proclamation.[162] I should also like to raise the possibility that his asceticism likewise had a persuasive dimension.

"Built into the repertoire of tactics and strategies of charismatics is the knowledge (intuitive or otherwise) that in a traditional setting the value of the message is judged by the personal qualities of the bearer. Thus it is through image-making and accentuation of personal qualities that the charismatic obtains a lever on the public and facilitates his recognition."[163] Now to wander about without purse or bag or sandals (Q 10:4)

159. Jesus' alienation also comes to expression in his ministry of exorcism, which was a central part of what he was all about. A world that is full of demons is a world of danger and disarray, not a world as it should be.

160. Compare William James, *The Varieties of Religious Experience* (New York: Mentor, 1958), p. 281: asceticism symbolizes "the belief that there is an element of real wrongness in this world. . . ." Swain, *Asceticism*, p. 145, asserts that "asceticism seems to increase as social and economic conditions in the world grow worse."

161. Stephen D. O'Leary, *Arguing the Apocalypse: A Theory of Millennial Rhetoric* (New York: Oxford, 1994), p. 4.

162. See Q 7:22–23; 11:15–23; Mk 3:22–27.

163. R. G. Waddell, "Charisma and Reason: Paradoxes and Tactics of Originality," in *A Sociological Yearbook of Religion in Britain*, 5, ed. Michael Hill (London: SCM, 1972),

was, within Jesus' context, a public and symbolic statement of absolute faith in God. As Q 12:22–31 plainly indicates, Jesus taught that the heavenly Father who feeds the birds and clothes the grass of the fields would take care of those who sought the kingdom of heaven and left off being anxious about food and clothing. One must ask how those who lived accordingly appeared to those without. An apparently carefree existence might have proved attractive to some. That happened with Francis of Assisi, who modeled his behavior upon the Synoptic Jesus. However that may be, asceticism is fairly good evidence of one's sincerity. For most people cannot seriously entertain living differently from those around them. Those few who can bear to be dissimilar, especially if that means doing without, demonstrate how sincere they are about what they are doing. So when Jesus and his disciples left behind their former lives, when they forsook their families and businesses to give themselves over wholly to their cause, they were not only calling attention to themselves and so creating a ready audience for their proclamation. They were also showing that they truly believed what they were saying. That is, they were offering proof of their earnestness and so initial evidence for their veracity.[164]

4. *Asceticism as a sign of judgment.* Gen. Rab. 31:12 attributes to R. Abin the sentiment, "If you see poverty and famine come to the world, regard your wife as menstruous." In other words, when one begins to hear the footsteps of the Messiah, it may be time to turn attention away from normal duties. Jesus demanded just such a turn. But he in addition called people to repent of their sins in preparation for the coming judgment.[165] This matters for our purposes, because one who calls to repentance cannot live a life of indulgence. If Jesus demanded repentance in the face of the end, his words would have found no audience if he did not somehow embody repentance in his own behavior. When the medium is the message, hypocrisy is not effective evangelism. It only makes sense that if he belittled those with fine clothing who lived in luxury (Q 7:25; Mk 12:38; Lk 16:19) then he himself must have done without (compare Q 9:58; 10:4).

Embodying repentance is precisely what Jesus did when he submitted

---

p. 5. Maimonides, in his letter to the Jews of Yemen (*Iggeres Teiman*), reveals that people believed in some Messiahs or messianic prophets because of their special character—they were "serene" or "pious."

164. For asceticism as a sign of sincerity within the context of personal piety note Jdt 4:8–15 (prayer with fasting and ashes); 1 Macc 3:47 (fasting with sackcloth and ashes and rending of clothes); 2 Macc 13:10–12 (weeping, fasting, prostration); Tob 12:8 ("Prayer is good when accompanied by fasting, almsgiving, and righteousness").

165. See above, pp. 103–104.

to John's baptism. For we may believe Mark when he tells us that immersion in the Jordan was "of repentance for the forgiveness of sins" (Mk 1: 4). We may also believe the tradition when it informs us that Jesus often took himself to the wilderness, a place for penance and awaiting the end,[166] and that he often occupied himself with solitude.[167] Further, one presumes that he traveled as he instructed others to travel—without purse or bag or sandals (Q 10:4). The upshot is clear. Jesus called others to repent, and he himself did not behave in a manner inconsistent with that call. If he believed that the presence of the kingdom involved some sort of celebrating (Mk 2:18–22), he equally believed that the coming of the kingdom demanded solemn preparation.

Ascetic practices are, in Jewish tradition, frequently associated with divine judgment. For judgment implies God's disfavor with human sin and hence the need for repentance. *b. B. Bat.* 60a says that "when the temple was destroyed for the second time, large numbers in Israel became ascetics, binding themselves neither to eat meat nor drink wine." *T. Mos.* 9: 6 tells of people fasting and isolating themselves in the desert before the eschatological judgment. Jewish legend has it that Noah and those in the ark were instructed to refrain from intercourse not only to avoid an unaccommodable increase of numbers but because of the principle that the individual must participate in the suffering of the community.[168] Already in the Hebrew Bible repentance involves such ascetical acts as fasting, putting aside normal garb, and sitting in ashes.[169] Joel 1:13–16 in fact commends fasting, prayer, and sackcloth as preparation for the Day of the Lord; and 2:16 tells "the bridegroom [to] leave his room, and the bride her chamber."[170] This raises the possibility that when the unencumbered Jesus and his fellow itinerants showed up in a village without money or shoes or wives, their austere appearance and unfettered way of life might have served, not as an invitation to party, but as a prophetic

---

166. See W. D. Davies, *The Gospel and the Land: Early Christianity and Jewish Territorial Doctrine* (Berkeley: University of California Press, 1974), pp. 75–90.

167. Texts that place Jesus in the wilderness and/or depict him seeking solitude include Q 4:1; Mk 1:35, 45; 6:31–44; 8:1–10; Jn 3:22 (on this verse see the fascinating article of Jerome Murphy-O'Connor, "John the Baptist and Jesus: History and Hypotheses," *NTS* 36 [1990], pp. 359–74); 6:15.

168. Ginzberg, *Legends of the Jews*, vol. 5, p. 188. The tradition goes back to the first century; see Philo, *Quest. Gen.* 2:49; and it was known to Christians: Ephrem the Syrian, *Hymn Nat.* 28:1. In *b. Taʿan.* 11a, there is to be no sexual intercourse during a time of famine.

169. E.g., Dan 9:3–19; Jonah 3:5; compare *T. Reub.* 1:10.

170. Compare the separation of the sexes in Zech 12:12–14.

sign, a warning that the normal course of things was about to change.[171] Jeremiah rejected family life in order to symbolize God's judgment (16:1–4). John the Baptist's rugged dress and desert way of life were presumably designed not as things to imitate but as ways of signaling a decisive break with the status quo—including the traditional religious authorities[172]—and so as ways of signaling that something new was afoot. Probably in analogous fashion Jesus' peculiar manner of life would have attracted attention and served as a sign that things were about to change: this man does not belong to the world as it is, because the world as it is is about to disappear.

5. *Asceticism as realized eschatology.* Some old traditions relate that the primordial Adam was neither male nor female.[173] Others (e.g., *2 Bar.* 56:5–6) tell us that Adam and Eve did not engage in sexual intercourse before their disobedience.[174] Both traditions presuppose that sex was not part of the primeval state, that it came upon the scene only later. Now the Jesus tradition, as we have seen, knows of an eschatological chastity, when human beings will, like the angels in heaven, neither marry nor be given in marriage (Mk 12:18–27). Because many hoped for an eschatological return to things as they were in the beginning,[175] it is possible that Jesus understood chastity as a replay of paradise and thus an anticipation of eschatological existence, in other words, as a proleptic recovery of "the glory of Adam."[176]

David Biale has written, in connection with some rabbinic texts, that "for those who believe that the ideal world will be asexual, one's behavior in this world [Biale is referring to moderate and modest intercourse] might serve as a *preparatio messianica*, a paradoxical nonascetic asceti-

171. Meeks, *Moral World*, p. 105, refers to the asceticism of those behind the Jesus tradition as a "prophetic symbol: a sign of the urgency of" the message of itinerants "and of the[ir] exclusive demand."

172. Michael Hill, *A Sociology of Religion* (New York: Basic, 1973), p. 164, observes that charismatic leadership may symbolize its break with traditional channels of authority through nontraditional behavior.

173. Philo, *Opf.* 151–52 (of the heavenly Adam); *Mek.* on Exod 12:40; *b. Ber.* 61a; *b. Meg.* 9a; *b. 'Erub.* 18a; *Gen. Rab.* on 1:26. See Wayne A. Meeks, "The Image of the Androgyne: Some Uses of a Symbol in Earliest Christianity," *HR* 13 (1974), pp. 165–208.

174. Full discussion in Gary Anderson, "Celibacy or Consummation in the Garden?" *HTR* 82 (1989), pp. 121–48.

175. This is a feature of millenarian movements in general; see Desroche, *Sociology of Hope*, pp. 91–92. On its importance within ancient Judaism and early Christianity see Nils A. Dahl, *Jesus in the Memory of the Early Church* (Minneapolis: Augsburg, 1976), pp. 120–40.

176. 1QS 4:23. For later examples of such thinking see Ephrem, *De paradiso* 7:5, and Nagel, *Motivierung*, pp. 55–62.

cism. By engaging in the sexual act of procreation in the properly chaste manner, one prepares the way for the asexual world to come."[177] What Biale conjectures with regard to some rabbis is just a more conservative version of what I am suggesting might have been the case with Jesus.

It may be pertinent in this connection to observe that, according to some old sources, Adam and Eve, before their disobedience, were angelic.[178] If Jesus expected to gain an angelic existence in paradise (Mk 12: 18–27), he could all the more readily have seen chastity—a quality of the unfallen angels—as a proleptic recovery of things lost by Adam and Eve. Such a view would be akin to how some modern exegetes[179] and many ancient readers[180] have understood Lk 20:35–36: "Those who belong to this age marry and are given in marriage; but those who are considered worthy of a place in that age and in the resurrection from the dead neither marry nor are given in marriage." The angelic life has become a present reality for the saints, who no longer enter into marriage. Certainly some early Christians thought in such terms.[181] Cross has written that the Qumran Essenes did too.[182]

177. David Biale, *Eros and the Jews*, p. 43.

178. E.g., *2 En.* 30:11; *Apoc. Adam* 5.64.15–20; 76.4–6; *Conflict of Adam and Eve* 1:10. We should also keep in mind that Gen 5:24, right before it tells us that the primeval Enoch was mysteriously swept up from the ken of his contemporaries, says that he walked with *'ĕlohîm*, which may mean that he walked with angels.

179. E.g., Turid Karlsen Seim, *The Double Message: Patterns of Gender in Luke-Acts* (Nashville: Abingdon, 1994), pp. 208–29. For some of Luke's ascetic tendencies see Gabriele Winkler, "The Origins and Idiosyncrasies of the Earliest Form of Asceticism," in *The Continuing Quest for God: Monastic Spirituality in Tradition and Transition*, ed. William Skudlarek (Collegeville: Liturgical Press, 1982), pp. 16–21.

180. See van Eijk, "Marriage and Virginity," pp. 209–35. For the Old Syriac text of Lk 20:35–36, which clearly refers to angelic life in the present, see F. C. Burkitt, *Evangelion da-mepharreshê: The Curetonian Version of the Four Gospels*, vol. 1 (Cambridge: Cambridge University Press, 1904), p. 386.

181. Some have argued that the Corinthians of Paul's time based their asceticism, including opposition to marriage, upon a realized or proleptic eschatology; see Margaret Y. MacDonald, "Women Holy in Body and Spirit," *NTS* 36 (1990), pp. 161–81. But for objections see Martin, *Corinthian Body*. Others, on the basis of 1 Tim 4:3 and 2 Tim 2:18, have divined behind the Pastorals "Jewish Encratites [who] proclaim that the resurrection has already taken place and that marriage should be abolished"; so G. Quispel, "Gnosticism and the New Testament," in *The Bible in Modern Scholarship: Papers Read at the 100th Meeting of the Society of Biblical Literature, December 28–30, 1964*, ed. J. Philip Hyatt (Nashville: Abingdon, 1965), p. 255. See further William L. Lane, "1 Tim iv.1–3: An Early Instance of Over-realized Eschatology?" *NTS* 11 (1965), pp. 164–67. The combination of celibacy and realized eschatology appears in the *Gospel of Thomas* (e.g., 51 and 75) and was part of Encratite thought according to Clement, *Stromata* 3:48 (Egyptian Encratites do not marry because they think they have already been resurrected).

182. Cross, *Ancient Library*, pp. 83–84. On these pages he uses, in connection with both Qumran and the early church, the term "apocalpytic asceticism."

One might also relate Jesus' prohibitions of illicit desire (Mk 9:43–48; Mt 5:28) to the imminence of the golden age. Rabbinic texts associate the evil *yēṣer* with sexual passion[183] and so see it as responsible for the perpetuation of the human race (e.g., *Gen. Rab.* 9:7). This is why they also, when they speak of the age to come, can say that the evil impulse will no longer be required and so will be slain.[184] Now if one were to believe, because of eschatological convictions, that the need for keeping the race going had ceased, then one might also see no more need for the evil *yēṣer*. So maybe Jesus thought that the time when the sexual impulse was needful had run its course. It was thus to be dispensed with (compare Ezek 36:26, where God removes "the heart of stone").

Jesus' free attitude toward property may also have had an element of proleptic eschatology. For Genesis 3 makes it plain that, before they succumbed to temptation, Adam and Eve did not have to toil in the cursed ground and eat bread by the sweat of their faces (compare *LAE* 4:1–2). Nor did they need clothing. Business and money, then, were not part of their world. One wonders whether Jesus' call to live without anxiety for food and clothing, which in Q 12:22–31 is so closely tied to the creator's care for the natural world, originally harked back to the primeval state.

This possibility is congruent with the argument in Mk 10:2–12. Here Jesus grounds his prohibition of divorce in what God intended "from the beginning of creation." Presumably the idea is that the Mosaic dispensation is giving way to the ideal, eschatological state, which will restore significant elements of the primeval state (compare Rev 22:1–2). In other words, Jesus wants some things even now to be as they were in the beginning because that is how they are going to be in the kingdom of God. So we should reckon with the possibility that matters may have been similar in connection with Jesus' ascetical renunciation of work and marriage: they were consistent with Jesus' attempt to regain the *Urzeit* in the face of the *Endzeit*.[185]

---

183. E.g., *b. Qidd.* 81a, 81b; *b. Suk.* 52a; *b. 'Abod. Zar.* 17a. Compare CD 3:2–3.

184. Texts in SB 4/1, pp. 482–83. But *Midr. Ps.* 146:4 declares that intercourse with menstrual women will be possible in the age to come (compare Commodian, *Instr.* 44).

185. Brown, *Body and Society*, p. 44, finds a contradiction between Jesus' prohibition of divorce (based on a recovery of paradise) and Mk 12:18–27, where Jesus foretells an angelic future without marriage. I concur that the discrepancy seems a bit vexatious, and I refrain (as did Matthew and Mark) from attempting harmonization. I do not, however, think this sort of disparity sufficient reason to deny one complex or the other to Jesus any more than I find the incongruity between Philo's admiration for the Therapeutae and his support of the traditional patriarchal household reason to doubt the integrity of the Philonic corpus. See further pp. 2–4 and 114–15 herein.

Final Remarks

Jesus is reported to have told his followers to take up a cross.[186] If he did so he was, as much of the *Wirkungsgeschichte* of the saying suggests,[187] asking them to do more than just endure the everyday sufferings that come to all people. He was rather enjoining them to enter, for a religious end, into some sort of voluntary suffering. This is precisely the demand that religious asceticism makes in all its forms. It requires genuine deprivation and sacrifice. The fact is consistent with the case I have been making.

But I want to return to the customary objections made against characterizing Jesus as an ascetic. There seem to be at least four. (1) Jesus did not fast as did John the Baptist. (2) He did not deny the goodness of the world.[188] (3) He associated with women.[189] (4) His harsh demands were directed only at some, not at all.[190]

I have already (pp. 173–74 above) indicated that (1) is hardly decisive. Here it may be added that Jesus could have been ascetic in some respects—with regard to mammon and sex, for example—but not in others. *The Gospel of Thomas* in its present form shows strong ascetic tendencies. Readers are told to "fast from the world" (27). They are to

186. Q 14:27; Mk 8:34; *Gos. Thom.* 55.
187. *Clem. Epit. A* 5:4 associates "take up your cross" with virginity. Evagrius, *Orat.* 17, links the imperative with giving away possessions. Theophylact, *Comm. on Mt.* ad 16: 24, says that "no one should have any friendship towards the body so that one can take up the cross." The Shakers used "Take up your cross" with reference to their celibacy; see Nardi Reeder Campia, *Mother Ann Lee: Morning Star of the Shakers* (Hanover: University Press of New England, 1990), p. 81. For the application to martyrdom see Luz, *Matthäus*, vol. 2, p. 146.
188. So Kretschmar, "Askese," p. 28.
189. Compare Hans von Campenhausen, "Early Christian Asceticism," in *Tradition and Life in the Church: Essays and Lectures in Church History* (Philadelphia: Fortress, 1968), p. 106: "Jesus himself does not hesitate to associate with the women who 'serve' him, and his first disciples returned later to their wives, even, like Peter, taking them, at times, on their missionary journeys. Here, therefore, there was no 'asceticism.'"
190. So Karl Suso Frank, *With Greater Liberty: A Short History of Christian Monasticism and Religious Orders* (Kalamazoo: Cistercian, 1993), pp. 17–18; Hans Kung, *On Being a Christian* (New York: Doubleday, 1976), p. 198; and Lohse, *Askese*, pp. 117–18. Kung offers additional reasons for holding that Jesus was not an ascetic, including this one: "He never demanded sacrifice for the sake of sacrifice, renunciation for the sake of renunciation." Does this imply that to be an ascetic one must embrace suffering for its own sake? If so, this would exclude the Essenes, people Kung himself labels "ascetics." It would also exclude the desert fathers, for "the monks went without sleep because they were watching for the Lord; they did not speak because they were listening to God; they fasted because they were fed by the Word of God. It was the end that mattered, the ascetic practices were only a means"; so Benedicta Ward, *The Desert Christian: Sayings of the Desert Fathers* (New York: Macmillan, 1975), p. xxiii.

become "passers-by," which may mean itinerants (42). Bodily existence is reckoned "poverty" (29). The poor are blessed (54). The well-to-do are rejected (64). And it is "solitaries," by which is meant the celibates, who are saved (16, 49, 75).[191] At the same time, *Gos. Thom.* 14 teaches that "if you fast, you will beget sin for yourselves." So *Thomas* is very ascetical about some things and yet in saying 14 opposes fasting. One wonders why matters could not have been similar with Jesus—if indeed he did not much fast—that is, why he could not have been ascetic in some respects but not in others. Further, if we do not hesitate, despite its rejection of the ascetic practice of fasting, to speak of *Thomas* as a document with strong ascetical tendencies, why should we hesitate, despite his apparent rejection of regular supererogatory fasting, to speak of Jesus as having similar tendencies?

The second objection regularly offered is that Jesus was not an ascetic because he did not deny the goodness of the world. If by this is meant that Jesus believed the world to have been created by God, then this criterion would also prevent us from calling the Essenes or the orthodox Christian monks of later times ascetics, for they professed God to have made all things. Even more significantly, one recalls that Francis of Assisi both fervently celebrated the creation and yet treated his body very harshly: the two things can be found in the same person.

But if the objection means that Jesus did not utter disparaging things about the body, matter, or the world, then several things may be said. (a) Mk 9:43–48, which counsels figurative amputation of hand, foot, and eye, certainly envisages the possibility of the true self being alienated from its own body.[192] (There is a parallel here with the alienation of Paul's "inmost self" from his "members" in Romans 7).[193] (b) Although his sayings relate God to the natural world in profound ways, Jesus nonetheless saw evil spirits round about him and believed that God would soon remake a world that was in its death throes. While the two things may sit uneasily side by side in our own minds, that does not determine what must have been the case for Jesus. Although a strong sense of cosmic anomie is patent throughout *1 Enoch*, chapters 2–5 and 72–82 go on at length

---

191. See G. Quispel, "L'Evangile selon Thomas et les origines de l'ascèse chrétienne," in *Aspects du Judéo-Christianisme*, pp. 35–52.

192. Compare Niederwimmer, *Askese*, p. 31.

193. On the Jewish background for this see Eduard Schweizer, "Die Sünde in den Gliedern," in *Abraham unser Vater: Juden und Christen im Gespräch über die Bibel*, ed. Otto Betz, Martin Hengel, and Peter Schmidt (Leiden: E. J. Brill, 1963), pp. 437–39. He cites *2 Bar.* 49:3; *T. Reuben* 3; *ARN* 16; and *b. Ned.* 32b.

about God's ordering of the world.[194] (c) Asceticism need not have its impetus in a dualism of body and soul or of the material and immaterial. The asceticism of the eleventh-century Jew Bahyā ben Yōsēf ibn Paqūdā did not derive from a negative view of the body or of matter.[195] Further, asceticism can, as the comparative materials collected throughout this chapter reveal, arise chiefly out of the perceived tension between the present world that is passing away and the new world that is soon to replace it. In Genesis 1–8, the created world is said over and over again to be good, and yet things get so bad that everything must be destroyed. Jesus' view of things was no doubt similar.

The third objection, that Jesus did not isolate himself from women, erroneously assumes that medieval Christian monasticism, with its monks separated from its nuns, is the only sort of social arrangement for sexual asceticism. Although some Essenes were celibate, 4Q502 praises various qualities of women, and the Qumran cemetery may testify to their presence among the men of the *yahad*. Perhaps the male Essene celibates did not completely isolate themselves from females. Certainly this may be said of the ascetical Encratites of the second and third centuries. They indeed often aspired to enter into so-called "spiritual marriages," in which husband and wives roomed together without engaging in intercourse;[196] and sometimes their missionaries, who proclaimed continence, traveled in pairs, one man and one woman.[197] Epiphanius wrote of the Encratites that they profess continence but "are to be found in the midst of women" (*Pan.* 47).

The fourth common objection to labeling Jesus an ascetic is that he imposed his strident demands only upon the few, not upon the many. The

194. Compare John J. Collins, "Wisdom, Apocalyptic, and Generic Compatibility," in *In Search of Wisdom: Essays in Memory of John G. Gammie*, ed. Leo G. Perdue, Bernard Brandon Scott, and William Johnston Wiseman (Louisville: Westminster/John Knox, 1993), p. 171.

195. Allan Lazaroff, "Bahyā's Asceticism against its Rabbinic and Islamic Background," *JJS* 21 (1970), pp. 11–38. On the varieties of asceticism in the ancient world and their various motivations see Vincent L. Wimbush, "Renunciation towards Social Engineering," *Occasional Papers of the Institute for Antiquity and Christianity* 8 (1986), pp. 1–20.

196. See Kathleen O'Brien Wicker, "The Ascetic Marriage in Antiquity," *Institute for Antiquity and Christianity Bulletin* 15 (1988), pp. 10–13 (with Neoplatonic parallels). Some have suspected that 1 Cor 7:36–38 already has to do with spiritual marriages; so recently Fox, *Pagans and Christians*, pp. 369–70. For a review of the discussion and critique see Deming, *Paul on Marriage*, pp. 40–47.

197. See Brown, *Body and Society*, pp. 92–102. Rosemary Rader, "Christian Pre-Monastic Forms of Asceticism: Syneisaktism, or 'Spiritual Marriage,'" in Skudlarek, *Continuing Quest*, p. 81, wonders whether 1 Cor 9:5 might refer to celibate women missionaries.

premise is true[198] even if the conclusion is false. There were two groups of Essenes, and the one that was far more isolated, strict, and austere than the other seemingly kept its higher standards to itself; for the documents from the desert recognize the legitimacy of those who live elsewhere, in the "towns" or "camps."[199] Similarly, most of the Christian monks of Egypt and Syria had no thought of remaking in their own image those who came to see them. They prayed, for example, that barren women might procreate,[200] and they adjudicated political disputes.[201] Clearly it was possible to live as an ascetic and not demand that everyone else do likewise. Indeed, it has been said that "asceticism has as its characteristic that its confessors do not regard . . . [their] discipline as of universal and perpetual obligation." They rather believe "that at most it is but a better way"; for them "its kernel consists not so much in the practice, that is the obedience to a law, as in the pursuit of a religious objective for which the ascetic practice prepares."[202] This generalization holds as much for Jesus as it does for John the Baptist.

A word of caution here, however: There are different sorts of asceticism. What Jesus practiced was much less extreme than what we often see in the history of religions and in the history of Christianity in particular. He did not go off by himself and practice the sorts of frightful self-tortures recounted in Theodoret of Cyrrhus's *Religious History*. By comparison with the bizarre and self-mortifying behavior of individuals such as Simeon Stylites and Henry Suso, Jesus' asceticism was relatively tame. There are no spiked belts in the traditions about him. What we sense rather with Jesus is an inner, psychological detachment from the world as it is, something perhaps reminiscent of the Stoic *apatheia*, as well as commitment to a cause that leads to outwardly ascetic behavior. Maybe, to

---

198. B. T. Viviano, "The Historical Jesus in the Doubly Attested Sayings: An Experiment," *RB* 103 (1966), p. 407, rightly observes that Q 17:31//Mk 13:15–16 says that "when the kingdom does come in its complete form the believers must drop what they are doing and run to meet it . . . from this one may conclude that Jesus expected the majority of believers to go on living a normal life in the interim."

199. The relevant texts are conveniently discussed in Geza Vermes, *The Dead Sea Scrolls in English*, rev. 4th ed. (London: Penguin, 1995), pp. 1–22.

200. See, e.g., Theodoret of Cyrrhus, *Rel. hist.* 11:4; 13:16; 26:21; Sozomen, *Eccl. hist.* 6:38.

201. Peter Brown, "The Rise and Function of the Holy Man in Antiquity," *Journal of Roman Studies* 61 (1971), pp. 80–101. On asceticism which does not withdraw from the world see further Wimbush, "Renunciation."

202. James A. Montgomery, "Ascetic Strains in Early Judaism," *JBL* 51 (1932), p. 184. This entire article remains instructive.

borrow from Vincent Wimbush's description of Paul, we should think of Jesus as a "worldly ascetic."[203] Whatever qualifications we may feel compelled to add, we must nonetheless acknowledge that Jesus and those around him were of more than temperate character. They practiced a rigorous self-denial for religious ends. They chose to forsake money and live in poverty. They elected to leave their homes and wander about without sandals. They decided to abandon wives and business. And some of them at least adopted celibacy. Surely such governing of themselves with extraordinary restraint, such denial of the usual amenities average villagers around them took for granted, deserves to be called "asceticism." Just as commentators have put too much distance between Paul and the Encratites,[204] so they have done the same with Jesus. The discontinuity between his practice and later Christian asceticism, especially of the sort practiced by some in second- and third-century Syria,[205] has been much overestimated.[206] The appeal to Jesus as ascetic model[207] was not altogether bereft of justification. One suspects that the desire of modern commentators to make Jesus stand out from his environment has here, as in so many other areas of life-of-Jesus research, come to expression at the expense of the truth.

203. See n. 86.

204. See Boyarin, *A Radical Jew*, pp. 158–79. Contrast Deming, *Paul on Marriage*, pp. 220–25.

205. On early Syrian asceticism see S. Brock, "Early Syrian Asceticism," *Numen* 20 (1973), pp. 1–19; Kretschmar, "Askese" (who concludes that asceticism emerged among early charismatic prophets and teachers who understood their radicalism in terms of the apocalyptic woes, their prophetic office, and the missionary instructions of Jesus); R. Murray, "The Features of the Earliest Christian Asceticism," in *Christian Spirituality*, ed. P. Brooks (London: SCM, 1975), pp. 65–77; and R. M. Price, "Introduction," in *A History of the Monks of Syria*, by Theodoret of Cyrrhus (Kalamazoo: Cistercian, 1985), pp. xx–xxiii (Price traces its origins to Matthew). Arthur Vööbus, *History of Asceticism in the Syrian Orient*, vol. 1 (Louvain: CSCO, 1958), pp. 3–30, argues for a connection with one stream of the earliest Palestinian Christianity.

206. Compare Mervin M. Deems, "Early Christian Asceticism," in *Early Christian Origins: Studies in Honor of Harold R. Willoughby*, ed. Allen Wikgren (Chicago: Quadrangle, 1961), pp. 91–101; also his earlier article, "The Sources of Christian Asceticism," in *Environmental Factors in Christian History*, ed. John Thomas McNeill, Matthew Spinka, and Harold R. Willoughby (Chicago: University of Chicago Press, 1939), pp. 149–66. Deems fully recognizes the eschatological factor in early Christian asceticism and also sees that the seeds of later monasticism are already planted in the earliest Christian sources.

If, as David L. Balch, "Backgrounds of 1 Cor. VII: Sayings of the Lord in Q: Moses as an Ascetic ΘΕΙΟΣ ΑΝΗΡ in II Cor. III," *NTS* 18 (1972), pp. 351–64, has argued, the Corinthians used some of Jesus' words to justify their asceticism, they may not have been too far off the mark.

207. On this see Nagel, *Motivierung*, pp. 5–19.

Western biblical scholars have little sympathy for eschatology and asceticism and so are not much good at finding either in the Jesus tradition.[208] We are more inclined to spot social concerns, to discover, let us
say, that Jesus showed a special affection for the disadvantaged, or criticized the oppressive social structures of his time. But Xenophanes long
ago observed that "the Ethiopians say that their gods are snub-nosed and
black, the Thracians that theirs have light blue eyes and red hair."[209]
Those of us who construct images of the historical Jesus always blend in
some our own features. More than that, we all too often uncover what we
like and cover what we dislike. It is no surprise that Clement of Alexandria, a sober Christian of Stoic temperament, thought that Jesus was an
exemplary ascetic (*Strom.* 3:6). It also does not surprise that certain
twentieth-century scholars with a different piety and of lesser orthodoxy,
at home in a world of comparative luxury, instead anachronistically envision Jesus as "the proverbial party animal." This may make him real to
us. But it is not the real Jesus.

Who we happen to be in the present is no good measure of who others
were in the past; and the contemporary antipathy for both asceticism and
millenarian eschatology has not helped us to interpret the original Jesus
tradition. Although much doubt remains about the details, it is pretty evident that Jesus and those around him lived with what we may fairly call
a millenarian vision or apocalyptic scenario. Moreover, in order to further their missionary goals, which were so closely related to that scenario,
they exited the course of a normal life and engaged in rigorous self-denial
of their natural inclinations. New Testament scholars who reconstruct a
Jesus without these two features have misconstrued the evidence.

208. F. Homes Dudden, in his old article on "Asceticism" in *A Dictionary of Christ and
the Gospels*, ed. James Hastings (Edinburgh: T. & T. Clark, 1906), vol. 1, pp. 128–31, was
so opposed to associating Jesus with asceticism that he interpreted Lk 4:2 to "mean merely
that He ate no ordinary food, but supported life on such means of subsistence as the wilderness afforded." The antipathy of Protestants to what they perceive as excessive asceticism in
the Catholic tradition has a long history; note already Calvin, *Inst.* 3:3:16. Jewish scholars, as Scholem, *Sabbatai Ṣevi*, p. 9, remarks, have also been reluctant to recognize the
significance of popular eschatology in Jewish history.
209. Frag. 16, preserved in Clement of Alexandria, *Strom.* 7:22:1

EPILOGUE

"Sometimes dreams are wiser than waking."
—Black Elk

HE DOES NOT COME TO US as one unknown. We know him well enough. Jesus is the millenarian prophet. He is Wovoka. He is Mambu. He is Birsa. What we think of the least of these, his brethren, we think, to large extent, also of him.

Jesus is the millenarian prophet of judgment, the embodiment of the divine discontent that rolls through all things. He sees those who go about in long robes and have the best seats in the synagogues while they lock others out of the kingdom. He sees a rich man clothed in purple and fine linen who feasts sumptuously every day while at his gate is famished Lazarus, whose only friends are the dogs who lick his sores. He sees people who are gorgeously appareled, who live in luxury in royal palaces, and who entertain themselves with the severed head of Elijah come again. What Nietzsche aptly if disparagingly called a "slave morality of chastity, selflessness, and absolute obedience" permits Jesus to see the truth about those who will power instead of justice. They are an evil generation, the blasphemers against the Holy Spirit, the first who will become last. Jesus knows that God promised never again to destroy the world through a flood, but he makes ready for the flood of the end-time anyway. He prepares for the baptism with which he will be baptized.

Jesus is the millenarian prophet of consolation and hope who comforts those who mourn. He sees the poor, the hungry, and the reviled, and he proclaims that the last will be first. He makes the best of a bad situation: things are not what they seem to be; everything will be OK. He declares, against all the evidence, that the oppressed and the destitute are not miserable but blessed. They will have treasure in heaven. They will be rewarded at the resurrection of the just.

Jesus is the millenarian prophet whose realism is so great that it must abandon the world, the lust of the eyes and the pride of life. He knows that we, being evil, cannot fix things, that the wall cannot climb itself. How bad is it? What is the world really like? God's envoy is reviled as in league with Beelzebul, and the city of the great king kills the prophets and stones those sent to it. Clearly all has gone irredeemably wrong. The kingdom of God suffers violence.

But with God all things are possible. So Jesus becomes the visionary, like Daniel. As he watches, thrones are set. He beholds the queen of the South rising from the dead. He sees those who repented at the proclamation of Jonah condemning those who have not repented at the proclamation of one greater than Jonah. Nothing will be hidden. Whatever is covered up will be uncovered.

Jesus' generation, however, passed away. They all tasted death. And it is not the kingdom of God that has come but the scoffers who ask, Where is the promise of his coming? For all things continue as they were from the beginning of creation. Jesus the millenarian prophet, like all millenarian prophets, was wrong: reality has taken no notice of his imagination. Was it not all a dream, an unfounded fantasy—a myth, in the derogatory sense of the word?

Once, long ago, Christ crucified was foolishness, the great rock of offense. For us, however, crosses are jewelry. Today it is Jesus' status as a millenarian prophet that causes those who believe to stumble. No wonder that the debaters of this age, orthodox and liberal alike, have tried to persuade us that we have troubled ourselves unduly. Jesus, they console us, was no fool about the end. He was no apocalyptic enthusiast. Such apologists for God's envoy either pluck out and cast from the tradition all parts that seem to say otherwise, or they wrongly divide the word of truth in overly clever ways. The result is the same. Whether the misunderstanding is that of his first followers or his latter-day interpreters, Jesus himself is exonerated. When he was near Jerusalem he did not suppose that the kingdom of God was to appear immediately. We can blame the students, who in their eschatological errors have not been like the teacher.

But not all was in parables, and maybe Mark was right when he wrote that Jesus explained everything in private to his disciples. Certainly Jesus was not a Delphian obscurantist, nor have the sources obscured him so much from us. He seems to have spoken plainly enough. And what he spoke plainly about was an old world made new, a corrupt world made incorrupt. It has not come. Will it ever?

And yet, despite everything, for those who have ears to hear, Jesus, the millenarian herald of judgment and salvation, says the only things worth saying, for his dream is the only one worth dreaming. If our wounds never heal, if the outrageous spectacle of a history filled with cataclysmic sadness is never undone, if there is nothing more for those who were slaughtered in the death camps or for six-year olds devoured by cancer, then let us eat and drink, for tomorrow we die. If in the end there is no good God to calm this sea of troubles, to raise the dead, and to give good news to the poor, then this is indeed a tale told by an idiot, signifying nothing.

INDEX OF ANCIENT SOURCES

1. In accordance with the hypothetical nature of Q and the convention of citing Q materials according to their Lukan chapter and verse, the references throughout this book to units from Q are entered here under Luke.

Greco-Roman Literature

Arrian

Discourses of Epictetus

Cicero

Balbo

Clitarcus

Sententiae

Dio Cassius

INDEX OF MODERN AUTHORS